From Roucan to Riches

From Roucan to Riches

The rise of the Glassell family

David McKenzie Robertson

Matador
9 Priory Business Park,
Wistow Road, Kibworth Beauchamp,
Leicestershire. LE8 0RX
Tel: 0116 279 2299
Email: books@troubador.co.uk
Web: www.troubador.co.uk/matador
Twitter: @matadorbooks

ISBN 978 183859 295 0

British Library Cataloguing in Publication Data.
A catalogue record for this book is available from the British Library.

Printed and bound by CPI Group (UK) Ltd, Croydon, CR0 4YY
Typeset in 11pt Adobe Garamond Pro by Troubador Publishing Ltd, Leicester, UK

Matador is an imprint of Troubador Publishing Ltd

In memory of Joan Glassell.
“Not a do-nothing body.”

Contents

List of Illustrations

Foreword

It was in Longniddry Primary School that I first heard of John Glassell, the 18th Century landowner who demolished my village in the course of agricultural improvements. Over half a century later I decided to investigate Glassell and his family in depth, and discovered a fascinating array of characters, all stemming from lowly origins in rural Dumfriesshire. Glassell himself made a fortune in Virginia and was able to join the landowning Scottish gentry. His talented daughter was educated in Edinburgh during its "Golden Age", married the heir to a dukedom and died tragically young. Glassell's brother became a plantation owner who founded an "aristocratic" Virginian dynasty encompassing Southern belles, millionaires and war heroes.

My thanks are due to Miss Dunbar who sparked my interest in local history back in the 1950s. Also to the staff members of the National Library of Scotland and the National Records of Scotland, who are unfailingly courteous and helpful. Thanks too for information and photocopies to Madison County Historical Society (Madison, Virginia), The Archives of the Virginia Historical Society, The Huntington Library (San Marino, California), and the University of Virginia Library (Albert and Shirley Small Special Collections Library).

David McKenzie Robertson
July 2019

I

Roots

AMERICA WAS VERY GOOD TO THE GLASSELLS. AMERICA ENABLED THE descendants of humble Scots tenant farmers to become plantation owners, war heroes, wealthy entrepreneurs, and titled aristocrats. One descendant married the daughter of the queen-empress of the most powerful empire on earth, another founded a Californian city, and yet another led triumphant armies over the Rhine to secure Nazi Germany's downfall. There was a darker side of course – ownership of slaves, tragic early deaths, duelling, and murder even. On the whole, however, America was very good to the Glassells.

There had been Glassells in the Scottish county of Dumfriesshire since at least the late 16th century.[1] The place in that county of particular interest to this study is the parish of Torthorwald, and three families living there in the mid-18th century. These were:

- A family headed by John Glassell in the village of Roucan.
- A family, also in Roucan, headed by Robert Glassell.
- A family headed by Adam Glassell in the village of Torthorwald.

1 "A history of Dumfries; An introduction to the history of Dumfries by Robert Edgar". Ed. R. C. Reid. J. Maxwell and Sons, Dumfries 1919. Page 19 mentions a John Glassell, merchant, who appears in the "Custom buik of Dumfries" for 1598.

John and Robert were probably brothers. Adam may have been another brother, but though almost certainly related, was perhaps a more distant connection.

The parish of Torthorwald lies immediately to the east of the town of Dumfries, separated from it by the Lochar Water, which was formerly bordered by extensive bogs, marshes and water-meadows. The handful of mostly modern buildings on the site of the old village of Roucan stand around a staggered crossroads just beyond the bridge where the road from Dumfries crosses the Lochar Water. Torthorwald, the "kirktoun" of the parish, stands on a ridge, half a mile uphill to the north-east. "Roucan" comes in many spellings in the records, "Ruchan" and "Ruken" most commonly, and occasionally appears as "*the* Roucan". Torthorwald is much more consistent, but is sometimes given as "Torthorell", reflecting the common local pronunciation.

James Anderson Russell's "Book of Dumfriesshire" describes Torthorwald in the mid-20th century thus: "It would be hard to imagine a less changed parish than Torthorwald; especially around the old tower of the Kirkton we seem far from the madding crowd, yet we are but three miles from Dumfriesshire's metropolis…".[2] In the second decade of the 21st century, however, due to the constant stream of traffic thundering along the busy A709 through the old "Kirkton" of Torthorwald, the atmosphere is rather less tranquil.

The name Torthorwald seems to be of Norse origin, and probably indicates a defensive site belonging to a man named Thorwaldr. In early mediaeval times the lands of Torthorwald came into the possession of the Carlyle family, who in spite of their name claimed descent from a celtic abbot of Dunkeld. A William Carlyle married a sister of Robert I (the Bruce), and at the Battle of Neville's Cross in 1346 Thomas Carlyle of Torthorwald was killed gallantly defending king David II.

At the end of the 16th century Torthorwald and its tower came into the possession of the Douglases of Drumlanrig. James Douglas pursued and slew the Earl of Arran in revenge for Arran's part in the beheading of Douglas's kinsman the Earl of Morton. Having avenged himself on his enemy, Douglas then displayed his head, spiked on a lance, on the

2 The book of Dumfriesshire – James Anderson Russell. Blacklock Ferries and Sims Ltd, Dumfries, 1964. Page 162.

battlements of the tower of Torthorwald.[3] The Douglases of Drumlanrig later became Dukes of Queensberry, and their estates passed to the Dukes of Buccleuch in the early 19th century. Torthorwald Castle, now a roofless ruin, was apparently occupied until 1715.[4] The only son of Torthorwald parish generally known to the wider world is William Paterson, the founder of the Bank of England, who was born in the farmhouse of Skipmore, Torthorwald parish, in 1660. The Rev. John Paton, a 19th century missionary to the New Hebrides who spent his boyhood in the village of Torthorwald, is less well known now than in his own day.

The (Old) Statistical Account of Scotland gives a description of each parish in Scotland as it was around 1790, and an account of the changes which had taken place within living memory. Since the Statistical Account appears to provide the only account of life in the parish of Torthorwald in the 18th century, it is an invaluable source of information. The account of Torthorwald was written by the minister of the parish, James McMillan. He sets the scene by detailing the geography of the parish. He describes the western part as very low-lying, forming part of Lochar Moss, and says the adjacent pastures and meadows are frequently flooded. A strip of sandy ground is then superseded by "fine till soil", then by "arable braes, banks and hillocks" interspersed by patches of moorland and "wet clay grounds", ultimately giving way along the eastern boundary of the parish to "high black hills".

McMillan recalls that until about 1770 the farmers of Torthorwald and Roucan "had a considerable part of their land at a distance from their dwellings". The landowner, the Duke of Queensberry, then removed 25 of them to other parts of the parish, built "good farmhouses" for them, and enclosed the land with stone walls and hawthorn hedges. This was a process which was being carried on all over Lowland Scotland at that time. Originally the arable ground belonging to any given landowner was shared among his people under the "runrig" system, where tenants were allocated "rigs" or strips of ground of varying quality, which were then reallocated on a regular basis, so that in theory everyone had a fair share of good and poor ground. At the beginning of the 18th century reallocation was generally no longer practised, but tenants still cultivated widely scattered and unfenced pieces

---

3 History of the burgh of Dumfries – William McDowal. 4th revised edition, 1986, T. C. Ferries and Son, Pages 30, 31, 279. (First published 1867).

4 Canmore http://canmore.org.uk/event729042.

of ground. By the end of the century improving landlords were striving to rationalise and modernise the system, consolidating their tenants' holdings into compact farms with neatly enclosed rectangular fields. The pattern laid down at that time persists in most of rural Lowland Scotland to the present day. The rationale of course was that tenants farming improved holdings with improved up-to-date methods, could pay the landlords higher rents than in the bad old days when the ground was "lying runrig". McMillan points out that the rental of the parish had more than doubled between1756 and 1790. In what had probably been an earlier attempt to get rid of a surplus of small tenants, five farmers were encouraged to move to the Isle of Bute in 1750. The scheme cannot have been entirely successful, as three of them returned ten years later.

According to the Statistical Account, farmland in Torthorwald by 1790 was particularly suited to growing oats and barley, and large quantities of potatoes. The parish supported 650 black cattle, and 280 "common or small sheeps" pastured mostly on the hills. Small flocks of other sheep, termed "pets" or "half mugs" were kept on the lower ground and grazed among the milk cows. Lime was being used to improve the soil, modern two-horse ploughs cultivated the fields, and produce and other materials were conveyed in carts, which had been uncommon before the middle of the century. The parish had 120 horses in 1790 to pull the new ploughs and draw the new carts.

The population of the parish had increased from 540 in 1742 to 660 in 1790. In the village of Roucan, the Glassells' ancestral home, there were 41 families, giving the settlement a population of 143. The inhabitants included a surgeon, a schoolmaster, 11 tenant farmers, 14 tradesmen, 6 apprentices, a blacksmith, a mason, 2 wrights, 5 shoemakers, 4 weavers, 3 male servants, 9 female servants, 2 labourers, and 13 "cottagers". What the "tradesmen" were if they were not blacksmiths, masons, wrights or weavers is a little puzzling. Cottagers or cottars were in the main sub-tenants who would rent a house and a small piece of ground from a farmer, or be given them in return for their labour. By 1790 most cottagers were probably farm workers with more or less constant employment on their landlords' farms.

A century previously the village of "Roucane" had 35 householders enumerated in a list made around 1691 of "The Duke of Queensberry's hearths in Torthorell and Mousewald".[5] Four of the heads of families had

5 NAS. GD/997/355.

more than one hearth, but it is not clear whether this means they lived in bigger houses than their neighbours, or whether they possessed more than one house. Roucan, then, was obviously a large and thriving village throughout the 18th century.

According to the Statistical Account, in the first part of the 18th century, since there were few carts, dung was carried out to the fields in creels. A labourer's daily wage in the 1730s was three or four pence sterling. Hens sold for four pence each, and eggs for one and a half pence a dozen. Butter cost four pence a pound, pork four pence a pound, and a leg of lamb seven pence.[6] A beef cow sold at Martinmas for two guineas, and in 1749 the best horse in the parish sold for seven guineas. At that time the people of Torthorwald extracted vast quantities of peat from Lochar Moss, both for their own use and for sale in Dumfries. Since carts were scarce the peat was usually transported on horseback in large sacks. The Rev. James McMillan regarded work in the peat mosses as very injurious to the health of his parishioners. Between 1734 and 1790 the commonest cause of death in the parish was "the asthma", with "rheumatic complaints" also an important cause of death. These of course are not necessarily what we would now understand by asthma and rheumatism. The terms almost certainly cover a wide range of breathing and musclo-skeletal problems, and digging peat would not necessarily be the cause of them. MacMillan's description, however, serves to underline the harshness of living conditions for the common man in 18th century Scotland: "The uncommon mortality of these diseases was occasioned by a great number of the inhabitants having been in the practice of employing the greater part of the summer, and even a good part of winter first in making, and then in carrying peats from the moss to their own homes and for sale in Dumfries. In this employment, besides being exposed to the vicissitudes of the weather, the labourers generally had their legs soaked in moss-water almost all the day: and as they performed this work not for wages but on their own account, they constantly wrought several extra hours at a distance from their own homes and without the convenience of warm victuals etc. Under the circumstances the frequency of the asthma and the rheumatism need not be wondered at."

6 It should be remembered that in the 18th century, 12 pence = 1 shilling, and 20 shillings = £1. There were therefore 240 pence in a pound, not 100 pence as at present. A guinea was £1 and 1 shilling.

Some might seek relief from their toil in the alehouses, of which there were four in the parish in 1790, "to which for the most part idle and loose persons resort to drink whisky…". In spite of the threats of ill health and injured morals, however, "The inhabitants," according to MacMillan, "are generally very sober, honest and industrious, and live comfortably and at an easy rate." Tellingly, in keeping with this present study's particular interest in the Glassells, MacMillan also observes, "Many young men have gone abroad in different lines, several of whom have been successful, and have done honour to the place of their nativity."

At the time of the Old Statistical Account the overwhelming majority of the dwellings in Torthorwald parish would undoubtedly have been cottages of the "cruck built" kind, where the full weight of a thatched roof was supported on three pairs of oak couples, and the rubble-built stone walls between the earthen floor and the eaves were not load-bearing. A sole remaining restored example of this type is preserved in Torthorwald village.

In the years immediately preceding the middle of the 18th century we find, as previously mentioned, three families of Glassells of interest in Torthorwald parish; one in Torthorwald village headed by Adam Glassell, and two in the nearby village of Roucan, headed by John Glassell and Robert Glassell.

Adam Glassell in Torthorwald was married to Marion Kelton, daughter of William Kelton, also of Torthorwald. Adam had a son John who died only one day old in 1749, a son William born in 1749, and a daughter Betty born in 1751 after her father's death.[7] There also seems to have been a daughter Marion, who is mentioned on William Kelton's headstone in Torthorwald churchyard.[8] Adam was an elder of the Kirk, and the record of his burial on 28th August 1750 states that he died of a "pleu. fever". It also describes him baldly as "old". However, the memorial stone to William Kelton and his wife also commemorates "Adam Glassell their son in law died 28th August 1750 aged 42 years. Also Mary Kelton his spouse died November 1793 aged 83." If the inscription is correct, Adam can hardly have been "old" when he died, even by the standards of the mid-18th century. Unfortunately, there is a gap in the Torthorwald records from the very early years of the 18th century until c.1730, and so Adam's parents cannot be identified with

7 O.P.R. Torthorwald baptisms and burials.

8 Memorials of Torthorwald Parish – George Gilchrist, Annan, 1968. Ref 217.

certainty. In the years around the end of the 17th century there were three Glassells in the parish, all in Roucan, who could have been Adam's father:

a. Robert Glassell in Roucan had a son Adam baptised on 1st November 1696. We might therefore be led to suspect that this is "our" Adam, and that the age given on the Kelton headstone is simply mistaken. This is quite possible, as the inscription was obviously engraved long after Adam's death. A birth date of 1696 would make him around 54 at his death, which might just qualify him to be considered "old", especially if his "pleu. fever" was a debilitating lung disease.
b. On the other hand, "our" Adam's name might suggest that he could have been the son of Adam Glassell, smith in Roucan, who had another son John born in 1701.
c. But then again, since "our" Adam named his eldest son John, and it was common practice to name the eldest son after the paternal grandfather, Adam may have been the son of John Glassell in Roucan who had a son John in 1699 and a daughter Janet in 1701.[9]

    It is impossible, then, to be absolutely sure of the exact relationship of Adam Glassell the Torthorwald kirk elder to his contemporaries John and Robert in Roucan, but it would be surprising if he was not related in some degree.

John Glassell in Roucan headed the second Glassell family of interest in Torthorwald parish in the mid-18th century. He married Marion Kirkpatrick on 2nd June 1730. He is described as living in "Townend of Ruchan", and Marion was also described as residing in Roucan at the time of her marriage. John and Marion had children Margaret (1731), John (1734), Margaret (1737),[10] Marion (1740), and Janet (1751). John, the head of this family, died on 17th April 1755, aged 55. He must therefore have been born around 1700. In the Torthowald register of baptisms we find a John baptised on 29th January 1699, the son of "John Glessel in Rouchan". This man is probably the John Glessel in Howgate who had a daughter Janet in 1701; Howgate was part of the village of Roucan. The Torthorwald Register of Marriages shows that John Glessell in Rucan married Marion Glessell there on 21st October 1697. Confusingly, however, the marriage is also recorded

9 O.P.R. Torthorwald baptisms and burials.

10 The second Margaret probably indicates that the first Margaret had died.

of John Glessell in Rucan and Margaret Burnet on 19th April 1698. The closeness of these two events surely indicates that here we are looking at two different John Glassells, both living in Roucan. To add to the confusion, Adam Glessel smith in Rucan had a son John baptised on 27th February 1701, who might have been the John who married Marion Kirkpatrick in 1730. "Our" John had a daughter Marion born in 1740. Perhaps this child was not named after her mother, but after her grandmother. This scenario would fit if her father John was the son of the John and Marion Glassell who married in 1697. As already mentioned, "our" John died in 1755. His wife Marion Kirkpatrick survived him for many years and died in 1771: "9th November 1771. Marion Kirkpatrick relict of John Glessell late tenant in Roucan Townfoot. She had been for many years much distressed with rheumatism. Nine days before her death she was deprived of the use of her left limbs. Her tongue was a little affected and her understanding impaired. The disorder was accompanied by a flux. Aged 65 years."[11]

The third of the mid-18th century families in Torthorwald parish was that of Robert Glassell in Roucan. Children of "Robert Glessil" recorded in the Torthorwald register of baptisms are Robert baptised 8th September 1734, John (28th November 1736), Andrew (8th October 1738), Robert (15th February 1741), and James (11th August 1748). It is from this family that the Glassells subsequently featured in this study descend.

The Torthorwald marriage register records that on 27th November 1735 "Robert Glassil in Ruchan was married to Mary Kelton daughter to William Kelton in Torthorwald Town". This leaves us with a puzzle over the infant Robert baptised in 1734. If he was the son of our "Robert Glessil" he must have either been born to a wife other than Mary Kelton, or been born out of wedlock either to Mary or to some other woman. However, there seems to be no record of the death of a wife previous to Mary. Nor is there any mention of illegitimacy in the record of Robert's baptism, as was almost always the case with children born out of wedlock. Also, it will become obvious as we pursue the family's progress that John, born in 1736, was regarded as the eldest son. The most likely explanation is that the Robert born in 1734 was the son of a different Robert Glassell. This of course highlights one of the bugbears of Scottish genealogy. When a surname is

11 O.P.R. Torthorwald baptisms, burials and marriages.

locally common, and children are allocated forenames from a very limited range, it is sometimes going to be difficult to tell who's who. Young married couples may be producing children while their fathers' younger second wives are doing likewise, and the fact that mothers' names are often omitted from baptismal records compounds the difficulty. Also, the widespread practice of "irregular" marriage meant that marriages were not always registered. And this is without even beginning to consider the cousins, uncles, and nephews who all may have had the same name as the particular father requiring to be pinpointed. Be that as it may, the likelihood that the infant Robert's father was a different Robert Glassell is supported by an entry in the Torthorwald burial register: "6th June 1771. Robert Glassell, shoemaker in Roucan aged 76. He had been of a healthy constitution. He was seized about a fortnight before his death with a general feebleness somewhat of the paralytic kind…". There were therefore two Robert Glassells in the small village of Roucan fathering children in the 1730s; Robert the shoemaker, and Robert the tenant farmer.

Robert Glassell and Mary Kelton, then, had children John (1736), Andrew (1738), and Robert (1741) – then Mary died only a year after the third child's birth: "11th March 1742. Buried Mary Kelton wife to Robert Glassil in Ruchan". Callous as it may seem, it was not the practice in 18th century Scotland for a widowed father to remain a "single parent" for long. Quite apart from the absolute necessity of childcare for a young family, the running of a tenant farmer's household comprised an endless round of duties. The position of "gudewife" was a full time job well beyond the competence of the bereaved farmer himself. Robert Glassell therefore took a second wife, Mary Coulter. Mary was presumably born during the 1701-1730 gap in the Torthorwald baptismal records, but may well have been the sister of "William Coulter in Greenhead Rukan" and "John Coulter in Townfute Ruchan". A James Glassell born in 1748, son to Robert Glassell, may have been Mary's child, but since he is not mentioned in subsequent family papers he presumably either died in infancy or was the son of the "other" Robert Glassell.

There seems to be no record of the marriage of Robert Glassell and Mary Coulter, so perhaps it was of the "irregular" kind where a couple simply agreed to take each other as man and wife. This was frowned upon by the Church of Scotland, but was very common and perfectly legal. Alternatively, they could have been married by a "seceder" minister from one of the Presbyterian sects strong in south-west Scotland. That Mary was in fact an actual "wife" is attested by a mention of "our father's wife" in a letter from Robert's son John to his brother Andrew shortly after their father's death[12], and by the record of the death in 1772 of "Mary Coulter widow of Robert Glassell, late tenant in Roucan".

The family of Robert Glassell, then, consisted originally of Robert, his wife Mary Kelton, and their sons John, Andrew and Robert. After Mary's death at an early age, Robert married Mary Coulter. Robert senior himself died in 1765. The Torthorwald burial register records: "24th January 1765. Buried Robert Glassell, tenant in Howgate Roucan. A [illegible] disorder accompanied by the spitting of blood. Age 62." A near-illegible word added looks very like "lunatic", but may not be. As already mentioned, Mary Coulter died in 1772: "14th July 1772. Mary Coulter widow of Robert Glassell late tenant in Roucan aged 67, astmatic and paralitic [sic]. A few days before her death took a swelling in her legs which continued to ascend till her death."

We see from the records that Robert's farm in Roucan was known as "Howgate".

Robert and his first wife are commemorated by an imposing stone in the South section of Torthorwald churchyard, which is inscribed:

"Sacred to the memory of Robert Glassell late tenant in the Howgate, Roucan, who died 2d January 1763 aged 61 years. And Mary Kelton his spouse who died 7th March 1742 aged 37. Here are also deposited many of his forebears who during some hundred years did successively inhabit the same house.

They aimed at no titles
But honest and unstained characters.
None of them were rich
Neither were they poor
But their own industry by the Divine blessing
Supplied them abundantly with the necessaries
Of life and with something else to relieve the
Distressed.

12 See Chapter 2.

As a testimony of filial gratitude this monument was erected by their son John Glassell, Merchant in Fredricksburg VIRGINEA.

A wits a feather and a chief a rod
An honest mans the noblest work of God.

The above Robert Glassell was proprietor of Slengebar & Westfield."

We shall hear much more of John, the merchant in "*VIRGINEA*". It seems a little odd that Robert was "tenant" in the Howgate and also "proprietor" of Slengebar and Westfield. We would usually expect a "proprietor" to be rather higher on the social scale than a mere "tenant". However, John had become a very wealthy man, as we shall see, and perhaps he had enabled his father to extend his farming beyond the Howgate with the purchase of other holdings.[13]

The intertwining of relationships between the Glassells and Keltons is underlined by another stone in the East section of Torthorwald kirkyard which commemorates William Kelton in Torthorwald who died in 1714, his wife Agnes Armstrong, and their sons William and John. Also their daughter Marion and her husband Adam Glassell. Adam's cotemporary, Robert Glassell, was as we have seen, also married to a Kelton – Mary, who died young. We might assume that here we have two brothers marrying two sisters. There is no proof that this was so, and we have already chewed over the possible relationship between Robert and Adam. However, a close relationship between them might be indicated by the fact that on 13th March 1741 Adam Glassell lent Robert Glassell £3 sterling.[14] At Adam's death only 3 shillings "annualrent" (interest) had so far been paid, and his widow Marion had to apply to the Commissary Court of Dumfries to enforce repayment of the £3.

It might be remarked in passing that in the mid-18th century the Keltons had not strayed far from their origins. "Kelton" stands on the banks of the River Nith, south of Dumfries, some four miles as the crow flies from Roucan.

Andrew Glassell, the son of Robert Glassell and Mary Kelton, founded an American dynasty. Its members have been proud of their Scottish

13 I have been unable to trace the whereabouts of Slengebar and Westfield.
14 Dumfries Commissary Court CC5/6, 13th June 1759.

antecedents, but what they believe about their ancestors, and what has been written about them online and on paper, complicates matters by not always being strictly accurate, and in some cases by being just plain wrong.

For example, we read in "A history of St Mark's parish, Culpeper County, Virginia"[15]:

"John Glassell of Eun-can, Scotland, m. Mary Coalter, a warm Covenanter, and their son Robert m. Mary Kelton, and their son Andrew Glassell was born at Galway, Dumfriesshire, Scotland, near Torthorwald 'Castle of the Douglases' October 8th 1738 and emigrated to Madison County, Virginia in 1756."

To deal with the obvious howlers first; Dr Slaughter seems to be suggesting that Torthorwald means "Castle of the Douglases", which of course it does not. There is no such place as "Galway" in Dumfriesshire, and there has presumably been some confusion with Scotland's south-western district of Galloway. The bizarre placename "Eun-kan" is no doubt the result of a mistaken transcription of one of the spellings of "Roucan". We should not judge Dr Slaughter too harshly however. He is unlikely to have ever been in Scotland, and his knowledge of its geography was probably fairly rudimentary. His information, including the reference to the "warm Covenanter" Mary Coalter, would be gleaned, we might guess, from family traditions or papers handed down by the American Glassells. These were expounded later in greater detail in Horace Edwin Hayden's "Virginia Genealogies".[16]

The American Glassells are descended from Andrew, born in 1738 to Robert Glassell, tenant farmer in Howgate, Roucan, in the parish of Torthorwald, Dumfriesshire. Both "Virginia Genealogies" and "A history of St Mark's Parish" agree that Robert, Andrew's father, was the son of a John Glassell in Roucan, and if this was a family tradition, it was probably correct. We have already seen that the Torthorwald registers show a John

15 " A history of St Mark's Parish, Culpeper County, Virginia, with notes of old churches and old families, and illustrations of the manners and customs of the olden time" – Revd Philip Slaughter D.D., Rector of Emmanuel Church. Culpeper County, Va. 1877. Page 132.

16 "Virginia Genealogies – a genealogy of the Glassell family of Scotland and Virginia. Also of the families of Ball, Brown, Bryan, Conway, Daniel, Ewell Holladay, Lewis, Littlepage, Moncure, Peyton, Robinson, Seat, Taylor, Wallace, and others of Virginia and Maryland" – Rev Horace Edwin Hayden, Wilkes-Barre, Pennsylvania, 1891. (Reprinted for Clearfield Company inc. Baltimore, Maryland. 2004.)

Glassell in Roucan at the end of the 17th century. Unfortunately, although the records show the baptism of his son John and daughter Janet, a gap of about thirty years in the records makes it impossible to prove with absolute certainty that he also had a son Robert. In the absence of written proof, we can only accept what seems to be family tradition. It seems probable, then, that this turn-of-the-century John was the father of Robert, and grandfather of Andrew.

Details beyond the mere fact of grandfather John's existence, are difficult to track down, however. Hayden's "Virginia Genealogies" states confidently, "John Glassell, a descendant of John 1620, lived in Rucan, Dumfries, Scotland. He married Mary Coalter as per family records. It appears from the Torthorwald parish records that he also married his cousin Marion, who was probably his first wife."[17] We do indeed find in the register of Torthorwald marriages that on 7th October 1797 "John Glessell in Rucan and Marion Glessell yr gave up yr names to be proclaimed in order to marriage and gave in yr dollars and after proclamation were married this twentieth and first day of October 1697." There is no mention of Marion being John's cousin, but she was almost certainly related to him in some degree. Confusingly, however, only six months later on 19th April 1698, "John Glessell in Rucan and Margaret Burnet being proclaimed in order to marriage, were married." These two marriages are so close together that they are most unlikely to indicate a second marriage following the death of a first wife, and must relate to two different John Glassells living in Roucan at the same time. So which of these two Johns was Andrew's grandfather?

Then there is the problem of Mary Coalter, grandfather John's wife "as per family records". Mary Coalter is a colourful figure in the American Glassells' family history. Horace Hayden writes in "Virginia Genealogies" that Andrew Glassell "knew his grandmother Mary Coalter Glassell who lived in the time of Charles II and James I [sic] during the persecutions of the Covenanters, and who often related how she frequently attended services in the hollows and caves of the mountains when the snow was two feet deep, her servant carrying a piece of carpet for her to stand upon, and while worshipping, sentinels kept guard for fear of Claverhouse and his dragoons. It is also narrated of her that on one occasion she secreted some Covenanting preachers in her house. Their whereabouts being suspected by

17 Virginia Genealogies, Page 4.

Claverhouse, he sent a party of dragoons to search her house. Being warned of their approach Mrs Glassell quickly made a large peat fire which so filled the house with smoke that the troops were unable to stand it, and soon left in disgust without making the search."[18]

Regarding the same woman, Slaughter's "History of St Mark's Parish" tells us, "John Glassell of Eun-kan, Scotland, m. Mary Coalter, a warm Covenanter."[19]

The first problem, but one easily disposed of, is that there is no record whatsoever of the surname "Coalter" in the parish of Torthorwald. This is not surprising, as it would be a most unusual surname in Scotland, if indeed it exists at all. However, the surname "Coulter" appears frequently in the Torthorwald registers, and "Coulter", with its variants "Coultart" and "Coultard", is a fairly common Scottish surname. Obviously "Coalter" is a mistake, arising either through Virginian pronunciation, or from a misreading of an entry in a family bible or some other family papers.

We are therefore dealing here with a woman called Mary Coulter, who was supposedly the wife of John Glassell in the late 17th century, and was also the grandmother of Andrew Glassell who was born in 1738. However, there is no record of a marriage between a Mary Coulter and John Glassell. Of course that is no proof that such a marriage did not exist. It might have taken place during the gap in the registers between the early 1700s and 1730, or in the years before the register began in the 1690s. On the other hand, we would expect to see a record of the burial of "Mary Coulter, relict of John Glassell" sometime around the middle of the 18th century. There is no such record, however, unless we allow the entry on 4th April 1748 noting the burial of "Marion Couter in Roucan aged 84". It is not beyond possibility that this is the Mary Coulter supposedly married to John Glassell, mother of Robert, and grandmother of Andrew the Virginian. The names "Mary" and "Marion" were sometimes deemed interchangeable in 17th/18th century Scotland, just as "Peter" and "Patrick" almost always were. However, although Marion Couter is approximately the right age, why is she not designated "relict of John Glassell" or "spouse of the deceased John Glassell" as was the custom of the time? It seems rather more likely that "Marion Couter" was an unmarried woman.

18 Virginia Genealogies, Page 6.

19 History of St Mark's Parish, Page 136.

Then again, if we consider the family story of Mary's Covenanting associations, the persecution of the Covenanting religious dissidents came to an end with the so-called "Glorious Revolution" of 1688 – the exile of James VII and the accession of William and Mary. The story of the smoke-filled house has Mary Coulter already a housewife during the Killing Times of the 1670s and 80s. This would give her a birth date of around 1650, in which case she would be rather unlikely to be bearing children to John Glassell in the first decade of the 18th century. There was, however, a "Marion Coulter spouse to the deceast Robert Glessil in townfoot in Roucan" who was buried on 7th April 1701. As already mentioned, "Marion" and "Mary" were sometimes treated as variant of the same name. Perhaps, then, it was this Marion Coulter who was the woman with Covenanting sympathies. Perhaps her husband Robert was the father of John, making her the great-grandmother, not the grandmother, of Andrew the Virginian. But then, "Virginia Genealogies" has it that Andrew "knew" his Covenanting forebear, which he obviously could not have done if she died in 1701.

A more plausible solution to the "Mary Coalter" problem is that Mary the teller of Covenanting tales was in fact Mary Coulter the second wife of Andrew's father Robert Glassell. We know that Robert remarried after the early death of his first wife Mary Kelton, because a letter to Andrew from his brother in 1765 mentions provision for "my father's widow"[20]. This widow is not named, but her death is recorded thus in the Torthorwald burial records: "14th July 1772. Mary Coulter, widow of Robert Glassell, late tenant in Roucan, aged 67, astmatic and paralitic. A few days before her death she took a swelling in her legs which continued to ascend till her death." There would be nothing more natural than Mary telling her young stepsons tales of her family's past, since Glassells and Coulters inhabited the same village, shared a common heritage, and had previously intermarried. She herself would have been born long after the persecution of Covenanters ceased, but the Killing Times would still be vivid in local tradition. The incident of the smoke-filled house has the feel of a folk-tale about it, and indeed similar tales have been told regarding revenue officers seeking contraband, and redcoats hunting Jacobite fugitives. Gatherings for worship in the hills had been frequent enough, but "mountains" are something of a Virginian exaggeration in the context of the countryside around Roucan.

20 National Records of Scotland, Register of Deeds RD274, Page 526.

The square of carpet to stand on in the snow rings true as someone's childhood memory. Surely a farmer's wife would have brought her own square of carpet if she thought her footwear unsuitable for standing an hour or two in the snow, but a servant might have carried one for a small child. We need not balk at the idea of a humble tenant farmer having "servants". The duties of the mistress of the house were many and onerous, and it was normal to have a girl or two to assist. Often they were young nieces or cousins. The Covenanting past of "Mary Coalter", then, may have been a melange of genuine family traditions and stories that typified a traumatic era, related by Andrew Glassell's stepmother, passed on by him, and seen by his Virginian descendants through the misty lens of 19th century romanticism. Incidentally, the description of "Mary Coalter" by Philip Slaughter as a "warm Covenanter" is ironically ill-chosen for someone who supposedly worshipped while up to her knees in snow!

A similar veil of romanticism obscures the Glassells' origins. In his "History of St Mark's parish"[21], Philip Slaughter states confidently, "The Glassell (originally Glasele) family went from Poitiers, France, with Mary Queen of Scots on her return to her native country." A 21st century amateur genealogist repeats the story online as follows: "The Glassell (or Glassele) family is of French descent. The first of the name went from France to Scotland with Mary Queen of Scots on her return to her native land in 1560. The name supposedly was originally spelled "Glassele". John Glassell, a descendant who followed the fortunes of Mary Stuart, lived on his estate called "Runcan" in Scotland…".[22]

Unfortunately, in his "Virginia Genealogies" Hayden quotes a letter dated 22nd November 1889 from George Burnett of the Lyon Office in Edinburgh in which Dr Burnett says he had searched the Exchequer Rolls from Queen Mary's reign "where we would expect to find payment to all her retainers and attendants", but had not found any mention of the surname Glassell. "In fact," says Burnett, "I do not find the name of Glassell in any records except in the parish records of Torthorwald and adjoining parishes in Dumfriesshire, and one in a retour of that county."[23] Slaughter

21 A History of St Marks Parish etc – Rev Philip Slaughter D.D., Culpeper Co., Va., 1877, Page 136.

22 Biography of Frances Toy Glassell Ware – Judith C. Ware, 2009. Updated 2013.

23 Hayden, Virginia Genealogies, Page 3.

presumably got the suggestion of the Glassell family's French origins from the Glassells themselves. What evidence they had for any such thing is unclear to say the least. However, in a Scottish or English context a surname of French origin might hint at aristocratic forebears, and thus might be attractive to an amateur American genealogist. The Glassells had become "somebody" in Virginia, and it would be more fitting to have ancestors who were also "somebody", than to be descended from mere peasant farmers. The dignifying of the Glassell farm in Roucan as an "estate" is an obvious example of the same mindset. And associations with "Mary Queen of Scots" would of course appeal to Americans susceptible to a romantic view of Scottish history.

We can probably accept as highly likely that Andrew Glassell's grandfather was a John Glassell living in Roucan at the end of the 17th century. As previously noted, "Virginia Genealogies" claims that this John was "a descendant of John 1620". This statement is presumably based on Glassell family tradition, but it is very difficult to prove, as there are no Torthorwald registers of baptisms, burials and marriages before the last years of the 17th century. Other documentary evidence is sparse to say the least. A "List of the Duke of Queensberry's hearths in Torthorell & Mouswald" exists, which the National Records of Scotland catalogue dates as "c. 1691".[24] There are no Glassells listed under "Torthoral toun", but under "Roucane" we find Adam Glassell, John Glassell, James Glassell, and Robert Glassell. Interestingly, although almost all the householders of Torthorwald and Roucan possess one single hearth, Adam Glassell is listed as having three. It is impossible to tell whether this means that he occupied a large house with three hearths, or was the proprietor of three properties, but he is clearly rather better off than his neighbours. There were also Coulters resident in Roucan: Michael, James, and a Matthew whose almost illegible surname may be Coulter. James Coulter is listed as being in possession of two hearths. We are catching a glimpse here of two men, Adam Glassell and James Coulter, who would seem to be above the level of mere peasantry, and their slightly superior status might by association have included their close relatives.

Continuing the search for 17th century Glassells, we find two entries of interest in the Register of Testaments in the Commissariot Record of Dumfries, both

24 National Records of Scotland GD26/7/355.

dated 1657. First is the testament dative and inventory of the goods, gear, sums of money and debts belonging to "Umqll Jon Glassell daitit 28 March 1657".[25] John died in January 1657 in "Ruiken foot", leaving an ox worth £8 Scots,[26] a cow worth £8, a mare worth 10 merks,[27] and ten pecks of seed corn estimated capable of producing a threefold increase, and therefore worth £15. There was also six pecks of seed beir (an early form of barley) estimated to produce a fourfold increase worth £18. John owed nothing to anyone, and had no debts owing to him. The inventory of his goods and gear was made by his eldest son Adam, and the inheritance was to be divided equally between two other children, Robert and Elizabeth. It should not be assumed, however, that the eldest son Adam received nothing. In all probability his inheritance was his father's house and landholding in "Ruiken foot".

Rather more intriguing is the testament dative and inventory of "Umqll Robert Glassel daitit first Appryll 1657".[28] His executor was his eldest daughter Jannet, and the list of his goods and gear was given in by Robert Mair, a relative of Robert's wife. At first glance, Robert's situation would seem to differ little from that of his presumed kinsman John. Robert died in "Ruken" leaving "thrie nolt" (three bullocks) worth £8 each, and "ane auld naig" estimated at £8. There were six pecks of beir estimated to produce a fourfold crop worth £15, and twelve pecks of oats capable of producing a threefold crop worth £12. There were also three bolls of malt worth £24. Robert's clothes and the contents of his house were reckoned to be worth £20. The only debt he owed was £33-6-8 to "William Cairlell late taylour of Dumfries". The striking difference between the inventories of Robert and John Glassell, is the astonishing number of sums of money owed to Robert. These are:[29]

John Mair, his father-in-law	*£82-30s*
Peter Potter in Cokfield	*£40*
Archibald Bell in Lynes	*£20*
James Halliday in Lynes	*£17-16s*
John Cowter in Rukine in Midtoune	*£6*

25 National Records of Sotland CC5/6/3, Page 203.

26 £1 Scots was reckoned to be worth one twelfth of a pound sterling.

27 A merk was two thirds of a pond Scots, i.e. 13s 4d.

28 National Records of Scotland CC5/6/3, Page 207.

29 All sums of money are in pounds Scots.

John Richardsone in Rukine	*£12*
Thomas Glassell in Rouken	*£33*
Margaret Young spouse to Wm Mutch	*£23*
William Bowie in Dumfries	*£5*
Margaret Coupland there spouse to Harbert Burges	*£15*
Elizabeth Clark in Dumfries	*£16*
Issobell Gilchrist there	*£4*
Elizabeth Gib £4 to umqll Wm Craik merchant there	*£30-13-4*
James McMillane indweller there	*£6-6-8*
John Newall smith there	*£5-5s*
John Glencross cutler there	*£8*
Robert Rae mason there	*£6-16*
John McKulie in Tinwald	*£6*
Elizabeth Couland in Dumfries	*£15*
Robert Glassell younger, merchant there	*£120*

Thus the deceased Robert Glassell was owed twenty sums of money ranging from £4 to £120. The previously noted valuation of a cow at £8 gives a rough idea of the relative contemporary value of each debt. The two largest debts are owed by Robert's father-in-law John Mair and by Robert Glassell "younger", a merchant in Dumfries. It might be assumed that the deceased was comfortably well-off, had acquired some capital, and was in the habit of lending out small sums of money. This is always a possibility, but it seemed perhaps more likely that Robert was selling something, that each debt represented an article or articles bought by the debtor, and that Robert, like his namesake in Dumfries, was a "merchant" of some description. Nowadays we are inclined to imagine "merchants" as wealthy men dealing in silks, spices, and other luxury goods, but it should be remembered that "merchant" was a term covering many levels of commercial activity and degrees of status. The proprietors of small general stores in 19th and early 20th century Scotland still habitually described themselves as "merchants". Although there is no direct indication in the inventory of what Robert was selling, there is a clue in his possession of two bolls of malt. A boll was not a measure of weight, but a dry measure of capacity. The standard boll of Linlithgow was equivalent to 145.145 litres.[30] The exact amount of a boll

30 Scots Concise Dictionary.

varied from burgh to burgh, but the variations were small. Robert therefore was in possession of just over 290 dry measure litres of malt at the time of his death, which is a fair amount. Six of his debtors were women, and an important part of the housewife's duties was brewing ale for the household. The implication is that Robert was a dealer in malt.

The interesting debtor on the list is "Robert Glassell younger, merchant in Dumfries". Does the "younger" indicate that his was the deceased Robert Glassell's own son, or was Robert Glassell "elder" somebody quite different? At the foot of Robert's inventory are two or three lines of mostly illegible scrawl, but it can be made out that a "Robert Glessill merchant in Dumfries" was "sworne", presumably indicating that he was witness to the registration of the inventory, or testified to its accuracy. His involvement certainly suggests a relationship of some sort to the deceased.

We can gather, then, that Robert Glassell who died in Roucanfoot in 1657, as well as being a small farmer in Roucan, was engaged in commercial activity, probably in the manufacture and sale of malt, and had a commercial connection with a Robert Glassell who was a merchant in Dumfries and was almost certainly a relative of the deceased, possibly even his son. Thus, although Robert's testament dative and inventory do not expressly state that he was a dealer in malt, it seems highly likely that he was. We cannot be sure that any one of the two Glassells, Robert and John, who died in 1657, was a direct ancestor of the 18th century family whose son Andrew became a wealthy Virginian, but it is highly probable that they were all closely connected, and that Andrew's direct ancestors were either engaged in commercial activity in the mid-17th century, or were closely related to those so engaged.

Reaching further back in time, we come to another interesting document in the National Records. This is a "Precept of warning" by the advocate Adam Cuninghame, proprietor of the lands of Dargavel, addressed to a list of people who are "pretended tenants and occupiers" of parts of Cuninghame's "meadow of Rowken, with pertinents lying of the south and southwest sides of the Water of Lochar adjacent to his lands of Dargavel." These occupiers of portions of Roucan Meadow are commanded to "flit and move therefrom at Whitsunday 1619" and the document is dated at Edinburgh 28th March 1619.[31]

Those named are:

31 National Records of Scotland GD86/446.

James Lawsone in Rowken
John Glassell
John Glassell, wobster[32]
Michell Cowter
Patrick Neilsone
Patrick Mair
Jonat Burnet
Johnne Mair
Robert Glassell
John Lawsone
John Glassell, smith
John Glassell, maltman
Katharein Kirkpatrick
Thomas Glassell
John Wichtman
Agnes Johnstoun
Thomas Cowter, callit Ridcloik
Mathew Cowter
John Burnet
Thomas Burnet
Edward Haliday
Edward Cowter
Margaret Ceirlell
Jonat Potter, widow
James Suan
Andro Potter
James Clark
Edward Johnstoun, all in Tounfut of Rowken.
John Ritcharsone in Torthorwald.

What we have here is almost certainly a list of every householder in Roucan Townfoot. Their interest in Lochar Moss was most likely as a source of fuel. Each household would have customary rights to cut peat, and possibly also the right to graze livestock. Cuninghame is seeking either to deprive them of these rights, or possibly to rearrange them within new legal parameters

32 weaver

favourable to himself. In the list we find several of the surnames which appear frequently in the 18th century parish records, including three "Cowters", one with the intriguing nickname of "Red Cloak". There are no fewer than six Glassells – one a weaver, one a blacksmith, and one a maltman. It can be presumed that the others were peasant farmers. Of the six Glassells in Roucan in 1619, four were named John. If the Virginia Glassells believed themselves to be descendants of "John 1620", which one was their ancestor? One John was a smith, one a weaver, one a maltman, and the other presumably a tenant farmer. We might guess that John the maltman was the father of Robert Glassell whose testament dative and inventory of 1657 indicates that he too was a dealer in malt. We might also guess that this John is very likely to be the Virginian ancestor, but admittedly there is no proof. And of course all of these Johns were probably related to each other in some degree.

1619 seems to be as far back as we can get with the Glassells in Roucan. However, the Dumfries registers also show Glassells in that town and parish throughout the 17th century. A John, son of Thomas Glassell, smith, was buried on 1st April 1622, and a Thomas Glassell, probably the same man, had a daughter Janet baptised on 19th March 1618. This Thomas must have been born in the latter years of the 16th century. There is no proof that he was born in Dumfries, but it would hardly be surprising if he was. Robert Edgar, c. 1667-1757, clerk to the Incorporated Trades of Dumfries, mentions a John Glassell who appears in the "Custom Buik of Dumfries" for 1578.[33] In that year John Glassell declared a dozen "blew bonnets" at 12d per dozen, eleven pounds of pepper and ginger at 6d per pound, and a dozen papers of "prenis" (pins) at 6d per dozen. If this John Glassell was active as a merchant in 1578, we would expect him to have been born at the latest around the middle of the 1500s.

Since there were so many Glassells in Roucan in 1619, it would hardly be straying into the realms of fantasy to suggest that they too would have Glassell ancestors, or an ancestor, living around the middle of the 1500s, in Roucan.

If there were Glassells already living in Dumfries and Roucan in the

33 A history of Dumfries: An introduction to the history of Dumfries by Robert Edgar, Ed. R. C. Reid, J. Maxwell & Sons, Dumfries 1915, Page 263.

mid-16th century that fact must cast serious doubt on the Virginian family myth that the Glassell family progenitor was a Frenchman who came to Scotland with "Mary Queen of Scots". It was 1561 before Mary returned to her native land from France.

There must, of course, have been an original bearer of the surname Glassell. It is not a surname with an obvious origin, like "Brown", "Robertson" or "Hunter", so how did it arise, and from where, if not France? The Ordnance Survey map shows "Glassel" and "Mains of Glassel" on the Burn of Canny some three miles north-west of Banchory in the Mearns. However, Deeside is a very long way from Dumfriesshire, and it seems an unlikely place of origin for our first Glassell forefather. If the surname derives from a place, it might rather be from some other "glas allt" (grey stream) in Dumfries and Galloway, wide areas of which were Gaelic-speaking in the Middle Ages – perhaps even from the Lochar Water itself, running between Dumfries and Roucan. Or then again, perhaps the name was descriptive, bestowed on a "glas 'ille" (grey boy or grey servant). Another consideration is: did the Dumfries Glassells come originally from Roucan, or did the Roucan Glassells stem from Dumfries? But here we are entering the realms of speculation where no definitive answer is possible. My own feeling is that the original Glassell progenitor was a peasant farmer living within sight of the "grey stream" of Lochar, but who can tell?

It may be worth remembering that in early records the name is often given as "Glessell". It might be assumed that this is just the Scots pronunciation of "Glassell". But what if, on the contrary, "Glassell" is an anglicisation of an original surname "Glessell"? This could send us scurrying for a whole new set of derivations.

Finally, what if the Virginian tradition of French origins is more than mere myth? We might imagine a scenario something like: "Grandpa always said we had been French originally."

"Oh? How would a Frenchman get to be in Scotland?"

"Who knows? Maybe he came over with Mary Queen of Scots."

In subsequent generations this is remembered as, "They used to say we were French and had come over with Mary Queen of Scots", and finally becomes, "The Glassells were originally French, and came to Scotland with Mary Queen of Scots."

This admittedly is not impossible, but, as already suggested, seems unlikely in view of the large number of Glassells securely established in Dumfriesshire only half a century after Mary's return in 1561. But what if the original Glassell was not a French retainer of some sort in Queen Mary's household, but a French merchant who settled in or near the port of Dumfries in the early 16th century or previously, bequeathing an entrepreneurial heritage to his descendants? The Glassells always seem to have had merchants among them. The rest were mostly tradesmen or farmers. Few if any seem to have been mere hewers of wood and drawers of water. Dumfries was a busy port in early modern times, and might well attract foreign merchants, just as Scots merchants were drawn to settle on the Continent. Of course this is all speculation. Personally, I would take the French origin with a pinch of salt, and settle for the humble farmer by the "grey stream".

Torthorwald Churchyard.

Headstone of "Robert Glassell, tenant in the Howgate, Roucan".

The site of Roucan today looks very different from its 18th century aspect.

A surviving "cruck house" in Torthorwald. 18th century Glassells might well have lived in a house like this.

2

"The large business I am engaged in..."

AROUND THE MIDDLE OF THE 18TH CENTURY, JOHN GLASSELL, SON OF Robert Glassell, a tenant farmer in Roucan in the Dumfriesshire parish of Torthorwald, crossed the Atlantic to begin a career in commerce in the British colony of Virginia. What were the circumstances that would impel a teenage boy to forsake home and kindred for a strange land so far away?

It is difficult nowadays for the casual visitor to the town of Dumfries to grasp that this was once a busy port, but the River Nith on which the town stands is tidal up to the weir below the Old Bridge of Dumfries, and allowed access to the Solway Firth into which it flows. The Solway in turn allowed access to the Irish Sea and Atlantic Ocean, and to the wider world beyond.

Access to the wider world was not without its problems, however. The channel of the Nith was prone to shifting within its banks, particularly where its widening estuary meets the Solway. Swift running tides exposed miles of mudflats and sandbanks at low tide, and covered them at high tide to trap unwary navigators who strayed from the main channel. Around the beginning of the 18th century, therefore, buoys were placed in the lower reaches of the Nith to guide ships up the deeper and safer river channel, and in 1710 obstructions were removed from the channel by blasting at Castledykes on the outskirts of Dumfries.[34] Harbour facilities were still rudimentary, however, until mid-century. In 1746 the Earl of Nithsdale gave land and supplied stone from his quarries to build a quay and necessary associated buildings at Glencaple, some five miles south of Dumfries, and the following year a quay was built at Kingholm just beyond the southern edge of the burgh.[35] Eventually there were five quays on the Nith: Glencaple, Kingholm, Laghall on the opposite bank facing Kingholm, Castledykes on the edge of Dumfries, and Dockfoot in Dumfries itself. The quays at Glencaple and Kingholm survive, and the Dumfries dock remains as the frontage of a riverside walk extending from the weir down to Dockfoot Park.

A programme of improvements meant that during the first half of the 19th century the port of Dumfries was able to receive ever larger vessels including the new steamships. There was not only a busy coastal trade to England and Ireland, but regular shipping to and from a wide range of European ports, and Virginia and New England across the Atlantic. Dumfries reached its peak as a port in the 1840s. Its facilities had never been able to match those of Liverpool to the south, and the Clyde to the north, and the coming of the railway in the mid-19th century began a slow but steady decline, as goods could now be quickly delivered anywhere in the country from these large efficient ports.

In the middle of the 18th century, however, all was optimism. Dumfries had established lucrative links with the American colonies, and so much tobacco was being imported that Dumfries merchants were beginning to harbour illusions of their burgh becoming "the Scottish Liverpool".[36] Several Dumfries merchants were not only trading regularly across the Atlantic, but maintaining permanent establishments in Virginia.[37] These Virginian depots and offices would obviously have to be staffed with trustworthy literate and numerate employees, to whom weighty responsibilities were delegated.

---

34 Dumfries's Story – David Lockwood, T. C. Ferries & Co. Ltd., Dumfries 1988, Page 65.

35 Lockwood, Page 65.

36 Lockwood, Page 64.

37 Scotus Americanus – William R. Brock, Edinburgh University Press, Edinburgh, 1982.

Scotland was more fortunate than many European countries in that it had an effective education system which allowed bright boys from the "middling" ranks of society, and even on occasion a particularly determined product of the "lower orders" not only to become literate and numerate, but to attain a university education and enter a range of professions. Admittedly, the glories of Scottish education have been exaggerated in the past, and the humble "lad o pairts" was more of a rarity than is often claimed, but education and progress was at least a possibility for the poor and low-born.

The system of parish schools envisaged by the protestant reformers had more or less come to fruition in the lowland parishes of Scotland, although less successfully in the remoter areas of the Highlands and islands. In addition, the burghs had their grammar schools and high schools, and Edinburgh, Glasgow, Aberdeen and St Andrews had their "colleges" preparing candidates for careers in the ministry, in law, and in medicine.

Private schools were also common, and parents would also club together to employ a teacher, as Robert Burns's father famously did.

Fees for the parish schools were deliberately kept low to ensure that schooling was available to as many children as possible, and indeed kirk sessions often took upon themselves to pay the fees of the poorest pupils. This did not mean of course that all children were educated to a high standard. Although it is likely that "schooling formed part of the lives of most of the Lowland population, at least for a brief period",[38] it was regarded as less of a necessity for girls, and was something of a luxury for the poorest ranks of society whose labour was required from a very early age. For many children, education, in the words of the old cliché, must have been "nasty, brutish and short". It has been estimated that by the end of the 17th century, a majority, perhaps as many as 75 per cent of the male population could sign their names, with the female population trailing far behind at 25-30 per cent.[39] Obviously the ability to sign ones name does not necessarily indicate any degree of ability and fluency in more advanced writing skills. The ability to read was anecdotally much more

38 A history of everyday life in Scotland 1600 to 1800 – ed. Elizabeth Foyster & Christopher A. Whatley, Edinburgh University Press, Edinburgh, 2010. (Chap. 6 "Communicating" – Bob Harris.) Page 168.

39 Harris, in Foyster & Whatley, Page 167.

widespread, but whereas the relative incidence of signatures and "marks" gives some basis for calculating the ability to writs, evidence for the ability to read is more ephemeral.

From the later 17th century the range of the curriculum available in at least some parish and burgh schools widened significantly to include, for example, book keeping, geography, arithmetic, mathematics and navigation. Parish school education had probably always included elementary arithmetic, and the basic raison d'être of the grammar schools and high schools was to drill their pupils in Latin. By the mid-18th century a bright boy who had ability and aptitude, and whose parents were willing and able to bear the expenses, could find himself in his early teenage years able to read and write fluently, calculate accurately, and have some knowledge of the wider world and its workings. He could then take steps to enter the world of commerce, or, if armed with a little Latin, could proceed to college to prepare himself for one of the professions.

Judging by his later career, it can be assumed that John Glassell was just such a youth. He left behind no references to his education, but we might assume he attended Torthorwald parish school, and may also have had a spell at the High School of Dumfries. It was well known in 18th century Scotland that America was the land of golden opportunity, but education and ambition were seldom enough to guarantee success there. Opportunity and progress were highly dependent on connections.

John Glassell would not take ship for Virginia, venturing into the complete unknown in the fond hope that somebody somewhere would offer him a job, or that an opportunity to set up as an independent trader would suddenly present itself. At the very least he would go with letters of introduction and recommendation, but more likely he would go to a pre-arranged employer, with the terms of his training, working conditions and remuneration already fixed. As Brock says in "Scotus Americanus", "many young men (or fathers acting on their behalf) took out indentures with merchants to serve for a period in the colonies as clerks, book-keepers, store keepers, or assistants to factors. The wages offered were usually low, but sometimes a limited trade on their own account was allowed. Bed, board and laundry were usually promised, and sometimes the merchant accepted responsibility for training the young man in business practices… Merchants with expanding interests relied upon this means to attract and train able young men who might eventually become key men in the operations at home or abroad."[40] There was a network of Scottish merchants in the American colonies, particularly in Virginia and Maryland, who did much of their business with fellow Scots. Even when trading to London, Liverpool, or the West Indies, they tended, if possible, to deal with Scotsmen.

The ever-flowing fount of wealth was the Virginia tobacco trade, in which Glasgow with its "Tobacco Lords" occupied a leading role. As already mentioned, however, Dumfries was also profitably involved. The owners of the huge tobacco growing estates established on the eastern seaboard of Virginia during the 17th and early 18th centuries tended not to be Scots, but by the mid-18th century the country to the west was being opened up and settled, and many Scots, often those who had made money in commerce, bought land and commenced as tobacco planters. It should be emphasised that the cultivation of tobacco relied completely on the captive labour of thousands of black slaves.

Obviously the tobacco planters needed buyers for their crop, but they also needed the necessities of life and the accoutrements of civilised living. In the American colonies the production of manufactured goods was still in its infancy, and almost everything in that vast range had to be imported. A network of stores spread across Virginia to supply the landward communities and plantations with their every need. The owners or their agents usually supplied goods on credit founded on the prospect of the next crop of tobacco. Much of this trade was in the hands of Scottish merchants, their "factors" (managers), and employees.

Just as John Glassell left us with no details of his education, neither did he leave a progress report of his career in Virginian commerce. But we might hazard a guess at an initial approach to a friend or relative of his family – someone engaged or with contacts in the Virginia trade. A position would be secured for young John as a clerk in the employ of a Scots merchant. He might go on to manage a store, and eventually break out to acquire one of his own, all the while learning the "tricks of the trade", and extending his contacts with planters, merchants and suppliers.

Who might have provided the opening for the young John Glassell to make

40 Scotus Americanus – William R. Brock, Edinburgh University Press, Edinburgh, 1982, Page 17.

his way in the American colonies? We have already heard of Glassells who were "merchants". There was the John Glassell who appears in the Custom Book of Dumfries in 1576, dealing in pepper, pins, and blue bonnets; and the Robert Glassell, merchant in Dumfries, who is mentioned in the 1657 inventory of the goods, gear, and debts owing to the late Robert Glassell, the dealer in malt in Roucan.

The Register of Deeds in the National Records of Scotland records a John Glassell, merchant in Edinburgh in 1696[41] and 1707[42], and John Glassell, merchant in London in 1700[43]. Although these could be two completely different traders, it would not be surprising if the references are in fact to the same man.

The Register of Deeds also makes mention of Thomas Glassell, merchant in Glasgow in 1695[44], 1697[45], 1698[46], 1699[47], and 1707[48]. Thomas is also named in the "List of the several persons resident in Scotland who have subscribed as adventurers in the joint-stock of the Company of Scotland". This was the enthusiastically supported but drastically ill-fated attempt to establish a Scots colony in Darien. Thomas invested £150.

There is no proof that John and Thomas were connected to the Dumfriesshire Glassells, but given the extreme rarity of the surname, it is surely not stretching conjecture too far to suggest that they belonged to the same family as John (1576), Robert (1657), and the 18th century Glassells in Roucan. John and Thomas would be long dead before young John's entry to commerce in the mid-18th century, but their children, grandchildren and friends might well still have been useful contacts, and their memory might provide encouragement and an inspiring example.

Although there is no doubt that there was something of a mercantile tradition among the Glassells, it is perhaps more likely that young John's benefactors were his Coulter relatives. One of their descendants summarises their history and achievements thus: "The Coulters came [to Glasgow] from Dumfriesshire about the end of the 17th century, and were soon leading

41 Dal LXXXX. i, 304, 417; Mack LXXIX, 648.
42 RD 2/74, fol. 733.
43 RD2/92 fol. 555, 721; RD4/86 fol. 519.
44 Dal LXXXVIII 1030, 1200.
45 RD2 81/1/232.
46 RD2 81/2/773.
47 RD82/215, 630, 657, 667. Also several mentions in RD3, RD4.
48 RD2/94 fol. 733.

merchants. James Coulter died in 1708, leaving a legacy to the Merchants' House. Michael Coulter was a merchant and bailie and died in 1732 doing likewise. John, the proprietor of "The Grove" was a capital citizen always active in the service of the city, and Lord Provost in 1736. James Coulter, another of the family, was an encourager of art and manufacture and at his death left a sum of money to fund an annual prize for the most artistic production. Lawrence Coulter, or Lawrie Coulter as he was familiarly called, was known to everyone in his day. He is a prominent figure in one of Kay's prints published in 1793."[49]

A present-day Coulter descendant, Warren Coulter of Arkansas, posted an interesting communication in 2003 on the genealogical website "Rootsweb". Mr Coulter believed himself to be descended from a James Coulter who lived from 1655 to 1713 and had connections with Roucan, Dumfries and Glasgow. James was a merchant, had a brother Robert who lived in Roucan, and another brother Michael who was also a merchant, and a burgess and Baillie of Glasgow. Michael's son became provost of Glasgow and his daughter Janet married Lawrence Dinwiddie, a merchant importing tobacco from Virginia into Glasgow. Dinwiddie's brother Robert was governor of Virginia from 1751 to 1758. Warren Coulter writes of his ancestor James, "James had a sister Mary who Married John Glassell of Roucan in about 1677. They had a son named Robert Glassell whose son John Glassell emigrated to Virginia sometime before 1776." This last of course is the young John Glassell whose motives for moving to Virginia we are currently pondering. It is not clear how Warren Coulter could be sure that his ancestor James "had a sister named Mary who married John Glassell of Roucan about 1677". There are no Torthorwald marriage records surviving from that time, and the difficulties of placing "Mary Coulter" in the Glassell family have already been discussed at length in Chapter 1. One suspects that Warren Coulter is drawing a conjecture based on "Virginia Genealogies" or something similar. Mr Coulter goes on to say that his ancestor James's brother Michael had descendants Michael and Hugh who "were in Virginia c.1730-1763". These two, Michael and Hugh, would seem prime candidates for the role of young John Glassell's mentors and benefactors. Unfortunately, an e-mail to Warren Coulter requesting further

49 Early records of an old Glasgow family. – "W.H.H.", Printed at the University Press, Glasgow, 1902.

information failed to get through, and it later transpired that Mr Coulter had died.

An early history of Glasgow,[50] referring to a period around the beginning of the 18th century, records, "Next there was another great company arose undertaking the trade to Virginia, Cariby-islands, Barbadoes, New England, St Christophers, Monserat and other colonies in America." Listed among those involved were James, John, and Michael Coulter[51]. A James Coulter, merchant in Dumfries, is also listed among the subscribers to the Darien Scheme, risking the substantial sum of £500.

Finally, the Torthorwald registers record the baptisms of Elizabeth (19th October 1745), daughter of "Michael Coulter merchant now in Ruchan, late in Maryland", and Janet (8th May 1747), "daughter to Michael Coulter, merchant in Liverpool, at present in Rucan". Michael died shortly after Janet's birth, and the burial register records, "10th July 1747; Buried Michael Coulter, merchant of Liverpool, late in Rucan, formerly Maryland."

As well as the mercantile Coulters, in the mid-18th century we find in the Torthorwald registers William Coulter at Greenhead, Roucan, who fathered seven children between 1738 and 1753, John Coulter in Roucan, and John Coulter in Kirkland near Torthorwald village. That all the Coulters were not wealthy merchants is underlined by the fact that the Torthorwald kirk session minutes record that a Michael Coulter was receiving money from the Poors' Fund in 1701.

It is stating the obvious to say that it is not easy to make sense of this maze of Coulters, and in the absence of definitive information it is possibly not worth trying. There can be no doubt, however, that as John Glassell, born in 1736, grew up, he had as near neighbours in Roucan men named Coulter closely related to merchants who were "movers and shakers" in Glasgow, trading regularly across the Atlantic. There had previously been at least one marriage between the Coulters and the Glassells, and John's own stepmother was a Coulter. In addition, there had previously been merchants among the Glassells, so Coulters and Glassells may well have had commercial as well as family ties. Suffice it to say that there would have been no shortage of helping hands able to give the young John Glassell the start he needed. Someone somewhere must have been not only able, but willing.

---

50 "The History of Glasgow", John McUre, "A new edition", Macvean & White, Glasgow, 1830. (First published 1735).

51 Ibid, Page 170.

Unfortunately, from the standpoint of the 21st century researcher, John seems to have risen to prosperity without visible trace. Hayden, in "Virginia Genealogies", makes no reference to John's early career, saying only that "Mr Glassell came to Fredericksburg, Virginia, before the Revolutionary war".[52] An article posted on the internet after the restoration of Glassell's former home in Fredericksburg says that "he had come from Galloway, Scotland prior to 1770 to open an export business involved in the sale of tobacco".[53] Another internet posting informs us, "Glassell emigrated in 1756 from Haddington, Scotland, to Virginia".[54] Yet another internet article, "Virginia Ghosts" by Jenny Lee and Margaret du Pont Lee, makes the same statement. Given the obvious confusion over John Glassell's origins, we might be sceptical over the dates given for his arrival in Virginia. "Before the Revolutionary war" and "prior to 1770" are hardly helpful. "In 1756" must be about right, but unfortunately the authors of the statement quote no source to back it up.

In the Register of Deeds in the National Records of Scotland there is the copy of a letter dated 13th July 1765 sent from John Glassell in Fredericksburg, Virginia, to his brother Andrew back in Scotland. The copy seems to have been made as evidence in a legal process of John's ongoing in the 1790s.[55] It is worth giving the full text of this letter, as it throws light both on John's situation in Virginia and family matters at home.

Fredericksburg July 13th 1765.

Dear Brother,

I duly received yours of 25 January, 14th February, 24th March advising me of our dear father's death. That melancholy event has laid me under the deepest concern, & now in spite of reason it hangs heavy on my spirits. But however affecting the dispensation is, we ought with due composure and resignation to submit to the will of the supreme being who orders all things for the best, and although he has left us to mourn the loss of

52 Virginia Genealogies, Page 4.

53 Fredericksburg.com 3/11/2006 :The Chimneys. HITI Success story – Ellen Makarechian.

54 "An unlikely ghost", The way it was, – Barbara Crookshanks. Town and Country. The Free Lance Star, Saturday Oct 26, 2002. (Newspaper article).

55 RD2/274, Page 525.

an affectionate father, I hope that he has not only freed him from a world of pain and anxiety but translated him to the heavenly mansions where there is neither pain nor death, but will enjoy consummate bliss through the ages of eternity. I observe the manner he has disposed of his affairs, which I apprehend he has deemed equitable, therefore I am satisfied. Had the whole estate he was possessed of fallen into my hands, none of you would have fared the worse for it, as I never would have taken from you what you depend upon and I could want.[56] *I must own (however independent I am of such a fortune as my father could give me) that not only my Birth right but my situation in life might I think have given me a nominal claim to the lands in the will, this I always expected and no more. I should have been better pleased had the land been burdened with twice the cost and left to me. In that case you might have kept possession of it as you do now, for I never should have sold it or taken one shilling of its rents, and at my conveniency I might have cleared it of every encumbrance when it would have been more beneficial among you. As for the small legacy left me, you may make yourself very easy about the payment of it, for in place of distressing you, your necessitys may always command my assistance. The large business I am engaged in requires a capital of some thousand pounds, which makes money to three times the value to me it can possibly be to you, otherwise I would cheerfully discharge every claim against you. In the meantime, whenever you are apprehensive of a pinch, advise me, and I will by my letter to some port in Britain support your credit; tho' by the collection of debts and your own industry I hope you will soon get clear. I shall write Commissary Goldie to assist you in the settlement of the Haugh yard. If I have time I shall also write my father's widow. In the meantime, however indiscreet her pass'd conduct may have been, let it now be buried in oblivion, and endeavour to make her live happy for our father's sake. Should she not be content with the annuity for her [BLANK]*[57] *and insist [BLANK] one third of the moveables consult Mr Goldie on what you are to take. However I'll endeavour to [BLANK]date her from such an attempt. I recommend to you and my brother Robert [BLANK] to live together in peace and friendship without [BLANK] superiority which never fails to feed contention [BLANK] strife, as you live together you*

56 i.e. do without.

57 Several spaces in this part of the copy of John's letter presumably indicate illegible words in the original, or damage caused by folding or a broken seal.

ought jointly [BLANK] the profits of your labour, nor can you reasonably expect Robert to work for nothing [BLANK] you should take our uncle into the family with you. He must be too old to cultivate the same spot of land he has, and when he lives with you he will not have the same care upon him [BLANK]. As for my paying you a visit, you are not to expect it for several years (unless my business obliges me to take the tour of Britain) and then my tarry cannot be many days. If I don't settle for life in this Colony, it is very probable I may fix in some one of the most considerable trading towns in Britain, tho' from every circumstance I rather think my residence will be here. I am every day sinking a property in the Country and it requires all my attention. I wish you and my brother were both here. I could soon settle you on a good tract of land, and with your money purchase negroes to labour for you; and your fortunes, with half the industry you use, wou'd increase much faster. However, I don't mean to persuade you to anything contrary to your inclination, only I should be glad you were near me that my influence might be a service to you. Let me hear from you frequently. Remember me to my uncle, brother, and all friends.

I am truly, Dear Andrew, your affectionate Brother,
Signed John Glassell Junr.
P.S. Intend is a letter...

[A short P.S. appears to be about the upkeep of "my father's widow", but blank spaces and illegible words make it difficult to unravel.]

Addressed to Mr Andrew Glassell.

At the time of writing, John Glassell was 29 years of age, and would have been in Virginia for around ten years. He was already engaged in "large business", and we can probably take "sinking a property" to mean that he was investing in real estate. He was apparently successful enough to be able to be indifferent to the size of his inheritance from his late father, and to be able to offer financial assistance to his brothers. We can detect a mild tone of pique, however, in his observation that as the eldest son he might have expected to have been willed his father's lands, but he labours the point that had this happened, he was in a position to have cleared the lands of debt for the benefit of his brothers, and left them in possession.

Obviously, then, John was financially secure. He was able to commemorate his father with the impressive headstone mentioned in Chapter 1, which describes the deceased as not only "tenant in the Howgate", but "proprietor of Slengebar and Westfield". It would seem that Robert Glassell had prospered enough to be able to buy land in addition to his tenancy. It is clear however from John's letter that these acquisitions were encumbered by debt, so perhaps Robert had not been as prosperous as the word "proprietor" might suggest. John's intriguing mentions of "my father's widow" do not suggest a very warm relationship with his stepmother Mary Coulter. What her "indiscreet past conduct" might have been, we have no way of knowing. Certainly, it was not the kind of indiscretion that was commonly recorded in kirk session minutes. Whatever it might have been, John was anxious that she should be provided for, for his father's sake, if not for her own.

Of greatest import for the future of the Glassell family, is John's invitation to his brothers to join him in Virginia, where he was in a position to settle them on a "good tract of land". There, he promised, they would prosper much more quickly with much less labour than they ever could by remaining at home. As we shall see, Andrew Glassell decided to take advantage of John's generous offer, while the youngest brother, Robert, opted to remain at home. Crucial to Andrew's success in America of course would be the "negroes" whose purchase John would arrange.

By 1765, then, John Glassell was plainly in a position of financial security. It will become obvious that over the next ten years or so, this became a position of considerable wealth.

Virginia was the first English colony in mainland America. In 1607 the "London Company" established the first permanent settlement and named it "Jamestown" in honour of the King. After the bankruptcy of the London Company in 1624 Virginia became a crown colony. The first area of settlement was the "Tidewater", the coastal plain comprising the eastern shore and the river estuaries of Chesapeake Bay. The colony was at first a precarious undertaking. Indian wars, famine, and a chronic shortage of labour all contributed to hinder development and progress. However, tobacco proved to be the colony's salvation. An insatiable demand in Europe for tobacco led to the establishment of vast plantations in the Tidewater, cultivated originally by indentured labour. After the mid-17th century however, tobacco production became increasingly dependent on the labour of African slaves. Native American tribal lands were gradually appropriated by a combination of force and treaty, and the "Indians" were decimated by the common European ailments to which they had no resistance. Many of those remaining were gradually assimilated into the "white" population, and today only 0.5% of Virginians classify themselves as Native American. White settlement quickly pushed westwards from the coast to the Blue Ridge Mountains, and beyond into the Shenandoah Valley. By the mid-18th century attempts were being made to trade and settle west of the Appalachian Mountains, leading to conflict with a French – Indian alliance.

The Rappahannock River has its source in the Blue Ridge Mountains and flows into Chesapeake Bay some twenty miles south of the Potomac River, widening into a tidal estuary for the final fifty miles of its course. Early in the 18th century Alexander Spotswood, Governor of Virginia, encouraged the development of the Rappahannock Valley, and many Swiss and German emigrants settled in the area around the confluence of the Rapidan River with the Rappahannock.

The town of Fredericksburg, named for Frederick, Prince of Wales, was established at the head of navigation on the Rappahannock as Virginia's frontier shifted westwards. A new county was formed, Spotsylvania, (named for Governor Spotswood) with Fredericksburg as its port and county seat. Fredericksburg, then, was the depot from which the recently settled inland areas could be supplied, and to which the settlers could send their produce for export to the wider world. Since business on the coast was likely to be already sewn up, Fredericksburg was just the sort of place to attract entrepreneurs eager to take advantage of recently settled country ripe for exploitation. It is hardly surprising then that John Glassell should have made Fredericksburg his base.

As we see from John's letter to his brother in 1765, when he was already engaged in "large business", he was writing from Fredericksburg. A few years later, obviously still prospering, he moved into a new house commensurate with his wealth and status. Colonial Fredericksburg was laid out on a grid pattern with its streets named after members of the British royal family. John Glassell's house survives to this day on Caroline Street. Known as "The Chimneys", it is one of the architectural gems of Fredericksburg's historic centre, and is listed in the National Register of Historic Places. The Chimneys is thought to have been built around 1771 by Charles Yates and sold to John Glassell shortly afterwards. It is a typical Georgian colonial house of two storeys, constructed around a strong hardwood frame, the beams of which are each marked by a Roman numeral and secured by wooden pegs. The outer walls are of white painted boards, and there are stout stone-built chimneys at each gable end. Inside, The Chimneys is notable for its panelling and decorative woodwork, typical of the Colonial era. The carved chimney pieces by Thomas Miller, a Scots cabinet maker, are judged to be particularly outstanding.

It might be worth mentioning in the passing that The Chimneys has acquired a reputation as a haunted house, bedevilled by the sounds of footsteps, crashing china, and opening and closing doors. There is the story of a girl playing the piano who felt an invisible presence sit down beside her and lay its hand on her shoulder. Also, there is the tale of a mother who looked in on her sleeping son, and was taken aback to find another boy in bed beside him. Oddly, she did not feel it necessary to wake them to account for the presence of the stranger, but left the room. In the morning the son denied that anyone else had been with him, and the bed showed no sign that it had been occupied by anyone else.[58]

"The Chimneys" was not the only property in Fredericksburg owned by John Glassell. When his assets in the town were finally sold in 1803 they were advertised in the "Virginia Herald" as "four lots on which are an elegant and spacious dwelling house and store, kitchen etc." There was also "a large warehouse with a store and counting room", "the tobacco warehouse", and "sixteen acres of land beautifully situated…on which have lately been built a wharf and warehouses that will be sold with two acres of land".[59] Hayden's "Virginia Genealogies" confirms[60] that "John Glassell owned several houses, store and warehouses in Fredericksburg, and a wharf…". Obviously, John was a man of substance.

"Virginia Genealogies" declares[61] that Glassell "was a merchant of large enterprises and fortune. He had branch establishments in Culpeper and Fauquier." Culpeper is both a county and a town lying some 30 miles west of Fredericksburg. Fauquier County lies north-west of Fredericksburg, running down from the Blue Ridge Mountains to a point on the

58 Information on "The Chimneys" from Wikipedia; and online articles "Virginia Ghosts" – Jenny Lee and Marguerita du Pont Lee, "The Magazine Antiques", and "Rootsweb: Janet Ariciu, family Bush".

59 Virginia Herald, 1st April 1803.

60 Virginia Genealogies, P. 44.

61 Virginia genealogies, P. 4.

Rappahannock River adjoining Spotsylvania County. An article in "The Newfoundlander" over a century after John had left Virginia claims that he had stores in Dumfries, Fredericksburg and Madison.[62] A decade after John's departure from Virginia, letters from his relative William Glassell (of whom much more anon) mention "our back store", saying, "All the honest Dutch[63] in that neighbourhood supply themselves from it, and it yields twice the ready money that the Fredericksburg store does."[64] William talks of making "a long tour over the ridge to the back counties where there are many weighty sums due".[65] A list of debts owed to British merchants in the former American colonies after independence[66] shows a myriad of mostly small debts owed to John Glassell. The correspondence of James Robinson, "superintending factor" for the Glasgow firm of W. Cuningham & Co. makes several mentions of Glassell: "Mr Balfour was up at Fredericksburg lately and bought some tobacco from J. Glassell at 20s stg." (1790). In 1772 after a James Robb had been offering to pay 20s for tobacco, Robinson remarked, "Mr Henry Mitchel and Mr Glassell are much piqued at the wanton manner Mr Robb has taken the lead, saying they could not support their engagements with the planters without giving them as much as they could procure in town." In July 1774 Robinson complained that there was "not much" tobacco for sale, but "Simon Fraser from Urbanna bought lately 70 hogsheads at 10s stg from John Glassell and Daniel Payne." In 1774 Robinson asked his bosses to honour a bill he has drawn on them in favour of John Glassell for £50, and in 1775 a bill in favour of John Glassell for £10-3-2.[67]

The key word in Robinson's letters is "tobacco". Tobacco underpinned the whole economy of colonial Virginia. The owners of the vast plantations of the coastal plain could afford to make their own arrangements to export their tobacco, but the smaller-scale planters of the more recently settled inland areas relied heavily on their local stores. The stores supplied them

62 The Newfoundlander, May 18th 1883. Dumfries in Prince William County, Virginia, is meant here, not Dumfries in Scotland.

63 i.e. German settlers.

64 "Intimate society letters of the eighteenth century", Ed. Duke of Argyll; Stanley, Paul & Co, London 1910. Letter from William Glassell to John Glassell, 24th December 1786, P. 483.

65 Ibid. Letter to John Glassell's wife, 14th August 1789.

66 "British Mercantile Claims", as published in The Virginia Genealogist.

67 Scottish History Society, 4th Series, Vol. 20. "A Scottish Firm in Virginia – W. Cuninghame & Co. Ed. T. Devine Ph. D., Clark Constable (1982) Ltd, 1984.

with the necessities and luxuries of life and advanced them credit, and at harvest time the owner of the store received the produce of the plantation and disposed of it for export. Basically the planters ran up annual bills which were set against their tobacco crop. In a good year, when the bill was deducted from the value of his tobacco crop the planter made a profit. In a bad year the shortfall was added to his debt. The successful planter could invest in more land, acquire more slaves, and buy better implements and tools; his less successful neighbour led a life of weary struggle and constant debt. Most of the stores were operated by a handful of highly successful British merchant companies such as William Cuninghame & Co., but there was also room for smaller-scale entrepreneurs like John Glassell, with his three or four stores centred on Fredericksburg. Much of this British commercial activity was in fact owned and operated by Scotsmen.

We find occasional mentions of John Glassell in the diary of John Harrower, a Shetlander who was forced by extreme poverty to engage as an indentured servant in Virginia, where he served as schoolmaster in a school on the estate of a Colonel Dangerfield at Belvidere, south of Fredericksburg. Harrower records for Sunday 12th June 1774, "This day at church at Fredericksburg and at same time settled a correspondence at Glasgow for getting letters from home by their being past under cover to Messrs Anderson & Horsburgh Merchts in Do. And the expense charged to Mr Glassell mercht in Fredericksburg." Similarly, on Saturday 10th December 1774, "This day after 12 o' clock rode to Town and delivered my letter to Mr John Glassell to be forwarded to Britain per first ship." On Monday 17th April 1775 Harrower wrote a love letter for a Mr Anderson, then, "After that I went to Mr John Glassell's store to enquire for letters from home but found none." On Saturday 27th May 1775 he noted, "Received a letter from my wife dated 1st March 1775. It came under cover to Mr John Glassell merchant in town, and cost me 1/3d." Apparently, then, providing a postal service between Virginia and Britain was another function of Glassell's stores. A more mundane commercial transaction is recorded in Harrower's entry for 24th June 1775: "This day I went to town at noon, and... bought from Mr John Glassell 1 yard black ribbon for my hair at 1/- and two yards figured do. At 1/- per yard to give to Nancy Beck [?] to altering my 2 vestcoats for me."[68]

68 Diary of John Harrower 1773-1776. American Historical Review.

Another glimpse into John Glassell's commercial activities can be obtained in the "Special collections and archives" section of the James Branch Cabell Library in Richmond, Virginia. There, incredibly, we find "John Glassell's Ledger", Glassell's invoice book for autumn 1769 and spring 1770. Unfortunately it has been used as an album for someone's collection of 19th century newspaper cuttings, which have been pasted over the 18th century handwritten records, obscuring many of them. Enough remains however to illustrate the vast range of goods Glassell made available to his customers. Page 1 is headed, "For Fauquier Store", but it is not clear whether all or only some of the records in the book refer to that establishment. Page 6 mentions rum from the Dumfries store that has been "entered in the Old Books & Inventory".

Bearing in mind that most of the ledger is obscured by newspaper cuttings, we can decipher on page 7 a reference to textiles in the form of German dowlass (coarse cotton cloth), brown sheeting, white sheeting, rolled sacking, and hempen rolls. There are also check handkerchiefs, blue printed linen handkerchiefs and spotted cotton handkerchiefs. Items of haberdashery include coloured thread (light drab, dark drab, blue, and red), quality binding (dark blue, light and dark drab, cream, claret, brown), and snuff, mohair, richest silk twist, white jeans[69], 7 bags of twist buttons and flat metal coat buttons. Also listed are books (6 bibles, 6 testaments, 4 prayer books and 1 history), plaid hose, worsted hose, women's worsted stockings and men's worsted stockings (white and "ribbed knit Aberdeen"). There were shoes (details obscured), coffee pots, loose salt (20 bushels), and West Indian rum (quantity obscured).

Visible on the mostly obscured parts of page 8 are padlocks, saddlers' tacks, women's brass thimbles, common needles, hats and combs. Displayed in greater detail are the records of Dutch ovens, candles, frying pans, glue, gunpowder, drop shot, green tea, Bopea tea, alum, hair lifters, gauze "searches" [sieves], saltpetre, grindstones (one 36 inch and two 25 inch), stone 1 gallon bottles, chamber pots, water jugs (gallon and half gallon), crown linen for bags, and refined sugar. White West India rum is marked "from D Store" with a freight charge of ten shillings, and two grindstones also marked "D Store" have four shillings "carriage paid here". The "D" presumably refers to

69 It is unclear whether "jeans" refers to the twilled cotton cloth or the thread from which it was woven – probably the latter.

the store at Dumfries.

Page 11 is the "Invoice for Spring 1770 continued", and although mostly obscured carries references to curry combs, forks and table knives. Page 14 shows only a reference to bridles, but page 15 enumerates Stoneware: custard cups, butter bottles, cream coloured sugar boxes, flat plates, and chamber pots blue and white. Glassware: common wine, wine and water, cruets, pint decanters, half pint tumblers, and pint tumblers. Also shown on page 15 are brown sheeting, white sheeting, Scots dowlass [coarse linen], thread hose (brown, marbled, and white), handkerchiefs, horn and ivory combs, "Russia drill red"[70], "Pomerania"[71]. Indian chintz comes in a variety of colours and patterns; red and black, purple, "lutestring", copper plate red, Japan chintz, purple ground, and green ground. There is also Argyleshire Osnaburg, tweel, and "brown rolls".

Page 16 records nails, broad hoes, chamber pots, women's fashionable bonnets (coloured, black, and velvet), women's hats (laced and coloured), ribbons, coat binding, "Barcelona", cinnamon and nutmegs.

Page 17 lists brown thread, Russian drill, camblett [?], pens, necklaces, cambric, mohair, silk twist, Glasgow check, spirits of turpentine, leather breeches (sheepskin, "shammy", and shambock), pins, sleeve buttons, gilt trunks, lintseed oil in jars, and axes.

On page 18 there are three boxes of window glass, Scotch snuff, nankeen, thread lace and egrets. There are also several different sizes of grindstones, a hogshead of West India rum, striped Holland, women's gloves and mittens, 6 bottles of Burlington balsam, and 6 bottles of Weston's snuff. The goods come in bales, trunks, casks, and boxes. Casks seem to have been charged for.

Considering this vast range of goods, and bearing in mind how much in the ledger must be hidden by 19th century newspaper cuttings, there is very little that the rural Virginian planter could have desired, from leather breeches to chamber pots, that could not have been supplied from one of John Glassell's stores.

Basically, then, John Glassell's business consisted of supplying up-country tobacco planters with their every need. It would seem, however, that this was

70 Drill – a stout twilled linen or cotton cloth.

71 Presumably another textile, as the entry refers to two 60 yard pieces.

not his only connection with tobacco production. It will be remembered that in 1765 John wrote to his brother Andrew advising him to come to Virginia. "I could soon settle you on a good tract of land," he wrote, "and with your money purchase negroes to labour for you."[72] Andrew did indeed follow his brother's advice, and in later life was a wealthy and greatly respected tobacco planter who founded a quasi-aristocratic Virginian dynasty. However, there is some evidence to suggest that for long, Andrew was merely managing a plantation for his brother John, or perhaps operating it as a junior partner. A decade after John's return to Scotland, his relative and agent in Virginia William Glassell wrote to him saying that Andrew was talking of "selling the Plantation Negroes". It might be thought significant that William does not write "*his* plantation negroes", but "*the* plantation negroes" as if "the Plantation" was something in which John still had an active interest. William goes on, "The mode of settlement therefore which in my idea would be most beneficial to you both would be to let him have the Plantation Negroes &c at a fair price...". Later he emphasises, "This again I beg leave to repeat, that it will be to your interest that your brother become the purchaser of the Culpeper Plantation negroes &c." Here again, not *his* Culpeper Plantation, but *the* Culpeper Plantation. [73]

In essence, John is being advised to allow his brother to buy him out, and presumably this is in fact what happened. The implications are that John, both before and after his return to Scotland, as well as carrying on business as a merchant, was the owner of a tobacco plantation managed or perhaps co-owned by his brother Andrew. Since tobacco production was based solidly upon slave labour, John was therefore, like all other tobacco planters, a slave owner. Indeed, although no actual mentions have come to light, John as a proprietor of stores and warehouses would almost certainly have had slaves to do the manual labour and heavy lifting involved, and as owner of a fine new house in Fredericksburg, would also have had domestic slaves. This would have caused him no qualms. In Virginia a man of his wealth and status would have been a slave owner as a matter of course.

It is worth mentioning that there was another source of cheap labour for planters and businessmen in Virginia. It is well known that British convicts were transported to Australia in the early years of settlement

72 National Records of Scotland, RD/2/274, Page 525.

73 "Intimate society letters of the eighteenth century", Page 483. Letter from William Glassell to John Glassell.

there, but perhaps not so well known that before Independence the American colonies were also used as a dumping ground for Britain's undesirables. Those of them who had special skills, or even physical strength alone, were valuable assets who could be bound to a master as indentured labour and exploited for many years for no more than the cost of board and lodging. On 1st October 1772 the "Virginia Gazette" carried the following advertisement:

> *"Fredericksburg Septr 12th 1772 run away from the subscriber the 11th instant John Osborn a convict imported in the "Breckdale", Captain Wood. He is about five feet seven inches high, of a pale complexion, strong made, had on a dirty flannel jacket and drawers, a check shirt, a pair of shoes tied with strings, and a round hat bound with osnaburgs. He passes for a runaway sailor, is artful and of few words. All masters of vessels are desired not to employ him, and whoever delivers him to me shall have forty shillings reward if taken within 40 miles, and if at a greater distance, three pounds.*
> *John Glassell."*

Many convicts bore their time of servitude stoically and became good and valued citizens afterwards, but obviously the prospect of several years under the thumb of John Glassell had not appealed to John Osborn.

By the early 1770s John Glassell's business interests appear to have been going from strength to strength. Unfortunately for him, however, as he was preparing to move into his new home on Caroline Street, Fredericksburg, the winds of political change were already beginning to blow. The American colonies had no representation in the British parliament, and bitterly resented taxes and laws imposed on them by the mother country. Perhaps the manifestation of this discontent which is best known in Britain today was the 1773 "Boston Tea Party" where local Patriots emptied a cargo of the British East India Company's tea into Boston harbour. A harsh response by the British government hardened American attitudes, and by the spring of 1774 clashes between Patriot militias and British troops escalated into open warfare. Independent administrations were set up in each of the thirteen colonies, and General George Washington took command of a united American army. A Continental Congress issued the historic Declaration of

Independence in 1776, officially breaking the bonds of British rule. France and Spain aided the Patriots, while American Loyalists fought along with the British Army. The Treaty of Paris in 1783 officially ended the hostilities which in fact had effectually concluded with American victory two years previously, and the United States of America were recognised as an independent country.

It is plain from John Glassell's letter to his brother in 1765 that he then saw his future as most likely lying permanently in Virginia. However, this was not the case with many members of the Scots mercantile class in Virginia, who had no intention of becoming permanent residents, but rather were intent upon exploiting the colonies to make as much money as possible before returning home to set up as "gentlemen". Thus, as discontent progressed to open conflict, many Scots saw the Loyalist side as being more favourable to their interests. This of course did not make them popular. There was already an undercurrent of anti-Scots feeling in Virginia, rather reminiscent of anti-Jewish prejudice in Eastern Europe. This was due, in the words of the historian T. M. Devine, to "their perceived grasping and rapacious nature, which threatened a kind of Scottish hegemony in the colonies. Indeed, in terms of Scottish success in the tobacco trade in the south, there was more than a degree of truth in such accusations. In November 1777, for example, the president of Yale, Ezra Styles, fulminated that 'the Scotch had got two thirds of Virginia and Maryland mortgaged or otherwise engaged to them, or was owned in Scotland'. He went on to assert, 'I have heard it often suggested to me by Scotch merchants and factors that the Scotch would in a very few years have all the property in Virginia, if not in general of North America'."[74] A favourite Revolutionary toast apparently became, "A free exportation to Scotchmen and Tories!"[75]

It is not surprising, then, that political events and popular prejudice led John Glassell to consider his options. Sometime around the 1980s, in pursuit of his Scottish roots, a descendant of the American Glassells appeared in the village of Longniddry, East Lothian, where John Glassell settled. This man mentioned to the postmaster and the local councillor that at the time of the American War of Independence two Glassell brothers had been in

74 To the ends of the earth – T. M. Devine, Allan Lane, London, 2011. Page 135.
75 Ibid. Page 135.

business together in Virginia. To safeguard their interests they decided that one would support the Revolutionaries and stay in Virginia; the other would make known his support for the Loyalists and return to Scotland. That way, whichever side won, the Glassell business interests would be kept safe.

Whether such a deliberate plan was ever conceived is debateable, but certainly, for whatever reason, in 1775 John Glassell deemed it expedient to leave Virginia, and had the following notice inserted in the Virginia Gazette:

> *"Fredericksburg June 19 1775.*
> *As I intend to leave the colony for a few months, all persons who have any claims against me are desired to call and have them settled. I must request all those who are indebted to me to pay off as far as they can, and give bond for the balance. Mr Lachlan Campbell will carry on the business in my absence, and he is properly authorised to receive all sums due to me, and to settle every just demand against me.*
> *John Glassell."*[76]

Subsequent references to John Glassell always label him a "Loyalist" who returned to Britain at the outbreak of the American War of Independence, presumably because his political stance made him no longer welcome in Virginia, or because his own political beliefs made it impossible to live any longer in a colony which was about to break its ties with the motherland. Whether his principles were really as strong, or whether his leaving was actually a hard-headed strategy as described by his brother's 20th century descendant, or whether indeed he actually intended to leave permanently at all is impossible to tell. In any event, in 1775 John Glassell returned to Scotland.

Horace Hayden, in his "Virginia Genealogies", states concerning John Glassell, "At the beginning of the revolutionary War he deeded all his property in America in fee simple to his brother Andrew [and] returned to Scotland…".[77] However, on Page 444 of the same publication Hayden corrects himself, saying, "The following facts came too late for insertion in note to [the chapter on the Glassells]. Dr Grinnan corrects his statement about the estate of John Glassell." Quoting Dr Grinnan, Hayden explains,

76 J387 mediahistory.weebly.com/uploads/6/4/2/2/642481/virginia_gazette2.pdf
77 Hayden, "Virginia genealogies", Page 4.

"John Glassell did not deed any bonds or property to Andrew Glassell before the Revolution. His properties were not confiscated because he returned before the time named in the Virginia Act of Confiscation. After the Revolution the valuation of the Madison property was referred to Mr Robert Patton of Fredericksburg, and Andrew paid his brother the amount of appraisement. John Glassell owned several houses, store and warehouse in Fredericksburg, and a wharf up to 1804. Daniel Grinnan sold them for him or his estate. They were valuable."

Hayden's source "Dr Grinnan" was the son of Andrew Glassell's daughter. She had married the wealthy Virginian businessman Daniel Grinnan mentioned in the quote, who was instrumental in sorting out the herculean task of settling American debt to British subjects after Independence. It is perfectly plain from Dr Grinnan's statement that although after 1775 John Glassell resided permanently in Scotland, he kept ownership of his American property and business concerns, which were left, as the notice in the Virginia Gazette makes clear, in the hands of Lachlan Campbell. David Dobson, the compiler of "Scottish transatlantic merchants 1611-1785", informs us that Campbell was "a merchant from Glasgow who settled in Fredericksburg Va. as a factor for John Glassell." Campbell would presumably keep business ticking over during the hostilities of the War of Independence. As already briefly mentioned, and as we shall see subsequently at greater length, after the peace John Glassell sent his young relative William Glassell to Virginia to oversee his American interests. The "Madison property" refers to the tobacco plantation managed or part owned by John's brother Andrew. Grinnan makes clear that Andrew became sole owner of the property after the war, remitting the full value to his brother. The rest of the property was eventually sold in the early 19th century.

John indicated in his Virginia Gazette notice that Lachlan Campbell was properly authorised to receive all sums due. If he imagined that his Virginian debtors would conscientiously settle up with Mr Campbell in the boss's absence, he was rather wide of the mark. As we shall see, after Independence an immense backlog of debt remained, to be painstakingly sifted through and processed along with thousands of other "British Mercantile Claims".

3

The laird of Longniddry

When King James VII and II fled into exile in 1688, support for the Stuart dynasty did not just evaporate, and at his death loyalties were transferred to his son James, known as "the Pretender" to his enemies. When Queen Anne died in 1714 and was succeeded by her nearest Protestant relative, the German George I, Jacobite feeling began to come to the boil. Scottish Jacobite support was concentrated in the Highlands, but there was a covert network of aristocratic Jacobites in the south of Scotland, of whom one was the rather offbeat and eccentric George Seton 5th Earl of Wintoun. His ancestors claimed to have been landowners in East Lothian from the time of King Malcolm Canmore, and the Setons had at one time been one of Scotland's most distinguished aristocratic and political families. Their compact East Lothian estates were centred on the Palace of Seton and comprised some of Scotland's richest farmland. Rich coal seams lay beneath the village of Tranent to the south, and salt was processed from the sea at Cockenzie to the north, where there was a good harbour, and another half a mile to the east at Port Seton. The Seton estates had potential for enormous wealth, but had been managed unwisely.

On September 6th 1715 the Earl of Mar raised the Jacobite standard at Braemar and moved quickly to capture Perth. Various suspect Jacobite landowners were then summoned to appear at Edinburgh Castle to give a guarantee of their loyalty to King George. One of those summoned was the Earl of Wintoun, and when he chose not to appear he was sentenced in his absence to a £500 fine, a year's imprisonment, and the lifetime forfeiture of his estates. An attempt to raise his tenants in rebellion fizzled out, and the Earl went on the run, arriving at Moffat shortly afterwards to join a small Jacobite army under Viscount Kenmure.

With his army augmented by Highland and Northumbrian reinforcements, Kenmure launched a rash invasion of England, resulting in ignominious surrender at Preston in Lancashire. The Earl of Wintoun was taken prisoner, lodged in the Tower of London, and put on trial for high treason. An attempted defence of insanity failed, and he was sentenced to death, his estates to be permanently forfeited to the Crown. However, Wintoun contrived to escape from the Tower on 4th August 1716, fled abroad, and died in Rome in 1749 as the Pretender's oldest Scottish pensioner.

That the Setons were no longer masters of their ancestral lands must have seemed almost inconceivable to their inhabitants. Such, however, was the case, and the Government proceeded to sell the forfeited Wintoun possessions, together with the estates of the other rebel Jacobite landowners. On 6th October 1719 the Wintoun estate was bought by the agents of the York Buildings Company for £50 000. The York Buildings Company originated in a 17th century scheme to establish a waterworks in the grounds of York House in London, but having acquired the right to buy land and issue shares, the company evolved after the 1715 Rebellion into a property business whose main purpose was the acquisition and exploitation of forfeited estates. The policy in most cases was to lease the estates to middlemen, thus saving the Company the bother of collecting from farmers, cottars, and villagers a multiplicity of rents large, small, and often trifling.

Thus, the York Buildings Company kept the potentially lucrative coal and salt producing villages of Tranent and Cockenzie in its own hands, but leased the lordship of Seton and the baronies of Wintoun and Longniddry to the Company's "confidential correspondent" in Scotland, George Buchan of Kello, for a rent of £1 500 per annum.[78]

78 Information on the York Buildings Company from "The York Buildings Company, a chapter in Scotch history" – David Murray, Maclehose and Sons 1883.

Buchan was descended from the Buchans of Auchmacoy in Aberdeenshire. His father was a younger son of the family who became an advocate. George Buchan was also an advocate, but had various business interests, and bought the lands of Kello in Berwickshire. His son John Buchan, another advocate, acquired the estate of Letham near Haddington in East Lothian.

George Buchan's lease of the Wintoun estates was for 29 years. On his death in 1760 he was succeeded by his son John Buchan of Letham, and when the lease expired John continued as proprietor by mutual agreement with the York Buildings Company.[79]

From the beginning, however, the finances of the York Buildings Company had been shaky, and its plans for the exploitation of its possessions ill-conceived and unrealistic. By the late 1770s the baying of its creditors could no longer be resisted. The York Buildings Company collapsed into bankruptcy and its extensive landholdings had to be sold off for the creditors' benefit. Thus, in 1778, Parliament passed "An Act for expeding the sale of the estates in Scotland belonging to the York Buildings Coy for the relief of their creditors".

It was decided that the value of the Wintoun estates in East Lothian was such that it would be difficult to dispose of them as a single entity, and even its individual constituent baronies were likely to be too much for a prospective buyer to take on. The various parts of the former Earldom were therefore divided into lots to be exposed for sale by public roup[80], and plans and descriptions of each lot were prepared for the perusal of prospective buyers. The Court of Session ordained that the sale should take place in Parliament House, Edinburgh, on 15th February 1779. The Lordship of Seton was to be offered in three lots, the Barony of Winton as a single lot, the Barony of Tranent and Cockenzie in three lots, and the Barony of Longniddry, in the parish of Gladsmuir, in four lots.

The sale duly went ahead under the supervision of the judge Lord Monboddo. A "half-hour glass" was set up for the sale of each lot, and the highest bidder "at the outrunning of the sand glass" secured the land in question. The sole bidder for Lot 1 of the Barony of Longniddry was William McKillop, a writer[81] acting on behalf of John Glassell. McKillop's

79 The York Buildings Company, a chapter in Scotch history.

80 auction

81 lawyer

offer of £1200 sterling was accepted, and he duly signed the purchase over to Glassell, who registered his ownership in the Books of Council and Session on 2nd March 1779.[82]

It is not clear where the new laird of Longniddry had been since he left Virginia in 1775. We might hazard a guess at Glasgow, Scotland's mercantile centre, or Edinburgh, then embarking on its Golden Age as an intellectual powerhouse. Perhaps, though, he was more likely to have been living quietly among his kin in Dumfriesshire, since he was apparently "almost totally unable to attend to his affairs in consequence of a complaint of which he had been long ill".[83]

In spite of leaving his business behind, Glassell seems to have been able to bring a substantial portion of his wealth with him from Virginia. A rather cynical article appeared in the "Newfoundlander" of 18th May 1883 on "How the Marquis of Lorne came to have an American ancestor". The Marquis of Lorne, eldest son of the Duke of Argyll, was then Governor General of Canada, and was, as we shall see, a direct descendant of John Glassell. The "Newfoundlander" claimed, "When the revolution of '76 broke out, or before it had interrupted the commercial relations with the mother country, John Glassell invested all his funds in tobacco, shipped it to Glasgow, and there realised what was considered to be an enormous fortune from its sale at three Scotch shillings per pound, thus becoming the richest commoner in Scotland." The "Newfoundlander" gives no source for this statement, but given the knowledge displayed elsewhere in the article of Glassell's Virginia relatives, it presumably came originally from that quarter. It is of course very unlikely that in 1775 Glassell would be selling his tobacco in anything other than shillings sterling, and it is even more unlikely that his transactions made him the richest commoner in Scotland. However, the basic suggestion that he brought his wealth home in the form of tobacco has the ring of truth about it.

82 National Records of Scotland: Register of Deeds RD3/238/1 and Session Papers CS/235/G/17/2 for details of the sale.

83 NRS: Court of Session records CS/235/G/17/2.

Longniddry House, John Glassell's "Manor Place of Longniddry".

Whatever the merits of the "Newfoundlander's" claims, there are two undeniable facts about John Glassell as he took up residence on his newly purchased estate: ill health prevented him engaging in business, and substantial wealth meant that he had no need to do so.

Mid-18th century Longniddry was a large straggling village in East Lothian some thirteen miles from Edinburgh, and around half a mile from the southern shore of the Firth of Forth. The layout of many Scottish communities at that time is a mystery or a matter of conjecture, but in the case of Longniddry the plans prepared for the 1779 sale give a meticulous representation of the village and its surroundings. The land was still "lying runrig" – that is, mostly unenclosed, and cultivated on a system derived from mediaeval agriculture where "rigs" or strips of ploughland were theoretically arranged so that each tenant had a fair share of both good and poor land. At one time their holdings were periodically swapped around to ensure this, but by the late 18th century such exchanges were a thing of the remote past. However, the scattered nature of individual holdings was still a feature of the landscape. The principal tenant farmers of Longniddry all held consolidated blocks of rigs interspersed with those of their neighbours in wide-open, unenclosed, irregularly shaped fields. Their ground was sometimes far from their homes and barns, and mingled with the scattered patches cultivated by smaller tenants and cottars. It would seem that under Mr Buchan, the York Buildings Company's tacksman of Longniddry, little had changed from the days of the Earls of Wintoun in the 17th century.

Longniddry, however, was on the brink of radical change. An interesting article by Betty M. Third in the East Lothian Antiquarians' "Transactions", Volume VI,[84] compares two maps in the possession of the Earl of Wemyss. One is the pre-sale plan surveyed in 1778, and the other is a "Plan of the estate of Longniddry" surveyed twenty years later in 1798. Even the most cursory glance at the maps is enough to confirm the writer's statements: "By 1798 Longniddry had shrunk to the proportions of a hamlet", and, "Enclosure had taken place and the straight lines of drystane dykes, ditches and hedges can be seen outlining a field pattern which is the obvious foundation of that existing today". As Ms Third further comments, "The village had become a shadow of its former self." The New Statistical Account confirms that local inhabitants in the 1830s remembered several rows of houses being swept away "without a stone remaining". One old man, indeed, claimed that seventy houses had been demolished.[85]

The barbarity of the Highland Clearances is well known in modern Scotland, and it is easy to jump to the conclusion[86] that similar callousness was enacted in Longniddry in the name of agricultural improvement. Given that 18th century households tended to be rather larger, to say the least, than modern families, the demolition of seventy houses could easily have rendered well over 300 people homeless at a stroke. However, before we denounce the laird of Longniddry, John Glassell, as a heartless monster guilty of wholesale evictions, it may be wise to examine his affairs more closely.

Glassell took up residence in what he later liked to describe as the

---

84 Transactions of the East Lothian Antiquarian and Field Naturalists' Society, Vol VI, D. & J. Croal, Haddington, 1955.

85 NSA, Vol 2, P. 194, Parish of Gladsmuir, 1836.

86 As I did in "Longniddry" – D. M. Robertson, East Lothian District Library Department, 1993. Pp. 17-21.

"Manor Place of Longniddry", now known as "Longniddry House". Today it is a Listed Building, described as a "17th century laird's house of complex building history". It is thought to have possibly originated as an L-shaped single storey building, probably thatched, which was later raised to two storeys and extended in the mid-18th century. Further alterations and additions were made in the 19th century to the rear, and a porch added.[87] Since by the 17th century there was no resident laird in Longniddry, the original house must have been something rather less prestigious than a "manor place", but presumably something more impressive than the usual run of humble dwellings. Perhaps it was built for the Earl of Wintoun's baron baillie in Longniddry, or for one of the more substantial tenant farmers. If the eastern addition is indeed *mid* eighteenth century rather than a *late* eighteenth century improvement by Glassell himself, this would date from the time of Buchan of Letham's tack from the York buildings Company, and again, may have been for a prosperous tenant, or for Buchan's factor. Or possibly the house was kept as a second home for occasional visits by Buchan himself.

The late 18th century was a time of enthusiastic agricultural improvement in Scotland. Basically, this involved getting rid of a landed estate's many peasant farmers with their irregular scattered holdings, enclosing the land into regular square or rectangular fields bounded by hedges or walls, and leasing the improved ground to two or three tenants who would operate by using up to date methods and pay rents commensurate with the value of their modernised farms.

The entry for the Parish of Gladsmuir in the New Statistical Account, written by the Rev. John Ramsay in 1836, says of Longniddry, "In former times four tenants lived in it – one in Coopers Close, one in Burnfoot Close, and one on each side of the road about the middle of the village." The cultivation of the barony by at least four tenants is confirmed by a legal case involving "Robert Pillans, John Dodds, Peter Keppie and James Sibbald tennents in Longniddrie… tennents and possessers there by tacks or agreements with Mr George Buchan of Kello, lessee"[88]. (Their crops had been commandeered by the Jacobite army after the battle of Prestonpans in 1745.) Perhaps, however, Mr Ramsay should have said "four *major* tenants",

87 http:portal.historicenvironment.scot/designation/LB126.
88 NRS: E780; CS 781.

for the 1778 description of the Barony of Longniddry prepared for the sale of the York Buildings Company's Wintoun estates listed sixteen tenants and one "feuer" in the village. These were:

- John Dods: Setonhill or New East Mains of Longniddry + three acres.
- Peter Bairnsfather: Redcoll Mains + part of Burnfoot.
- George Ronaldson: A farm of 5½ ploughgates + some lands and houses.
- John Cleugh: Links and Rabbit warren. Boglehill. 3½ acres of cotlands.
- James Mitchel: Burnfoot and Harelaw; other lands, a yard, Ladies' Yard.
- Thomas Rennie: The brewery. A farm.
- Mr Buchan: Hepburn's Croft and Loan Park (Natural possession of the principal tacksman).
- Mrs Buchan: Two little parks.
- Robert Burn: A farm with a dovecot – 3½ ploughgates. Stoneylees. A piece of land in Hyneward Park.
- Hugh Reoch: A farm 3½ ploughgates. Cadger Burn Park.
- Peter Burn: 2 acres formerly the Officer's. One third broken plough. An acre at the Dean. Lands formerly belonging to Christy Bone, Janet Bone, William Glover; six acres. ½ of the grass at Cadger Burn.
- William Keppie: 2 acres.
- George Fairly: 2 acres.
- William Bain: 7 acres.
- George Pow: 2 acres + 3 acres rent free as salary for being Baron Officer to Seton, Longniddry and Winton.
- James Harley: About half an acre.
- James Mylne: Fuer [Sic]. 4 merk and 20 penny land of the town and lands of Longniddry with houses etc. held in blench ferm for payment of ½ pair of white spurs or 6 silver pennies at the feast of John the Baptist if asked.

Dods and Bairnsfather presumably resided on their farms of Setonhill and Redcoll which were outwith the Lot 1 of Longniddry purchased by John Glassell, but they obviously also rented ground within the bounds of Lot 1.

James Mitchell's farm of Harelaw was also beyond the boundaries of Lot 1. The Buchans of course were resident at Letham near Haddington. James Mylne was farmer at Lochhill, well beyond the boundaries of Longniddry. The "4 merk and 20 penny land" of Longniddry does not seem to be shown on the 1778 plan. As a fuar, Mylne would have rights of ownership, unlike a mere tenant, so if his land fell within Lot 1, Glassell would have had to come to a separate arrangement with him to acquire it. Mylne, incidentally, was a local poet who had much to say about agrarian reform and "greedy lairds".

As well as the agricultural tenants listed, there would have been the usual run of rural craftsmen – smiths, shoemakers, tailors, wrights and others. Certainly, there were handloom weavers who had several pews in the Longniddry Loft of Gladsmuir Kirk. Also, there had been a school and schoolmaster in Longniddry since at least the end of the 17th century. And we must not forget the many labourers who would hire themselves out for a wide range of tasks as required. All must have occupied houses in the village. Some may have paid rent to tenant farmers, some may have rented from the "principal tacksman", and it is not unlikely that some may have occupied houses which belonged to their family by use and wont, with no written agreement. Most of these "humbler sorts" would have a "yard" or garden, and might well have cultivated a rig or two in the Cotlands, or rented scraps of ground from tenant farmers.

On the face of it, then, John Glassell came to a large, sprawling, irregularly shaped village of rubble-built thatched or pantiled houses and outbuildings; a busy hive of activity with a large and varied population. Between Glassell's arrival in 1779 and the drawing up of his estate plan in 1798, all this, it seems, was swept away.

Glassell's first action as laird of Longniddry was to assert his position as "master of the ground". On 22nd February 1780. Peter McIntyre, Sheriff Officer, arrived in the village to summon Glassell's tenants to appear before the Sheriff to hear an "action of removing" lodged against them at the instance of the new laird. Named in the action were:

- John Buchan Esqr of Letham,
- Peter Bairnsfather tenant in Harperdean and Redcoal Mains,
- John Cleugh, tenant in Boglehill.

- George Ronaldson, James Mitchel, Thomas Rennie, Robert Burn, Peter Burn, Hugh Reoch, tenants in Longniddry,
- William Keppie, indweller there,
- William Bain, mealmaker there,
- Peter Clark, wright there,
- James Harley, day labourer and indweller there,
- George Pow, Baron Officer, day labourer and indweller there.

It was ordained that those named, "Ought and should be severally decerned & ordained by Decreet of Court to flit out and remove themselves, wives, families, servants, cottars, subtenants, and dependers, furth and from the occupation and possession of such parts of the several subjects above contained in the pursuer's titles… and that upon the 26th day of May next as to the houses yards and grass, and at the separation of the crop from the ground in the present year 1780 as to the arable land, and to leave such their several possessions void, redd, and patent at the said terms to the effect that the said pursuer or others on his account may then enter to the peaceable possession thereof and possess the same in time coming."[89]

Glassell was to say many years later that when he "made his purchase he was almost a stranger in this country, being newly come from America where he had passed the greater part of his life. He was besides almost unable to attend to his affairs in consequence of a complaint of which he had been long ill, and from which he did not recover till many years after. In this situation after his purchase he let the whole estate except some parks around his house at cumulo rent to the same tenant who had formerly possessed it, and hardly took any other concern than to receive his rent."[90]

The tenant referred to is Robert Burn, and of course in reality he was only *one* of the former tenants of Lot 1 of the barony, rather than "the same tenant who had formerly possessed it". That Burn was the sort of progressive farmer approved by the age of agrarian reform is indicated by the plan of 1778 which shows that he had already made several "inclosures" to the southwest of the village, outwith the boundaries of Lot 1. Burn, therefore, farmed most of Glassell's Longniddry estate, and he was almost certainly

89 NRS. Haddington Sheriff Court records SC40/20/22.

90 NRS. Court of Session records CS/235/G/127 – John Glassell v. Earl of Wemyss.

based at what is now Longniddry Farm on the south side of the village. Legal references through the 1780s and 90s make it obvious, however, that James Mitchell[91] also farmed a substantial part of Glassell's land. For example, in a boundary dispute of 1800 Mitchell deponed that, "he was a tenant on the Longniddry estate from 1749 to Whitsunday last 1799". In the same process a witness testified that he "frequently challenged the herds of Burn and Mitchell, tenants of Longniddry".[92] By 1800 Mitchell was "tenant in Trabroun"[93] and may well have been already based there while farming ground in Longniddry.

John Glassell, then, being debarred by ill health from the hands-on management of his estate, simplified matters by removing his tenants and leasing the ground to Burn and Mitchell. We should not jump to the conclusion, however, that this transfer marks the time when "over 70 houses" were swept away. Nor need we believe that all those named in the "action of removing" were necessarily in fact evicted. Glassell had taken legal steps to "clear his feet", as it were. The impression given is that as long as Burn and Mitchell paid the rent, what happened on the ground was of little concern to the laird. Burn and Mitchell might have been quite happy to allow the occupants of the many houses on their land to stay at an appropriate rent, and may even have been prepared to sub-let pieces of ground. In the 1790s, for example, George Pow, the former Baron Officer named in the "action of removing", was still living in Longniddry in a house for which he paid rent to Robert Burn.[94]

Thus, the disappearance of the "Town of Longniddry" shown on the 1778 plan was probably not the sort of cataclysmic event we see in the Highland Clearances, where an entire community would be evicted from their homes in a single day, and their houses demolished. It is more likely to have been a slow long-drawn-out process, as happened elsewhere in the former Earldom of Wintoun. After the forfeiture of the 5th Earl's estates, the entire Barony of Winton, near Pencaitland, was leased by its new owner to a local man James Clark in 1725. At that time there was a substantial village on the estate. A "List of the Rental, Cotland, and Cot Houses on the

---

91 Sometimes spelled "Mitchell", sometimes "Mitchel".

92 NRS. Court of Session records CS235/G/127.

93 NRS. Sheriff Court records SC/40/1/41. Trabroun lies to the south of Longniddry, well beyond the boundary of the former barony.

94 NRS. Court of Session records CS235/G/127.

Barony of Winton, Whitsunday 1780" shows that by then half of the listed properties were standing empty, and six were ruinous. In 1804 a lawsuit over who should have kept the buildings in repair revealed that no repairs had been done since the Earl of Wintoun's forfeiture. It is obvious that by the end of the 18th century the village of Winton had been in decay since1715, that some of the houses were empty, some ruinous, and most in poor repair. Eventually what was left of the village was demolished, and the remaining inhabitants rehoused in "New Winton", a purpose-built hamlet on the edge of the estate.

A similar process of decay seems to have also operated in Longniddry. In the "old" Statistical Account of 1793, the Gladsmuir minister George Hamilton wrote, "From the appearance of *ruined houses* on the north side of the parish, an opinion has prevailed that the inhabitants were once more numerous that they are now."[95] The "north side" of Gladsmuir parish is of course Longniddry.

As we shall see, it seems to have been only towards the end of the 1790s that John Glassell began to take an active interest in running his estate, and yet already, before the sweeping away of "over 70 houses", according to the Statistical Account parts of Longniddry were ruinous. We can imagine a situation where houses fell vacant, and Robert Burn and James Mitchell found it more bother than it was worth to re-let them. Old houses would begin to crumble, thatch to deteriorate and leak, and the greater the deterioration, the less Burn and Mitchell would be inclined to bear the cost of repairs. Since the master of the ground showed no interest, why should his two tenants put themselves out? Indeed, this may well have been a process ongoing since 1715, as in Winton. After all, Mr Buchan of Letham was an absentee landlord who leased not only Longniddry, but other parts of the former Earldom, and also had his own lands of Letham. Would he necessarily have been punctilious in doing repairs and re-letting vacant houses? The 1778 plan shows a large village comprising many buildings, but that does not guarantee that all the buildings were occupied, in use, or in good repair.

By the mid-1790s John Glassell seems to have stirred to take his estate in hand. In 1796, Robert Burn, claiming to have lost the paper detailing the terms of his lease, was forced to submit to arbitration to

95 My italics.

settle various matters, including "the condition under which said lands and houses should be left and what part of the said lands ought and should be surrendered to the said John Glassell and what retained by the said Robert Burn".[96] The adjudicator Charles Brown of Coalston[97] (related to Glassell by marriage) decided Burn was entitled to possession of Longniddry Farm until 1799. Glassell was awarded immediate possession of 30 acres of links, and other ground near his house "in order to straight his enclosures adjacent thereto". He was also to be entitled to take off land to the south of Longniddry House in order to alter the line of the road through the village. It is likely that the object of this exercise was to take in and enclose land around Longniddry House in order to improve the laird's privacy as befitted his status. Also, Glassell was to be "entitled to enclose what part of the farm he should think proper" as long as he compensated Burn for any ground he was unable to crop while the enclosures were being carried out. Finally, Burn was to be entitled to a reduction in his rent "for each house the said John Glassell has taken into his own possession at the west end of the Town of Longniddry".

Thus, in 1796, Glassell was taking into his own hands land formerly possessed by Robert Burn. He also seems to have been compulsorily enclosing Burn's fields for him. According to George Pow, the former Baron Officer, who had rented a house from Burn, Glassell had ordered Burn to evict him around 1795 because he kept a horse against the Laird's wishes, and because "Mr Glassell wanted to take the whole houses into his own possession"[98].

Burn's lease ended in 1799, and in May of the same year Glassell initiated a "process of removing" against James Mitchell.[99] By July of the same year Thomas Howden was "tenant of the Farm of Longniddry". Howden represents the culmination of John Glassell's programme of improvements. He was now the sole tenant farmer on an estate which had once carried multiple tenants. His landlord lived secluded in the "Manor Place of Longniddry", surrounded by parkland, with the road to Edinburgh diverted away from his mansion. It must have been just prior to this that the remains of the old "Town of Longniddry" were demolished. It was probably

96 NRS. Register of Deeds RD4/260.

97 Nowadays "Broun of Colstoun".

98 NRS. Court of Session records. CS/235/G/127.

99 NRS. Sheriff court records. SC40/1/41.

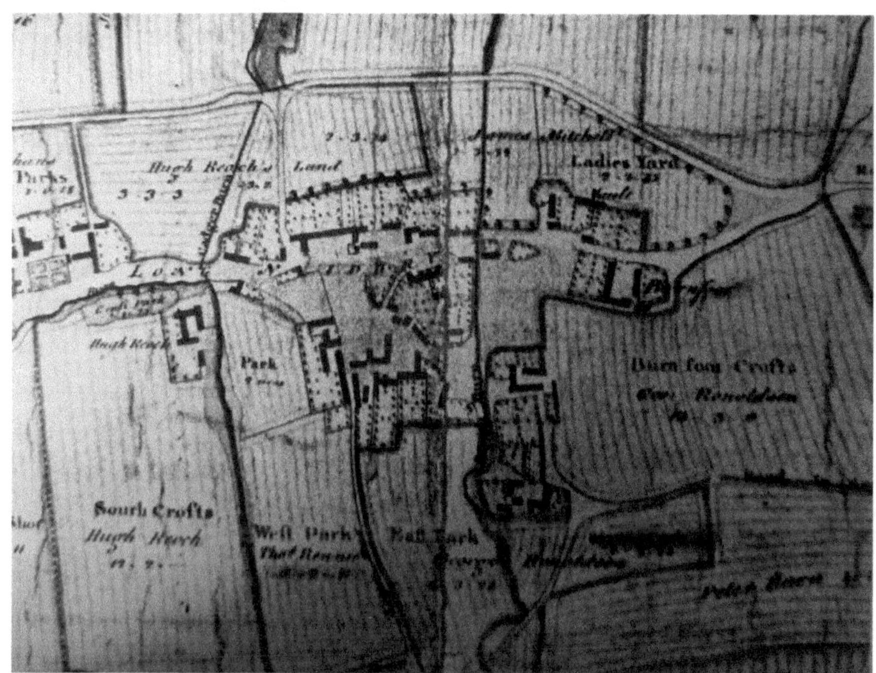

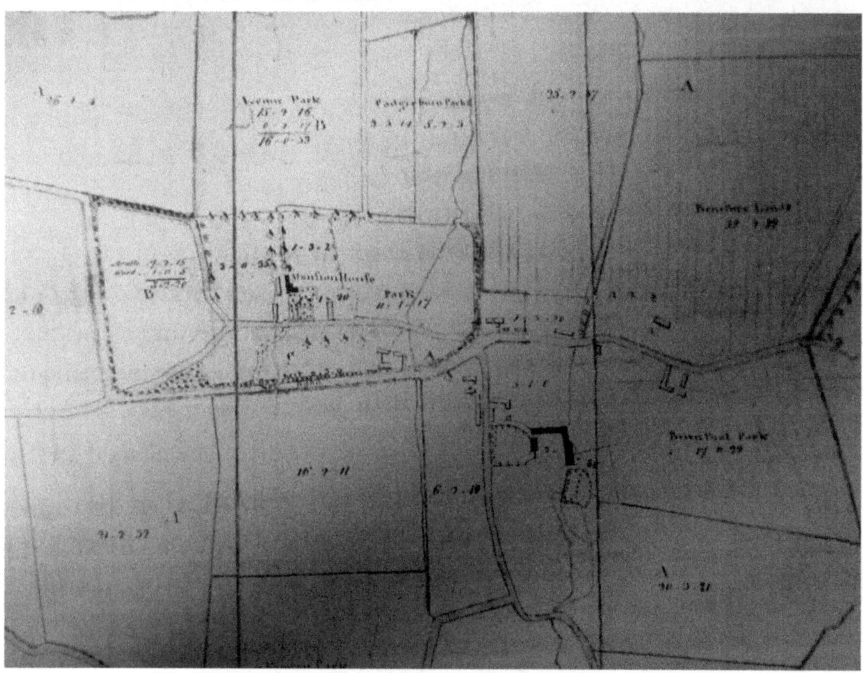

Longniddry in 1778 (above) and in 1798 (below).
(Details from maps in the possession of the Earl of Wemyss, with the written permission of Wemyss and March Estates.)

done without much fuss. Most of the houses would already be empty or in ruins. Those of the inhabitants who were not housed in the hamlet that remained would go to neighbouring communities or to the many large "improved" farms nearby. There is not a whisper recorded of a mass eviction. Rather, what we seem to have is a long process of running-down, followed by a tidying-up exercise.

Even so, the face of the landscape had changed forever, and what was once a large thriving community had all but vanished, along with its memories, customs and traditions. James Mylne of Lochhill, in a bitter poem entitled "A Scots Song", paints a gloomy picture of the effects of agricultural "improvements" on "Lothian's groaning swains", contrasting a happy and idyllic rural past with a wretched and poverty-stricken present, and unhesitatingly points an accusing finger at the culprits:

"But ken ye whence our sorrows spring?
Our greedy lairds bear a' the blame.
What once made many a tenant sing
Now barely steghs ae landlord's wame.
While sumptuously ye eat and drink,
Does it ne'er sting your conscious breast,
Oh cruel luxury! To think
He starves whose toil produced the feast?"

Although John Glassell's health had not permitted him to take much interest in business affairs until many years after his return to Scotland, he did not waste much time in putting his domestic affairs in order. The Scots Magazine for November 1780 carried among its marriage announcements:

"18th November 1780.

At Letham Haddingtonshire. John Glassell Esq. of Long Niddery to Miss Helen Buchan, daughter of John Buchan Esq. of Letham."

Glassell's new bride, therefore, was the daughter of the former lessee of Longniddry – one of those on whom he had served a notice of eviction in February of the same year as his marriage. The fact that Glassell and Buchan remained on friendly enough terms to link their families in marriage might suggest that the "eviction" of the former lessee from the parts of Longniddry he farmed on his own account, was a mere legal formality. So might it have been, as previously hinted, with others of the "evicted" tenantry.

Helen was a descendant of the Buchans of Auchmacoy in Aberdeenshire. Her father was an advocate and East Lothian landowner whose estate of Letham lay just outside the county town of Haddington. He had married firstly Elizabeth Hepburn, by whom he had five children. The Hepburns were an ancient family of East Lothian gentry. (Queen Mary's third husband the Earl of Bothwell was a Hepburn.) Elizabeth was of the Hepburns of Smeaton, and her son George eventually inherited that estate as Sir George Buchan Hepburn.

John Buchan of Letham married as his second wife Ann Brown, sister of George Brown of Colstoun.[100] This second marriage apparently produced six sons and seven daughters, including Helen, who married John Glassell, and Mary, who married Glassell's near neighbour John Cadell of Cockenzie.[101] John Glassell's place among the county gentry of East Lothian was now well secured. He was not only the wealthy owner of a small estate, but related by marriage to the Buchans of Letham, the Hepburns of Smeaton, the Brouns of Colstoun, and the Cadells of Cockenzie.

According to Hayden's "Virginia Genealogies", Helen Buchan was born "c. 1750".[102] If this is the case, she was, by the standards of the day, rather late in embarking upon marriage. Her husband of course was himself well beyond the first flush of youth. Born in November 1736, he must have married around the time of his 44th birthday in November 1780. It seems just a little odd that he had never married in Virginia – his brother Andrew certainly did – but there appears to be no mention or record of any such thing. The sexual exploitation of black slaves was of course rife, but to suspect John of seeking consolation in that quarter would be mere speculation.

Although John Glassell's marriage to Helen Buchan may have been a passionate love-match, the fact that she was a single woman of child-bearing age was probably John's principal motivation, and her kinship to

100 Or "Broun of Coalston".

101 Details of the Buchan family as supplied to Hayden's "Virginia Genealogies" by Sir Thomas Buchan Hepburn, 1891.

102 According to the online website "The Peerage" (thepeerage.com/p.2212.htm#c22112.2) Helen Buchan was born 28th April 1754 and baptised 3rd May 1754 at Haddington. However there is no mention of this in "Scotland's People", the website of the National Records of Scotland, and therefore obviously no record of it in the parish records of Haddington. It is not clear what the source of the information in "The Peerage" could be.

a network of East Lothian gentry would certainly not detract from her desirability.

Helen, unfortunately, is a woman about whom little or nothing is known. Hayden's "Virginia Genealogies" quotes a letter written in 1804 by Walter Colquhoun of Glasgow to Daniel Grinnan in Fredericksburg, Virginia. He describes a visit to "my old friend Mr Glassell" at Longniddry. "Mrs G.", he says, "is an amiable well-informed woman – active, industrious, extremely attentive to her husband and to her domestic concerns." If any other description of Helen exists anywhere it has yet to come to light.

If the provision of an heir was indeed the prime purpose of Helen's marriage, the couple had to wait a surprisingly long time for that happy event. The register of baptisms for Gladsmuir parish informs us:

"Glassell

John Esqr of Longniddry and his wife Helen Buchan daughter of John Buchan Esqr of Letham his spouse [sic] had a daughter born at his house in Longniddry Thursday 9th June 1796 & was baptiz'd the 1st of July following by the Revd Mr George Hamilton minister at Gladsmuir and named Joan in presence of John Cadell Esqr of Cockenzie, Messrs George & John Buchan Hepburn, John Buchan Esqr writer and Dr Richard Somner."

Sixteen years is a long wait for a first child, and we might suspect a history of discouraging miscarriages over that time. There is also the question of John's chronic ill health, the nature of which we cannot now know. The Gladsmuir Kirk Session cash book[103] baldly records a payment in 1799, "By cash from Mr Glassell for erecting a tomb-stone in the church yard for his infant son." If Helen was indeed born "c. 1750" she would be 49 in 1799 and her husband would be 63. The death of this unnamed infant must have been the last crushing blow to Glassell's hopes of a male heir.

After Glassell's old friend Walter Colquhoun visited Longniddry in 1804, he mentioned Glassell's only child thus in his letter to Daniel Grinnan already quoted: "Their daughter and only child, about eight years of age, is a fine looking healthy promising girl – she will have a handsome fortune." As we shall see, Joan not only had a handsome fortune, but an unusual education, a prestigious marriage, and was a most interesting woman in her own right. A fairly wide selection of her adult correspondence survives

103 NRS. Church records, CH2/169/10.

in the Campbell Papers in the National Library of Scotland. Her lively letters and journals have much to say about her friends and acquaintances, contemporary events, literature, art, science and cultural matters, but nothing about her parents, and next to nothing about her childhood. Indeed, that a woman of such wide interests and obvious intelligence, perception and self-awareness should have almost nothing to say about her childhood seems just a little odd.

When Joan was sixteen, her mentor Mrs Grant wrote her a frank and in places rather brutal assessment of her strengths and weaknesses.[104] Mrs Grant includes among "external disadvantages" for which Joan "cannot be blamed", "A very irregular and imperfect education, owing partly to adventitious circumstances & very much to the injudicious indulgence of one who like Othello 'Lovd not wisely but too well'. This is lamentable but not irremediable." Mrs Grant also mentions "the very little control under which you have hitherto lived".

In 1819 Joan wrote to her future husband, "I was much amused with a very grave epistle of my own in my 7th year I found t'other day. I suppose my governess had seized my weak side to reduce me to order (as the one I had then made a devil of me) for this letter was written from Somebody telling me my Father had determined to send me to an English school, & I began saying I never would do good anywhere but Scotland, as I never would like any country but my own, & saying my hand was shaking so with fright I could not write well. Poor wreckin! Much I knew then about 'all the nameless ties that in the name of country lies'... I daresay when I wrote that letter I thought it was impossible to have a sorer heart than the prospect of a few months in England."

It was not unknown for the children of 18th century Scottish landowners to have part of their education in the local parish school, but by the end of the century this was less common. In any case the parish school of Gladsmuir was around two miles away from Joan's home at Longniddry House. Parish records show that there had been a village school in Longniddry since at least the late 17th century, and it is possible, but not very likely, that Joan might have had a spell there. As a wealthy self-made man her father might have been wary of the dangers of social backsliding inherent in his daughter attending a mere village school.

104 NLS. Campbell Papers Acc508/38.

When Joan wrote of "the one I had then" in relation to her governess, it would appear to hint at a succession of such teachers. We can probably assume, then, that Joan received a basic education at home, albeit an education dismissed by the exacting Mrs Grant as "irregular and imperfect".

Joan's adult correspondence includes only one or two passing references to what are probably childhood memories. In another letter to her future husband she mentions the Longniddry gardener trying to convince her of the necessity of removing some old elder trees which were "nae ornament", and replacing them with fruit. Joan commented, "I acknowledged all he said was very reasonable, but I liked the old things. I had sometimes seen the birds feeding on them in hard snowy winters. The fruit must take its chance, I can't part with them. I'm seldom there, but nowhere like to see changes.[105]

In another communication, after referring to her estate as "Longstuffery", Joan continues, "Seriously though, I mind walking sometimes on the shore on a misty morning when the fleet of oyster boats was invisible, and then the dredge song sounded something fine and wild. And what a beautiful thing it is seeing boats emerging from a mist, their sparkling oars seen before the distinct shape of the whole is visible."[106]

An amusing incident, perhaps from Joan's early teens, could be taken as an example of "the very little control" under which she had supposedly lived as a girl, according to Mrs Grant. In 1927 W. B. Dunlop of Seton Castle, Longniddry, wrote to the "Scotsman" newspaper after he had seen a letter from Lady Frances Balfour "re that charming and most engaging personality Miss Joan Glassell". Mr Dunlop's very long letter was not published, but a copy of it is in the Campbell Papers in the National Library of Scotland. He mentions Joan's "charming buoyancy of spirit and enthusiasm of youth", and goes on to illustrate this with a story he had heard from Colonel Cadell of Cockenzie. Cadell had got the tale from his father, who was Joan's cousin Hugh Francis Cadell. When Hugh was a boy, Dunlop related, "He and some friends were bathing on the sands at Bogle Hill, a small hamlet existing just below Longniddry House where Miss Glassell lived. She happened to be riding on the sands and recognising either the boys in the sea or their clothes, she stooped from her horse, gathered up all their garments, and

---

105 NLS. Campbell Papers Acc8508/47, Letter 7.

106 NLS. Campbell Papers ACC8508/37, Letter 3. The oyster fishermen of Cockenzie and Prestonpans sang as they dredged for oysters. The "dreg songs" are now lost, and recent attempts at reconstruction by an American academic are unconvincing.

made off with them, leaving the bathers in a state of nature to make their way back over a mile to Cockenzie house as best they could. Fortunately they met some fisherwomen whom they knew and they stripped themselves of their manifold petticoats and cloaks and so the boys eventually reached their destination."[107]

These meagre details seem to comprise all the remaining records of Joan Glassell's childhood.

Though we know next to nothing of the family life of the Glassells of Longniddry, we get occasional glimpses in the records of John Glassell performing the kind of social obligations incumbent on the rural landowners of the day. He also makes an appearance in legal disputes with his neighbours and others. He would appear above all to have been anxious that his family should be firmly established socially among the landowning elite, and took several legal steps to ensure that this should be so. Not least, it is possible to trace his ongoing involvement in his American business affairs.

---

107 NLS. Campbell Papers Acc8508/37, bundle 6, item 3.
Boglehill was in fact over a mile from Longniddry House, and Cockenzie House a good two miles away. At low tide a vast tract of sand is exposed, and this is where Joan would be riding. The traditional fishwives' costume comprised several layers of petticoats.

4

Obligation and litigation

John Glassell's position as a landowner in the parish of Gladsmuir came with social expectations attached. It was the responsibility of the landowners or "heritors" in a parish to finance the upkeep of the parish church and school, supply the stipends for minister and schoolmaster, and provide their accommodation. The buildings would need regular maintenance and repair, and sometimes extension or indeed replacement, and it was the duty of the heritors to provide the necessary funds. Each parish church had a poors' fund to maintain parishioners unable to earn a living. Church collections helped with this, as did the fines imposed on offenders against church discipline. However, when these resources were inadequate, as they almost always were, it was the duty of the heritors to supply the shortfall. Basically, the minister and elders of the congregation, meeting as the Kirk Session, ran the affairs of the parish, and the heritors supplied them with the money to do so. It goes without saying that generosity was not always the guiding star of a parish's heritors.

As already mentioned, when John Glassell bought Lot 1 of the Barony of Longniddry in 1779 his health was poor, and that is probably why he does not appear in the records of the Gladsmuir Heritors[108] until 1783. In the early 1780s the heritors were meeting several times a year, but thereafter

108 National Records of Scotland HR115/1

a single annual meeting seems to have been thought sufficient, unless particular business made additional meetings necessary. There were around a dozen heritors in the period 1780 – 1810. Those who did not attend meetings personally would usually send a proxy, or delegate a fellow heritor to speak for them. Two female heritors, Lady Ross and Lady Stewart, of course never attended meetings, and always sent proxies. The grandly titled landowners in the parish, the Earl of Haddington, Lord Elibank, the Earl of Hopeton, and later the Earl of Wemyss, were almost always represented by their factors. Some heritors seem to have hardly ever attended and did not even bother to send proxies. Others were regular attenders who presumably had a genuine interest in parish affairs.

John Glassell's first appearance at a heritors' meeting was on 25th April 1783. Present were "Mr Law of Elvingston, Dr Barclay of Middleton, Mr Glassel of Longniddrie, Mr Mason for the Earl of Hopeton, Mr Frazer for Lord Elibank, Mr Clark for Capt Hamilton of Pencaitland, Mr Lees for the Earl of Haddington and Mr Craig of Seton Hill". The minister Francis Cowan and three elders were also present. Mr Law was chosen "preses" or chairman, as he subsequently usually was. Perhaps the fact that his estate was only a mile from the parish church made him a more reliable attender. The matters discussed at this meeting were support for the poor and repairs to the manse. It was reckoned that the sum necessary for supporting the poor for the next half year would be £36-1-8. Mr Law had £26-6s in hand of the Kirk Session's money, and the heritors agreed to assess themselves for the balance. A committee was formed consisting of Mr Law, Mr Glassell, Dr Barclay, Mr Gray[109] and Mr Mason, who were to consider the repairs necessary to the manse and its outbuildings, and to receive estimates from tradesmen. They were also to consider repairs required to make the church roof watertight. A quorum of three was considered sufficient for the committee to conduct its business. Glassell, Law, and Barclay duly visited the manse on 9th May with two wrights and a mason who were instructed to prepare estimates, and a figure of £46-18-8 for all joinery work and for the re-roofing of the manse "offices" was accepted on 24th June.

By that time Glassell found himself on another committee charged with selling the kirkyard trees.

A heritors' meeting of 7th July considered the allotting of the church

109 Mr Gray of Southfield. Presumably drafted onto the committee in his absence.

of Gladsmuir's seating among the heritors "according to their valued rents". The total area of church seating, 1809 square feet, was divided into sixteen shares, ranging from the Barony of Penston with 316 square feet, to Gladsmuir with 6½ square feet. The second largest share, 255 square feet, went to "Mr Glassel Longniddrie" who was allotted "the whole west part of the Longniddrie loft, and in the east part of it 102 square feet from the north gable of the ayl southward, being the whole of said loft except the front seat in the east side of it, and the seat at the back of the said front seat." In other words, Glassell was awarded the whole Longniddry Loft apart from two pews at the front of one side which were allotted to Mr Craig of Setonhill. Although each heritor's seating was based on the rental value of his estate, since the seating was of course meant to accommodate people, it must have been felt that rental value reflected population. Indeed, perhaps the phrase "their valued rents" might refer to the seat rents of the pews rather than the rental value of the heritors' estates. In either case the indication is the same, that in Gladsmuir parish at that time Longniddry was still second only to the thriving coal-mining village of Penston in population.

There were two heritors' meetings in 1784, and John Glassell was absent from them both. He was also absent from the only meeting in 1785, on 9th April. The probable reason was his health. A letter survives among the papers of Professor William Cullen, which may throw some light on this.[110] Dr Cullen was the Professor of the Practice of Medicine at Edinburgh University, and has been described as "almost rivalling Boerhaave and Hoffman as Europe's leading medical teacher".[111] In 1785 he was in receipt of a letter written on 17th August from Dumfries beginning, "Mrs Glassell takes the liberty of troubling Dr Cullen with a few lines to inform that Mr G is now free of swelling and pain in the ankles, but feels stiffness in his feet…". He had been troubled with headaches for the preceding three weeks, and was frequently vomiting up his food. He had been advised to drink the waters at Gilsland, which were reputed to be good for stomach complaints, and he had also been advised to drink trefoil. Mrs Glassell added that her husband had been "jaunting" for twenty or thirty miles every day.

110 The Cullen Project. www.cullenproject.ac.uk, Doc ID 2689.
111 Edinburgh and the Golden Age – Mary Cosh, Birlinn, Edinburgh 2014. Page 109.

Now, certainly there may still have been several Glassells in the Dumfries area, but Mrs Glassell asks Dr Cullen to send his reply "care of Mr Macmillan, Dumfries". James Macmillan was actually, as previously noted, the minister of Torthorwald, the Glassell "heartland" adjacent to the town of Dumfries, and as we shall see, John Glassell made him one of the trustees charged with administering his estate. John Glassell and James Macmillan were obviously on friendly terms. Also, it is perhaps unlikely that any of the Glassells remaining in the Dumfries area would be consulting a physician based in Edinburgh, far less one of Europe's medical stars. It is more probable that Professor Cullen's patients would reside in the Edinburgh area, and be rather wealthier than any of the Glassells remaining in Dumfriesshire. Also, Mrs Glassell signs herself "H. Glassell", and John Glassell's wife's name was of course Helen. On balance, it seems likely that "Mr G" is John Glassell of Longniddry who is on an extended holiday in his native county, probably for health reasons, and probably based with his contemporary and family friend the minister of Torthorwald.

Cullen replied to Mrs Glassell saying that in his opinion the recent wet weather was the cause of her husband's headaches and stomach problems. He thought the exercise of travelling would do more good than the water of Gilsland itself, and that the water at Buxton was better for drinking and bathing than the water at Gilsland. If the weather continued wet Glassell would be better to travel to the east or the south of England where conditions were drier. As for the trefoil, Cullen didn't advise it, as "medicines without necessity are improper for the road".

Poor Glassell's health may have been a constant bugbear, but at least he was wealthy enough to be able to seek the advice of Scotland's top doctor.[112]

Glassell was able to attend the 1787 heritors' meeting. Support for the poor was discussed, and it was decided that before applicants could be admitted as "pensioners" their furniture and possessions must be signed over to go to the Kirk Session at their deaths. Also, heritors were warned that if they did

112 The mineral springs at Gilsland in Cumbria became a popular spa during the latter part of the 18th century, which was visited by Robert Burns in 1787 and Sir Walter Scott in 1797. Buxton is a Peak District town in Derbyshire. The Romans built baths there to take advantage of thermal springs, and it was an established spa by the 16th century, visited by Mary Queen of Scots during her captivity at nearby Chatsworth. Its boom period as a fashionable spa began around 1780.

not pay their due assessments within ten days, they would be prosecuted. Glassell was then absent from heritors' meetings until 28th September 1790, although he had been nominated in 1789 to serve on a committee to consider repairs to the "additional school". As well as the parish school at Gladsmuir, there were "additional schools" at Longniddry and Samuelston. Although the heritors' minutes do not say which of the schools is meant, Glassell's nomination would indicate that it was Longniddry. He was also nominated on 18th June 1790 to serve on a committee to assist in collecting a levy on the heritors to finance repairs to the manse and its garden walls.

On 28th September 1790 Glassell was present at a well-attended meeting where the roof of the church was "minutely inspected". Although "several of the gentlemen present were of the opinion that there is no immediate danger of the roof falling" and that it was good for another twenty years, they agreed to an inspection by a wright and an architect. It also appears that the floor of the church was now far below the level of the ground outside, which of course would cause severe dampness, and it was decided that the clerk should employ labourers "to remove the earth all round the Kirk to the distance of three feet from the walls, where it can be done without interfering with any of the graves". A further meeting in October of the same year sanctioned repairs to the roof. John Glassell's name was added to a committee to take estimates for plastering the church ceiling and walls, levelling the church floor, installing fixed communion tables, and taking forward the repairs to the roof. Unfortunately, this committee apparently fell apart, and a new committee, including John Glassell, was appointed on 5th April 1791.

Over the next dozen or so years Glassell was able to attend nearly all the heritors' meetings, considering such matters as "the poverty of the schoolmasters in Samuelston and Longniddry", the rebuilding of the Gladsmuir "schoolroom" which was judged "very injurious to the health of the children by the lowness of the roof and the dampness of the floor", which was apparently *three feet* below the level of the ground outside. Another important undertaking was the rearrangement of the church seating and the various shares of it allotted to each heritor. Glassell, was one of the committee dealing with this, and his share was now slightly adjusted to comprise the whole Longniddry Loft except the front seat on the east side. He also served on a committee considering an extension to the manse in 1804.

John Glassell attended the meeting of 2nd July 1805 which considered the parish's inability to find men for the army reserve. He sent a proxy to the meeting of 1st April 1806, and died a fortnight later.

We can probably assume that as a parishioner and heritor, John Glassell would attend Gladsmuir Parish Church as often as his health allowed. The Kirk Session minutes, however, contain an interesting example of a different aspect to his dealings with the church. Even in the late 18th century, kirk sessions were still keeping a close eye on the moral welfare of their parishioners, and were legally empowered to process offenders for such lapses as profanity, Sabbath breaking, and fornication. Gladsmuir Kirk Session at its meeting of 2nd August 1789 considered a letter from John Glassell "wherein he strongly charged his manservant David Bain as guilty of fornication with his maidservant Janet Scot". Not only that, but he had been informed that they "had used means to cause abortion". In a note to the Session David Bain declared his innocence. The Session summoned Janet and interrogated her closely, but she strenuously denied everything, claiming that "she had sent to the doctor for some drugs, but it was for another cause, and that Mr Glassell knew of it and advised her thereto". Having no evidence to allow them to proceed further, the Session decided to let the matter rest "until Providence should give more light on it". Providence presumably did no such thing, as the records contain no further reference to the case.

Incidentally, Glassell's servants were not the only Longniddry residents accused of moral lapses. The sole agricultural tenant of Glassell's estate, Robert Howden, who would certainly have been expected to behave more circumspectly, found himself in very embarrassing circumstances in 1802. At a Kirk Session meeting on 26th December of that year Elizabeth Lugton appeared before the Session and "declared that she had brought forth a child to Robert Howden farmer in Longniddry". At a subsequent appearance she was sharply rebuked for her offence. There seems to be no record of action taken against Howden.

According to the 19th century local historian John Martine[113] John Glassell was also a Justice of the Peace, and in that capacity was present in Glen's

113 Reminiscences and notices of the parishes of the County of Haddington – John Martine. East Lothian County Library Service, 1999. (Originally published in two volumes in 1890 and 1894.)

Inn, Tranent, at the fateful meeting of the JPs and Deputy Lieutenants of the county on 25th August 1797. This meeting had been called to receive lists of men in the western parishes of East Lothian who were qualified to serve in the Militia, a sort of Home Guard to be used as back-up for the regular army. It was not fully understood among the local people that the Militia could not be sent to serve abroad, and an angry crowd gathered outside the inn to make their displeasure felt. As the demonstration became more threatening the Riot Act was read, troops brought in to keep the peace panicked and opened fire on the crowd, then rampaged out of control through the town and surrounding countryside shooting and sabring, killing and maiming. It was not the British Army's finest hour, and the local gentry must bear at least part of the blame for allowing the situation to get out of hand. A subsequent inquiry resulted in what would nowadays be termed a "whitewash job", and no-one was ever brought to book for the bloodshed.

John Glassell would have little sympathy for the Tranent rioters. After all, he had left Virginia at least partly because of his opposition to American revolutionary principles. Since then the ideas spreading from revolutionary France had become vastly more radical and intimidating to Britain's ruling classes. Glassell may have sprung from a humble background, but he was now a wealthy landowning Tory, who would equate liberal politics with mob rule and chaos. Martine gives an amusing example of this in his "Reminiscences and notices",[114] where he draws a flattering pen portrait of David Aitken, who "was for over sixty years a principal merchant in Tranent... kind, affable, hospitable and courteous, he was for many years the head man in Tranent". By "merchant" we should understand "shopkeeper" rather than someone engaged in international trade. Some proprietors of small rural general stores in Scotland were still describing themselves as "merchants" well into the 20th century. Aitken, says Martine, "was a keen Liberal all his days, and in his younger days, an extreme one".

John Glassell was in the habit of dealing with Aitken for groceries and hardware, but eventually called on him to tell him he intended to withdraw his custom, "as he could not think of dealing any longer with a person of republican principles who wanted to subvert the government of the country". Aitken took no offence, but quietly and calmly expressed regret to Mr Glassell that he should think of withdrawing his custom after so many

114 Ibid. Page 223.

years. He thanked Glassell for his previous patronage, and agreed that he was perfectly free to deal with whomsoever he pleased. However, Aitken reminded Glassell, his account had been standing unpaid for many years, and he would be obliged if the account was settled before Glassell took his custom elsewhere. Martine remarks, "This was rather a clincher for Mr Glassell, who went off not too well pleased. His custom with Aitken was continued."

Scots of course have always delighted in seeing the high and mighty taken down a peg, but it is unlikely that paying Mr Aitken's bill would have made too serious a hole in John Glassell's funds. He had certainly brought a fortune out with him when he left Virginia, but he had not completely abandoned his business there, and since Britain had made peace with what were now the "United States of America", it was possible once more to exert some control over what remained. As previously noted in Chapter 2 John's brother Andrew took over the brothers' tobacco plantation and remitted the value of John's share to him. John Glassell's business interests had been left in the hands of his factor Lachlan Campbell, and much later his property in Fredericksburg was sold on his behalf by Daniel Grinnan who eventually married Andrew Glassell's daughter. It was presumably with a view to supervising all this that John's young relative William Glassell was sent out to Virginia.

When John Glassell advertised his immanent departure from Virginia, and indicated that his factor Lachlan Campbell was authorised to receive payment of all debts due, he would be well aware that not all of his customers would rush to make payment. The outbreak of war and its duration over several years made payment even more unlikely, especially in view of Glassell's status as an absent enemy alien. However, when the Peace of Paris brought hostilities to an official close in 1783, it was again possible for John Glassell to give closer attention to his business interests in Virginia, and to the substantial sums of money still owing to him. To this end, William Glassell was sent to Virginia in 1785.

It is not clear exactly who William Glassell was. The website "Founders Online" quotes a footnote to a letter sent to James Madison, which says William was "apparently a nephew of John Glassell", and this may be correct. It is possible that he might have been a son of John Glassell's younger brother Robert, but according to the National Records of Scotland's website "Scotland's People" there is no record of the birth or baptism of a William Glassell in the Old Parish Records between 1750 and 1780. A William Glassell is commemorated on a stone in Torthorwald churchyard, but since that William died in 1804, he cannot be "our" William, as we shall see. A letter from a William Walker of Madison County in Virginia refers to William as John Glassell's son,[115] but Walker may well just have been jumping to conclusions. A Dr John K. Read of Norfolk, Virginia, making a statement regarding a small debt of his to John Glassell, remarked that he had been in the habit of visiting Fredericksburg regularly, and "was intimate with the present Mr Glassell's father, and often in association with him in his own house".[116] If we take "the present Mr Glassell" to be William, it is certainly significant that a man who had been on friendly terms with John Glassell in Fredericksburg, perceived them to be father and son. The obvious difficulty of course is that there appears to be no mention anywhere of any marriage of John Glassell's prior to his marriage to Helen Buchan in 1780. There is, however, a rather suspicious lengthy period of apparent celibacy before those fairly late-in-life nuptials. Might William have been an illegitimate son? Unfortunately, that possibility is not encouraged by the fact that a few of William's letters have survived[117] and in none of them does he address or refer to John as "father" or "my father". Instead, he refers to him as "Mr G" or "my benefactor". It remains more likely therefore that William was a more distant relative, possibly a nephew, or perhaps the son of a cousin. Whatever the relationship, William seems to have been commissioned by John Glassell to go to Virginia to oversee his remaining business interests there, and undertake the collection of debts owed by creditors since before the war.

Among the Campbell Papers in the National Library of Scotland is a "Journal 1785 of a voyage by Will Glassell from Liverpool to Virginia on board the brig *Alexandria*, John Watkins, master". Each page of William's journal bears tables of the course taken by the "Alexandria", with details of winds, distances, latitude and longitude. There are also "remarks" on the

115 "British Mercantile Claims". A series of articles in the "Virginia Genealogist". Letter of William Walker 30th Sept. 1792; Vol 27, No 2, April-June 1963.

116 Virginia Genealogist: April-June 1980, Vol24, No 2.

117 "Intimate society letters of the eighteenth century" – Edited by the Duke of Argyll K.T. in 2 Volumes, Stanley, Paul & Co, London, 1910.

events of each day. William's obvious knowledge of the technicalities of operating a sailing ship would suggest that he himself had been a seaman, or at least someone used to frequent sea voyages. He left Liverpool on 23rd August 1785, and reached Urbanna on the Rappahannock River on 4th November.

While much of William's journal is pretty mundane stuff, some entries remind us that a voyage across the Atlantic in the late 18th century was not all plain sailing. On 30th August petrels were seen, "a sure sign of approaching storm". On the evening of the 31st a sailor burst into the cabin crying that "he'd be damned if Davie Jones was not perch't upon the mast head". Lights like candle flames were observed in the rigging, "a certain token of bad weather and impending storms". These discouraging omens proved correct. A "violent hurricane" blew up on 1st September, persisting for several days, during which William noted, "The vessel very leaky. Pump constantly going." Then on 6th September arose "a great storm… which is allowed by all on board to exceed the hard gale we met on 1st inst". William observed, "Chaos itself was not darker unless when it lightened, the glowing flashes of which only served to discover the greatness of our danger. The sea was astonishingly high and the reflection of the lightning on the white foam rendered the scene altogether awful." Squalls and gales continued for a week, then on 21st September the "Alexandria" was pursued all through the day by "a large vessel astern crowding all sail and standing after us". This they took to be a "Moorish Corsair", but fortunately they were able to give it the slip after darkness fell.

The crew were in the habit of spearing dolphins when the opportunity arose. In the gut of one they found two "animals" which appeared to be leeches. To ascertain whether this was what they really were, one was applied to the cabin boy's arm, "where it immediately fixed, and could not be taken away till glutted with blood". William does not say how willing a participant the cabin boy was in this little experiment. On 19th October another dolphin was speared, and the meat made into a stew. Having eaten some of it, William was immediately seized with "strange pains", and his "whole frame relaxed greatly". He noted on the following day, "I have been extremely ill, having excruciating pains in my bones accompanied by a burning fever, brought on (as I apprehend) by eating a part of that poisonous dolphin. I took an emetic and other remedies and am now much recovered."

By the end of October the crew were spotting land birds, and drifting trees and fence rails. On 1st November they sailed into Chesapeake Bay where they made contact with a Rappahannock pilot boat. William struck a bargain with the master of the pilot boat to ferry him and his baggage to Urbanna, a little way up the river, where he landed "in perfect health".

William, obviously, was none the worse for his adventures. In fact, he must have been well used to the hazards of sea voyages. At one point in his journal, discussing a species of fish known as "old wives", he remarks that he has often seen them for sale in the fish markets of Jamaica. Similarly, after observing quantities of "gulph weed" drifting past the ship, William comments that he has "seen this gulph weed as far to the eastward as the Azores". William, then, seems to have been an experienced traveller, probably in a mercantile capacity. It was no doubt this that qualified him for the position of John Glassell's factor or agent in Virginia.

William lost no time in getting to work. In a letter to John Glassell of 24th December 1786[118] he advises John that there is little risk of the confiscation of British owned property in Virginia, advises him against selling his house and warehouse, and talks of shipping tobacco from the Fredericksburg warehouses. He also, as previously mentioned, recommends that John's brother should be allowed to buy the Culpeper plantation "negroes". Business, said William, was going well, particularly the "back store", and Mr Campbell was a very satisfactory partner.

In letters to John's wife Helen in 1789 he talks first of winding up his partnership with Lachlan Campbell, and then of Campbell's death.[119] William speaks also of making a long tour to "the back country over the ridge" on a debt collecting exercise.

William married Sarah Buck, the sister of Anthony Buck, a "highly esteemed" Fredericksburg auctioneer.[120] He was a member of the old established Fredericksburg Masonic Lodge No. 4, and if he did not actually live in John Glassell's house "The Chimneys", ownership of it certainly seems to have passed to him.[121] His status in Fredericksburg society, however,

118 Intimate Society Letters of the 18th century, P483.

119 Ibid, Page 492.

120 Website: Librarypoint. Central Rappahannock Regional Library, "Alum Spring Park – a walk through history".

121 Wikipedia: The Chimneys, Fredericksburg, Virginia. "Ownership of the Chimneys passed to William Glassell to whom John Glassell had given power of attorney. An insurance policy written in 1792 showed William as the owner."

caused him to become involved in a shocking incident which gained him embarrassing notoriety.

In or around March 1790, Lodge No. 4 held a ball in Fredericksburg. Glassell escorted to the ball a young, attractive, and respectable orphan girl who was living in his household, perhaps a relative of his wife's. During the course of the evening she was insulted in some unspecified manner by one Robert Ritchie. Ritchie was "somewhat under the influence of wine" and refused to apologise when requested to do so. William, therefore, no doubt conscious of his standing as a "gentleman" in Fredericksburg circles, sent him a formal challenge. Ritchie accepted, and rather rashly chose pistols as the weapons to be used in the duel – "rashly", because William was reputed as an expert marksman.

William offered Ritchie every opportunity to withdraw, all to no avail. The two met at Alum Spring, a sequestered spot outside Fredericksburg, and Ritchie fell mortally wounded. William rushed to his aid, requesting forgiveness, but was rebuffed. Following Ritchie's death William was arrested on a charge of murder, but on 31st march 1790 he was unanimously acquitted by a special session of the Spotsylvania Court[122] If news of this adventure ever reached John Glassell at home in Longniddry, he is unlikely to have been best pleased about it.

William Glassell features prominently in the records of British Mercantile Claims owed to John Glassell. After John's departure for Scotland on the eve of the American War of Independence, (or "the Revolution", as Americans like to call it) many of those who owed him money would pay their debts to his manager Lachlan Campbell. Others, the records show, made their payments to John's brother Andrew. Of course, not everyone was so honest, and many debts remained unpaid. Certainly, sometimes this was due to the straitened circumstances of the debtors, or due to illness and death. Many debtors, though, seem to have regarded John's absence as a good excuse to renege on their obligations. Such attitudes of course were commonplace, and after the Revolution a British Mercantile Claims Commission was established to track down those who owed pre-war debts to British merchants. "Jay's Treaty", named after James Jay the American Chief Justice,

122 Librarypoint: Central Rappahannock Regional Library, "Alum Spring Park – a walk through history".

was signed on 19th November 1794 to settle the many ongoing disputes, and provided for payments from the U.S. Government where necessary. Congress guaranteed that courts would process the recovery of bona fide debts, and a joint commission was set up to hear appeals. Unfortunately, it proved more difficult than anticipated to solve the many problems arising, and it was not until 1802 that the United States agreed to pay the British government a sum of £600 000 to cover all outstanding claims.

The tabulation and settlement of debts owed to British merchants was a herculean task. Details of the labours involved in the Commonwealth of Virginia were published in the "Virginia Genealogist" between 1962 and 1992, and it is possible to extract from this mountain of information the details relevant to John Glassell. These articles on "British Mercantile Claims" show in the region of 126 debts owed to him, 65 for unspecified amounts.[123] The greatest sum claimed was £839 owed by William Walker of Madison County, who, it transpired, had paid the principal sum with interest then due to John's brother Andrew in 1778. The remaining interest owed had since been paid to William Glassell. The smallest debt owed was £1 due from John Price and Alfred Williams, formerly of Spotsylvania, and subsequently of Kentucky.

Out of those debts where the amounts were specified, twelve debts were for sums over £50, and all the rest were below £50 – the vast majority well below that figure. We might guess that the debts for unspecified sums would be of similar proportions. Many of the debtors had moved elsewhere in Virginia. Others had moved to other states, particularly Kentucky. Many others were dead. Of the surviving debtors, some were insolvent. Others had died in good financial circumstances, but their estates had been squandered by their heirs.

The following examples will give some idea of the extreme difficulty of recovering some of the sums of money owed to John Glassell:

"John Murray £4-5-6. Aquia Store. He died many years ago possessed of a handsome estate, the greater part of which he devised to his relation James Murray, a young man much addicted to intoxication, who after dissipating a considerable part of his fortune died. P. Payton of Stafford is his executor."[124]

123 Figures are approximate, because photocopies requested were of all pages where debts to John Glassell were listed. However, it is possible that debts owing to him appeared on other pages without actually mentioning his name.

124 Virginia Genealogist, Oct – Dec 1970, Vol 14, No 4.

"Joseph Chapman, Louisa. Absconded from Louisa County before the war, and supposed to have gone to one of the southern states. Several writs were issued against him before his elopement, none of which could be executed."[125]

"Thomas Breedlove, Albemarle. This claim was in suit before the war under the direction of John Walker, attorney for the claimant. The papers in this suit among many others were destroyed by Col Tarleton in his expedition to Charlottesville, and no directions have been given to Mr Walker since the peace to renew the suit."[126]

"James McAlister, Culpeper. Was killed by lightning during the war, and his estate was entirely wasted before the peace."[127]

"William Clatterbuck, Culpeper. Died in Culpeper about eight or ten years ago, insolvent. He was never able to pay anything, being always a poor man. His widow is now and has been supported by the parish ever since his death. There was a judgment for John Glassell's debt in 1772; if Mr Clatterbuck had been able to pay, the creditor would doubtless have compelled him."

"Phillip Lipscomb, Spotsylvalia, £116-19-4. …In 1788 and now he had in his possession a house and lot in Fredericksburg with about £200, with a few slaves and other personal estate, but it was generally said that the whole of his slaves and personal estate were under encumbrances and had been so since the peace, as not to be held liable for his debts. It is said the slaves were settled on his children by the relation of his wife. He is a bricklayer by trade, and during the war made by his industry a considerable addition to his estate, but before the peace, having taken to hard drink (which habit he still pursues) it was thought necessary by his friends to save her estate from being taken by his debts. …It is the opinion of Thos. Cochran, merchant of Fredericksburg, that …he would not have given him credit for any amount, believing that his circumstances were too doubtful to justify it."[128]

"James Isbal, Albemarle. £1-4-3 by account. He removed to North Carolina during the war and settled in Walker County and possessed a very good estate. Before the peace he became deranged in his mind and shot himself. His estate after

125 Virginia Genealogist, July – Sept 1983, Vol 27, No 3.
126 Ibid, Jul – Sept 1982, Vol 27, No 3.
127 Ibid, Oct – Dec 1983, Vol 27, No 4.
128 Ibid, June – Sept 1985, Vol 29, No 3.

his death was squandered among his children, most of whom are settled in the same neighbourhood."[129]

A number of the debts in the list of John Glassell's claims had in fact already been paid over to John's brother Andrew. These debts may perhaps have been owed by people well known to John and Andrew, or people on friendly terms with them, men who would have thought shame to renege on a debt to a neighbour. Thus, for example:

"Fisher Rice, Culpeper, £60-17-4. He removed to Kentucky before the peace, but before he went away he paid the whole of this debt to Andrew Glassell, except about £8."

"Jesse Thomas, Culpeper, £5-13=10. He removed to South Carolina during the war, but his father John Thomas assumed the payment of this debt, and about four or five years ago paid it together with his own to Andrew Glassell of Madison."

"John Thomas, Culpeper. £3-1-6. This debt was paid to Andrew Glassell about 4 or 5 years ago in full."

"Daniel Baynham, Culpeper, £4-12-0. This debt was paid to Andrew Glassell of Madison about ten years ago."[130]

Andrew Glassell, as we shall see, was regarded as something of a pillar of the community, and his recorded actions occasionally reflect his sympathy for the less fortunate. When James Garriot "ran away from Culpeper before the peace and left his wife and children not worth a penny, Andrew Glassell contributed to their support to keep them from starving".[131] Andrew also intervened in the case of Yowell Boston, who was "universally reputed insolvent for more than 20 years past". Boston had been overseer on the estate of Col. John Baylor in Orange County. As such, he was entitled to a share of the proceeds of the crops, but he was in the habit of squandering his payments in advance by drinking and gambling. Andrew Glassell had appealed to the steward of Baylor's estate to keep back as much of Boston's

129 Virginia Genealogist, Oct – Dec 1987, Vol 81, No 4.
130 All Virginia Genealogist, June-Sept 1985, Vol 29, No 3.
131 Ibid.

money as would pay his account with John Glassell, but this tactic failed, "as Boston being always in debt drew the proceeds of the crop out of his hands in favour of other persons".[132]

William Glassell appears to have been assiduous in the collection of debts owed to John Glassell, which presumably was the point of his being sent to America in the first place. It is stated quite plainly in the list of Mercantile Claims, "William Glassell had powers to receive the debts due to John Glassell in Virginia, and Col. Abram Maury was appointed by Wm Glassell collector of these debts."[133] Mention of payments to William are frequent in the list of Mercantile Claims:

> *"Joshua Ransdall, Culpeper… Col. Maury his account put into his hands by William Glassell for collection, who shortly afterwards withdrew it, as was the case with several of the accounts which the debtors paid off to William Glassell himself."*[134]
>
> *"James Willis, Orange. All that was due on the bond of James Willis to John Glassell was paid by Mr Willis to Col. Maury in September 1790 by transferring to William Glassell a bond on James Colleman for £37-0-0, and a note on George Heywood for £2-16-0, which bond and note William Glassell received as payment."*[135]
>
> *"John Williams Jr, Culpeper. William C. Williams long since the peace paid to William Glassell upwards of £300 in part of this debt. Mr Glassell received from him several slaves at valuation in payment, a receipt for which is in possession of his brother Philip Williams, clerk of Shenandoah County…"*[136]
>
> *"Dr Thomas Walker Sr, Albemarle. £15-9-0… In 1791 Francis Walker who had the sole management of his father's business (whose*

132 Virginia Genealogist, April-June 1980, Vol 24, No 2.
133 Ibid. April-June 1982, Vol 27, No 2. (Debt of Zecharia Herndon.)
134 Ibid. April-June 1983, Vol27, No 2.
135 Ibid. Oct-Dec 1983, Vol 27, No 4.
136 Ibid. April-June 1983, Vol 27, No 2.

> *great age and infirmity rendered him unable to do it himself) paid to William Glassell the full amount of this debt, with fourteen years interest."*[137]

Debt collection did not always go so smoothly, however:

> *"Thomas Walker Jr, Albemarle. £19-2-6. He died intestate in Albemarle County about 3 years ago possessed of a considerable estate. His administrator is his brother Francis Walker, now of the same county, who is confident this debt has been paid. About 1792 his brother had delivered a quantity of wheat to William Glassell for the purpose of raising a sum of money to satisfy some pressing demand. Meeting with Mr Glassell a short time afterwards at Orange Court House, he applied to him for the money arising from the wheat he delivered. Mr Glassell told him in the presence of Mr Francis Walker that he had appropriated part of it to the discharge of his old British debt to John Glassell, and refused to pay for the wheat until the amount of that debt was deducted, upon which a violent quarrel ensued. Mr Thomas Walker was willing to pay the debt to John Glassell, but wished to postpone it until his other demands, which were more urgent, should be satisfied."*[138]

William's diligence in debt collecting seems to have caused irritation in some quarters. The case of Thomas Walker is the only "violent quarrel" mentioned, but a comment by Andrew Glassell, the respected planter, hints at widespread grumbling. In a note following references to several debts which had been paid to Andrew, the Mercantile Claims administrator observes, "N.B. Altho Mr Glassell is brother to the claimant, and as such must necessarily feel some degree of interest in his affairs, yet he highly disapproves of the conduct of Wm Glassell in respect to these claims. Andrew Glassell is a man of excellent character, and is in possession of a very valuable tract of land, and having moreover intermarried with a citizen of this Commonwealth, he is sensibly affected by the prospect of injustice which will be done to the United States by a general admission of the claims of British creditors. He has long had the management of the debts of John Glassell due in his neighbourhood."

---

137 Virginia Genealogist, April-June 1986, Vol 30, No 2.

138 Ibid. April-June 1986, Vol 30, No 2.

William's will was probated on 26th September 1801 before Fredericksburg Hustings Court,[139] so presumably his death occurred shortly before that date. The cause is not known. It is possible that his strenuous efforts in debt collection were more for his own benefit than for John Glassell's. A letter quoted in Hayden's "Virginia Genealogies" was written in September 1804 from Walter Colquhoun in Scotland to Daniel Grinnan in Virginia. Colquhoun was an old friend of John Glassell's and had visited him at home in Longniddry. In his letter Colquhoun affirmed that Glassell, "cannot speak with patience of W's management, and no wonder – not a shilling was remitted of his collections and receipts from rents. And besides this, Mr G had to pay several thousand pounds sterling in this country for goods which W had failed to remit". Colquhoun, however, assures Daniel Grinnan that Glassell "holds you in much esteem, and flatters himself with your being able to make beneficial sale of his property, as also to gather something respectable from the wreck of his debts".

Daniel Grinnan Sr had a large estate in Culpeper County on the Cedar Run watercourse, and served in the American War of Independence. His second son, Daniel Grinnan Jr moved to Fredericksburg as a young man around 1792, and became clerk to James Sommerville, a wealthy Scots merchant who had lived in Fredericksburg for nearly half a century. On Sommerville's death Daniel Grinnan took over his extensive business interests. In 1798 Grinnan was appointed to meet the British Commission tasked with recovering the many British Mercantile Claims still remaining unsettled. The negotiations took place in Philadelphia, and apparently Grinnan took three wagon loads of account books and papers with him. He went on to become a successful and very wealthy merchant trading at home and abroad, and although based in Fredericksburg, the owner of several estates. On 20th November 1815, he married Helen Buchan Glassell, the daughter of Andrew, John Glassell's planter brother.[140]

This was the man, then, who was charged with making "beneficial sale" of John Glassell's American property, and gathering "something respectable from the wreck of his debts". To this end, the following notice appeared in the Virginia Herald on 1st April 1803:

139 Will Book A, 1782-1817. Pages 267, 268.
140 Details from Hayden's "Virginia genealogies".

"To be sold at Public Auction, to the highest bidder on the 29th of April next, upon the premises, that well known and valuable real estate of John Glassell Esq in and adjoining the town of Fredericksburg, consisting of near four lots, on which are an elegant and spacious Dwelling House and store, kitchen etc, now occupied by Wm C. Williams Esq.

A large warehouse with a store and counting room

And the tobacco warehouses occupied by the public

Sixteen acres of fertile land beautifully situated, bounded by the river, the lower line of the town of Fredericksburg, the lands of John Minor etc, on which have been built a wharf and warehouses that will be sold with two acres of land, and the balance to be divided into lots of two acres each. Six, nine, and fifteen months credit will be given to purchasers on securing the payment of the purchase consideration, bearing interest from the date if not punctually paid'

John Grinnan, attorney in fact for John Glassell Esq.

Fredericksburg Feb. 20th 1803."

Grinnan was obviously making a determined effort to achieve for his client what William Glassell had failed to do. This was to be a lengthy process. It is obvious from a deed lodged in the National Records of Scotland, that later in 1803 John Glassell still considered himself heavily involved in Virginia:

"Conserning I have belonging to me in the said Province of Virginia sundry lands houses and hereditaments, and likewise sundry debts and sums of money and other estate real and personal belonging to me in the said province or other provinces of North America..."[141] This document, originally signed in 1797, became part of the update of the entail of his lands and estate, and among much else instructs that after his death all his American possessions are to be sold, and the proceeds brought to Btitain. Glassell died in 1806, but there is evidence that the disposal process was only completed much later.

After his death John Glassell's estate was managed by trustees on behalf of his only daughter Joan. On February 6th 1820, she wrote to her fiancé Lord John Campbell that she was now a "free woman", as the trustees had recently had their final meeting. Under the laws prevailing at the time, on

141 RD3/311/1111.

her marriage her estate would be put in her husband's hands, and it would seem that Lord John's opinion had been asked about the appointment of "an American agent". Joan wrote to John, "Whenever your answer about the American agent's name comes, Kermack is to write to Grenan. He I believe is an honest man from what Kermack says was Cathcart's opinion of him. But General Shaw who was left in charge of some property in another state is a scamp by all accounts, and perhaps would be the better of a little rough handling. Since 1813 Steuart has received £1050 from America, I suppose all from Grennan, but I am not sure. £150 I think was within these 6 months. Now judging by the effect on Steuart himself I think it may have a very good effect on the American agents too, knowing they have no longer to deal with trustees or a woman..."[142]

Thus, far from John Glassell's American business affairs being wound up at his death, his trustees were still receiving substantial sums from America fourteen years later. Grenan/Grennan, the "honest man", is of course Daniel Grinnan, who by that time was married to Joan's cousin. The fact that her affairs would soon be in the hands of her husband Lord John obviously led Joan to expect that her American interests would be attended to more scrupulously in the future.

The National Records of Scotland have preserved many of John Glassell's legal papers. These record his disputes with neighbours and local government, and other more mundane matters, but of particular interest is the deed of entail of his estate, with its subsequent updates and alterations.[143] By the latter years of the 18th century it must have been obvious to Glassell that there was now going to be no "male heir of his body". He was getting on in years, his health was poor, and his sole surviving child was a girl. It was therefore absolutely crucial that his house, lands, and financial assets, and the succession to them after his death, should be made as secure as the law could possibly allow. Any laxity, any loopholes, could plunge the results of his lifetime's work into chaotic oblivion, and John was too shrewd an operator to allow the least danger of any such thing.

Glassell would be well aware that wealthy widows and rich heiresses were prime bait for unscrupulous ne'er-do-wells seeking to repair lost

142 Campbell Papers, National Library of Scotland. Acc8508/46, Letter 20.
143 Register of Deeds RD3/311/1111, RD3/311/1530, RD3/311/1235.

fortunes, finance fantastical schemes, or give themselves a leg-up on the social scale. It was therefore essential that his wife, daughter, and estate should enjoy foolproof protection from any such predators. To that purpose Glassell enacted a Deed of Entail on 3rd January 1797, and set up the trust already mentioned to manage his estate in the event of his death. The Trustees named were:

Helen Buchan his wife, during her "widowcy",
Charles Brown Esq of Coalston, advocate,
Rev James MacMillan, minister of Torthorwald,
William Cadell Jr of Cockenzie,
Charles Stuart, Writer to the Signet,
John Dodds, farmer at Myerton near Ballencrieff,
Robert Cathcart, Writer to the Signet.[144]

In 1800 "Rev Mr Bryce Johnston minister at Holywood" was added to the list.[145] Any three of the Trustees made a quorum, and if death reduced their numbers even to a single member, that one was still a quorum. The duties of the trust were:

- To pay Glassell's debts on his death,
- To provide for any possible children apart from the heir, up to a limit of £3000,
- To settle an annuity of £300 on his widow, reduced to £200 if she remarried,
- To settle an annuity of £20 on his brother Robert and his wife,
- To provide for Robert's children, if Longniddry should be inherited by an heir not of John's body; and if the heir should be one of Robert's children, to top up Robert's annuity by a further £30.

The trustees were also appointed Tutors and Curators to John's children, a provision that was modified in 1800 "to be Tutors and Curators to Joan Glassell my only child". It was specified that on his death all John's American assets were to go to his Trustees. Everything was to be sold, and the money

144 RD3/311/1111.
145 RD3/311/1530.

was to be brought to Britain and put under the care of a manager appointed by the Trustees. Similarly, at his death any land, houses, stocks and shares, and debts owed were to be converted into money, and put at the disposal of the Trust. The exception was the estate of Longniddry which was to be held in trust for the heir. If necessary, however, the rents of Longniddry could be used to top up the funds of the Trust.[146]

Glassell's revised deed of entail of 3rd February 1800 sets out the line of succession to the estate of Longniddry. First the heirs male of his body lawfully begotten (by then a forlorn hope); next, his only child then living, Joan Glassell, and the heirs of her body; next Robert Glassell, tenant in Corbally in the parish of New Abbey, and his heirs; finally, Andrew Glassell, merchant in Virginia, and his heirs. It was stipulated that heirs succeeding to the property "shall be holden and obliged to assume and constantly retain use and bear the surname arms and designation of *Glassell of Longniddry*," and that female heirs "shall only be at liberty to marry a man of the name of Glassell".[147] John obviously wished to establish a "county" family. It was quite common for a man marrying the heiress of such a family to adopt the wife's surname. As far as "arms" are concerned, John was rather over-reaching himself, as no Glassell coat of arms has ever been matriculated.

Provision was also made to safeguard the "manor place of Longniddry", with the "gardens, woods, plantations, and 50 acres of ground most adjacent", and limitations were placed on leases and liferents of the property. Any contraventions of any of the conditions would render the title to Longniddry null and void, and the estate would then pass to the next heir.

Also in 1801, and by ratification in 1803, John empowered his Trustees to take up to £500 out of Trust funds to lay out a garden at Longniddry, to use £500 to build houses at Longniddry, and to use £50 to £200 to enclose a burial ground, erect a monument, or build a vault in Gladsmuir churchyard. John further directed that his Trustees should pay £5 per annum to his cousin Mary Kelton during her lifetime.

Dealing particularly with his daughter Joan, the revision of 1800 stipulates, "My daughter Joan Glassell shall not be considered of age nor entitled to take any management nor relieve my trustees of the Trust until she is 25 years of age." As far as concerned her maintenance, "I direct that

146 RD/311/1430.
147 RD3/311/1530.

my daughter Joan Glassell's expense shall not exceed £200 stg. a year while she is under 12 years of age." Her allowance was to be increased to £300 between the age of twelve and sixteen, and would rise to £400 per annum between sixteen and twenty one. In the event of John's death he wished his wife and daughter to reside "in Town", as it would in his opinion be "improper" to live at Longniddry. Instead, the house was to be let, with its gardens, offices and parks, until his daughter's marriage.[148] Finally, it was enacted that if Joan was under the age of 25 at her father's death, she could marry only with the consent in writing of the majority of the trustees. If she married before the age of 25 without the Trustees' consent, she would forfeit all right to Longniddry and the funds held by the Trust, until her eldest son attained the age of 25. In such a turn of events, the Trustees were to pay Joan a yearly allowance of £500, to be continued by her eldest son when he came of age and inherited. Joan's husband was to have no rights to this annuity.[149]

Thus, by the time of his death in 1806 John Glassell had firmly fixed the line of succession, provided for his wife and daughter and other relatives, and made it impossible for any fortune hunter to get the estate into his clutches by seducing a naïve teenage heiress into marriage.

The Firth of Forth formed the northern boundary of Glassell's estate, approximately a mile of foreshore between two small water-courses. All along this stretch of coast the sea recedes a great distance at low tide, exposing vast tracts of firm flat sands formerly used as short cuts by travellers, and shown as such on old maps. Today, the coast road from Port Seton to Aberlady stays fairly close to the shore, separated from it for the most part by a strip of low sand dunes covered over in places by brier, hawthorn and buckthorn bushes.

To the south of the road is a well-manicured golf course, typical of those strung along what East Lothian Council likes to call "Scotland's Golf Coast". In John Glassell's day this was Longniddry Links, described at the time as being "in a state of nature". It is of course difficult to square that description with today's busy coast road, closely mown fairways, and seaside car parks, but we must try to picture a wide strip of dunes or "benty hillocks" fronting the shore, with a flatter expanse behind, stretching back several

148 RD3/311/1111.
149 RD3/311/1530.

hundred yards to the raised beach with its "link dyke" where the arable land of Longniddry began. The Links would be well covered with rank grass and patches of scrub, pocked with "heichs and howes" and with occasional boggy patches. It was used as pasture for the livestock of the Longniddry tenants, roaming more or less freely supervised by cowherds. In a prominent position by the shore was the house of Boglehill, where prior to the sale of 1779 dwelt the "cunningar" or lessee of the extensive rabbit warrens in the Links.

In 1796 the "Trustees of the Northern District of Roads in the County of East Lothian" decided to build a new road through Longniddry Links as part of the coastal route from Prestonpans to North Berwick. The old road seems to have been a mere track, and it was obvious to the Trustees that it had taken different courses at different times. This was probably because the sand dunes would not be as stable as they are today, and would be liable to shifting at the whim of wind and weather.[150] Little wonder that travellers often preferred the tidal sands. In the eyes of the Trustees the Links were of little agricultural value, but John Glassell did not agree. In his opinion the ground was "very valuable", and he had intentions of converting it to arable use. Thus, he objected to the initial line of road suggested by the Trustees, and they eventually settled on a line closer to the shore than originally intended.

The Trustees were legally entitled to take stone for road building from any convenient source, as long as they avoided gardens, plantations, avenues, and built-up areas, and as long as they compensated landowners for the stone extracted and any damage done. From Boglehill, roughly the mid-point of Glassell's shoreline, a reef of hard whinstone runs out in a westerly direction towards Port Seton. This reef is covered at high tide, but exposed for most of any given day, and is easily accessible. It seemed to be the ideal source of road-building material, and the Trustees' contractor George Dunlop began to exploit it.

Glassell, however, objected strongly, and took out a Process of Suspension against the Trustees in the Court of Session. He argued that many places along the East Lothian coast were vulnerable to erosion. When the east wind blew and at the time of spring tides "the encroachments of

150 In the decades after World War 2 the dunes were planted with marram grass by East Lothian Council to stabilise them and to prevent coastal erosion.

the sea are great and frequent", and in fact much ground had been lost in this way on the estates of Seton and Preston to the west of Longniddry. The reef from which the trustees' contractor was removing his road metal formed a bulwark against the force of the sea, and weakening the barrier was putting Glassell's shoreline in danger. The Trustees replied sarcastically, "The Suspender seems to have taken up a most erroneous opinion that he is entitled to protect his property without regard to any injury he may do the Public." Glassell in turn observed, "The powers of the Trustees are not without limits." He had been a Trustee himself, "and knows the nature of his duty on the public good". He claimed that there was good stone available from alternative sources, to which he was perfectly willing to allow access.

Suspension of quarrying was ordered and arbitrers appointed to decide what was to be done. The final decision agreed by all parties was that the Trustees were forbidden to take rocks and stones from "within sea water mark", and that Glassell was to allow the Trustees to work alternative sites.[151] Work on the new road proceeded, and its winding course along behind "Longniddry Bents" is still with us today.

The Barony of Longniddry had been an integral part of the Seton family's earldom of Wintoun since at least the early 17th century, and after the forfeiture of the 5th Earl in 1715, Longniddry and Seton continued with a single owner as parts of the York Buildings Company's Wintoun Estate. At the sale of 1779, as we have seen, John Glassell bought Lot 1 of the Barony. Lot 1 of the Lordship of Seton, immediately to the west, was bought by Alexander McKenzie, the York Buildings Company's agent who had been responsible for making the arrangements for the sale.

Previous to the sale, Glassell's purchase and McKenzie's purchase had both been leased by George Buchan, the York Buildings Company's factor in Scotland. After Buchan's death the lease was continued by his son. Following the sale, for the first time in a century and a half, Longniddry and Seton had different owners. Thus it was that a boundary which had meant little or nothing since far beyond living memory, became a matter of some importance.

McKenzie, in a shocking act of vandalism, demolished the vast and derelict ancient Palace of Seton in 1790, and replaced it with a modern Adam mansion. However, questions were raised about his conduct of the

151 Court of Session CS232/G/12/31, and Register of Deeds RD270, page 263.

sale in 1779, where he had in effect arranged to sell Seton to himself, and no sooner was his new house completed, than McKenzie was forced to sell Seton to the Earl of Wemyss, who already owned Gosford to the east of Longniddry.

On 4th July 1800 Lord Wemyss petitioned the Lords of Council and Session informing them that a dispute had arisen between himself and his neighbour John Glassell over the boundary between their properties. Glassell, or his tenants, had made "considerable encroachments" on the north eastern corner of Lord Wemyss's Seton estate, and to cover this Glassell had diverted the course of the burn which he "erroneously" conceived to be the boundary. Wemyss claimed that the true boundaries of his property and Glassell's were unambiguously shown on the plans produced at the time of the sale. These boundaries were not necessarily the same as those of the former baronies, but any discrepancies were clarified by the plans, which were "the final indicators of the buyers' possessions".

John Glassell, however, contended that Alexander McKenzie, who made the arrangements for the sale, had resolved to make the boundaries between the lots as obvious and unambiguous as possible by altering them if necessary to run along "roads, rivulets and the like". Advice was taken from the former lessee Mr Buchan Hepburn and others, and the "Longniddry Den Burn" was fixed upon as the boundary between the Longniddry and Seton estates. In the written description of Glassell's property, it plainly said that "the Burn of Longniddry Den" was its western boundary.

A "den" (or "dean" as it more usually is in East Lothian) is a deep narrow valley, usually wooded to some extent, with a stream running through it. "The Dean" is the western boundary of present-day Longniddry, full of fine mature trees, running from the eastern end of the dual carriageway on the A198 down towards the sea. Some 300 metres from the shore the Dean opens out fairly abruptly to flat sandy links, and the burn turns westwards before making another almost right-angled turn to run under the Coast Road and out to the sea.

Whereas John Glassell claimed that the written description of his property, and the title deeds, showed that the burn was the boundary, Wemyss's position was that the plans showed the boundary running along the east side of the Dean, and that the authority of the plans trumped the written description. This boundary as shown on the plans and favoured by the Earl, was almost identical with the ancient "march" between the baronies.

The Lords of Session gave their *interloquitor* (interim decision) in favour of the boundary as shown on the plans, and dismissed John Glassell's claim that the burn was the boundary. This decision served only to provoke a flurry of claims and counter claims from both parties. The documentation produced was vast,[152] but amongst the reams of dense repetitive legalese there are occasional interesting glimpses of Longniddry life at the time.

The thorniest part of the problem was the course of the boundary from the foot of the Dean to the sea. The road from Longniddry to Port Seton came down the east side of the Dean along the top of the bank. Where the valley opens out onto flat level ground the road had formerly turned sharp left, crossing the burn on an old bridge, and then made its way westwards through the links. As we have seen, however, the East Lothian Turnpike Trust had constructed a new coast road, and as part of the work had built a new bridge over the Dean Burn, nearer the sea and considerably west of the old bridge. The road from Longniddry now came down the side of the Dean, ignoring the old bridge, and continuing straight forward to a new junction with the coast road.

From the Old Bridge, the boundary in Glassell's opinion followed the burn to the New Bridge and on to the shore. In Wemyss's opinion the boundary as shown on the plan was identical to the line of the new road from the foot of the Dean to the coast road, but of course this stretch of road did not exist when the plans were made. And between the coast road and the shore there was little apparent in the way of any obvious boundary apart from vague traces of an old track and former water course. Complicating matters was the fact that between the sale in 1779 and the turn of the century the Dean Burn had changed its course several times.

Thus, the situation was that after a century and a half where the boundary was of no great significance, there was confusion as to where it actually was. For most of its length there was a clear-cut choice – it was either the course of the Dean Burn, or it was along the eastern edge of the valley. Between the Old Bridge and the shore, however, if the boundary was not the burn, it was less than obvious where it was.

James Wright, tenant in Seton East Mains[153] from 1780 to 1799, considered the disputed patch of ground at the foot of the Dean to be part of

152 Court of Session CS235/G/17/2.

153 In those days there were two farms on the site of present-day Seton Mains – East Mains and West Mains.

his farm, but Mitchell and Burn, Glassell's tenants, considered it to be part of Longniddry Links. If Wright saw Mitchell and Burn's herdsmen grazing cattle on the disputed ground he would chase them off, but eventually, as he became better acquainted with the Longniddry tenants, they seem to have come to an agreement that their cattle should be "allowed to pasture indiscriminately without regard to marches". It might be thought that here the farmers were showing more common sense than the lairds.

Lord Wemyss was convinced that Glassell had attempted to strengthen his claim to the disputed patch of links by deliberately diverting the course of the burn. Several witnesses testified that around 1783 a Mr Renton, either on behalf of Alexander McKenzie, or with his permission, had made an attempt to find coal just to the west of the Old Bridge at the foot of the Dean, and had dug a "level" or drain to carry off the water from his excavations. Some time after that, the burn, already prone to changing its course, had turned into the cut of Renton's drain. It had followed that course ever since, and it was over that channel that the New Bridge had been built.

George Pow was able to throw some light on this final change of course. Pow had been Longniddry's Baron Officer before the sale, and had lived all his life there until Glassell had him evicted around 1795. He testified that the course of the burn had been altered by Renton's mining activities, but that Glassell had also diverted the course of the burn sixty yards above the New Bridge by throwing up an embankment, causing the burn to take its present course. In addition, Glassell had another embankment built below the New Bridge to stop the burn turning east.

John Pow (presumably a relative) testified that he had been employed by Glassell to make the stone embankment above the New Bridge "to turn the burn from its easterly course". He explained that "he cut the ground from the embankment where the new bridge now is on Mr Glassell's orders and the water now runs east in that cut". It is difficult to escape the impression that Glassell was making a deliberate attempt to define the disputed boundary to his advantage.

Complicating all this was that some of the plans bore signs of erasures and corrections. The original surveyor John Home explained that the plans had been prepared by his assistant, who had shown the final part of the boundary as following the course of the burn in 1779. Home had then altered this to what he thought was "the most eligible boundary".

All the fuss was over a piece of ground little over an acre in extent – the roughest of grazing growing upon pure sand. One cannot help feeling that such a display of pig-headed stubbornness on the part of the landowners over such a paltry scrap of ground was hardly worth the bother, particularly in view of the expense incurred by parading their wrangling through the Court of Session. In the end the Earl of Wemyss was victorious. Indeed, half a century later Longniddry itself was to be added to the extensive Wemyss domains.

In his book "Virginia Genealogies", Horace Edwin Hayden quotes part of a letter written in October 1804 from Walter Colquhoun of Glasgow to Daniel Grinnan in Fredericksburg,[154] which throws some light on John Glassell's final years:

> *"…Last month I went on a visit to my old friend Mr Glassell and passed eight days with him at Longniddry, where I was treated with much friendship and hospitality. Mr G, who looks fresh and well, is infirm and of late afflicted with an astmatic [sic] complaint which hinders him from walking much. He however rides almost every day, which exercise we uniformly took from two to three hours each forenoon while I was there. You may believe we talked much of Virginian affairs. He inquired kindly about a number of old acquaintances. Among them was your father…" (Here Colquhoun goes on to talk of Glassell's displeasure at William Glassell's mismanagement, in the passage already quoted.) "He holds you in much esteem, and flatters himself with your being able to make beneficial sale of his property, as also to gather something respectable from the wreck of his debts. I felt myself warranted in confirming his belief that his affairs could not have been in better hands. He spoke of the remittance you made him not long since.*
>
> *Mrs G is an amiable well informed woman – active, industrious, extremely attentive to her husband and his domestic concerns. Their daughter and only child, about eight years of age, a fine healthy promising girl – she will have a handsome fortune. The Estate of Longniddry, excellent soil, all arable, cost Mr G about 24 years by-gone £1200 Str. It now yields him, estimating the part he cultivates, about £1400 per annum, of which the tenant pays £1100…".*

154 Virginia Genealogies, Page 5.

It may have been Glassell's habit of riding daily that brought about a process raised against him in Haddington Sheriff Court. In the summer of 1798, John Oswald, tenant in Harelaw to the east of Longniddry, claimed that his sheep had been killed by Glassell's dogs. It is something of a cliché, but probably real enough, the image of the bluff country squire or laird riding out accompanied by his dogs. Did Glassell ride out one day and fail to stop his dogs bounding off in pursuit of Oswald's sheep? Or did his dogs merely escape one day from the "manor place of Longniddry" and go ravaging through the countryside? However the incident came about, on 16th August the Sheriff's *interloquitor* found the accusation "not proved", and on 4th October he refused petitions from both parties and confirmed his "not proved" decision.

On 4th February 1806 John Glassell wrote to his lawyer Robert Cathcart about his tenant Robert Howden's rent.[155] He then revealed, "I have been a good deal distressed and shaken within these 10 days past, and I have this day given leave to Mr Williamson to order out Dr Gregory. Altho I do not flatter myself I shall profit much by his advice, it may be some satisfaction to Mrs G." He went on to ask Cathcart to see to his Trustees making provision for his brother Robert's family, and three of his own cousins. In a postscript he added, "Advise when you are able to be out. I am much debilitated…".

On 18th May 1806 Walter Colquhoun wrote again to Daniel Grinnan, "I ought to have written, because among the things I had to communicate to you [was] the death of my old friend Mr John Glassell which took place at Long Niddry on the 15th of last month… I presume that his only daughter now about ten years of age will inherit all, which in lands, money &c will at least amount to fifty thousand pounds sterling. Nay, the Estate of Long Niddry itself would sell for £45000 or upwards. Mrs Glassell who is only a few years turned of fifty will no doubt have a handsome jointure, and seven or eight years hence Miss will have numerous admirers."[156]

John Glassell would presumably be laid to rest in Gladsmuir churchyard. A walled enclosure there is probably the Glassell burial ground, but in spite of the instructions to his Trustees, and the provision made, there is no monument or memorial tablet to commemorate him. His name is only

155 Register of Deeds RD3/311/1935. Copy: Letter of Instructions.
156 Virginia genealogies Page 5.

preserved locally in "Glassel Park"[157], a 20th century housing development in Longniddry. It might be thought rather ironic that whereas Glassell demolished a village to create farmland, that farmland was itself destroyed to create a new settlement bearing his name!

157 John spelled his name variously Glassel, Glassell, and Glassels. His daughter always spelled her surname Glassell. The American Glassells invariably spell the name with the double "l". When the Longniddry housing development was built, for reasons best known to themselves, the "powers that be" preferred "Glassel".

5

"Not a minute for spleen or lassitude"

THE BIRTH AND BAPTISM OF JOAN GLASSELL, DAUGHTER OF THE LAIRD of Longniddry and his wife Helen Buchan, are recorded thus in the registers of the parish of Gladsmuir:

"Glassell, John Esqr of Longniddry and his wife Helen Buchan daughter of John Buchan Esqr of Letham his spouse[158] had a daughter born at his house in Longniddry Thursday 9th June 1796 & was baptiz'd the 1st of July following by the Revd Mr George Hamilton minister at Gladsmuir and named Joan in presence of John Cadell Esqr of Cockenzie, Messrs George and John Buchan Hepburn, John Buchan Esqr writer, & Doctor Richard Somner."

Joan, as we have seen, was an only child, and the heiress to her father's substantial fortune. As also previously mentioned, her adult correspondence reveals next to nothing about her childhood. She had been educated at home by governesses, apparently not too successfully, and presumably lived with her parents in "the manor place of Longniddry" until her father's death in 1806 not long before her tenth birthday.

158 At first glance this is rather confusing. The clerk, in writing "his spouse" has obviously forgotten that he has already written "his wife".

John Glassell had expressed the wish that in the event of his death Longniddry House should be let, and his daughter and her mother should live "in Town". Whether this did in fact happen is not obvious. There is no reference to any such thing in Joan's adult correspondence. Indeed, there appear to be no references to her mother at all in Joan's many letters, apart from a very brief mention of her death while Joan was on a European tour. (This, like the absence of anything substantial about her childhood, might be thought just a little odd.) Joan's mother was one of John Glassell's trustees, and if she had been determined to stay on in Longniddry, it is perhaps unlikely that the other trustees would have stood in her way. After all, her nearest relations were all in East Lothian. On the other hand, if Mrs Glassell aspired to a more stimulating social life in Edinburgh she could certainly have afforded it.

The only tenuous clue as to whether or not Joan and her mother shifted their quarters, is the story already quoted about her stealing her cousin's clothes while she was riding on the sands at Longniddry. It might be thought that this was the sort of prank likely to be played by a girl rather older than the age of nine, but who knows? Certainly, by the summer of 1811, when she would be newly 15, Joan was indeed resident in Edinburgh, in the household of Mrs Anne Grant of Laggan, where she had been placed to continue her education. We must not for one moment conceive of Mrs Grant as some sort of mere governess, however.

Mrs Grant of Laggan was born Anne Macvicar on 1st February 1755. Her father Duncan Macvicar of Craignish in Argyllshire was an army officer, and her mother was a Stewart of Invernahyle, also in Argyll. Shortly after Anne's birth her father was sent to America with his regiment, the 77th Foot, and his family joined him the following year. The Macvicars spent the next ten years in America, mostly in Albany in what in now New York State, but with occasional spells in more remote and wilder places. Anne was educated at home by her mother, but there was also input from an old Scots sergeant who gave her a taste for Blind Harry and the "uncouth and rugged Scots verse of a bygone age". A Dutch lady, Mrs Schuyler, was an important influence on her, and also took a hand in her education. Anne wrote of Mrs Schuyler later in life, "Whatever culture my mind received, I owe to her." Certainly, Anne seems to have been a precocious child, as by the age of six she had apparently read through the entire Old Testament, and half-way through Milton's "Paradise Lost".

Duncan Macvicar had acquired property in Vermont and intended to remain permanently in America. However, ill-health necessitated a return to Scotland. This was intended to be only temporary, but the deteriorating political situation in the American Colonies, and the outbreak of open warfare between Britain and the Colonists made going back impossible. After a spell in Glasgow, Macvicar was appointed to Fort Augustus as Barrack Master, and there his daughter Anne met and married the chaplain to the garrison, the Rev James Grant. Shortly after their marriage in 1778, Grant was appointed minister of the Inverness-shire parish of Laggan. Anne was married to James Grant for 23 years and bore him twelve children.

Mrs Grant, influenced by the fervour for all things Celtic caused by the publication of Macpherson's "Ossian", was an enthusiast for Highland culture. Not only did she master the Gaelic language, which of course was the native tongue of the parishioners of Laggan, but she insisted that Gaelic was used at home in the manse, and it was the first language of all her children. Her bilingualism was certainly a praiseworthy achievement, but even though she had grown up in America Mrs Grant cannot have been unfamiliar with Gaelic. Both her parents were from Argyll, and in the context of the mid-18th century would almost certainly have some degree of fluency in the language. Even if her first language was English, it would be surprising if Anne was entirely ignorant of Gaelic before her move to Laggan.

Maternal and domestic duties, and what was expected from a lady of the manse, do not seem to have imposed over-strict limits on Mrs Grant's active mind. She was keenly interested in literary matters and corresponded regularly with a wide circle of friends and acquaintances.

In 1801 James Grant died suddenly, leaving his widow all but penniless with their eight surviving children, the youngest two years old, and the eldest 21. Two rather difficult years followed, but in 1803 Mrs Grant moved to Greenend near Stirling, and commenced her literary career with the publication of a volume of poems, which was well received and enabled her to pay her debts. She had always been a prolific letter writer, and she was now persuaded to publish a selection of her correspondence, which appeared as "Letters from the mountains" in 1806 and was universally praised. Her next literary effort, "Memoirs of an American lady" was basically a biography of her mentor Mrs Schuyler, mingled with reminiscences and observations of her own. This too was a success. By then Mrs Grant's literary reputation was solidly established, and her financial situation greatly improved. She had moved into the town of Stirling, and supplemented her income by taking in a few pupils from suitably genteel backgrounds.[159]

She began to consider a move to London, and on 15th December 1808 she wrote to her friend Mrs Hook[160], "You wish to know my plan of removing to England, and I told you I would explain it ... My purpose, then, is to take a house fit to accommodate a few young ladies, the children of wealthy persons in the upper circles of life." On 6th July 1809, however, she wrote to Mrs Fletcher in Edinburgh, "I am not certain that after all I shall remove to England. Mary [her daughter] is now there receiving much kindness and making many preparations. She is however by no means sanguine, and rather alarmed at the great expense of living and house rent."[161] Presumably the "great expense" alarmed Mrs Grant even more than it did her daughter, for on 6th August 1809 she wrote again to Mrs Hook in Winchester, "I know that it is best to me to be where I am; and am certain if it were otherwise this plan of moving to England would have answered. What I meant to do in London I shall do in Edinburgh."[162]

Mrs Grant finally made her intended move to Edinburgh in the spring of 1810 into a commodious newly-built house at 2 Heriot Row in the New Town. Her new home commanded a view of the Firth of Forth to the rear, while private gardens sloped up in front to Queen Street. Henry Mackenzie, the celebrated "Man of Feeling", was a near neighbour, and Mrs Grant was already acquainted with several other nearby residents. She was immediately showered with invitations and besieged by visitors, including Walter Scott and the "Archcritic" Francis Jeffrey, editor of the renowned "Edinburgh Review". On 17th March she wrote to John Hatsell in London, "I arrived

159 Information on Mrs Grant taken from
Sheffield Hallam University, Corvey women writers on the web, CW3. Biography of Anne Grant – Pam Perkins.
www.electricscotland.com. A Group of Scottish women: Mrs Grant of Laggan (1755-1838).
Wikipedia: Anne Grant.
Possibly the Pam Perkins biography is the most concise and informative.
160 Memoir and correspondence of Mrs Grant of Laggan – Ed. by J. P. Grant in 3 volumes; Longman, Brown, Green, Longman; London, 1844. Vol. 1, Letter 73.
161 Ibid, Vol. 1, Letter 91.
162 Ibid, Vol. 1, Letter 92.

in Edinburgh ten days ago, and I found all things in far better order than I could have expected, and my house in the best possible regulation. I find it an exceeding good and pleasant one, though so large that the furnishing of it was pretty serious… Were I to go on in my way of taking under my tuition all that could pay me well for so doing, I could soon, I am sure, fill a larger house than this. But I see daily more reason to adhere steadfastly to my first intention of restricting the number of my pupils to 3 or 4."[163]

It is difficult to exaggerate the ferment of intellectual activity in Edinburgh at this time. This was "The Modern Athens" in its "Golden Age", where writers, critics, philosophers and thinkers thrived in a hotbed of speculation, argument and genuine inspired attainment. Edinburgh had always been Scotland's prime centre and training ground for the Law and the Church, and to this had been added a flourishing reputation in the fields of medicine and surgery. In addition, there was now a vigorously burgeoning interest in every aspect of science and discovery. Edinburgh was small enough for all the lions of literature and academia to know each other, and to be known by a wide circle of friends, admirers and emulators. Into this exhilarating scenario stepped Mrs Grant, with a reputation of her own, already acquainted or on friendly terms with the Great and the Good, and in a position not only to expose her pupils to the upper echelons of society, but to what were considered some of the finest minds in Europe.

It would be fair to say that what was being offered to Mrs Grant's "young ladies" was almost equivalent to a modern liberal tertiary education. Although they were not of course offered a degree at the end of their tuition and studies, their educational experience, formal and informal, was infinitely more wide-ranging and interesting than what was being offered to the exclusively male undergraduates in many a university in the early 19th century.

Mrs Grant was 55 at the time of her move to Edinburgh. Her surviving children at this point included Duncan who was in India, and Mary who seems to have been in London. Her daughters Moore, Isabella, and Anne, and her second son John Peter, were presumably with her in Heriot Row. Two pupils who made the move with her from Stirling were Elizabeth Boyle, daughter of the Earl of Glasgow, and "an amiable young lady to

163 "Memoir and correspondence of Mrs Grant of Laggan", Vol 1, Letter 99.

the last degree docile and artless" who was the daughter of Sir Hedworth Williamson of County Durham. [164] By the summer of the following year these two pupils would seem to have departed, and Mrs Grant now had three young ladies under her wing. On 14th August 1811 she wrote again to Mrs Hook, "Now to go on with the progressive history of our establishment, Miss Gardener thinks herself quite recovered, but I have painful doubts, and fear I shall be obliged again to carry her to the countryside[165] Isabella Smythe is the beloved of my heart and I believe loves me with a quiet enthusiasm;[166] and our lively heiress Miss Glassell is truly a fine creature, and will I trust, be all we wish. She has a pure and generous mind, a warm heart, and excellent abilities. Our three graces, though very different, love and suit each other, and combine with the family to form a happy household in which there is not one jarring string."[167]

Joan Glassell gets another mention in Mrs Grant's correspondence a few months later in a letter of 17th December 1811 to Maria Fanshawe in London.[168] "Our young heiress Miss Glassell improves upon us daily; that is to say, she softens, and without affecting, seems visibly to acquire that attention to acquisitions, and that gentleness of manners, which from the unrestrained liberty she enjoyed, and the unbounded vivacity of her untamed spirits, were before much wanted. She has noble and excellent qualities; a strong mind, quick perceptions, good feelings, and much generous enthusiasm. We do everything to make her sensible that her wealth is not considered by us as entitling her to any pre-eminence; and no creature can be more obliging, nor labour more to be useful and pleasing to the rest, whom she seems exceedingly to like".

"Unrestrained liberty" and "untamed spirits" certainly indicate a childhood of what might nowadays be termed "light-touch regulation", and "unbounded vivacity" and "generous enthusiasm" suggest that Mrs Grant would have to work hard to inculcate the decorum and refinement expected of young ladies in early 19th century Edinburgh.

That Mrs Grant was uncompromising in her determination to mould

---

164 "Memoir and Correspondence of Mrs Grant of Laggan", Vol 1, Letter 99.

165 Mrs Grant had taken her to Newbattle, near Dalkeith in Midlothian, no doubt in the hope that the country air would aid her recovery. (Ibid, Letter 96.)

166 Isabella was the daughter of an Irish landowner. She returned to Ireland in 1812, and died two years later, leaving Mrs Grant a legacy of £1000.

167 "Memoir and correspondence of Mrs Grant of Laggan", Vol 1, Letter 115.

168 Ibid, Letter 121.

Mrs Anne Grant of Laggan (Source: "Memoirs and Correspondence" – P. J. Grant).

young minds into socially acceptable form is obvious from a letter written by her for Joan's benefit on 13th October 1812. This can be taken as a "report card" summing up the first year in her mentor's household.[169] Mrs Grant's rather ponderous prose is perhaps a little tedious to the modern ear, but it is worth bearing with her as she examines the character and conduct of her sixteen year old pupil with "painful accuracy":

> *"2 Heriot Row Octr 13th 1812.*
> *My dear Charge,*
> *bear with me patiently tho I resume a subject near my heart & not*

169 National Library of Scotland, Campbell Papers, Acc8508/38. Correspondence 1812-1819 of Joan Glassell. Letters from Mrs Grant of Laggan to Miss Glassell, Letter 1.

the less so that I am sensible I must appear to you tiresome and abundant in repetitions. The more you need advice the less you will care for it, and when your ripened judgment and experience render it necessary your value for it will increase.

Pray attend steadily while with perhaps painful accuracy (painful both for you to bear and me to inflict) I draw a map of your possessions natural and acquired. And forgive me if in this definition if I mark with a steady hand both your redundancies and deficiencies. I shall begin with those gifts of nature and Providence which you possess in a superior degree and for which you must be awefully responsible. You are endowed by nature with the invaluable blessing of a sound and firm constitution, equal and lively animal spirits, a warm and liberal heart, a vigorous and clear intellect, a quick apprehension and more judgment and discernment in matters of importance than could well be expected from your ungoverned faculties and defective education. I say in things of importance for in trifles your exuberant spirits and unregulated habits do not permit you to give fair play to your judgment. In addition to these rich endowments of nature among which may be included taste and sensibility to feel all that is grand and all that is lovely either in moral or physical views of the Divine beneficence, Providence has blest you with ample means to gratify every reasonable wish & indulge every generous or compassionate feeling. Not only the decent comforts and simple elegance of life is placed within your reach, but the means of that diffusive good which many an elegant mind, many a generous and tender heart vainly wish to bestow. Add to this a far more equivocal privilege which may or may not be a blessing as you use it, a degree of liberty of will and choice such as rarely falls to the lot of any female at your early age. Why now must I shade this brilliant picture where the colours tho so rich and lively are all so true? Say rather why should I not shade and chasten it, that it may be more true to general nature, and more faithful to individual likeness. To be an honest witness it is not enough to say nothing that is not true. I must say all that is true, and you will find within you an impartial judge whose assent will justify me where I am right.

What then are your natural defects and redundancies which it is my duty to point out and yours to remedy? They are superabundant rashness; and impetuosity, impatience, anger and transport alike disproportionate to their object. Resentment too readily entertained, and too inconsiderately shown, which others will remember to your disadvantage when you have forgot it. Want (a grievous want) of application to pursuits that by a little steadiness & self constraint you might excel in. Want of self government in general and great want of indulgence and accommodation to the feelings and manners of others unless they happen to be those you either love or admire. Observe dear girl how very few there are worthy of such love or admiration, and how little merit there is in being civil to these few. Observe too how very limited our humane politeness would be if we reserved it for these chosen few. Observe what a charm that general good breeding is which is perfectly consistent with sincerity & is the result of innate benevolence softened by delicacy and exalted by refinement. Above all observe that deeper rooted good will to our fellow creatures which proceeds from a conviction of our great imperfection, a fellow feeling of infirmity & thorough belief that without ample reliance on the great remedy provided for us, we shall all share the same condemnation. Where this belief truly exists, it will not fail to strike a deep root downwards in humility, and to spread upwards and blossom into all these gentle graces that ripen into the fruit of righteousness which is peace. Sweet inward peace that is blest in blessing and shines like the sun on the righteous and unrighteous.

I go now to speak of external disadvantages; these for which you cannot be blamed, but which you must seriously feel and ought speedily to remedy. These are a very irregular and imperfect education, owing partly to adventitious circumstances & very much to the injudicious indulgence of one who like Othello "Lovd not wisely but too well". This is lamentable but not irremediable. The ardour of your mind, your early independence & the very little control under which you have hitherto lived will very naturally stimulate you to enter further and earlier into the world than is compatible with redeeming this lost time. Depend upon't however, if you do not resist this most natural wish and devote your time and attention to this redemption of the past with a steadiness worthy [of] the strength of your character and the importance of the object, you will hereafter long & vainly regret the omission. Another thing I must represent to you very earnestly, and urge you to give it your most serious consideration. It is the shadow which prosperity and good ability never fail to cast before them unless early discipline of mind or most uncommon self government prevent it. The shadow I mean is an air of decision or determination unsuitable to early years and modest pretensions. Being in the right is not enough for anything young, gentle and female; one must be properly and decorously in the right. You may be very wrong in your mode of showing yourself to be very right. It is hard to judge of a young and unsubdued character merely by manner. Manner however, will always by the generality of people be considered as the index to mind. Anything that in the least degree indicates self opinion or borders upon arrogance in you will be more liable to misinstruction than in almost any person I know. I think I can very safely acquit you of what is called purse pride; for that mean insolence your mind is too strong & your heart too generous. My entire consciousness of how little you deserve this charge would add much to my vexation seeing it imputed to you. Yet depend upon it, if you do not moderate this vivacity of your feelings in the expression of them, that vehemence which is merely the result of ungoverned ardour will appear to common minds the insolence of wealth which is always revenged by secret ill will and open misconstruction. This class of persons you may console yourself by despising. Yet they are a body too numerous for contempt, and very capable of giving that bias to public opinion which none of us would like to have against us. There is another less formidable because smaller class whom it would be less dangerous but still less pleasant to offend, and this because they are good and estimable & their opinion is far more valuable. They are worthy & modest people of humble pretensions and whose intellects are neither singularly powerful nor highly cultivated. They will have too much candour and discrimination to ascribe imperative language and an air of decision to so base a motive as conscious abundance of what only derives its value from its use. But supposing you to overvalue the powers of your understanding & the degree of taste and information it might have led you to acquire…"

The rest of Mrs Grant's letter is missing, but after such a thorough examination of Joan's strengths and weaknesses there surely cannot have been much more to say. It is difficult to imagine such a candid and uncompromising critique going down well with many 21st century teenage girls, who are more usually boosted with "Yes you can!" or "Go for it!" Indeed one suspects that the attention of today's cool and confident Material Girl would possibly begin to wander shortly after "pray attend steadily". Mrs Grant's frankness, however, was well meant, and though Joan may have been temporarily discomfited, she obviously bore no resentment. She remained in Mrs Grant's household for at least another five years, and was on friendly terms with her for the rest of her life.

In fact Joan had probably become well used to such improving advice and guidance, as is indicated by another two surviving letters of Mrs Grant's which Joan obviously felt were worth keeping. The first is addressed to Joan at Drum, the house of her guardian Robert Cathcart,[170] and is probably from September 1812, as Mrs Grant mentions being upset at the news of the burning of Moscow. Mrs Grant hopes that Joan does "not wish to overbear anyone with intrinsic or external superiority" and wishes her to "escape the common fate of these young persons to whom wealth, liberty and talents have become fatal snares…". After much more of this, Mrs Grant continues (with some perceptiveness), "I see your colour rise, and I hear you say to me, 'What need of this harsh lecture to one who has been invariably kind to you and yours; from whom you have never experienced anything but the most cheerful submission?'." Mrs Grant then explains at some length that it is all for Joan's own good, and goes on to say how fortunate she is to have a faithful and amiable guardian like Cathcart, so qualified "to supply to you the want of a father and the sweet counsels and affectionate intercourse to be to you as a brother." This letter ends on a lighter note, as Mrs Grant compares the achievement of self-mastery to the smoothing-down of an untidy head of hair.

Lighter notes were perhaps not Mrs Grant's forte. Her usual standpoint of high seriousness left little room for the frivolous or the merely amusing, as demonstrated in another letter addressed to Joan at Heriot Row. "I am disgusted at the panegyric[171] on masquerades. These things have been merely endured, but never till now were they publicly praised and vindicated. It is a most unhappy argument which he uses for their justification, their being so much approved in the South of Europe; that is, today in Italy, which even the witty and worldly Chesterfield calls 'that foul sink of liberal manners and vices'."[172]

170 Campbell Papers Acc8508/38, Letter 2. The beginning of the letter is missing, and it is archived as part of what is in fact a separate letter from Mrs Grant to Joan at Cockenzie.

171 Presumably something she has read in a magazine or newspaper.

172 Campbell Papers Acc8508/38, Letter 3. Undated but obviously before 1815 when Mrs Grant moved from Heriot Row to the west end of Princes Street.

In spite of such uncompromising earnestness, and the constantly recurring spells of ill health among Mrs Grant's daughters, the household at Heriot Row, (and after 1815 at the west end of Princes Street), seems to have been a happy one. After Joan's fellow pupil Isabella Smyth returned to Ireland she wrote a series of letters to Joan where she made it plain that she regarded her days at Heriot Row as almost blissful. "Indeed I am gratified more than I can express by the affection my friends at Heriot Row now bear to me and my sister. Few in the world can boast of such friends, but what I value more than I can tell, is that I know that when they do bestow their affection it is not transient but lasting. Oh my dearest friends, what I would give to get a sight of you all… When I was out today I wished to bring myself to Heriot Row."[173] From Dublin a few weeks later,[174] "I wish you joy of your return to Heriot Row and to all those whose society forms so great a portion of the happiness of your life. Indeed your letters are particularly dear to me from their containing (besides the opinions of your regard) so much about those who are equally dear to us both. You know we used to agree what a bond of union it made between us as we walked and sat together, our having no friends we could so well speak to on the subjects we liked as ourselves. The letters I get from Edinburgh spoil me for any other I read or receive, if I except Miss McMorine's." Isabella had apparently been praising Heriot Row to the skies in letters to her correspondent Miss McMorine, who replied that some authors strike a chord that quickly fades, "But with your Mrs Grant it is far otherwise. I feel something for her which certainly bears a strong family resemblance to affection, and after your own family, you cannot give me greater pleasure than by communicating what you know of her and hers, all of whom deserve[?] my sincere good wishes."

Poor Isabella died a tragically early death in 1814, showing her regard for Mrs Grant by leaving her a legacy of £1000, a considerable sum in the early 19th century. This was not strictly binding, as Isabella was still a minor, but it was sanctioned by her elder brother, the heir to the family estate and fortune.

Joan has little or nothing to say in her surviving adult correspondence about her time with Mrs Grant, but we can glean something of it from

---

173 Campbell Papers Acc8508/38, Letters from Isabella Smyth to "Iris". Letter 1. ("Iris" seems to have been Joan's nom de plume at the time.) From Isabella at Mount Henry, the family home, 19th September 1812.

174 Ibid, Letter 3, 4th October 1812.

other sources. Mrs Grant, as previously noted, had a prodigiously wide circle of friends and acquaintances, including all or most of the Lions of Literature and the Great and Good in Edinburgh. Excursions out of town and short stays with friends in the country were common, and much of each day in Edinburgh was spent in paying calls and receiving visitors. That her pupils were much involved in this social round is more than likely, as demonstrated by a letter from Isabella Smyth to Joan, dating from the early Heriot Row days, in September 1811. Joan is staying with her Cadell relatives in Cockenzie, and Isabella is keeping in touch from Heriot Row. Mrs Grant has left for a few days away and Isabella describes what must have been fairly typical Edinburgh days:[175]

> *"Miss Grant and I have spent several hours of the days in walking, paying visits &c. Tuesday we were out till dinner time, yesterday from eleven till two, and after dinner had Miss A. Thompson and her little [illegible]. The former supped here. Today we went before breakfast to the dentist, and took breakfast at Mrs Hay's, and sat till past twelve, and after different calls was home in time for the Abbey[?] and [illegible] had Miss James, and then was glad to lie down till dinner. After dressing and playing an hour, Mr Turnbull not coming we all went to Miss Lowe's… We are just come in at nine o' clock. I am going to work in the drawing room, having told you some of our doings and will add some more after supper… ". After supper Isabella continued, "I wonder you did not tell me what you thought of the Review. I believe when you compare it with others that it is very favourable indeed… I think the first few lines very good, but Mrs and Miss Grant do not. My sister has written me a long letter, two pages Italian, two French and two or three English, and I will read some of it to you, for a good deal is about the superstitions."*

The references to "the Review" and the "superstitions" are interesting. Mrs Grant had just published her "Essays on Superstitions of the Highlands". She had become great friends with the "Archcritic" Francis Jeffrey, co-founder and editor of the prestigious Edinburgh Review. Mrs Grant was therefore puzzled when it seemed to her that Jeffrey was avoiding her. All became clear however when Jeffrey admitted that he was about to publish a

175 Campbell Papers Acc8508/38, Letters to Iris, Letter 5.

critical review of her "Essays", saying that he always liked to let friends know "before they were led out to execution". The review was indeed not entirely favourable, but Mrs Grant diplomatically agreed that she was "satisfied he had done justice to the *subject*", and they remained friends.[176] Presumably Isabella is referring to this minor controversy in her letter.

Mrs Grant dwells on the warm supportive family atmosphere at Heriot Row in a letter of 4th June 1812.[177] Her mother had just died, and her daughter Anne was in London:

> *"Had my three inmates stood in the same relation to me as the rest, it would be impossible for them to have shown more tender sympathy or more active exertion in aid of the family. Miss Glassell, my little heiress, with whom, I suppose, Anne has made you acquainted, was invited to pass the holidays with a gay social family of her relatives in the country. Nothing however would prevail in her to leave us till the funeral was over. It is difficult to conceive of attachment warmer than these creatures have for every individual of the family. I cannot imagine warmer hearts and purer minds to meet in one place, and the consequence is that without the aid of forced gaiety or studied amusements, they are always happy, and seem not to have a minute for spleen or lassitude. I only regret that in the nature of things this innocent happiness cannot always continue. They will of course separate and enter upon other scenes that will promise more and perform less…".*

The main purpose of Joan Glassell's residence in this garden of delights, however, was her education. An indication that this was wide-ranging can be found in Mrs Grant's statement, "Our young ladies have seven wise masters attending them for as many branches of polite and useful sciences."[178] Unfortunately, she does not tell us what these polite and useful subjects were. Joan's adult fluency in writing, and her rich and extensive vocabulary, would suggest that grammar, spelling, and English composition must have had an important place. In later life Joan expressed herself in writing with ease, and her spelling and grammar are nearly faultless. On the other hand, her punctuation is erratic, to say the least, and her handwriting

176 Edinburgh, the Golden Age – Mary Cosh, Birlinn, Edinburgh, 2014. Pages 281-282.
177 "Correspondence", Vol 1, Letter 121.
178 "Correspondence", Vol 2, Letter 135. 19th November 1812.

frankly dreadful, and sometimes indecipherable. English literature would certainly have been considered an important topic at Heriot Row, and in later life Joan displayed a wide knowledge of it, and was an eager buyer of books. "What a deal you spend on books!" her correspondent Elizabeth Mure remarked in 1825.[179]

The fact that Isabella Smyth's sister wrote to her in French and Italian surely indicates that Isabella was expected to understand what was written. In her travels abroad as a young woman Joan showed some competence in both languages, so we might expect that two of the "wise masters" were language teachers. There may also have been a basic grounding in Latin, although since Mrs Grant's "little heiress" was not destined for the Law, the Kirk, or for Medicine, Latin would not have been considered to be of prime importance. Music and singing would certainly have been part of the curriculum, as would drawing and painting. Although Joan's later correspondence makes little or no reference to any claim to musical abilities, bizarrely she seems to have had some skill at whistling, and her son recalled his parents whistling duets together.[180] As for drawing, the few rough sketches surviving from Joan's European tour display little artistic ability. Well-bred young ladies would be expected to be competent in basic arithmetic, since after all they would probably have to supervise household accounts after marriage, and it might well have been deemed fitting to touch on more unfamiliar branches of mathematics.

Ladies active in Edinburgh society would be expected to have not only some knowledge of what was going on in the world, but to have at least a little knowledge of the background to current events. History and geography would therefore be essential. And since early nineteenth century Edinburgh was in a fever of excitement over scientific progress and discovery, there may well have been lessons in elementary physics, chemistry, and natural history. Ladies after all were not only expected to *know* about the modern world, but to be capable of intelligent conversation about it – although the expression of too much enthusiasm and the demonstration of too much knowledge might lead to the dreaded designation of "bluestocking", particularly if the intellect of the lady in question was not accompanied by a sufficiency of physical "charms".

179 Campbell Papers Acc8508/25, Letters from Elizabeth Mure, Letter 9.
180 George Douglas, Eighth Duke of Argyll, Autobiography and Memoirs, Ed. The Dowager Duchess of Argyll, New York, Dutton &Co. 1906. Vol 1, Page 91.

Surviving in the Campbell Papers is an "Undated draft letter from Joan Glassell and others thanking someone for his interesting classes".[181] The intended recipient is not named, the sender's address is given only as "Edinburgh", and as the caption says, the letter is undated. The list of names, which is all in Joan's hand, is marked "To be omitted." The letter reads as follows:

"Sir,

We think it unnecessary to apologise for doing what, tho it may appear forward and intrusive, is in reality intended as a testimony of respect and gratitude for the great obligation conferr'd on us in the unremitted exertions you have made for our improvement during the time we have attended your class. Our principal motive, however, for addressing you is to express our united and most earnest wish that you would (if perfectly suitable to yr convenience) still continue your valued instruction for another course to commence at the usual season. We are particularly desirous to advance further in astronomy than the short time before the present class will admit of, and will most gladly accommodate ourselves to whatever hour, and follow any course of study you assign. Whither [sic] you can comply with our request or not, we trust you will at least forgive our having presumed to suggest a measure the expediency and utility of which you are a much more competent judge. Permit us again to express the lively sense we feel of your endeavour to improve and inform us, which we may venture to say have not proved altogether ineffectual. With the highest feelings of respect and gratitude we subscribe ourselves

Joan Glassell	*Harriet Cathcart*	*Mary Rolland*
Moore Grant	*Elizabeth Cathcart*	*Mary Wood*
Jane Scott Moncrieff	*Catherine Walsh*	*Margt Simpson*
Anne Scott Moncrieff	*Jane Balderson*	*– Scott*
Eliza Innes	*Mary A. Dinwoody*	*Jane Cheyne*
Mary Cathcart	*A. Witherspoon*	*Aloise Smith."*

Although the letter has been drafted by Joan, we might well suspect "suggestions" from Mrs Grant in its composition.

181 Campbell Papers Acc8508/36, Letter 13.

Obviously the intended recipient of the letter was giving the benefit of his expertise to more than just Mrs Grant's household, and it is likely that the pattern of Joan's education would include not only private tuition by the seven "wise masters" but a diet of external classes similar to the one mentioned above.

The identity of Joan's teachers is not known, except perhaps for one. In one of Mrs Grant's letters of improving advice to Joan[182] she says, "I want you to exercise self government in small matters. Sitting two hours on a stretch with the family, steadily preparing for Mylne and all such quiet stationary duties that are merely the parade before the battle."

"Mylne" is likely to have been the Rev. Andrew Mylne, "a gentleman long eminent as a teacher in Edinburgh, and the author of several valuable works in education".[183] Mylne was regarded as an expert in the field of education, and was the author of

"The first book for children." Price 2d.

"A spelling-book upon a new plan, for the use of schools. In two parts." 1/6 each.

"An epitome of English grammar with a variety of exercises." 1/6.

"Outlines of modern geography for the use of schools." 2/6.

"Exercises on the history of England, containing a regular series of questions on all the important facts of the history." 2/6.

"Exercises on the histories of Greece and Rome." 2/6.

"An elementary treatise on astronomy: or an easy introduction to a knowledge of the heavens, intended for the use of those who are not much conversant in mathematical studies." 9/-.

Mylne's authorship of "An elementary treatise on astronomy" makes it not unlikely that he was the intended recipient of the young ladies' letter requesting a further course on that subject. Regarding his publications, the Edinburgh Review[184] wrote, "The celebrity which Dr Mylne long enjoyed as a teacher in Edinburgh renders it unnecessary to say much in recommendation of these elementary works. They are the result of long experience and are distinguished by condensation, arrangement and perspicuity, which render

182 Campbell Papers Acc8508/38, Letter 2. 1812.

183 The Monthly Magazine, January 1st 1819.

184 For October 1821-February 1822.

them alike intelligible, systematic and comprehensive. They are now used by some of the ablest teachers in Edinburgh and other parts of Scotland." In 1815 Mylne was appointed minister of Dollar, where he was the main mover in setting up Dollar Academy, of which he became the first rector. If all Joan's teachers were of similar calibre, her education would be in capable hands indeed.

Joan remained with Mrs Grant into her early twenties. As the years passed the informal social side of her education would take on increasing importance. She was a wealthy young heiress connected to several landowning families in East Lothian, but it was vital for her future to extend her social contacts not only among the Edinburgh gentry and intelligentsia, but as far and wide as possible. In the beginning, when the Great and Good came to call on Mrs Grant, or when she took her pupil with her on the daily round of calls and longer visits, Joan's role would be that of an observer and learner, speaking when spoken to, and being modestly deferential. Eventually, she could hope to become accepted as an equal, and then her personality and talents would be given the chance to shine, leading to a comfortable niche in the upper echelons of society. This process was expressed succinctly by Joan's son when he wrote, "Among the young women with whose education she [Mrs Grant] was charged, my mother soon took a high place, as distinguished by the vivacity of her mind, and by her charm of conversation. Mrs Grant spoke and wrote of her to friends in terms which made them anxious to secure her acquaintance."[185]

By early 1816, when Joan was aged 19, Mrs Grant was writing to her friend Mrs Smith of Jordanhill,[186] "Miss G. does really great credit to the pains bestowed on her. She is a very fine creature; her faults are merely those of habit and a vigorous uncultured mind – those in short that belong to considerable strength of character in which the process of refinement has scarcely begun. She has however a good temper, a good understanding, and that rare union of ardour and perseverance before which difficulties vanish, and by which seeming impossibilities have been accomplished." Later that year she wrote to another Glasgow friend,[187] "Miss Glassell… is that

185 Autobiography and memoirs – George Douglas, 8th Duke of Argyll, New York, Dutton &Co, 1906. Page 51.

186 Correspondence, Vol 2, Letter 174.

187 Correspondence, Vol 2, Letter 181. 3rd July 1816.

good wine which, according to the old saying, needs no bush. Her quick observation, strong sense, and cordial frankness make way[188] at once; and it does not detract from the merit she really possesses to say that they make way the faster from that affluence of which she really makes a very good use. Her manners would not do so well with a person whose heart could not show itself by effects; she has many good qualities and some noble ones."

In the autumn of 1816 Joan wrote from Cockenzie to her friend Janet Dunlop,[189] telling her that she had just returned from Roseneath, and that there was to be "great gaiety" in Edinburgh the following week, with the renowned actor Edmund Keane appearing for six nights, and the Caledonian Hunt races to be run at Musselburgh. However, the main purpose of Joan's letter was to tell Janet about the unexpected friendship she had struck up with the famous actress Eliza O' Neill. Joan was apparently a great fan, and had attended the theatre every night during Miss O Neill's appearance in Edinburgh during the summer. She had been introduced to Miss O' Neill, who enjoyed an aura of unblemished respectability unusual for one of her profession, and subsequently called on her with friends. Being rather overawed in the presence of greatness, Joan said little, and came away "very much mortified at the impression of my dumbness and stupidity". However, a day or two later, as she and Moore Grant were passing Miss O' Neill's lodgings in George Street, the actress saw her from a window, recognised her, and invited her in. Joan and Eliza felt an immediate rapport, and saw each other every day for the fortnight that Miss O' Neill remained in town.

Lady Dalhousie, a renowned amateur botanist, and a distant relative of Joan's through the East Lothian Brouns of Colstoun, had invited Joan to bring Miss O' Neill to view the gardens at Dalhousie Castle in Midlothian. Eliza was due to leave Edinburgh, but postponed her departure until the Sunday so that she could spend Saturday at Dalhousie with Joan. Lady Dalhousie's husband had just been appointed governor of Nova Scotia, and she herself had left for London, but Joan and Eliza were allowed the run of the conservatory and gardens. "She had left order with the gardener to give us fruit there, and desired her compliments to Miss O'N and to say how happy she would have been had she been at home to receive her, and that she would feel honoured by Miss O' Neill taking a bouquet of the

188 By "make way" Mrs Grant means "draw attention", not "step aside".

189 Campbell Papers Acc8508/37/2. Bundle IV, Letter 4. Typewritten copy of Joan Glassell's letter to Janet Dunlop (afterwards Mrs Cathcart of Auchendrane).

heaths and geraniums." The two passed a pleasant forenoon at Dalhousie, then spent the evening together. Joan was very much impressed by Eliza's singing. "She has all the Irish melodies and every Scots song you can name by heart." Before Eliza left Edinburgh she and Joan exchanged locks of hair. "She asked me for a lock of my hair!!!!" Joan emphasised with four exclamation marks. A very few years later Eliza prudently married an Irish landowner and left the stage forever.

In his memoirs, Joan's son throws further light on his mother's friendship with Eliza:[190]

"On seeing the famous tragedienne Miss O' Neil performing the part of Juliet, my mother was so carried away by her emotions that she at once bought a diamond ring and sent it anonymously to the object of her enthusiasm. Miss O' Neil, concluding or suspecting that it came from a man, never wore it until she discovered the real donor, and then wore it for the rest of her long life as Lady Beecher in loving memory of her young friend. I have this anecdote from Lady Beecher herself…".

There can be no better illustration of Joan Glassell's secure place in the scheme of things than the fact that she could not only befriend with ease one of the era's brightest stars of the stage, but could entertain her at the country mansion of a great lady with a scientific reputation. Little wonder that Mrs Grant felt that Joan did "really great credit to the pains bestowed on her".

190 Autobiography and Memoirs, New York 1906. Page 51.

6

Background to a love story

AS HER SON WROTE IN THE PREFACE TO HER PUBLISHED correspondence, “Mrs Grant mixed extensively in the literary and other circles of Edinburgh, where her house was the resort of many eminent characters, both of her own and foreign countries.” Her oldest and most intimate friend, however, was Isobel Euing,[191] the companion of her early years in Glasgow, and whose friendship was a lifelong joy and consolation to her. Isobel’s sister Jane was also a valued friend, and Mrs Grant corresponded regularly with both. In the formal style of the early 19th century she invariably addressed Isobel as “Mrs Smith” and Jane as “Mrs Brown”. They were the daughters of William Euing “Deacon Convenor” and baillie of Glasgow.

Jane Euing married James Brown, of the Browns of Broadstone near Beith in North Ayrshire. He became a much respected merchant in Glasgow, and seems to have had an artistic bent. A well-known view of the Trongate in 1778 is attributed to him. The Browns’ three sons Francis, Robert, and William all became prosperous merchants with interests in the Caribbean, with all that implied. Francis was the proprietor of an estate in Trinidad named “Jordan Hill”, and was involved with his brother in buying 156 slaves in Dominica in 1819 and shipping them to Trinidad to work at

191 Also spelled “Ewing”.

Jordan Hill. When slavery was abolished in the British colonies in 1834, the brothers were compensated for the financial loss by the British government. Robert eventually became Robert Brown "of Fairlie", and William was known as William Brown "of Kilmardinny".[192] Jane Euing's husband James Brown died in 1808 at the age of c. 59, so during the time when Mrs Grant was writing from Edinburgh, Mrs Brown was a widow of mature years in comfortable circumstances, with adult sons already making their way successfully in the world.

Isobel Euing married Archibald Smith, a younger son of the laird of Craigend in Strathblane, Stirlingshire, just beyond the northern fringes of present-day Glasgow. As young men, Archibald and his two brothers, like John Glassell, went to Virginia and engaged in the tobacco trade. Also like John Glassell, they returned to Scotland before the outbreak of the American War of Independence. They began trading to the Caribbean and were very successful. Archibald was partner in the firm "Leitch and Smith", and around 1800 was able to buy the estate of Jordanhill, then lying in the countryside a few miles to the west of Glasgow. During the years when Joan Glassell resided in Mrs Grant's household, Mrs Grant was in the habit of paying an annual visit to her old friend at Jordanhill, often remaining for several weeks.

Archibald Smith and his three sons continued to have business interests in the Caribbean, and on the abolition of slavery James and Archibald Jr. received substantial sums of money in compensation for freed slaves on estates in Grenada mortgaged to them by their owner James Stuart. William, the brother of James and Archibald Jr., had a commercial interest in his cousin Francis Brown's "Jordan Hill" sugar plantation in Trinidad, which in 1822 relied on the labour of 173 slaves.[193]

The foundations of the wealth and social status of many affluent and prominent Glasgow families of unimpeachable respectability basically rested on the misery of faceless droves of enslaved fellow humans. It is only in recent years that the extent of these connections has become apparent, after two centuries of "out of sight, out of mind", and we would have to search long and hard to find to find any reference to such uncomfortable links in the contemporary correspondence and records of the 19th century.

192 www.ucl.ac.uk/lbs – Database "Legacies of British slave ownership".
193 www.ucl.ac.uk/lbs : Database – "Legacies of British Slave Ownership."

Here is how Mrs Grant refers to her good friends the Smiths and Browns:

> *"That family consists of Mr Archibald Smith, who has made a fortune in business, and has retired to enjoy and to employ it on an estate in the country, a fine place five miles below Glasgow. He is one of those people on whose countenance, sentiments, and manners, the stamp of gentleman is visibly impressed: such a taste for literature, such pleasant conversation, such an easy, disengaged manner, that looks as if he were serenely happy himself, and wished without saying so, that everyone about him should be the same. His wife, my friend of forty years standing, is a pure-minded, meek, and amiable being, has an excellent and kind heart, an informed mind, and much delicacy of feeling; as a wife and mother she is unequalled, but as a friend and companion she is less perfect, because from a certain diffidence of herself, she is too anxious and always too much afraid of failing in some of her duties, to have that delightful tranquillity, that animated peace, that diffuses such charm around her mate. Her sister Mrs Brown, is a widow, a faithful mourner, yet comforted by three excellent sons, who honour her with no common love and deference. Mrs Brown cannot have more worth and truth, more heart, piety, and purity of mind than her sister; yet though her lot in life has been circumscribed to a more confined range of duty and society, hers is the stronger and more comprehensive mind. Her sister too, would do as kind a thing, if she had the occasion, but Mrs Brown would sooner discern where or how it might be done."*[194]

Amidst all this pleasant conversation, delicacy of feeling, and delightful tranquillity, it is perhaps worth remembering once again the lines of the East Lothian poet James Mylne:

> *"While sumptuously ye eat and drink,*
> *Does it ne'er sting your conscious breast,*
> *Oh cruel luxury! To think*
> *He starves whose toil produced the feast?"*

James was the eldest son of the Smith family, but had little interest in business.

194 "Correspondence", Vol 1, Letter 36, to Mrs Gorman, Kilmore, Ireland, 19th December 1815.

The firm of "Leitch and Smith" eventually evolved into "James and Archibald Smith & Co." but after the death of Archibald Sr. in 1821, James's younger brother Archibald Jr. was almost solely responsible for conducting business, and James had probably been pretty much a "sleeping partner" well before then. James's passions were yachting and geology, and he was not only one of the earliest and most illustrious practitioners of sailing as a leisure activity, but came to be known as the "father of yachting" on the Clyde. To facilitate his nautical activities James and his wife Mary Wilson rented a property from the Duke of Argyll at Rosneath on the west side of the Gareloch, near its opening into the Clyde. A short distance away, on the eastern shore of the loch, was Ardencaple Castle, the residence of Lord John Campbell, brother of the Duke of Argyll. Let Lord John's son take up the story:

> *"In the last year of my grandfather's*[195] *life, early in 1806, when he was living at the old Castle of Rosneath, it took fire, and the greater part of it was destroyed. But a portion of the building was saved. It stood on the top of a very steep bank rising above a little bay of the sea, and close to the point which may be considered as the opening of the Gareloch. As my uncle*[196] *very foolishly began to build a new Italian palazzo about a hundred yards further inland from the shore, and as the great expenditure he lavished on this house at a time when everything was very costly, soon plunged him into embarrassment, the remains of the old castle were roughly fitted up as a temporary residence, and were finally let to anyone who wanted a place in one of the loveliest spots in Scotland, with peculiar charms of quietness and cheerfulness, together with great seclusion. As Mr Smith of Jordanhill had taken to yachting, the place exactly suited him, and he became the tenant in 1812. The two castles of Ardencaple and Rosneath were exactly opposite each other, and only separated by a narrow strait which could be crossed in a rowing boat; my father*[197] *and Mr Smith were thus very near neighbours, and an intimate friendship was soon established between them.*
>
> *Miss Glassell was a favourite guest with Mr Smith and his wife…".*[198]

195 The 5th Duke of Argyll.
196 The 6th Duke.
197 Lord John Campbell.
198 "Autobiography and Memoirs", Vol 1. E.P. Dutton & Co., New York, 1906. Pages 52, 53.

The link between Rosneath and Joan Glassell was of course Mrs Grant, the lifelong friend of James Smith's mother. Mrs Grant, as previously mentioned, was in the habit of paying an extended annual visit to her old friend at Jordanhill, and also kept in touch with her friend's sister Mrs Brown. It would seem that Joan, and other "young ladies" accompanied Mrs Grant on at least some of these visits, and certainly Joan and Moore Grant stayed with Mrs Brown in the early summer of 1816. It was after this visit that Mrs Grant described Joan to a correspondent as "that good wine which needs no bush".[199] It would be quite natural for James Smith to extend an invitation to a charming young heiress of impeccable credentials, already known to his family, and Joan's lively and attractive personality would ensure that one invitation to Rosneath led to others. Indeed, Joan's son wrote in his memoirs, "My mother had often lived there with the Smiths who were her earliest and most intimate friends."

If Joan was a favourite and frequent guest at Rosneath, it would follow naturally that she would be introduced to James Smith's neighbour from across the Gareloch, Lord John Campbell. Their first meeting was certainly at Rosneath, but it is difficult now to know exactly when. Late in life the 8th Duke of Argyll placed it "around 1815 or 1816",[200] but as we shall see, it may have been slightly later.

John Douglas Edward Henry Campbell, known by the courtesy title "Lord John Campbell", was born in London in 1777, the son of the 5th Duke of Argyll. The 5th Duke was a military man who at his death in 1806 at the age of 86 was the oldest field marshal in the British army. John's mother Elizabeth Gunning was a famed beauty, the daughter of an Anglo-Irish country squire in Co. Roscommon. She was the young widow of the Duke of Hamilton, who had died after only six years of marriage, leaving her with three children.

John was the youngest of his parents' surviving four children. His elder brother George became 6th Duke of Argyll on his father's death in 1806. John's sister Augusta married a Colonel Clavering, but separated from him after having three children, and lived a retired life in a villa on the Rosneath peninsula. His other sister Charlotte was another noted beauty. She married

199 "Correspondence", Vol 2, Letter 47.

200 "The Intellectual Duke; George Douglas Campbell 8th Duke of Argyll" – Kirsteen Mulhern. Ph. D. thesis, University of Edinburgh, 2006.

John Campbell of Shawfield and had a large family. Her relatives were not best pleased when as a middle-aged widow she married a penniless but artistic Church of England clergyman much younger than herself. Charlotte became a popular novelist, celebrated in her day, although nowadays almost completely forgotten.

John's childhood was spent mostly at home in Inveraray Castle. He was educated by tutors, and "was accustomed during all his boyhood to life in the open air", fishing and shooting in a wild landscape of lochs, moors and mountains. He also "had imbibed a very early taste for the physical sciences, and specifically for chemistry and mechanics".[201] This idyllic boyhood was rudely interrupted, however, when John was uprooted from Argyll, and sent to Christ Church college in Oxford, an institution still mired in traditional classicism, where he found little stimulus for his talents and interests, and apparently relieved his boredom by taking potshots with an airgun at flower-pots on the quadrangle window sills.

In 1797, when John would be aged around 19, his father agreed to him joining the 3rd Foot Guards as an ensign. There was little difficulty involved – the regiment had been formed in 1641 as the Marquis of Argyll's Royal Regiment, and John's father was its colonel.[202] Very soon afterwards John found himself in Ireland where his regiment was involved in putting down the Irish rebellion of 1798, an uprising inspired as much by the radical ideals of the French Revolution as by Irish nationalism. Apparently John spoke little about this interlude in later life, but one incident seems to have made a deep impression on him. A band of rebels had been captured in possession of a cache of pikes. It was decided that some of them should be hanged on the spot, and that the victims should be chosen by lot. John never forgot how the losers accepted their fate stoically and calmly, while those who escaped with their lives were "violently agitated".[203]

John's military career did not last long, however. In 1799, serving in the Netherlands as a captain in a campaign against the French Revolutionary Army, he fell ill, as he believed, "in consequence of wading through the canals".[204] Writing many decades later, John's son wrote that his father

201 "Autobiography and Memoirs" – 8th Duke of Argyll, Page 31.
202 "Draft: John D.E.H. Campbell, 7th Duke of Argyll." – Ann Galliard.
203 "Autobiography and Memoirs" Page 32.
204 Letter from John to the Duke, 30th September 1799. Quoted in Ann Galliard's "Draft".

had fallen victim to "Walcheren fever". This is a mistake however. The "Walcheren Expedition" in 1809 was long after John's brief spell of military service. A British expeditionary force sent to the Dutch island of Walcheren to counter the French occupation of Antwerp, was decimated by disease. By February of the following year 40% of the force had succumbed, and 60 officers and 3900 men had died. This mystery killer disease was dubbed "Walcheren fever", and is now thought to have been a deadly combination of malaria, typhus, typhoid and dysentery[205] which could largely be attributed to "sanitation issues arising from the presence of thousands of men sloshing about on a semi-flooded island".[206] Significantly, many of the soldiers who recovered from Walcheren fever continued to relapse for years afterwards.

John, who fell ill in 1799, cannot have had "Walcheren fever" which broke out in 1809, but he presumably had fallen victim to something very similar, and suffered from recurring bouts of ill health throughout his life. He was judged unfit for further service, and his brief military career came to an abrupt end. Fortunately, around the same time, John's uncle Lord Frederick Campbell retired as Member of Parliament for Argyllshire, and John was able to step into his shoes. He remained as M.P. for Argyllshire until 1822 representing, it must be said, not so much the people of Argyll as the interests of the Ducal family of Argyll.

Soon after the beginning of his hardly distinguished political career John committed the unfortunate misjudgement of making an "unhappy marriage". This, not surprisingly, is veiled in obscurity, and John's son in his "Autobiography" merely observes hurriedly that he "knows nothing of the details". Probably somewhere in the archived correspondence of the early 19th century clues will lurk as to why the union with Elizabeth Campbell of Fairfield was so "unhappy", but nothing has as yet come to light. It is possible, however, to trace something of the circumstances of the marriage and its speedy demise.

Elizabeth was the daughter of William Campbell of Fairfield in Ayrshire. Campbell was an advocate, and served as provost of Ayr. He was "gentry", but of course far below the son of a Duke in terms of social status. There is no obvious clue as to how Lord John and Elizabeth became acquainted, but

205 B.M.J. 18th Dec 1999: "Walcheren 1809 – a medical catastrophe." – Martin R. Howard.

206 Military Medicine: "The lessons of Walcheren fever 1809." – John Lynch.

some evidence survives as to the circumstances of the marriage in statements given four years later by two Writers to the Signet.[207]

Mr Harry Davidson W.S. testified that he was asked to attend a meeting on 20th December 1803 between Lord John and Elizabeth Campbell, in his capacity as a Justice of the Peace. At this meeting John declared that Elizabeth was his lawful wife, and had been so since August 1802. Elizabeth confirmed his statement, and Mr Davidson gave them a written certificate confirming the marriage. Also present at this meeting were Elizabeth's father William Campbell, Adam Gillies advocate, John Farrier W.S., John Hunter W.S., and Hunter's sister Agnes.

Mr Hunter testified that the meeting took place in the house of his sister Agnes in Queen Street, Edinburgh, where Elizabeth was living at the time. He said that some time previously Elizabeth had told him that she was married to Lord John Campbell and that he had given her a written acknowledgment of the fact. It was then thought advisable by Elizabeth's "friends" that there should be a public acknowledgment of the marriage. It was eventually agreed by Lord John's friends and Elizabeth's friends that a meeting should be convened for that purpose in the presence of Mr Davidson, Sheriff Substitute of Edinburgh. A marriage certificate was duly made out and signed by the Sheriff Substitute and lodged in Hunter's hands at Elizabeth's request. At the meeting Lord John acknowledged that Elizabeth had been his lawful wife since August 1802, a statement which corresponded to the written acknowledgment in John's handwriting which Elizabeth had shown him, and of which he had made a copy.

It should be said here that in the eyes of the Law and the Church there was only one form of "regular" marriage, which was marriage conducted by a minister of the Church of Scotland before witnesses, and after the calling of "banns" (a public announcement from the pulpit of the couple's intention to marry). However, the law also allowed for "irregular" marriage, which in fact was widespread in early 19th century Scotland. "Irregular" marriage could take the form of cohabitation followed by acknowledgment, or it might consist of an agreement to accept each other before witnesses, perhaps with another party officiating – Gretna Green marriages conducted by the local blacksmith are a famous example of this. In Edinburgh there were several

207 National Records of Scotland: Edinburgh Commissary Court. CC8/6/1330. Process of Divorce, Statements by Harry Davidson W.S. and John Hunter W.S.

disreputable so-called "priests" operating at the time who made a living by charging a small fee for marrying couples who, for whatever reason, might not want to expose themselves to the scrutiny of their parish minister and kirk session. Indeed, witnesses, or a "celebrant" of any kind, or any written record, were unnecessary for the validity of an irregular marriage. It was enough that the parties had accepted each other as man and wife. When the news reached their kirk session, however, ordinary mortals were expected to submit to church discipline to receive a rebuke for flaunting the "regular" procedure. It will be obvious that the widespread practice of irregular marriage left much room for uncertainties, doubts and grey areas.

Returning to the meeting of 20th December 1803, what are we to make of it? It can hardly be called a "wedding". It was an admission before an array of lawyers that John and Elizabeth had been man and wife since "August 1802". This vagueness suggests that there had not been much of a "wedding" in 1802 either, but more likely the beginning of a sexual relationship in August of that year. At the time of the meeting in December 1803 Elizabeth was living with Agnes Hunter. Had she ever actually lived with Lord John? And if she had, why was she not living with him in December 1803?

The answer is that Elizabeth had been deliberately abandoned by Lord John, who had deserted her early in 1803 and spent at least half the year abroad. Late in life, John's son wrote that in 1802 his father "before the end of the year had discovered and had suffered from his mistake – not only in spirits but in health, and his family and friends advised him to go abroad". He adds, "My grandfather seized the opportunity to send his son abroad", thereby suggesting that the trip was financed by the Duke of Argyll.[208]

The Peace of Amiens made it briefly possible for British citizens to travel safely in Europe. In his "Autobiography and memoirs" John's son states that he was in possession of a "careful journal" kept by Lord John during his travels, and that he left England on 16th February 1803. That he was indeed abroad during the first half of 1803 is confirmed by the fact that he wrote frequent letters to his father describing his experiences.[209] Lord John was accompanied on his tour by Dr Robert Robertson, an older friend and medical advisor. In Paris John met Napoleon, and in Geneva struck up a friendship with the renowned Madame de Staël, famed in her day for her

208 "Autobiography and memoirs", Vol 1, Page33.

209 "Draft: John D.E.H. Campbell 7th Duke of Argyll" – Ann Galliard.

literary salons, and with an international reputation as an author in her own right. John suspected that she was romantically attracted to his travelling companion Robertson. Comments made at the time make it plain that John was suffering from more than just the after effects of "Walcheren fever" or a disappointing love-life. In Geneva he was "under the shadow of a trouble which saddened his spirit"[210] and Mme de Staël remarked to Robertson "that she was conscious of a depressing influence from what she called my father's *mauvaise honte*".[211] Another Swiss lady, presumably in an attempt to show sympathy and raise his spirits, "told him she had once been under the influence of a gloomy sorrow which destroyed all the enjoyments of life. She exhorted him to struggle against it by forcing himself to take an interest in a variety of subjects and in Nature. He told her this was exactly what he was doing, but theretofore with little success."[212] In spite of the change of scene and the stimulating social round in Geneva, it was obvious to others that John was "under a shadow". It would not be surprising if this would nowadays be diagnosed as "clinical depression".

To add to John's troubles, war was resumed between Britain and France while he was still in Geneva, which at that time was under French control. Napoleon ordered the arrest of all British citizens, and the fact that John was the son of a prominent Duke made him a particular target. Being fresh-faced, slightly built and short in stature he was able to make a daring escape dressed in women's clothes in the carriage of his acquaintance Mme de la Chaude, disguised as her maid. Poor Robertson was left behind. John subsequently made his way down the Danube to Vienna, where he was rejoined by Robertson who had been released as a person of no value to his captors. From Vienna they travelled home by way of Dresden, Berlin, and the Netherlands, arriving in England in September 1803.[213]

Thus, after beginning a relationship with Elizabeth Campbell in August 1802, and subsequently giving her a written acknowledgment of marriage, John took off for Europe only four or five months later, in ill health and suffering from depression, and spent more than half of 1803 abroad. Then, bizarrely, just before Christmas of that year he attended a meeting with Elizabeth and her "friends" and made a public

210 "Biography and memoirs", Vol 1, Page37.

211 Ibid, Page 39. Mauvaise honte : bashfulness, extreme shyness.

212 Ibid, Pages 44, 45.

213 "Draft: John D.E.H. Campbell 7th Duke of Argyll" – Ann Galliard.

acknowledgement of their marriage. Perhaps even more surprisingly, he seems to have lived with Elizabeth for a short time after his public confirmation of their marriage, as the lawyer James Hunter testified that "from that period [he] considered the parties as married persons and he afterwards visited the pursuer [i.e. Elizabeth] in Lord John's lodgings both in Edinburgh and London, and the deponent's wife has called on Lady John both in Edinburgh and London at said lodgings".[214] It would seem therefore, that John and Elizabeth did make an effort to save their marriage – or perhaps the apparent rapprochement was only for the sake of appearances. Whatever the motive, it was in vain, as we shall see. But the marriage was probably doomed from the start. It is surely significant that no member of the Argyll family was present at the Queen Street meeting. It seems the family was against the marriage, which came about "despite the best efforts of the Duke"[215] who, it was rumoured, had tried to buy Elizabeth off with an offer of £10000.[216]

The whole sorry business has the air of an impulsive sexual encounter, or a furtive hole-and-corner affair, where the young woman, feeling herself compromised, asks for and receives a written acknowledgment of marriage as an insurance policy. The immature young man then bolts abroad, and on his return a public declaration of the validity of the marriage is demanded by his betrayed partner's "friends" – her outraged father and near relations.[217] A half-hearted attempt is then made at reconciliation, but all in vain.

The mystery at the heart of all this of course is, what was it that made the couple so incompatible? Had Elizabeth been briefly pregnant, giving rise to feelings of entrapment in one or both parties? Or conversely, did John find himself impotent as a result of his ill-health? Was one of them infected with a sexually transmitted disease? When Mme de Staël spoke of John's *mauvaise honte* – his bashfulness or extreme shyness – what lay at the root of it? Was John simply naturally reticent, or was there something more sinister making him wary of female company? There is a piece missing in the jigsaw here, which has probably been deliberately hidden, and is now

214 National Records of Scotland. Edinburgh Commissary Court CC8/6/1330, Statement by John Hunter.

215 "Draft" – Ann Galliard.

216 "The History of Parliament: The House of Commons 1790-1820." – R. G. Thorne, Secker and Warburg, London, 1986. Article on Lord John Campbell.

217 "Friends" (freends) often had the meaning "relatives" in Scotland, and indeed sometimes still does.

unlikely to be found. But then, perhaps it was just that John and Elizabeth didn't really like each other very much.

Whatever the cause, the couple soon parted, and after living separately for a few years, brought their ordeal to a formal and official conclusion. On 8th January 1808, after deliberating for four months, the Commissary Court of Edinburgh granted Elizabeth Campbell a divorce on the grounds of her husband's adultery. Reflecting as it does on Lord John's questionable behaviour, this divorce is never mentioned in his son's "Autobiography", nor in any other accounts of Clan Campbell or the House of Argyll. It has been quietly erased from history.

The "Summons of Divorce" issued on 28th August 1807[218] made the accusation that

> *"...the said Right Honourable John Douglas Edward Henry Campbell commonly called Lord John Campbell, casting off the fear of God and disregarding his matrimonial vows and engagements whereby he stood bound and obliged to preserve the marriage bed inviolated, has for a considerable time past alienated his affections from the pursuer and has given up himself to adulterous practices, fellowship, and company with women one or more other than the pursuer, his lawful wife, and more particularly the said Right Honourable John Douglas Edward Henry Campbell, commonly called Lord John Campbell, having become acquainted with Etienette Roucie formerly of the Rue de Mont Blanc à Paris, afterwards of No. 9 Bolton Street Picadilly in the liberties of Westminster, has deserted the fellowship and society of the Pursuer and formed a criminal connection with the said Etienette Roucie, and has for many months past been in the practice of visiting and associating with her...".*

The affair with Etienette had apparently been going on from 1805 up to the issuing of the summons in August 1807, and John stood accused of "having carnal knowledge and adulterous conversation, intercourse, and dealing" with her and possibly other women.

In the course of legal proceedings the statements already quoted from Henry Davidson and John Hunter were submitted as proof that John and

218 National Records of Scotland: Edinburgh Commissary Court CC8/6/1330/1.

Elizabeth were indeed man and wife. Various other witnesses testified to John's engagement in jiggery-pokery. James Gordon, a former waiter at the Cross Keys, Kelso, testified that one Sunday in 1806 a lady and gentleman had arrived in a chaise from the Tankerville Arms at Wooller and shared a room at the Cross Keys. The gentleman had identified himself as Lord John Campbell. Gordon had seen the same gentleman on a subsequent occasion at Inveraray (probably when the summons of divorce was delivered), and heard him answer, "I am", when asked if he was Lord John Campbell.

Barbara Rae, who had been a chambermaid at the Cross Keys, remembered the couple arriving the Sunday after Kelso Fair. The gentleman asked for two beds, but the inn was so busy there was only one bed left. The gentleman replied, "Very well, that will do." His companion was a "well-made stout little woman", and since there was no other bed in the room, the chambermaid had no doubt they had both slept in it. The waiter told her next morning that the gentleman was Lord John Campbell.

The innkeeper George Yule confirmed that the inn had been so busy that night that only one bed was available for the lady and gentleman. Before the couple left in the morning Yule asked his guest whether he intended to attend Kelso Races that year, and added, "I presume you are Lord John Campbell?", to which he got the reply, "Yes, I am." He described the lady as a "plump ruddy-faced good-looking woman". The couple had ordered a chaise and travelled on to Cornhill.

Two servants who had been in Elizabeth's household for the previous fourteen months testified that Elizabeth had no contact with Lord John during that time. At the time Lord John and his companion had turned up at the Cross Keys, "Lady John resided at Levenside from the 18th of June to the 9th of September last, and never slept a single night from the house during that period" – the inference being of course that Lord John's companion at the Cross Keys could certainly not have been "Lady John".

The outcome of the case, pronounced on 8th January 1808, was not surprisingly:

> *"The Commissaries having resumed consideration of this cause with the proof adduced on the part of the pursuer, find facts, circumstances, and qualifications proved relevant to infer the defender's guilt of Adultery. Find the said Defendant guilty of Adultery accordingly, therefore divorce and separate, find and declare in terms of the pursuer's lybel and decern.*

Find the pursuer entitled to the expenses of process and ordain an account to be given up."

One cannot help feeling sorry for Elizabeth, who by any standards seems to have been treated abominably not only by her husband, but by the few fleeting written references to Lord John's "bad" and "unhappy" marriage which always give the impression that its demise was due to some flaw or failure on her part. She survived another ten years after regaining her freedom, and died in 1818. Let us hope that decade of freedom brought her some recompense.

John's son, the 8th Duke, placed the first meeting of Lord John Campbell and Joan Glassell "around 1815 or 16". However, in a letter she wrote to John in September 1819,[219] Joan says, "So you won't get a picture done because you are getting 'uglier every year'. Pray how many years has this process been going on? I think it must be at most a triennial change, as you were quite as ugly I'll swear on the first of Feby1817 as you are now…". This sounds very much as if by "1st February 1817" Joan simply means "When I first saw you". In February 1817 Joan was a young woman of 20, and John at 39 was almost twice her age. He was also, as we have seen, a man with considerable marital, sexual, and possibly psychological "baggage".

However, John did have something in his favour which might have made him quite a catch in the eyes of many a young lady. He was the heir to a dukedom. When the 5th Duke of Argyll died in 1806, Lord John's elder brother George succeeded to the title and the estates. Born in 1768, George had long made his life in London, and was not one to emulate either the soldierly devotion to duty of his father or the stern Calvinism of his earlier forebears. He was one of the set of wits, dandies, and hedonists orbiting around the extravagant and selfish debauchee George Prince of Wales, or "Prinny" as he was known to his friends and hangers-on. George Campbell was Member of Parliament from 1790 to 1796 for St Germans, a notorious "rotten borough" in Cornwall, where a handful of "freemen" elected not one but two M.P.s to the House of Commons. When he succeeded to the Dukedom in 1806 George entered the House of Lords. He very seldom deigned to visit his Argyll estates, which were administered by trustees and

219 Campbell Papers Acc8508/48. Letter 8.

used as a cash cow to finance a life of leisure. He was in fact the archetypal absentee Highland landlord.

In 1810 George, then in his early 40s, married Elizabeth Villiers, daughter of the Earl of Jersey. The nuptials took place a mere three weeks after her divorce from George's friend Lord Uxbridge. The marriage produced no children, although a previous mistress, Harriet Wilson, had dumped George after discovering that he had impregnated her sister.[220]

George's nephew the 8th Duke wrote of him:

> *"Of my uncle Duke George who held the Dukedom for 35 years, I have unfortunately nothing very favourable to record. He was very handsome, of dignified and most courteous manners, and naturally of a kindly disposition. But in his early life he fell into companionship with the society which surrounded the Prince of Wales, and from sheer carelessness, idleness and want of purpose in life, did nothing but dilapidate his great inheritance. For many years he was never able to live at Inveraray, and the estate was put under trust…during all the years of my boyhood he lived always in England…".* [221]

George 6th Duke of Argyll has been described more succinctly as a "dissipated playboy"[222] and "as black and wicked a rake as ever lived".[223] The point is, that whatever his personal qualities or lack thereof, around the time that Joan Glassell and Lord John Campbell became acquainted, John's brother the Duke of Argyll had been married for several years, and the marriage was still childless. That state of affairs made it more than likely that at some point in the future John would become Duke of Argyll.

---

220 "The magnificent cheek of Harriet Wilson" – www.lifetakeslemons.wordpress.co. [Among others.]

221 Autobiography and Memoirs, 8th Duke of Argyll – Vol 1, Page 28.

222 "Stately Passions: the scandals of Britain's great houses" – Jamie Douglas Home, Michael O' Mara Books Ltd, London, 2012.

223 The Telegraph, article by Adam Nicolson, 7th August 2004.

7

"The omen of a more serious feeling"

MANY DECADES AFTER JOAN GLASSELL'S DEATH, HER SON WROTE, "My mother was not a beautiful woman in any definable sense."[224] It is difficult to understand this statement. A portrait of Joan made in her early twenties shows her to have been what any 21st century observer would instantly perceive as physically attractive. Admittedly however, the standards of what constituted a "hot babe" may have been different in the early 19th century. Physical "charms" apart, Joan had a lively and attractive personality, and was well educated and highly intelligent. She was also heiress to a considerable fortune held in trust for her. All this would most certainly make her a valuable prize in the matrimony stakes.

Only one hint remains of the attentions of what must surely have been numerous admirers. In 1825, several years after her marriage, Joan received a letter from "M. Lappenberg" in Hamburg[225] informing her of his engagement, and sketching out his career so far. He had been an envoy to the court of Prussia, and was now "Archivarius" in charge of the records of the city of Hamburg. Lappenberg muses that Joan may be "altogether indifferent" to

224 "Autobiography and Memoirs" – 8th Duke. Vol 1. Page 53.
225 Campbell Papers Acc8508/6, Letter 5.

his memory, or perhaps "may still continue to recall occasionally… the pain and sorrows that we both have been designed by mysterious Providence to inflict upon each other." He says he is "…very happy now, that the last traces of these deep afflictions are obliterated", and he only wishes to know that Joan too is happy, and hopes that one day he may have the opportunity of seeing her again. His success in his career Lappenberg attributes to "the energy excited by my former relations[226] in Edinburgh when very young for such a situation". What "pain and sorrows" Lappenberg and Joan inflicted on each other is an intriguing puzzle. Possibly Lappenberg was not an admirer after all, but a tutor – perhaps even one of Mrs Grant's "seven wise masters" – and the pains and sorrows may have been more academic than amorous. Even so, the roles of tutor and admirer are not mutually exclusive, and the tone of the letter seems to show something of the nostalgic regret of an old flame. It may be significant that Joan did not immediately bin the letter, but kept it.

As we have seen, Joan first met Lord John Campbell through her mentor Mrs Grant's friends the Smiths, probably at Rosneath. In a letter to Lord John written in 1819[227] Joan says, "I was 20 nearly before I saw your face." This would indicate a first sight of him sometime in 1816. In the same letter Joan recalls, "I mind when I was first coming to Arden[228] saying to Miss Grant who had brought me to Dumbarton, 'I would be quite happy if these men were not there. Rawdon[229] is such a stick, and as for Lord John, I'm sure he'll detest me…'." Returning after the visit, she had obviously changed her tune, and told Miss Grant that Lord John had been making her laugh "12 hours out of the 24". Miss Grant reminded her that not so long before Joan had said, "Oh that weary Lord John, I can't tell you how frightened I am for him!!!"[230] Until her first visit to Ardencaple, then, Joan had found Lord John rather intimidating, thinking him "the gravest person on earth", as she admitted in the same letter, but after getting to know him on his "home turf" she was pleasantly surprised. Could this have been the

226 i.e. social contacts and relationships.

227 Campbell Papers Acc8508/47, Letter 1.

228 Ardencaple, John's home outside Helensburgh.

229 Rawdon Clavering, son of Lord John's sister Augusta.

230 Acc8508/47, Letter 1. "Frightened for" is a Scots idiom equivalent to "frightened of" in Standard English. The three exclamation marks are Joan's.

previously mentioned meeting on 1st February 1817 when John was "quite as ugly as you are now"?

There are occasional vague references to social contact between the two after that. John and Joan were now moving in the same social circle, and invitations and meetings at the homes of mutual acquaintances would be quite natural. In her "Continental Journal", Joan wrote on 29th March 1819, "I took my skirt and observed in another place a tear that it got at Kilmun in October 1817! That was the day we were so late you thought we had pipes and whisky over Lady Augusta."[231] Writing on 7th November 1818, having seen a string of mules, Joan observed, "They reminded me of an assemblage I saw at the high dairy at Inveraray the first time I was ever up there with you, spring before last." "Spring before last" would be the spring of 1817. The indications are that during 1817 there was at least occasional contact between John and Joan, and a deepening friendship. Looking back three years later, Joan wrote to Lord John, "I think the time in all my life when my own feelings were brighter and all nature looked most beautiful to me was that time when you and Bessie Mure came back from Edinburgh in November 1817. There was a week at that time of perfect heaven after I had resolved to go to Inver."[232]

The week of "perfect heaven" was the prelude to an extended winter break at Ardencaple and Inveraray in late 1817 and early 1818, during which Joan began to realise (if she had not been aware of it before) that she had come to regard Lord John as much more than a friend. Part of a diary she kept at this time has survived in the Campbell Papers.[233] Joan did not note the month or the year, but a letter to Mrs Smith written in January 1818[234] indicates that she is writing of events more or less contemporary with the diary, and entries in her Italian journal in autumn 1818 make it plain that the diary refers to December 1817.

From the diary we learn that on Thursday 12th December Joan, Mr Lauder, Miss Mure and Lord John went up the hill behind Ardencaple. The

231 Campbell Papers Acc8508/41. Joan's journal was kept for Lord John's benefit. "You" is therefore Lord John. Kilmun is the Campbell burial place at the head of the Holy Loch.

232 Campbell Papers Acc8508/46, Letter 9.

233 Acc8508/35.

234 Acc8508/37, Letter 4.

whole firth was "in a flood of glory" while the Cowal hills were shrouded in mist. The party had music in the evening and on the following day, Friday, Joan went to Rosneath and was rowed back by Lord John. In the evening Mr Lauder sang, and Lord John whistled "For the lack o gold", and "Queen Mary". Joan wrote, "It is not in my nature to lock up my feelings, and who indeed can say to the heart, 'Thou shalt not love' and be obeyed?" On the Saturday Joan observed that Lord John was "more delightful than ever". However, the company was not all similarly delightful. "Miss C." was "cold and sarcastic", and later "very haughty". It is not absolutely clear who Miss C. was, but she may have been Miss Clavering, the daughter of Lord John's sister Augusta.

On the following day, Sunday, the party embarked at 9.15 in the morning by coach on the long journey to the Duke of Argyll's castle of Inveraray. The route lay up the east side of the Gareloch, and on up Loch Long to Arrochar at the head of the loch. From there the party followed the military road up Glen Croe, over the Rest-and-Be-Thankful, down Glen Kinglas to Cairndow at the head of Loch Fyne, and on down the west side of the loch to Inveraray Castle. Unfortunately, early on in the journey Lord John mentioned the possibility of his going abroad, thus reminding Joan that "in a few weeks' time the only light that can ever give happiness is to vanish, perhaps for ever". Joan goes on to rhapsodise in her diary over "the joy of awaking in the morning and knowing I must soon see that beloved countenance, soon hear that voice which is to my ear the soul of music". She feels that she "could live forever under the influence of that beautiful smile". Joan slept part of the way to Arrochar with her arm pressed against Lord John's heart. Ironically, at Arrochar John asked her if she felt "plagued" with him "hanging on" her. He sometimes rode, and sometimes took a seat in the carriage, where he eventually fell asleep. "I could forever have found fullness of occupation of heart and mind," Joan wrote, "gazing on that tired brow, so mild, so calm, so eloquent... How will the memory of this journey forever haunt me." The party arrived at Inveraray about five o' clock, having been on the road for nearly eight hours.

Monday featured an expedition up Glen Shira to a waterfall with Lord John and Mr Lauder. Lauder had a talent for amusing mimicry, but all Joan's attention was on Lord John, "so beautiful, so free of all bitterness and buffoonery... What an elegant creature he is!! But it is the beauty and elegance and spirit of the mind that turns within more than the beauty of that perfect form." In the evening after tea there was music in the hall. "Oh it is enchanting to stand by him and listen to music. He was more delightful than ever."

The following two days were taken up with excursions into the countryside, the first spoiled by John dwelling on his plans for going abroad. On the Tuesday also, Miss C. was "in the most freezing humour" with Joan, and on the Wednesday was "giving cuts" in the morning. This came to a head in the evening:

> *"Miss C. would scarce speak to me at night. Late in her room, such a speech. Good God, how strong above all feelings is that which can endure my spirit bear this! [sic]… Oh heavens, and how I indeed made myself odious to every creature in the house, and can I live and look up after being told in the most gross manner that I throw myself at and run after any man – and can he see too in this revolting and shocking light the natural wish I have to enjoy the conversation of the person who certainly has more mind and feeling than all the others together… There is a feeling of deep and dreadful humiliation, not in loving, for he is worthy of the warmest devoted love, but he is, alas, brother of the Duke of Argyll. I feel that my motive even by himself may be suspected. She can never know how fondly & triumphantly I would devote myself to him, were he the most obscure of his race, for he is by right of mind 'one of God's nobility'… There is something most dreadful in the first accusation of a gross misconduct, and some of the epithets she applied to me were really too dreadful. Had I been trying to wile away her own lover she could not have spoken with more vehement detestation. It was dreadful to have a bursting heart and not be able to tell anyone my wretchedness."*

The next morning, presumably still rather shaken, Joan refused to go out, and stayed in the hall while Miss C. and Miss Mure played billiards. Surprisingly however, in early evening Joan and Miss C. walked up to Carlunan Bridge by moonlight. Later there was waltzing and singing with Lord John and Mr Lauder. "He was more delightful and attentive than ever."

On Friday there was a jaunt to Furnace on horseback. If Miss C.'s hostility had been soothed by the previous evening's moonlight walk, the claws now came out again. "Miss C. sneered at me. I at last after ten said something that quieted her. She went to bed before supper." It would have been interesting, to say the least, to know what the "something" was that stopped Miss C. in her tracks, but Joan makes us none the wiser. The Duke himself joined the company later in the evening, and amused himself playing billiards. Joan made a deliberate effort to be less in John's company, but "there is such pleasure in seeing him come over to me. Was there ever an eye that could beam with such full benevolence?", and John claimed for himself a drawing Joan had made of Ardencaple. Cryptically, Joan concluded her account of the day's events, "After I went to my room her Ladyship followed me. I wrote about it." Since the Duchess of Argyll would properly have been "her Grace", "her Ladyship" is more likely to have been Lady Augusta, who had appeared to Joan "very sulky" early in the evening. If Miss C. was indeed Lady Augusta's daughter Miss Clavering, "her Ladyship" had no doubt noticed the tension between Joan and her daughter, and wanted to know what was going on. But what did Joan write? And where did she write about it?

Joan's brief journal ends on the Saturday:

> *"Preparing for the play all morning, then at Theatre for scenes. Exquisitely happy there, for he kept always by me. Can there be any joy like watching with hope signs of those we love loving us? But the delusion will be dissipated, and I much fear will leave me without the power [of] enjoying less exquisite pleasures"*

In Italy the following year, Joan wrote,[235] "I think about the happiest half hour of my life was one in the theatre at Inver on the 19th of December last. I don't know why, as many others might have been the same, but trifling circumstances in some minds make an age of happiness in a few short minutes." Elsewhere in her Italian journal Joan recalls other scenes from the fairly fraught interlude at Ardencaple and Inveraray – going to Furnace, being amused by Mr Lauder, the Duchess drinking John's health on his birthday; but significantly she also wrote,[236] "I recollect trying to shake off the impression given me on New Year's Day of a parting being the first event of a new year. I don't think any other can now cost me as much."

Joan had certainly, as the old cliché goes, *lost her heart* to Lord John, but she perceived many hurdles on the course of true love. John was a Member

235 Campbell Papers Acc8504/41. Continental Tour 31st October 1818.
236 Ibid. 1st November.

of Parliament who spent much of his time in London, and was now making plans to go abroad. He was the heir to a dukedom, and Joan, although wealthy, was certainly not of aristocratic birth. John was kind and attentive, but such was his nature, and if he was attentive to Joan was it necessarily significant? There was also the humiliating realisation that she had made her obsession with Lord John obvious to everyone, to the extent that she had been accused of throwing herself at him. Not least, he was a man of the world, verging on middle age, and Joan was very conscious of her youth and lack of sophistication. "I'll tell you what often comes into my mind, she wrote to John a year and a half later,[237] "One day in January 1818 when we were coming down the west walk of the wood, just at the Badger Knowe, and you had been making me firmly believe the most outrie nonsense, and I was in sic a fury, and said it was dreadful to be found out an idiot."

At some point in January 1818, feeling the need to confide in a friend, and possibly also to clarify her own feelings to herself, Joan wrote a letter to Mrs Smith. They had by then got to know each other well, and Mrs Smith was not so many years older than Joan. Just before her marriage Joan told Lord John that she had written the letter weeks before she dared to give it to Mrs Smith, and on the letter itself Joan later noted "To Mrs Smith first telling her. Written in January 1818. Found in the trunk I brought from Roseneath."

It seems worth giving the text of her letter in full, showing as it does the extent and force of Joan's emotional turmoil and mental anguish:[238]

> *"There is nothing I have always held in greater contempt than the childish desire of pouring out all ones feelings, of having in short something to make a confidant about. Other things too I have always held in derision and contempt, which I find I might have been more mindful on. My heart has been so very full I could have given the world to have unburdened it to you, but could never find words, as the light in which I myself view my feelings is so new to me, and to others I feel too bitterly it may appear humiliating. But indeed my dear Mrs Smith I have no fears of you judging coldly or harshly, even if it is much less if you knew all the circumstances that have attacked me insensibly. I trust quite well*

237 Campbell Papers Acc8508/47, Letter 1.

238 Acc8508/37, Letter 3.

that you see and know that I can [illegible] accustomed to speak of what I think of to those I really do love, and feeling the most perfect dependence on you, I have I know spoken 'out of the abundance of my heart' to a degree that may I fear make you think me very foolish at least. Oh my dear Mrs Smith, I fear now it will appear to you how it has always appeared to myself, a woman who says she loves any creature who has not asked her love, but consider at least the excuses – forever with a person whose character never can be appreciated till seen in domestic life; seeing and feeling the winning gentleness and kindness of his temper. But I will not say (I cannot indeed) all that gives him such dangerous fascination. I merely felt that I was happy. It was to be sure because he was very much with me, but vanity had no share in my feelings, and though I felt the effects like a constant sunshine, I never thought of his attentions as being particular. I had no anxiety for the future, no reflexion almost on the past, when some accidental mention of his going abroad made me feel I had not the same spring of independent happiness in myself I once had. However I soon forgot that the happy present would ever end. It was so customary to me to see him always near me, always delightful, that I forgot the time must soon come when the pleasure I was unconsciously making the sole one of my life would be taken from me. Miss C. and Miss Adair both spoke of my engagement with Lord John as a thing there was no doubt of, at least it was quite apparent that there was an attachment. I of course said, as was true, there was nothing between us. But the delight it gave me when Miss C. said (in answer to my saying Lord John was attentive to everyone) she knew his measure well, and never saw a man 'so undisguisedly in love', soon proved too strongly that on the truth of that assertion my happiness was staked. Miss Adair said yet more, and as I persisted in laughing it off, she desired me to say if ever a man followed anyone so constantly unless he loved them. Never were feelings so mixed as those with which I watched him after this. It was delightful to see that he did indeed forever seek me, stay by me, and often speak more seriously more of his own little-understood feelings to me rather than to anyone else, and all with a tone of confiding kindness more gratifying than a thousand direct compliments. But this was counterbalanced by the agony with which, whenever I was not just with him, I thought of my happiness hanging on any man's undeclared affection – and worse than all misery – the man the presumptive heir to a Dukedom! May no-one ever know the wretchedness of feeling that their most pure and disinterested affections may have their purity and disinterestedness doubted, and even perhaps too by the very being we feel we could forever love, tho' the most undistinguished of mankind. You cannot know what this dreadful thought has cost me. When I was with him I only thought of him as I felt him to be, the most delightful creature I ever saw, who whatever his faults have been, has still pure and warm feelings and the most serious and liberal heart. But whenever I was alone I hated myself and was wretched. But indeed they were to blame. I know that he has a sort of affection for me but it is in his nature to be kind and affectionate, and should I never see him again, I know he has never from vanity played with my affections. There has never been any parade of attention or commonplace gallantry with which I have seen men amuse themselves. All his attention seemed the involuntary impulse of the moment, and there was sometimes an embarrassment in his manner that alternately appeared to me the omen of a more serious feeling or the wish to repress it if he felt it. After they spoke to me I did sometimes feel that he gave me a look of affectionate kindness that made me for a happy moment believe that they spoke true, but should on pretence of excusing my own folly indulge in having over again [illegible] so bright that the rest of life must look dark and clouded in comparison. My dear Mrs Smith, not only from the circumstances of your already having seen into my mind do I wish to tell you, but when I was in all that doubt and misery at Inver I often thought that had I been within reach of you I would have told you all my feelings. There are so few, so very few one would not shrink from speaking to, and yet when it is bursting full it is such a blessing to have someone to tell its fullness to. I have every day determined to speak to you, as I saw you was under a wrong impression. You saw indeed that I was attached, but you imagined I know that he was too. It was dreadful tonight when you read to me "vous m'aimez, vous ne me le dites, et je soupire"[239]. How I detest how I have ridiculed the mawkish feeling sentimental love which is generally that which springs up unsanctioned, but I do feel (however my feelings may appear to some) you can make some allowance [for] the rational though strong affection that binds me to a person in whom one every hour sees something admirable and amicable,

239 You love me, you don't tell me, and I sigh.

and by living in the same house such a person gets so intimately connected with all ones ideas and feelings. To you I can confess what I little thought I ever would to any creature, that the bare idea of the separation which is now only delayed by my infatuation is misery. I do not say I will never regain the tone of mind I had before this too fascinating creature made me so dependent on him, but oh my dear Mrs Smith, there is unspeakable [illegible] in parting after such long intimacy, and being to him as if I had never been. There is no saying how I value every moment I can be near him. If you only knew him you would understand this. Then I am often miserable that from my incurable openness in shewing all my feelings, I shew my delight in him too much. I would not for worlds lose his esteem when he is gone forever. It would be hard indeed to think he should have a bad impression of me."

Joan is not always coherent, but there is no doubting the intensity of her feelings. Note that at the end of the letter she does not say "*if* I don't see him again", but "*when* he is gone forever". She seems to have convinced herself that she was fated to lose the "being she could forever love". Later, writing to Lord John[240] she recalled the day she wrote her letter to Mrs Smith, "I was in such a state I could not articulate a word even to Mrs S on the subject, and wrote in desperation a letter which I gave her and then ran down and got into the boat and crossed. It was that day that you and I tried to avoid Col. And Mrs Hastings, and you came over with me to Roseneath, dined and remained all night… I recollect fearfully well the state I was in, scarce able to drag myself up to the house at Roseneath. God only knows how I went through that dreadful parting." This seems to indicate that after leaving Inveraray, Joan had continued as a guest at John's home of Ardencaple, and parted with him at Rosneath.

Joan need not have worried. Miss C. and Miss Adair had not been wide of the mark when they observed that they had never seen a man "so undisguisedly in love". Although he had made no "parade of attention" or shown "commonplace gallantry", and had clearly made no declaration of devotion, John was indeed smitten, and was not about to let the prize slip through his fingers. Incidentally, as far as his heirship to the dukedom of

240 Campbell Papers Acc8508/37, Letter 1.

Argyll is concerned, it may have appeared as much of a handicap to him as it did to Joan. She was a wealthy heiress, and the Argyll finances were in far from good shape. If Lord John was seen to be too conspicuously in pursuit of young Miss Glassell, it was not only hardened cynics who might jump to the conclusion that his motives were more pecuniary than passionate. And of course, given his age and unimpressive sexual history, it is little wonder that he should be reticent in declaring himself unambiguously to an attractive young woman.

It is not clear what contact, if any, there was between John and Joan after the "fearful parting", but a few weeks later he sent her a cheery letter from the New Club in Edinburgh extolling the pleasures of eating "ginger nutts" in Princes Street.[241] "When will you come and eat gingerbread nutts on Princes Street?" he asked. There is also mention of a book which he tells her to send to Edinburgh when she has finished it, if she will not bring it herself. He seems to be about to leave for London, and the letter is addressed to Joan at "Ibrox near Glasgow", dated March 4th 1818. The date is written in such a way that the final "8" could easily be taken for a 6, giving the date 1816, and someone has noted on the letter in pencil, "Before the death of his first wife." This is a mistake however, as the postmark reads quite clearly "Mar 4 1818".

Nor was this a one-sided correspondence. On 28th March John wrote that he had received Joan's letter in which she had informed him that his ticket had won a prize in the "China Lottery". He tells her to keep the prize until he has the pleasure of seeing her. He is writing from Brook Street in London, and chats amicably about hearing a grand organ capable of imitating any instrument. He has been taking an interest in balloons, and hopes to build an "experimental apparatus".[242] On 6th April he writes about his intentions of joining with Sir George Cayley to have a balloon made. Joan seems to have been taking an interest in the fashionable "science" of phrenology, as John jokingly declines in his letter to "trust my unfortunate skull among the mathematicians and divines in your collection".

The next letter in this sequence is dated 9th May, also from London. John remarks slyly about Joan becoming indolent from keeping bad company at Inveraray and Ardencaple. His balloon is progressing very slowly, and he

241 Campbell Papers, Acc8508/23, Letter 1.
242 Campbell Papers Acc8508/23, Letter 2.

refers laughingly to the Argyll family as a "horrid lot" who are "somewhat more than half mad". Has Joan heard about his sister Lady Charlotte marrying her son's tutor? Duties in Argyllshire unfortunately mean that his Paris expedition must be "put off sine die", and he enquires, "How does your hopes of accompanying Mrs Smith come on?" Joan, it would seem, had left a necklace of some sort behind at Ardencaple, and had asked if John had seen it. "Truly I have the chains," he replied, "and never thought of them till I received your letter, but they are safe. I believe I shall hang them about your neck in Edinburgh rather than Paris, or if you come up, in London."

These letters are light-hearted and chatty. In spite of the "fearful parting" John and Joan are writing to each other frequently. There is still nothing in the letters to indicate anything other than friendship, so presumably both parties are playing safe by not committing themselves. John clearly has intentions of seeing her again, however, and even (Is there the merest hint of fleshly lust?) of personally hanging her chains about her neck. John's postponed Paris expedition is no doubt the trip abroad that John had been planning at Inveraray, the mention of which had distressed Joan so much. However, it is the reference to Mrs Smith which is significant.

It would seem from John's letter that as early as spring 1818 Joan had been discussing the possibility of a trip to Europe with the Smiths. It has been suggested that there had been gossip about Joan and Lord John, and that to avoid a looming scandal Joan was removed from the scene by the Smiths and taken on a long European tour.[243] However, this is predicated upon the misapprehension that Lord John was still a married man, albeit estranged from his wife; and as we know, John had been divorced by his wife Elizabeth Campbell in January 1808. Whereas divorce in England at that time was very difficult, and the Church of England extremely reluctant to recognise its validity, in Scotland marriage was regarded as a contract, not a sacrament, and divorce was relatively easier to obtain than south of the border – for those who could afford the legal process, at any rate. Thus, in the spring of 1818 Lord John was a single man, free to bestow his affections as he pleased. There may well have been tittle-tattle about Joan's "running after" Lord John, or Lord John's "attentions" to Joan, but the talking points are likely to have been his age, the rather humiliating circumstances of his divorce, and

243 Both Kirsteen Mulhern's PhD thesis and Ann Galliard's "Draft" make this suggestion.

the possibility of his being a mere fortune-hunter. The fact that his former wife was still alive in early 1818 (she died later that year) made not a whit of difference to the legal status of John's availability. It might have added spice to any circulating gossip, but was no barrier to any "intentions" Lord John may have had regarding Miss Glassell.

Rather than being spirited away by older and wiser friends to avoid a scandal, a more likely explanation is that Joan originally conceived the trip as a distraction to help her "get over" her infatuation for Lord John, or (more romantically) as a trial separation to test her feelings for him. A poem written by Joan in September 1819, which she describes as referring to September 1818,[244] portrays her saying farewell to John without yielding to "the heart's wild call" to tell him (predictable rhyme) "all".

"I dared not look on that beloved face
Without betraying all the dire disgrace
Of having given to thee, unwooed, unsought,
A heart that trust me, never could be bought!"

So as late as September 1818, on the eve of Joan's departure for the Continent, there had still apparently been no declaration of love, no commitment given. Joan still seemingly feels rather embarrassed about falling for Lord John with no open indication on his part that he is any more than a friend. In that light, it might appear that Joan, in true romantic vein, was tearing herself away in order to "forget" her heart's desire.

On the other hand, a letter to Joan from David Cathcart, who had succeeded his father as the most important of Joan's "curators", shows the European jaunt in a rather different light. It will be remembered that Joan, although a woman of 22, was still not "of age" under the terms of the entail of her landed estate and fortune. Cathcart's letter reads as follows:[245]

"My Dear Miss Glassell,
I received your letter and returned an answer in course of post under cover to Mr Norman[?] as you had not given your address. I entertained no doubt that your proposed visit to the Continent from which I had anticipated much pleasure and improvement to yourself had taken place

244 Campbell Papers Acc8508/46, Letter 8.
245 Campbell Papers Acc8508/38.

with the approbation of all your Friends, and that your communication to me was nothing more than polite information to me as one of your Curators. Of this measure I therefore wrote to you instantly what really occurred to me on the subject, most sincerely congratulating upon the prospect of so pleasant a tour. I was not personally acquainted with either Mr or Mrs Smith, but their very high respectability was well known to me from several of my friends who were upon intimate terms with them.

From some letters however which I have received last night, I am most extremely sorry to find that your friends and relations are very uneasy with your going to the Continent, and I am afraid that you had not sufficiently consulted them on the subject. Had I been in Town I certainly would have used all my endeavours to remove these impressions, and which could much more easily be done in conversation than in writing. But if I did not succeed I should certainly have tried to persuade you, not only as one of your Curators but as your sincere Friend, who on every occasion has felt the warmest interest in your welfare, not to give offence to your relations on this point. I have always expressed what I truly felt, the greatest confidence in propriety of your feelings and in the soundness of your judgment, so that I was in general ready to acquiesce in every proposal made by you, not only from my own mind generally according with yours upon most subjects, but from the high opinion I entertained of your good sense and of your good heart and intentions. When I therefore make any remonstrance against any measure proffered by you, I think that you may rely that I do so with great reluctance, and that nothing but a sense of my duty could compel me.

You will observe that my own opinion (from any information I possess) as to your going abroad with Mr and Mrs Smith is precisely the same as when I wrote to you last, but at the same time, if your relations have formed another opinion, and very decidedly so, I would not consider myself entitled to differ from them in opinion upon this point. They perhaps are unacquainted with Mr and Mrs Smith, and may not have the advantage of knowing their high character. And it is exceedingly natural and right that they should be most anxious to have you placed when in a foreign land under a Protector who in every respect enjoyed their confidence. This is a feeling I should most warmly enter into as a parent. I never doubted not only that your relations were well acquainted with Mr and Mrs Smith but had approved your plan. But whatever was my own opinion, I should certainly tell you, my Dear Lady, that you stood in that situation which required the utmost deference to the opinion of your relations, and especially in matters where your future happiness were not to be sacrificed. You have a very considerable Fortune, and providence has deprived you by the death of your Father and the very bad health of your mother of that most important protection which every lady in your circumstances so eminently requires. But your most respectable relations will do everything they can to supply as far as is in their power, the loss you have experienced, and this most important benefit must not if possible be thrown away. Indeed, I should consider it the most disastrous measure that could befall you.

Now I understand that your mother, Sir Geo B. Hepburn and your other relations are extremely grieved at the present plan of your going abroad. This I am extremely sorry for, but I am not at all surprised at it, as certainly they ought to be well acquainted with the persons to whom so near a relation is to be entrusted in a foreign country. Some reports have prevailed, which have even reached this distant quarter, of the great attentions of a person of high Rank. Perhaps the same reports may have reached them more strongly, and their feelings of propriety may have suggested it might be most unsuitable that you should go abroad, where he is most likely to be one of the party, until the truth of these reports were better ascertained, and especially when they are unacquainted with the persons under whose protection you must be placed. These reports must necessarily much exercise their anxiety.

I must therefore entreat you my good lady that you will not leave the country without the consent and approbation of your relations. And I earnestly recommend your immediately meeting both your mother and Sir Geo B. Hepburn, and that Mr and Mrs Smith should also have some communication with them. I urge this the more strongly as my co-curators view the matter in the same light with them, although I am confident their opinion would instantly be affected by that of your relations. I have been obliged to write this letter to you in a great hurry and with the house full of friends, so that you must excuse many errors which I have not time to correct. But believe me to be at all times

You most sincere friend

D. Cathcart."

Here we see the planned Continental trip from a rather different angle. Amid rumours of the "great attentions" of a "person of high rank", Joan is about to swan off to the Continent in the company of people nobody knows, with the attentive "person" a likely member of the party. Her mother, "Curators", and close relations have not been consulted, and are "very uneasy" and extremely "grieved". Cathcart's letter is couched in terms of the most tactful deference, but he makes it plain that Joan's "future happiness" (in other words, her all-important reputation for respectability) is at stake, and failure to appease her relatives would be "most disastrous". Obviously, far from the tour being organised by Joan's "Friends" to remove her from possible scandal, the planned trip has outraged them as an inevitable instigator of scandal. For all his deference and courtesy, Cathcart is in effect *ordering* Joan to seek her relatives' approval. He even manages a note of reproach at having to attend to the tiresome business when he has a house full of visitors.

Were Joan's "Friends" jumping to entirely unwarranted conclusions? Lord John, it will be remembered, had been making plans to go to Paris. Joan's European tour also included Paris on the itinerary. Perhaps they hoped, or even planned, to meet there, still pretending to each other that they were mere acquaintances. It is just possible that they had indeed concocted a deliberate plot to begin a sexual relationship in Paris, but in the light of their previous conduct, it would seem unlikely.

Whatever the underlying motives for the European tour, Joan was not stupid, and must have immediately moved to placate and reassure her family. The tour went ahead, and she remained on the best of terms with her relatives the Buchan Hepburns and Caddels, and with her "curator" Cathcart.

8

"So far, so very far, from ____"

Joan's Continental Tour began in September 1818, the intention no doubt being to avoid the overpowering heat of the Italian summer, while traversing Switzerland before the rigours of the Alpine winter. On 1st November, writing from Como to Janet, the wife of her cousin Hugh Francis Cadell of Cockenzie, Joan remarked that there had been only one rainy day since the party had set out from Dunbar.[246] It is not immediately obvious why Joan should name Dunbar as the starting point of the tour, rather than Edinburgh. We might have expected the party to proceed south by coach, but Dunbar was a seaport, so perhaps the first leg of the journey was by sea to Newcastle or some other harbour in the north of England. Certainly, by 19th September Joan was in Harrogate, as she recalled in a letter to Lord John a year later, and two weeks after arriving in Harrogate she crossed the Channel to Calais.[247]

After a very short stay in Paris, the party proceeded to Geneva and

246 Intimate Society Letters of the Eighteenth Century, Ed. The Duke of Argyll. Vol. 2, John Lane Company, New York, 1910, Page 631.
247 Campbell Papers, Acc8508/46, Letter 15.

Lausanne, then over the Simplon Pass and on to Como and Milan. Leaving Milan on 5th November Joan and the Smiths travelled on to Genoa, embarked there for Lerice by boat, then travelled by carriage to Lucca and on to "Leghorn" (Livorno). After a day of sightseeing in Pisa the party arrived in Florence on 18th November. The sights and social round of Florence detained them until 22nd December when they set off on the long journey to Rome.

The party spent two months in Rome, from 28th December 1818 until 27th February 1819, before travelling on to Naples, which they reached on 2nd March. After spending a fortnight there they headed back to Rome where they remained until 13th April. Travelling by way of Florence and Bologna the party reached Venice on 5th May. After a few days in Venice and Padua Joan and her companions proceeded by Verona and Milan to Turin, and on through Savoy, reaching what was then the frontier of France on 22nd May. The last stages of their journey took them to Lyon, and on to Paris, where they arrived on 29th May 1819. In another letter to Janet Cadell, dated 17th June, Joan informs her, "We leave on Monday next for Calais by Beauvais."[248] By the time Joan left Calais she would have spent nearly ten months abroad.

Joan was the guest of James Smith and his wife Mary. Smith was aged around 36 in 1818. As a wealthy, well-educated and mature man of leisure, he would be responsible for planning the itinerary and for making the travel arrangements. At the time of the tour the Smiths had three surviving children (although they were to have several more subsequently): Christina, born 9th July 1810, Archibald born 10th August 1813, and Isabella born 12th December 1814. An infant son had died the previous year.[249] Apparently the Smiths brought their family with them on their European tour. An acquaintance of Joan's writing to her on 22nd February while Joan was in Rome, asks to be remembered to Mr and Mrs Smith "and the dear children",[250] and elsewhere in the course of her travels Joan makes mention of "Christina" and "the children". Joan was accompanied by her maid "Aitken". There was also "poor Young" whose duties are never made clear, nor is it obvious whether he was Joan's servant or the Smiths'. Possibly he served in the capacity of a valet to Mr Smith. Mrs Smith would

248 Intimate Society Letters, Vol 2, Page 645.

249 Website www.clanmacfarlanegenealogy – James Smith of Jordanhill.

250 Campbell Papers Acc8508/38. Emmeline Cairns to Miss Glassell, 22nd February 1819.

undoubtedly be accompanied by a maid, and there would almost certainly be female assistance for the Smith children. The party, therefore, was large enough to travel in "carriages" rather than in a single coach. Some stages of the tour were undertaken with a courier, and in many places local guides were hired.

The main source providing the details of Joan's continental tour is the journal she kept during her travels, which can be found in the Campbell Papers in the National Library of Scotland,[251] and once its jumbled sequence has been mastered, it provides a clear and fascinating account of the tour with insightful comments from Joan on all she saw, and her thoughts on much else besides. The diary is written as if kept for the benefit of some reader other than Joan, and it quickly becomes obvious that this is Lord John Campbell, although he is never named. Despite the fact that at times Joan seems to have believed that John was "lost forever", there are many references to her hopes that she will see him in Paris at the end of her tour. She later claimed to John that her diary was "never meant to be for shew",[252] even to Mrs Smith ("the only thing we quarrel'd once about and she took the pet at it"), but she did indeed eventually show it to him, and in fact it is very probable that the reason she refused to let Mrs Smith read it was because it was so full of obvious allusions to Lord John.

Joan's son wrote towards the end of his life, "The Smiths of Jordanhill invited my mother to accompany them on a visit to Rome… her letters are full of the most lively and varied interest in Nature and in art and show great power of expression, and an enthusiastic and poetic temperament." Comparing his mother's letters to his father's, he comments that her letters show "perhaps a much more highly emotional disposition, perhaps a wider range of interests and certainly a much greater facility and copiousness of expression."[253]

On 18th November 1818 Joan's mentor Mrs Grant wrote to her "dear friend" Mrs Smith, mother of Joan's travelling companion, that her daughter

251 The journal is in two sections in the Campbell Papers – Acc8508/40 and Acc8508/41. However, as currently archived, the journal is presented in a rather disordered state. In sequence of time most of Acc8508/41 actually precedes Acc8508/40. The various bundles in Acc8508/41 are not in sequence, and the entries for 19th-27th May in Acc8508/41 rightly belong near the end of Acc8508/40.

252 Campbell Papers Acc8508/48, Letter 8. 2nd Sept 1819.

253 Autobiography and Memoirs – George Douglas 8th Duke of Argyll, Dutton &Co, New York, 1906, Page 54.

Moore "hears often from Miss Glassell". Never one to miss an opportunity for what nowadays might be regarded as mannered literary posturing, Mrs Grant allows that Joan's letters from abroad

> *"are very amusing, but, in substance, I think, much like those you receive, though the same objects may be more forcibly portrayed in her energetic, though careless language. It is in that negligence of order and precision that much of the merit of her epistolary style consists; not that careless rapidity in itself constitutes merit, but that it prevents certain demerits that distort or flatten the style of those who would be thought fine writers. Her fluency is not merely that of words, it is that of a fervid mind kindled by powerful emotion that speaks more to relieve itself than to inform, far less dazzle others: in short it is unstudied and original, amply compensating for the want of that elegance which is now become too cheap for admiration."*

Unfortunately almost all of Joan's letters from abroad seem to be now lost, but all the above observations from Mrs Grant and Joan's son could apply as much to the journal of her European tour as to her letters. Joan's handwriting is atrocious, and her punctuation erratic, but there is no denying her powers of expression, and her writing is indeed lively, enthusiastic and fluent. Perhaps too many scenes and occasions are "delicious" and "delightful", and she is obviously much influenced by romanticism and its grand panjandrum Byron, but we can forgive her the clichés of her day, and be thankful that she was not too much constrained by "order and precision".

It is clear from Joan's journal that she often suffered from homesickness, although in her mind "home" seems to have become not so much her native East Lothian and Edinburgh as the hills and sea lochs of Argyll and the Clyde. It would seem that she and John had agreed not to write to each other – an agreement which John broke, contacting her after she had been gone for two months. In a letter to him after her return to Scotland she recalled that she was "alive only after the 28th of Nov." which is when she received the first communication from him.[254] The journal is full of references to anticipating or receiving "home letters", and many are the expressions of disappointment or joy felt at the appearance or absence of a letter from

254 Campbell Papers Acc8508/48, Letter 8, 2nd Sept 1819.

the "you" addressed in the journal's pages. "I recollect the day well," Joan later wrote, "Mrs Smith thinking me drunk when she found me sitting up in bed combing my hair with my fingers and half mad with fear and joy... every letter from you, Dearest, left a brightness like a setting sun... and a midnight darkness had always gathered over me before another came."[255] And again, in another letter around the same time, reminiscing about her tour, Joan admitted, "God knows how bitterly I often felt when away from you... Oh, it was dreadful often."[256] Despite the many and varied marvels of Italy and the Alps, and despite the manifest fascination the exotic and unfamiliar held for Joan, nothing could for long distract her from the fact that all that was most important to her was far away. If the object of the tour had been to test the bond between Joan and John, it was an undoubted success. The bond was tested, strengthened, and made permanent.

Joan's journal begins in the Franche-Comté, in the foothills of the Jura Mountains. It is likely that there was a preceding section, now missing. Joan was writing in her room which opened off a gallery round the courtyard of an inn, probably in the town of Dole. She concluded the entry, "I feel especially now awakened to the reality of being indeed so far, so very far, from ___ ."[257] The following day, 20th October 1818, the party set off by coach, and from a hill above Dole had "a most glorious view of the whole of Franche Conté and Burgundy." The final post of the day's journey to Poligny was through a forest where they were told there were "multitudes of wolves".

From Poligny they ascended a mountain pass hundreds of feet above a valley bedecked with fine autumn colours, surrounded by "perpendicular mountains covered in gigantic pines". Joan began to attempt sketching the mountain scenery, although it is obvious from her later remarks that she had little talent in that direction. By 22nd October she was in Geneva. "We have seen Mont Blanc! ... I attempted two or three sketches, but I am a very bungler." Part of that day's journey had taken the travellers far above the clouds – "an ocean of white clouds" with "eternal snows towering above them". Joan was awestruck: "I was utterly unprepared for the sublimity of this most overpowering spectacle." But in the face of the sublime, the ridiculous is never far away. Joan's tomboy youth came to the fore, and where

255 Ibid Acc8508/46, Letter 22. Undated, probably 1820.

256 Ibid Acc8508/46, Letter 21. February 1820.

257 The blank is Joan's. She is almost certainly referring to Lord John.

the road descended through a tunnel in the rock, she "tried the effect of Queen Mary's Lamentation whistled under the arch".

In Geneva Joan met a M. and Mme. Saussure who had known John during his youthful Swiss exile. However, she "could not for my life find courage to speak to Madame in French". At the Saussures' home Joan met several guests including an Englishman "hot with the mania for everything Scotch", no doubt under the influence of "Ossian" and Walter Scott. Leaving Geneva on a "grey Gare Loch looking morning", the travellers proceeded to Lausanne, where in the evening Joan walked up a hill with Mr Smith to view a glorious sunset. The lakeside scenery reminded her of the Cowal coast on the Clyde. "I have seen scenes there quite as enchanting as anything we have yet seen," she remarked rather sourly.

From Lausanne the party followed the River Rhône. "I attempted a sketch," Joan admitted, "but there's such poverty in all the things I do, when I look at the glowing beauty of the original it quite discourages me." Near Sion they passed the scars of a disastrous avalanche which had destroyed 250 houses four months previously with the loss of a hundred lives. At Brig where they stopped for breakfast, Joan stumbled on the kitchen of the inn, "The nearest thing to the infernals I ever saw, round a peat fire in the middle, demon looking figures as black as soot and many with enormous goitres busily employed boiling milk etc. for us… and what with the darkness and dirtiness it was the most unappetising place I ever saw."

On 29th October, Joan's party, consisting of "three coaches and a wild goose string of horses", began the ascent to the Simplon Pass, climbing by "endless turnings", with gigantic mountains rising on the far side of the Rhône, the Jungfrau towering high above the rest. Glaciers were visible above "this glorious path across fathomless gulphs and along precipices overhung by vast rocks". There was a rather farcical incident later that day when Joseph, the party's courier, and the servant of a fellow traveller rolled a large tree trunk down the slope from the roadside. A band of ferocious looking woodcutters suddenly appeared from nowhere, seized Joseph, and seemed inclined to hurl him down after the log. However, tempers were soothed and the matter settled by the payment of a fine of 10 sous. The town of Simplon was reached in time for dinner, at which they were joined by two Scots travellers, a Mr Loch of Ratho, and MacNeill of Ugadale.

Passing over the watershed early next morning, Joan and her fellow adventurers descended the valley of the Divedro, where there was "no trace of life for many miles" until the wild and barren landscape developed into "the softness and beauty of this first and lovely Italian valley", and after Domodossola Joan began to see mulberry trees, vines, and fields of Indian corn, with hill villages and tiny chapels "perched like eagle nests above". Lake Maggiore, Joan observed, was lovely "but not as lovely as the Gare Loch". After an excursion by boat through the Borromean Islands of Lake Maggiore, the party arrived in Bavena,[258]

On 31st October Joan and her companions proceeded to Como, by way of Varese, in the company of "the most bandit-looking postilion I ever saw", who nonetheless turned out to be civil and intelligent, and able to speak good French. Joan seems to have been reasonably fluent in French, although as she admitted in Geneva, initially shy about using it. By the end of her Italian trip she had also acquired a fair command of Italian. Joan was impressed by the beauty of Lake Como, which reminded her of Loch Long, apart from the fact that on the steep sides of Lake Como "where a human foot can tread, are palaces, villages and vineyards". She commented that it was better to have the Alps behind her than before her, but alas, "they are between us and home". The following day after a visit to the cathedral and a walk through the streets of Como, Joan had a severe fit of "home seekness", remembering New Year at Inveraray and her sad anticipation of her immanent parting from Lord John.

After Como the tour continued to Milan through well-populated countryside, on roads busy with carriages, "diligences", and carts drawn by oxen and mules. All the ploughing in the roadside fields, Joan observed, was being done by oxen. Milan was a whirl of sightseeing and socialising – the opera, Leonardo da Vinci's "Last Supper", and the Cathedral with its tomb of St Charles, its "magnificence beyond description", and innumerable paintings and statues. Among the latter was a representation of St Bartholomew holding his skin. This, Joan acknowledged, was a masterpiece, but "Can anything be more absurd than a man standing upright in a firm and graceful posture with his skin thrown round him as drapery?"

Joan's party seemed to excite much curiosity on the streets of Milan. "I think it must have been our tartans, as strangers can be no rarity here," she mused. They visited a workshop to see mosaics being made, and a shed

258 Probably "Bavena". Joan wrote what looks like "Levano". Her spelling of Italian names can be erratic, and occasionally requires the reader's best guess.

where a now redundant tribute to Napoleon had been stored, consisting of a statue of Bonaparte himself, with his ministers and generals, attended by classical gods and goddesses. Joan's party had once again run into their "Scotch friends" Loch and MacNeill. "Mr Loch was much scandalised at my refusing to put my foot on his [Bonaparte's] head," Joan observed. "His feelings to him are childish and cowardly."

After two days in Milan the party set off for Genoa, which they reached on 10th November, travelling by way of Pavia, Novi, and Voltigno(?).[259] In Pavia, where there was nothing "the least worth seeing", Joan noted that "I began to attempt Italian today. I must endeavour to lay my head to it." On the way to Voltigno they dined at Tortona. Attracted by "some splendid picture frames", Mrs Smith entered a room in the inn to inspect them. "The smell was so dreadful she is quite sure she has got some fever from it." This stage of the journey seems to have been considered perilous (apart from foul odours that is). "We are now in the land of danger and suspicion," Joan commented. The courier Joseph had taken to wearing a sword and pistols, and their lodgings at Voltigno had a huge guard dog on a chain at the foot of the stair, much to the terror of Joan's maid Aitken. The travellers left in the morning in the company of a party of dragoons escorting a "treasure caliche". They made an impressive sight – the "treasure caliche" with driver and postilions, "the mounted dragoons with their enormous hats cloaks and carabines, our courier with a military looking cap, great surtout, a sword and pistols, then my caliche and the carriage behind". Seated on the "dicky" of the coach beside the driver was a soldier who had accepted a lift from the party. Joan was favourably impressed by his refusing a tip when it was offered by Mr Smith. Of the multitudes of natives encountered on the way, said Joan, every one of them could have sat as models for a picture of bandits.

Joan sailed from Genoa on 10th November, entered the Gulf of Spezia next morning, and disembarked at Lerice. The party travelled on to Lucca, stopping to view the marble workshops at Carrara. The inn at Lucca provided "beautiful rooms with every comfort, wax candles, and a band of 24 men serenading us." They were attended by "a nice mulatto boy who is waiter here and very anxious to display his English." Reaching "Leghorn" (Livorno) on 13th November Joan found most of her expected letters from home had been sent on to Florence. What remained was of little interest,

259 Joan appears to write "Voltigno", but I have been unable to find it.

apart from one from "Lady R." who mentioned that Lord John had been looking ill. Joan reacted to this piece of news with five lines in her journal which were later heavily deleted, rendering her thoughts on the matter totally illegible.

In Livorno Joan witnessed a service in a synagogue attended by "fine looking Greek and Turkish Jews in the costume of their country". She also attended the theatre. The play was "Saul", and "David strumming on his harp was by far the most miserable and childish exhibition I ever saw. There were many Turks and Greeks in the house, and tho' the Jews' Sabbath, half the boxes filled with their black visages." Joan made the acquaintance of an American couple, Mr and Mrs Carnes, who had been at "a Jews' party with their Consul, and saw the most extraordinary assemblage of all nations, the ladies dressed splendidly, blazing with diamonds and gold. The barbarians from Africa danced quadrilles and waltzes beautifully. Poor Mrs C. was taken for a Turk or Algerine. Someone spoke Arabic to her. The two nieces of the gentleman of the house were beautiful women and spoke French perfectly." No doubt Mrs C. from race-conscious America was mortified at being taken for an Arab, yet we should not necessarily read antisemitism into Joan's references to "black visages" and "barbarians", but rather a delighted appreciation of the exotic. On seeing a large Turkish ship unloading in the docks, she observed, "Her crew and the other wild looking figures constantly passing made the view very gay looking and interesting."

On 16th November Joan and her fellow travellers moved on to Pisa. On the way the courier Joseph ordered Joan's coach driver to speed up. He immediately took off at full gallop and "would inevitably have broken everything to atoms", had not Joseph sped after him with drawn sword, and with "furious threats" made him bring the coach to a standstill. The night before, Joan had dreamed of home, and once again three lines of her thoughts on the matter were heavily deleted. The whole of the following day was spent in seeing the sights of Pisa, after a night when Joan was "half eaten by mosquitos". She noted, "Fortunately my face was covered. Had it been blistered as my hand is, I must have laid in bed or worn a mask." She saw the Cathedral, Baptistry, Leaning Tower, and Campo Santo burial ground, which she learned had been filled with earth from the Holy Land. Their guide around the sights of Pisa was a man whose card pronounced him "antiquary and valet de chambre", and Joan observed, "To us this seems an incongruous mixture, and rather odd to see a man carrying away the breakfast things and then talking familiarly and with such a degree of judgment of the great masters, works of art, and the glory of a land now indeed too like a dream."

The next stage of the tour took the travellers to Florence, where they remained for over a month, from 18th November to 22nd December. Florence was of course one of the finest jewels in the crown of European civilisation, and familiarity with the city and its wonders counted as a prestigious qualification in the drawing rooms of Enlightenment Edinburgh. Joan's first journal entry in Florence declares, "We have been here two days doing nothing but seeing sights." Over a week was devoted to visiting galleries, churches, "innumerable palaces", appreciating works by Rafael, Leonardo, and Michaelangelo, and a "vast" collection of paintings of the Florentine school. Joan attended the opera, and an Italian production of "The School for Scandal" which she had also seen performed in Edinburgh three weeks previously. Alas, this time "the acting was wretched, Charles a vulgar monster, the others little better, and all sticks". She also visited the sculptor Bertolini, and "saw busts of nearly every English person who has been to Florence", and full sized sculptures of Eleanora, one of the daughters of Lord John's sister Charlotte, and two younger daughters Emma and Julia. "Emma is beautiful!" Joan enthused. (This piece, incidentally, supposedly portraying the Campbell sisters dancing a waltz, can be seen today in the National Gallery of Scotland in Edinburgh.)

Joan's party had been befriended by an Italian gentleman named Ombrosi, and they ran into Lord John's nephew Walter Campbell (another of Lady Charlotte's many offspring) with a Major McPherson who told them John's other nephew Rawdon Clavering was also in town. Rawdon found a house for them to rent, the Casa (or Palazzo) San Clementi, with "splendid" rooms, a fine garden, and commanding a marvellous view of Fiesole, the Appenine Mountains, and part of Florence. Joan had a small room decorated with frescoes and looking out into the garden. The house also had historical associations, for as Joan noted, "Our unfortunate Prince[260] lived here for some part of a life that once promised brighter days", and the emblems of the thistle and the rose were painted on the doors.

All was not well with Joan, however. Her first journal entry in Florence

260 "Bonnie Prince Charlie" – Charles Edward, the "Young Pretender".

has eight lines of one page and six of the next heavily deleted. The next entry mentions the arrival of a packet of letters, including one from John's sister Lady Augusta, and this entry also has five lines heavily deleted. After moving into their new quarters, Joan's party visited "Lord Bor"[261] in the evening. "Misery, misery," commented Joan, "how I hated it." As already mentioned in the previous chapter, Joan referred to "wretched Florence" in a letter the following year.[262] The problem was of course that in spite of all the marvels of Florence, and the round of visits, calls, and social occasions, she was homesick and depressed by her separation from John. It seems she had told John not to write to her, but with typical human inconsistency, spent months thereafter hoping that he would. Then on 28th November letters arrived, including a "stray one" from Lord John.

Joan later wrote that she was "alive only after the 28th of November",[263] and what undoubtedly brought her to life was John's "stray letter". This is likely to be his letter to Joan of 11th November, later included in "Intimate letters of the 18th century",[264] in which John expresses the hope that Mr Smith will continue to write to him during the Italian tour, even if Joan herself keeps to her "resolution of not writing". He continues,

> *"Perhaps I have done wrong in writing this letter to you after what you said in the last you wrote to me, but in the one I wrote to you from Riddlehowhope I told you that if you really wished me to write no more to you, you must say so in so many words and then I would plague you no more, so I shall obey your commands whatever they may be, and now I shall bid you farewell my dear Miss Glassell, begging you to believe me always*
>
> *Your sincere and affectionate friend*
>
> *J. D. Campbell."*

Joan recorded the arrival of another letter from John on 10th December. "You wish me to write," she exclaimed delightedly, and the following day wrote in her journal, "From this my journal will be less as a letter as I can

261 Possibly Lord Burghersh, the British representative in Florence.

262 Campbell Papers Acc8508/37, Letter 2.

263 Ibid Acc8508/48, Letter 8.

264 264 "Intimate society letters…": Ed. The Duke of Argyll. Vol 2, John Lane Company, New York, 1910.

write you direct." From then on they seem to have corresponded as regularly as vagaries of the postal system would allow.

The days now passed with sightseeing and socialising at a more relaxed pace. The party's new Italian friend Ombrosi was constantly attentive. Joan thought he had "all the reality of Scotch kindness with Italian politeness", although it was not long before she was writing, "Mr Ombrosi came in and I thought would never go away," and rather more forcefully, "Oh heaven be good to us, here is Mr Ombrosi again!" Joan was taking lessons from an "Italian master", went shopping, saw the ascent of a balloon, paid calls, and received visitors. Mr Smith befriended a Roman artist. "He seems a sneaking toadeater," Joan commented acidly, "and so desperately assiduous he must have some prospect of making *Milord Anglais* pay for all the fine things he says to him."

On the morning of 22nd December Joan's sojourn in Florence came to an end, and the party "left the Casa San Clementi about half past ten", reaching Poggibonsi on the road to Rome at sunset. The following day they continued by way of Sienna to Buonconvento, stopping in Sienna to view the cathedral. Joan was impressed there by a small sculpture of Christ by Michalangelo, and another of "The Graces" in the sacristy, one of whom looked surprisingly like her Edinburgh acquaintance Mrs Fletcher.

Writing on 24th December in Radicofani, Joan began that day's entry, "This is your birthday my dear...". She had walked several miles that day picking up geological specimens, and remarked in her journal, "You once had a passion for chappin stanes." That night there was a tremendous storm which was still raging as they set off in the morning. "The mules could scarce go on, and crossing a long gully in the mountains it was such a hurricane I thought the caliche would have blown over the precipice." Eventually the barren countryside became well cultivated and the road improved greatly. While the carriages were delayed at the border post of the Papal States, Joan walked on with the Smith children. She struck up conversation, presumably in Italian, with an old woman who pointed out all the features of interest in the landscape, and, saying that it was a very cold day for children to be out, produced a "little stoneware stove from under her plaid, and insisted on Christina warming her hands on it". She also met a bearded Franciscan friar who complimented her on her Italian, and seemed to be under the impression that Scotland was a Catholic country. As they parted he gave Joan a blessing, which she thought "though a heretic, will at least do me no ill".

Driving along the shores of Lake Bolseno they entered the town of the same name, where they were to spend the night. When they arrived at the inn, Mr Smith found the door of his room locked, and tried to force it, causing the landlady to scream at him "in no very gentle tone". As their hostess later became "all sweetness" Joan presumed that their courier Joseph had subsequently made her aware of the travellers' "dignity". In her room that night, Joan was "assailed by flees and mice". "After fighting with the first, my long walk made me fall asleep in spite of them, when a riot among the rats in the loft above awoke me. And then I heard the colony of mice in my bed running races with all their might... To prevent them coming over my face I made Aitken light the candle, and I soon left them to amuse themselves and forgot their existence to take a voyage to Scotland", (where as some small compensation, she dreamed about Lord John).

As for the town of Bolseno, although the lake was "bright in glorious sunshine" the following morning, the streets were "narrow, abominably dirty, smelling of garlic, and all contrived to hide the beautiful views around". Joan made little mention of the fact that it was Christmas Day, noticing only that the shops were decorated for the occasion. Of course, Joan had been raised in Presbyterian Lowland Scotland, where little heed was paid at the time to such quasi-Romanist fripperies.

From Bolseno the travellers proceeded to Viterbo, where Joan and Christina visited a shrine containing the perfectly preserved body of a saint, their courier Joseph having urged the attendant nun to open up the chapel specially for the "Signora Inglese". The night of 27th December was spent in Bracciano, only eighteen miles from Rome. Joan wrote in her journal that evening, "I always feel as if I am really telling you things, tho' you may never get it." "You" of course is Lord John. Of the journal itself she remarked, "If the malaria get hold of me on our return I shall certainly wish Mrs S. to give it to you, though I confess I don't think you would wade through it all." On the following day, 28th December 1818, the party arrived in Rome.

Rome is almost completely missing from Joan's journal. Either she did not keep a record of the two months spent there, or if she did, the entire section has been lost. Instead, the next part of Joan's chronicle begins in Velletri on 27th February 1819. It quickly becomes clear that in Rome Joan had become very friendly with Lady Charlotte Campbell, John's sister. Charlotte was a widow, the mother of a large family, who had caused something of a scandal by her recent marriage in Florence to Edward Bury, a penniless Anglican clergyman and talented artist, who had been tutor and travelling companion to her adult son Walter. Bury was not only a mere middle-class nobody, but was much younger than Charlotte, and was suspected by the Argyll family of being a calculating fortune hunter. The newlyweds therefore considered it prudent to continue to live abroad for the foreseeable future.

Joan relates how she had set off from Rome on 25th February, but the weather was so atrocious that the party turned back. The previous evening Lady Charlotte had expressed her dismay at Joan's planned departure, as she would have liked to keep her for another day to help her to arrange her papers. Joan wrote, "I was beyond measure delighted to do anything for her and have another day with her." The following day she did indeed arrange a "great heap" of papers for Lady Charlotte, and after finally departing on the 27th confided to her journal, "Leaving Lady Charlotte was like a second parting from home and all that I have loved. She has been the only sunshine I have seen in Italy. What would I give that I could stay and be with her as she wishes. It would be the delight of my life." While describing her last day in Rome Joan makes mention of giving advice to "Beau", whose "simplicity" was likely to make her vulnerable. "Beau" was Harriet Charlotte Beaujolois Campbell, another of Lady Charlotte's daughters, who would be newly sixteen at the time of Joan's visit. It is not beyond the bounds of possibility that Joan did indeed keep up her journal during her Roman interlude, but being on such intimate terms as she obviously was with Lady Charlotte and her family, what she wrote may later have been judged rather too revealing. It may therefore have been quietly disposed of.

From Velletri Joan's party journeyed through the "utter dreariness" of the Pontine Marshes, and spent the night in Terracina, where the waves of the sea washed the walls of the inn, and their landlord was said to be "a captain of banditti, and looks like it". "I wish I could draw him as the model of a ruffian," said Joan.

The party left Terracina early on 1st March. Joan was had just been thinking how much the countryside looked like Argyll when her maid Aitken remarked, "Mem, is na this like coming from Inveraray?" They were detained some time at the Neapolitan frontier for passports and Joan whiled away the time by picking up pieces of crystal and ironstone from the road. In the inn at Santa Agata that night a "very rough looking figure" who came into the dining room proved to be "Johnny Bell the surgeon from

Edinburgh", and as an interesting indication of the condition of the inn's bedding "a sort of thing like a balloon frame was placed over the brazier in the public room when we arrived to dry the sheets".

Joan arrived in Naples on 2nd March and took up quarters in the Largo del Castillo, "out of sight of the sea", where the landlady was an Englishwoman. The party spent a fortnight in the city, and perhaps this was the part of her tour that Joan found most stimulating. "I never in five days saw so much that was interesting," she wrote on 14th March.

The first thing Joan did on arrival in Naples was to send off a letter to her mother. This is the first mention of her mother in the journal. Indeed, in the journal and in Joan's correspondence in general, references to her mother are almost entirely absent. We can perhaps understand that there should be little mention of her father, who had been dead for many years, but it is strange that her mother should be such a shadowy figure. "Shadowy" in fact seems almost too solid a term to describe someone who seems to have been absent from Joan's thoughts, and to all appearances missing from her life.

Joan began her first full day in Naples by going for a drive around the bay. Later she went to visit American friends encountered earlier on her tour. She found they had climbed Vesuvius to the very brink of the crater, and they showed her pieces of lava into which coins had been stuck while it was still hot and soft. Next day she saw the royal palace with its fine collection of pictures, and was shown round by the Prince himself, whose identity she had not at first realised, taking him for a "young coxcomb". On 5th March the party went to Pompeii and Herculaneum, and Joan explored the excavated "long lines of streets sometimes opening to splendid squares". She noted that an apothecary's shop had been excavated a month before and "quantities of instruments found". The shops and houses seemed to her very small. Joan picked up an ancient button. Her guide told her he was supposed to confiscate it, but "had not the heart". At Herculaneum Joan spoke to "Salvatore the Vesuvius guide", who said he had just sent off some geological specimens to Sir Humphrey Davy, and asked if Joan perhaps knew "Signore Playfair".

Joan ran into a Mrs Barclay whose acquaintance she had made in Scotland, dined with her two days later, and the pair agreed on an expedition to Vesuvius. Thus, on 9th March a party consisting of Joan,

Mrs Barclay, Mr and Mrs Smith, and three acquaintances of the Smiths, disembarked from carriages at Portice at the foot of the volcano, and were immediately surrounded by a crowd of men and boys each with a mule or donkey. However, Salvatore, the overseer, already had "a very nice ass with a sidesaddle" prepared for her. She suspected he thought her a kindred spirit after their conversation about mineral specimens at Herculaneum. When they were all suitably mounted the party proceeded up a very rough path between vineyards. Preferring to walk, Joan dismounted, and her guide Phillippe "a fine boy about 16" began picking up geological specimens for her and collecting them in a large canvas bag she had brought for the purpose. Wine and provisions had been sent on to a Hermitage where "the great cone was now rising black and perpendicular very near us". During a volcanic eruption only two months previously the lava flow had gone around the Hermitage leaving it untouched. The party decided to press on, and eat on the way down. At the foot of the final ascent to the crater they mounted on mules waiting ready for them. The slope now before them was "formidable" and "the mountain was now and then uttering a low groan which rather shook Mrs Barclay's courage".

Once again Joan dismounted, preferring to pick her way up the slope with the aid of a stick. They continued along the edge of a four week old lava flow which was still warm and smoking. Meanwhile, there was "considerable noise and often blasts from the crater", and suddenly "a fine explosion with stones falling quite near". Towards the summit "the heat as we got near the lava crater was intolerable", as were the fumes of sulphur. A small crater was throwing up stones, and streams of red hot lava cold be seen from the main crater. Some gentlemen above her shouted to Joan to come up. "I went up, and certainly the mouth of the infernal pit could scarce look more terrible." She felt no fear (she claimed), but the fumes, the heat, and the difficulty of keeping her feet urged a quick retreat. From the highest point on the mountain Joan could see Naples, the bay, and the islands, with the result of the eruption that had overwhelmed Pompeii resembling "a calm black sea petrified". "We here looked literally into the crater," Joan later recorded, "and were fortunate in some fine bursts while we were up, the steam issuing all around us on the slope... I never felt fear except when I unwilling [sic] agreed to venture among those chimneys from the infernals, and fresh holes were falling in all around us and streams of vapour coming up... Never could I have imagined anything so magnificent. Going to see the crater is a boast." Obviously "Health and Safety" rules for tourists were rather more lax in the early 19th century than nowadays.

Joan descended quickly, and remounted her mule. At the Hermitage some of the party suggested going back up, but Joan "joined with Mrs B. in enforcing homeward orders", and the party moved on, with "a glorious sunset behind Ischia, the bay a flood of gold". Joan's donkey boy Phillippe "was very urgent with me to take him to England", but alas, he "ended I believe in stealing my bag with my stones. I never was more vexed than when I arrived and found my stones all gone."

After the Vesuvius expedition several blank pages follow in Joan's journal, but on 14th March she went to see the ascent of a balloon, which rose to a "vast height" before being landed skilfully on a vessel flying a white flag in the bay. The following day Joan pretended she was going to visit Mrs Barclay, but in reality hired a coach and a servant from her hotel and returned to Vesuvius. In spite of her former comments on his honesty, she re-engaged Phillippe, and ascended as far as the Hermitage, where the hired servant, "a fine intelligent creature" was soon "well loaded" with geological specimens. Back in Naples, she went shopping with Mrs Barclay, and arranged to have her stones shipped home.

On 16th March Joan's party left Naples, calling at Caserta, the King's colossal palace, where Joan had a misadventure with a "gazelle-like" animal in the palace grounds. Two or three of them, "the size of a small roe deer with black spiral horns" were grazing peacefully, and Joan walked towards another which was lying down. It rose and slowly approached her. She held out her hand to the seemingly friendly beast, when suddenly "he made a run at me with such force with his horns, he hurt my leg excessively and renewed the attack". Joan managed to seize the animal's horns, and hung on until help arrived. She seems to have been only bruised rather than wounded, and was apparently none the worse for the incident. The party travelled on by Santa Agata, Terracina, and Velletri, and reached Rome again on 19th March.

Joan remained in Rome until 15th April. She found a letter from John awaiting her, dated 27th February, and wrote in her journal, "How grateful I am to you for writing me so soon to tell me of my mother." The news, presumably, was of her mother's final illness, but Joan made no further comment. Surely Joan's relationship with her mother cannot have been so distant that her ill health was of little consequence, but all the same her detachment is noticeable. By contrast, she went immediately to see John's sister Lady Charlotte, causing "uproar" when she arrived unannounced. "I love to be missed, you know," she wrote, "so of course a hearty welcome is not thrown away on me."

Charlotte was the younger daughter of the 5th Duke of Argyll, born on 28th January 1775. In her youth she was considered a great beauty, as her mother had been before her. At the age of 21 she married her kinsman Colonel John Campbell, bearing him nine children before his death in 1809. After her husband's death Charlotte was appointed lady in waiting to Caroline Princess of Wales, who was increasingly at odds with her debauched and unpredictable husband the Prince Regent, the future George IV. Charlotte travelled abroad with the Princess until she deemed it wise to detach herself from her increasingly scandalous mistress. In 1817 she went to live in Italy with the younger members of her family, and the following year, as already mentioned, married the Rev Edward Bury. Charlotte, although over forty and the mother of many children, was still a very physically attractive woman, albeit perhaps a little "Rubenesque" for modern slimline tastes. She had already by this time published a novel and a book of poetry. She went on to publish many more novels, and a long poem "The three great sanctuaries of Tuscany" illustrated by her husband Bury. It was common knowledge that she was also the anonymous author of a "Diary illustrative of the times of George IV" which appeared in 1838 and was something of a best seller, dealing as it did with Charlotte's inside knowledge of the scandal-ridden royal court. She was a popular and highly-regarded writer in her day, although now almost entirely forgotten. Charlotte died at the age of 86 in 1861, having survived her second husband by many years.

Although Charlotte was twenty years older than Joan Glassell, they seem to have taken to each other immediately, forming a close bond during Joan's first visit to Rome, and during her second visit hardly a day went by without some contact between Joan and Lady Charlotte, or her teenage daughter "Beau".

"Beau", as already mentioned, was Harriet Charlotte Beaujolois Campbell – Beaujolois, because she had as godfather Louis Charles Alphonse Léodgard d'Orleans, Count of Beaujolais, brother of Louis

Philippe the future King of France.[265] Beau married into the Anglo-Irish aristocracy, having met Charles Bury, Lord Tullamoore, (no relation to Mr Bury, her mother's second husband) in Rome in 1819. They married in Florence in 1821, and Beau became Countess of Charleville when her husband succeeded as 2nd Earl in 1835. Intriguingly, the diary Beau kept on the journey to Italy in1817 with her mother and siblings was found on the floor of a London bookshop in the mid-20th century and published as "A journey to Florence in 1817".[266]

Beau was a perceptive observer and a more than competent writer. Regarding her mother's relationship with Mr Bury, she wrote that her governess Miss de la Chaux was increasingly jealous because Lady Charlotte was paying more attention to Mr Bury than to her. "I soon discovered that Mr Bury was in love with mamma, or rather that mamma sought to make him so by her endearing conduct to him," Beau wrote on 15th February 1817. Lady Charlotte admitted the relationship to Beau's sister Eleanora, who told her brother Walter, who as his father's heir was head of the family. "He was furious but kept the secret. About ten days ago he came to mamma and only from his suspicions taxed her with the whole." His mother could not deny it. Walter begged her to wait a few months before marrying Bury, and Lady Charlotte refused to commit herself. "Walter was so hurt that he fell upon his knees, and in violent hysterics implored her to think again. At that moment I entered perfectly ignorant of Walter's being there. I saw him crying violently and mamma standing perfectly cool desiring him to take a glass of water…". Walter left in a show of righteous rage, swearing never to enter the house again, and wrote to Edinburgh instructing his lawyers to cease payment of the allowance he made to his mother, as soon as her marriage was accomplished.

On 12th April 1818 Beau wrote, "The marriage was celebrated on the 21st of March. I was present. Miss de la Chaux has left us and Eleanora is gone to Naples… The last weeks have been a painful trial to me. I am far from happy…". However, by August Walter had apparently made his peace with Mr Bury, and at the end of November Bury, Lady Charlotte, and the younger children took up residence in Rome. Thus by the time of Joan Glassell's second visit to Rome, if all was not entirely sweetness and

265 "Beaujolois" is merely an archaic spelling of the more familiar "Beaujolais". C.f. anglois, écossois, j'avois, etc. all common at the time.

266 Ed. J. R. de Beer, Geoffrey Bles Ltd, London, 1951.

light in the Bury household, at least the time of "violent hysterics" was over.

Joan soon fell into a routine of sightseeing, shopping and socialising. On 24th March however Lady Charlotte received letters among which was one giving the news that her brother John was ill. "It is beyond endurance," Joan complained, "the casual way in which people mention things of the highest and most painful interest." The following day she came away early from a gathering at Duchess Braciano's, as she was "sick to the soul". "God grant your recovery," she wrote. "I can't bear to think you may be as you were two years ago." By 29th March there was still no news from home about John's health, and Joan wrote, "I dreadfully fear you are very ill." However, a letter from John himself arrived on 9th April, which must have reassured her. "I now begin to believe we will meet you in Paris," she wrote with obvious relief. "We are to go on Wednesday."

If Lord John's health was no longer a cause of anxiety, the same could not be said for one of the party's Scottish servants. "Poor Young has been very unwell and bled today," Joan wrote; then three days later, "In addition to Young's blistering and bleeding, my poor maid has got a fever. Joan's maid Aitken made a quick recovery, but the case of "Poor Young" proved to be much more serious.

In spite of such inconveniences the social round had continued throughout Joan's second stay in Rome. On 30th March Joan, Lady Charlotte and Beau went shopping, after which Joan and Beau accompanied a Miss Kay to hear a "miserere" in the Torre del Speccio Convent. "I expected to be taken to some crowded church and suffocated with garlic," Joan observed, but was in fact impressed by the singing, the playing, and apparent contentment and happiness of the small company of nuns. The composer was himself present among the musicians. By contrast, in the evening Joan was obliged to attend a social gathering in the house of a Mrs Austin, where the company engaged in silly party games and Prince Frederick carried Miss Austin in her chair all round the room. "I was very wearied and glad when it was over," commented Joan, who tended to find such frivolities embarrassing.

Incidentally, referring to the miserere performance, Joan noted, "We were the only English." It would strike a jarring chord with most modern Scots to hear themselves described as "English". It is obvious from Joan's correspondence that she felt a great attachment to Scotland, and indeed in her letters to Lord John she occasionally breaks into extended passages in literary Scots. However, it was common enough in the 19th century to equate "English" with "British", as notoriously exhibited in Lord Nelson's famous Trafalgar "England expects" message to his fleet, and Joan would certainly not feel any less of a patriotic Scot for her careless use of the adjective "English".

There were peaceful interludes amidst the flurry of calls, visits and great occasions. On 1st April Joan and Beau spent much of the day walking in the grounds of the Villa Borghese. "It is quite delicious just now round the little lake, the beautifully drooping willows throwing a curtain of the brightest green over some of the statues that are placed all round; they and the dark ilex reflected in the clear basins. There are the most magnificent deer here, some gigantic milk white stags, with such horns." But there was no lasting escape from social obligation: "The crowd of English tonight was most extraordinary and the Italians have now much the advantage. There were some really fine women tonight, and such a shabby set of English." Interestingly, Beau Campbell's journal is full of similar references to English travellers abroad appearing as vulgar, awkward, or embarrassing.

While in Rome Joan made the acquaintance of the celebrated sculptor Canova, who visited on the evening of 9th April. "We had much fun with Canova, and I am delighted by his liking me and my phisioginomy – surely he must be a judge." She had an even greater triumph the following day. "I had a private audience of Canova this morning, and a learned dissertation on craniology was interrupted by the Duke of Devonshire coming in. Not before Canova had time to take me and show me in a sanctum a fine head of Napoleon and one of Sapho. He told me he had told Napoleon if his head was ever dug up 1000 years hence, people would say it belonged to a great man."

Of course no visit to Rome could be complete without experiencing the pomp and splendour of the Catholic Church there at its very heart. On Ash Wednesday, 7th April, Joan attended mass in the Sistine Chapel, a splendid spectacle with the visiting Holy Roman Emperor present, and "ambassadors, multitudes of foreigners and English in fine uniforms". Joan noted that as was the custom in Holy Week, all the ladies were veiled, dressed in black, and separated from the rest of the congregation. All the cardinals were present, although the Pope himself was not. Mass was performed with "exquisite music", and as the Lamentations were sung, thirteen lamps representing the Virgin and the Apostles were gradually extinguished until only the Virgin's lamp was left burning behind the altar. After the lamps were put out Joan was struck by the glow from the orchestra falling on Michaelangelo's Last Judgment. "Then after a dead pause the miserere began, and never did such harmony ascend to heaven… I wished, painfully wished, you could have heard it. Many have an ear, but you have a soul for harmony." Although it was an impressive scene, Joan wrote that her mind was too preoccupied to feel the occasion as a religious experience. "A Presbyterian is too little accustomed to enter daily into the feelings that other people have about this time… But though I grieve to say my religion is not the governing principle of my life, yet when I do feel it speak to me through the medium of innocent pleasures I cannot think that I am bound to reject it."

The next day, Joan was again in the Sistine Chapel, where she saw "the splendid procession of the Pope, who goes under a white canopy supported by cardinals and followed by the whole train of them." Then, out in St Peter's Square where "countless multitudes" were kneeling, she stood waiting in the deep silence while the Pope blessed the crowds. Afterwards Joan wrote, "I was fool enough, perhaps you will think, to have a good deal of pleasure in feeling I was not excluded from it, as it was not confined to Catholics."

Finally, Joan Attended High Mass at St Peter's with Beau Campbell on Easter Sunday. "The spectacle was the most splendid imaginable: the church hung with crimson damask; lined with troops… I cannot go through all the ceremonial; the kneelings before the altar, and depositing his temporal crown on it by the Pope. Indeed everything he does is interesting." All this most certainly was a far cry from the cramped low-roofed country kirk of her childhood, or the serious Presbyterian piety of Mrs Grant the mentor of her teenage years. In the evening there was a spectacular firework display, intended to mimic a volcanic eruption – "Far beyond anything I could have imagined art could produce."

In Joan's company almost daily, Lady Charlotte's daughter Beau seems to have begun to look on her as a kind of elder sister in whom she could confide. This is in some contrast to the dismissive statement in her diary two years previously, when Beau wrote, "I found out that in all probability Rawdon[267] will marry Miss Glassell, a rich heiress, but who I believe has few other recommendations."[268] By contrast, when Joan stayed the night

267 Her cousin Rawdon Clavering, son of Lady Augusta.

268 A Journey to Florence in 1817: Sunday 28th September.

at Lady Charlotte's in Rome on 6th April 1819, she noted, "Beau and I from an accident obliged to sleep together and I never was in such misery trying to suffocate laughing at some of her confessions of faith." Joan had also observed the day before that Beau imagined herself "seriously attached to Lord ____. …Poor child, it is amusing." Joan of course was being a little forgetful here of her own agonisings over Lord John not so very long before. Was the mysterious "Lord ___" perhaps Lord Tullamoore, Beau's future husband whom she first met in Rome?

On 15th April Joan left Rome with the Smiths, after she had spent the whole of the previous day with Lady Charlotte and "the girls". The party travelled by Cività Castellano to Terni and Foligno, which they reached on 17th April. In the inn there Joan observed, "We are in the third hour of waiting for dinner. But now that spring has come and our faces are to home, nothing at present here has the slightest power to annoy me." As she was writing, two Englishmen gave up in disgust and took themselves off to another inn. The following day the travellers passed through Perugia and stopped for the night at an establishment in the village of Masiano, where Joan was allocated a "dungeon". However, she spotted that there was in fact "a nice airy front room with a bed" apparently vacant, and she managed to secure it after a "right battle" with the "little hump backed camariera". Alas, the nice airy front room was not all it seemed to be. Closing her journal entry for the day, Joan recorded, "But in truth I can scarce sit still, I am so devoured by flees."

By 20th April the party was back in Florence where they were detained for ten days by Mr Smith falling ill. Joan mentions him "putting on a blister", but does not mention what the health problem actually was. On arrival in Florence she found a letter from John written on 7th March informing her of her mother's death. Joan did not elaborate in her journal on this sad news, but instead went on to surmise from John's letter that he would not after all be coming to Paris. The day before the travellers left Florence another letter from John revealed, "You are again ill, and very doubtful of coming to Paris."

They finally left Florence on 2nd May, delayed till mid-morning by bad weather, and "going very fast with six horses, and Mr S too unwell to stop" when Joan spotted some brilliant green stones by the roadside. Over the next few days they proceeded by Corilago, Bologna and Rovigo. Of the flat intensely cultivated countryside where they crossed the River Po, Joan remarked, "I have no E. Lothian predilictions in favour of large farms. It is so delightful to see the multitude of small enclosures here..." Her feelings here of course are directly contrary to her father's actions as an "improving laird" in her native Longniddry. She commented also, "It is no saving travelling without a courier, and such torment and delay." She contemplated taking matters into her own hands, and hiring a courier from Venice herself "if I find Southfield is sold".[269]

The events of the next few days Joan wrote up in retrospect, having been "in such agony with toothache I cannot say a word". On the way from Rovigo to Venice it had been necessary to leave the servant Young at Padua,[270] presumably because he was too ill to travel further. After waiting for a thunderstorm to pass, the party embarked at Mestre in a "post gondola" with six oarsmen. "The first view of Venice is not as striking, from being seen from the low lands; it is after having got out into the great lagoon that it appears with most magnificent effect, the main part of the town and its attendant isles rising with innumerable domes and spires from the waters as we approached; the sound of bells coming softly over the sea suited well the mild beauty of everything round, the noiseless gondolas gliding past, for they use their oars so quietly that there is none of the splashing we have in rowing..."

Joan arrived in Venice on 5th May. After breakfast next morning she went to St Mark's Square, a space "vast, lofty and magnificent beyond anything I ever saw except the *place* of St Peter's." The church of San Marco seemed to her "mosque-like" and dark and gloomy inside. Joan visited the Ducal Palace, the Bridge of Sighs, then proceeded through "a labyrinth of canals" in a gondola to the church of St Peter and Paul, where she saw "the finest Titian in the world", a painting of St Peter the Martyr. Next came the Rialto Palace with "the finest collection of paintings I ever saw together". After this hectic schedule there was still time for shopping, and Joan bought some "fine chains" and a "bonnie opera glass, finely set, as a specimen of Venetian work".

Next day, Joan was sent for to Padua, as Young's condition had worsened.

---

269 Southfield, a large farm south of Longniddry, had not been part of John Glassell's original purchase. Presumably, he or his trustees had acquired it at a later date. The sale of such prime agricultural land would add substantially to Joan's wealth.

270 What Joan wrote looks like "Argua", but I have been unable to find any such place. "Padua" is probably meant, as will become apparent.

However, "the doctor saying it would be some days before Young's case would be decided, they proposed to me to go back to Venice". Since she could do little good by remaining in Padua, Joan returned to Venice, and on Sunday 9th May attended St Sebastian's church where "there was the most eloquent and intelligible Italian sermon I ever heard. He dwelt much on the gratitude due to Heaven by the Venetians, chiefly and fondly recalling the 13 centuries of glory and liberty. Of the present he said little." Joan here is probably quietly but justifiably congratulating herself on her improved ability to understand spoken Italian. After the service she entered a side chapel where a holy relic was kept. The priest took her for a Catholic, placed the relic on her forehead, blessed her, then offered her the relic (whatever it might have been) to kiss. This threw her into confusion, as she no doubt felt that relic-kissing was a step too far for a Scots Presbyterian, however open minded. "I felt as if the whole eyes of the church were on me."

In the early evening Joan and her fellow travellers crossed the Lagoon to Lido where Byron was living at the time, and she was privileged to catch a glimpse of the superstar himself, out riding under a brilliant sunset, with towering storm clouds over the Alps. The setting was suitably Byronic, and "he looked as fine and strong as the skies above him". However, when he saw the rest of Joan's party catching up with her, he signalled to his servant and "darted off to another part of the shore".

The next entry in Joan's journal laconically records a tragedy and leaves the rest of the page blank. "I heard Mrs Smith was ill, came off instantly, and found poor Young dreadfully ill. I was up with him till sunrise, which I went to see from the Tower. It was glorious. At half past six I left him and sent Aitken. He died half an hour after." Very few of Joan's letters from Italy survive, but one to Lord John is preserved in the Campbell Papers which sheds light on "poor Young's" harrowing last days:[271]

"I wrote to you yesterday from Venice to London and said I should write also to Paris in the chance of your having come. We are now certainly to go to Chamberay and Lyons. From the former I think Mr Smith would perhaps go to Geneva, but that our only way now, if you are in Paris, of seeing you there, is going straight on. We are at present in a most

271 Acc8508/48, Letter 4. Addressed to "The Rt Hon Lord John Campbell, Chez Opperman Maidnat &C, Banquiers, Paris. Pencil note on letter – "May 8, 1819 Young's illness and death in Padua."

distressing situation from the violent illness of the poor servant we had left here when we went to Venice. He is spitting blood and has been four times bled and blistered in two days. The doctor says he may die today, but if he is to recover it will be decided tomorrow at farthest. We can do nothing until there is some turn, but the moment the disease is removed, which is dreadful inflammation and cannot last, we are to go on with a courier and leave a servant with him who can speak English, and there is an English gentleman here and a very respectable Italian Doctor to whose charge he can be left, as it must certainly be weeks before he can travel. It is dreadful the idea of dying so far from his family, and I really don't think he will live. There seems fate against us ever getting cross the Alps again. Will you write a note to Chamberay and tell us if you are in Paris? I hope we may get there.

Padua May 11th.
The day I wrote the first half of this the Doctor told us it would be some days before Young's illness was decided. As I had seen nothing of Venice, and the American ladies we had been in company [with] were to be there till today, I took their advice and went back to [illegible] them for a day to see the Arsenal, and Canova's works and Lord Byron. Yesterday morning I heard Mrs Smith was ill and set off in a great hurry, my terror making me think she was in a fever. Thank God she is quite well now. It was only from having been up a whole night with Young she had got feverish. It is now all over. He expired this morning about 7 o' clock, poor soul. He was delirious all night. It was dreadful to hear him imploring me to let him go home. As none of the assistance understood him, one of us had always to be in the room to save him irritating himself. Mrs Smith and my maid had been quite worn out. It would have melted a heart of stone his ravings to get home, and talking of every place, appealing to me if I would like to be kept away all my life from Scotland, then praying I might die in a foreign land for using him so ill. I never saw anything more gentle and womanly than the people he had to attend him. Poor fellow. I heard him talking a great deal of you in the night, thinking he was defending something of yours, and saying he would complain to you…".

Joan then describes climbing a church tower to watch a beautiful sunrise. On her return the Doctor and her maid Aitken made her go to bed, and

Young died half an hour later. On the same day as she wrote the second half of her letter to John, Joan wrote in her journal, "Padua 11th May. We went Mr Smith and I to the Campo Santo with poor Young's funeral. After, we went to several sights…".

On 13th May Joan went to visit Petrarch's house and tomb with the Smiths' daughter Christina. Using the poet's own inkstand Joan wrote her name in the visitors' book, in which, she observed, Byron's name also had been inscribed in May 1817. "I never was so glad to leave any place as Padua today," Joan wrote on the 14th, having dreamed about John and Ardencaple during the night. "We took a last look at poor Young's tomb." Later that day the party arrived in Verona. Joan went on her own to ascend the cathedral tower, and the "chief canon" sent a man to see her up the stair. "Such a crazy stair I never ventured on, and certainly but for offending the Reverend Father I would have turned."

The travellers reached Breschia on 15th May. "The hills rise abruptly in an amphitheatre round the town, terraced with gardens, convents and houses." Joan walked out with Christina Smith to view the ramparts of the town, and "had a long conversation with an old man playing bowls about the varieties of the game." Obviously her earlier sessions with an "Italian master" had not been in vain. Next day, after a record trek of 60 miles, the party reached Milan, then on 17th May crossed the frontier into the kingdom of Piedmont, reaching Turin the following day. There was a slight mishap five miles outside Turin, when, "under a burning sun, and choked with dust, the wheel of Mr Smith's carriage came off, and after some difficulty getting it put on, we had to come along at snail's pace."

Joan was impressed by the regularity of Turin's street-plan, and found the inn "very comfortable". The son and daughter of Professor Young of Glasgow University were fellow guests in the same establishment, and came to see the Smiths. Joan had previously met the daughter at her relatives' house of Smeaton in East Lothian, but on this occasion "could na be fashed to go in" and passed up the opportunity to renew the acquaintanceship.

The party proceeded by Rivoli and Susa, and on 20th May reached Lancelebourg in Savoy, where the landlady was an Englishwoman. The road to Lancelebourg led through desolate countryside, and there had been a snow shower on the way. Now, Joan wrote, they were "once more in a tramontane country, snow above us and a wood fire, very comfortable. The ascent was magnificent, the snowy peaks, the great masses of fir, and below the glowing walnut green vineyards, and always in every little hamlet the grey spire of a small church." She continued optimistically, "We are not now far from Paris. Will we see you there?" The concluding three lines of this entry are heavily deleted.

Next day, on the road to Aiguebelle, the party "changed horses five times, some of the relays at great length". Their route followed the River Are, "the Alps rising on either side perpendicular". On the 22nd, coming down through countryside like "the vast debris of some former order", where Napoleon had begun a "gallery" to conduct the road by a "less fearful descent", Joan saw the plains of France spread before her. The travellers crossed the French frontier and put up in Pont de Beau Voisin. "We have just had the strictest visit of *Douanne* we have ever had, and poor Aitken is in such a fright."

Two days later, writing in Mâcon, Joan recorded a very narrow escape:

> *"Yesterday had very nearly put an end to my journal. After travelling the worst roads in Europe and coming down Mount Cenis at full tilt… we were near St Laurent two posts from Lyons overturned… I like a fool leapt out, and God knows how, found myself laid on my back on the hind wheel, the flat side of it being up… How only my leg was hurt, my back and head untouched, is a miracle. I did not know how much hurt my leg was till I got to the next post. When I tried to get down I could scarce move. I was half dead with the pain trying to move. Mrs Smith put on leeches and has saved me a long fit of lameness."*

For all her faith in Mrs Smith's leeches, however, Joan's leg was still troubling her several months later, long after her return to Scotland. On 30th August she wrote to her correspondent Mrs Fletcher, "My leg is better again almost. It was perfectly healed… and repeatedly been in warm water and rubbed. It was just a very feverish day did it, and it merely bled and had no appearance of festering, and you do me great injustice thinking I won't give it rest and care."[272]

In Lyon Joan spent the night in a hotel overlooking one of the quays along the River Saône. The cathedral was opposite her window. After her

272 Campbell Papers Acc8508/48, Letter 8. To Mrs Fletcher 30th August 1819.

accident there was none of the usual sightseeing. "I was quite in a fever the first short time, but after I had been bled it was delightful lying on the sofa and seeing the colours where the stars were beginning one by one to appear… I thought, or rather Aitken thought that I was going to share the fate of Seneca[273] (if she had ever heard of him), as after my wounds were bound up they persisted in so long bleeding, I was obliged to keep awake…" Closing her entry written in Mâcon, Joan again wrote wistfully, "In five days we will be in Paris… Will we see you?

On the way to Autun next morning, when the carriages had stopped at Tournus, the second post, Joan found, "My wounds were so feverish I went to a nice looking woman's house to get some vinegar to put on my knee." She was delighted with the woman's house: "The inside was exactly a Scotch cottage, and very clean." Later that day there was a terrific thunderstorm lasting for two hours. In Autun that night Joan concluded her journal entry for the day with, "In four days we shall be in Paris!!" and yet another heavily deleted phrase. She had a restless night. "I thought this morning I was going to have a leg to cut off, it was so ill. All night in such a fever and pain and extending over the whole leg." The inn at Avallon, that day's destination, on 26th May, was clean and comfortable. "I am reposing to save my leg. The last milestone I saw had 114 on it leagues from Paris."

On 27th May Joan arrived at Villeneuve sur Yonne, and found herself in "quite an English inn – carpets, clean blankets". A wood near Lucy le Bois had reminded her of woods at Inveraray thinned out on Lord John's orders. Joan was intrigued by the great rafts of timber floating down the River Yonne "50 in a string" with "two men on each directing them at the ends. They have small straw huts and fires on them." We can almost feel her mounting excitement as she closed the day's journal entry with, "The night after tomorrow at this time!"

Joan's next entry was written in Paris on 31st May. "I could not write any of the last days. We stopped at Melun which left a very short journey to Paris When I saw the letters I thought now Lord John is not coming but perhaps tomorrow he will be here. My leg has been sore. I have had a doctor, and that no other than my old friend Dr Spurzheim[274], so ardent

273 Roman statesman and philosopher, ordered by Nero to kill himself by opening his veins to bleed to death.

274 Johann Gaspar Spurzheim, a famous phrenologist in his day. He had visited Edinburgh in 1816.

and enthusiastic as ever... I am laid upon my bed taking care of myself, one of the most wearisome occupations I know." She had found letters awaiting her from various friends and acquaintances, but there is no mention of anything from John.

The Journal ends here. Joan wrote "1st June 1819" but made no entry for that day. The remainder of the notebook, around half of it, is blank.

It is disappointing, to say the least, to be deprived of an account of Joan's much anticipated stay in Paris. There is, however, a solitary letter[275] of hers surviving from that time. It is addressed to Janet, the wife of her cousin Hugh Francis Cadell, and is dated 17th June from the Hôtel Meurice, Rue St Honoré. "We arrived here on the 29th and leave it on Monday next for Calais by Beauvais. We had so little time in passing through before that we had almost all the sights to see now." Joan had been at the Jardin des Plantes, shown round by "the famous Cuvier"[276]. She visited Montmartre, attended a seminar at the "Institute", and enjoyed the Tivoli Gardens. She planned to see Versailles the following day. Her party had "delightful apartments in Hotel Meurice, overlooking the gardens of the Tuilleries". The hotel appeared to be overrun with English visitors, 160 of them when Joan arrived, and even more she thought at the time of writing. In the course of her letter Joan mentions nonchalantly but significantly, "We have met two Scotch friends since we came, Mr Smith's youngest brother and Lord J. Campbell."

Joan's hopes, then, had not been in vain. Throughout her Continental Tour John had never been far from her mind. We can only imagine with what relief and pleasure they met again after their separation. The course of their lives after their Paris reunion demonstrates that both were now well aware that their bond was one of more than mere friendship.

275 "Intimate Society Letters of the Eighteenth Century", Ed. The Duke of Argyll, Vol 2, Page 643. John Lane Company, New York, 1910.

276 Naturalist and zoologist. Major contributor to advancement in the field of palaeontology.

Joan Glassell.
(Source: "Autobiography and memoirs" – 8th Duke of Argyll.)

Lord John Campbell.
(Source: "Autobiography and memoirs" – 8th Duke of Argyll.)

9

“That stream of intelligence and amusement”

After her return from her Continental Tour, Joan Glassell went to live in the household of her relatives the Buchan Hepburns at Letham, just outside Haddington, the county town of East Lothian. Letham was some five miles from Joan's own property at Longniddry, to which she seems to have made occasional visits. She was not yet “of age” under the stringent conditions of her father's will, and so it would probably not have been considered fitting by her relatives and trustees, for her to live alone at Longniddry.

George Buchan of Letham was the half-brother of Joan's mother Helen. He was an advocate who became Judge of the High Court of Admiralty, and a Baron of the Exchequer. As well as being laird of Letham, on the death of his mother's brother George Hepburn of Smeaton, he had inherited the estate of Smeaton near East Linton, also in East Lothian. He then assumed the surname and arms of Hepburn of Smeaton, built a new mansion house at Smeaton, and took up residence there. He retired in 1814 and was created baronet in 1815, thus becoming Sir George. Sir George had one surviving son, John, also an advocate, who resided at Letham with his wife Mary

Turner Hog, the daughter of a West Lothian country laird. Mary was a grandchild of the Earl of Lauderdale, through her mother.

Sir George Buchan Hepburn died in July 1819, and his son John inherited the baronetcy and the estate of Smeaton. When Joan Glassell arrived at Letham, therefore, John and Mary had newly become Sir John and Lady Buchan Hepburn. Sir John was Joan's cousin, although since he was nearly twenty years older, their relationship was more like uncle and niece. The Buchan Hepburns had three children – Mary, Thomas, and John. By birth, background, professional and family connections, the Letham family was one of irreproachable respectability, eminently suited to oversee the final dependent months of a wealthy unmarried woman's "minority".

The widow of the recently deceased Sir George, Sir John's stepmother, continued to reside at Smeaton during Joan Glassell's months at Letham. She is mentioned several times in Joan's correspondence, not very sympathetically, and had a rather more colourful background than the wives of most East Lothian country lairds. "Old Lady Hepburn" had been born Margaretha Hendrina Beck, the daughter of a German immigrant to the Cape of Good Hope. Her father Johannes Zacharias Beck arrived at the Cape in 1715 and became a burgher in 1722. He seems to have been a brewer with a farm at Rondebosch named Welgelegen, where his steward and another white man were brutally murdered by three slaves. Margaretha had two husbands before she married George Buchan Hepburn, both Scottish army officers – Captain Alexander Grant who fought with Clive at Plassey, and secondly Brigadier General Simon Fraser who was killed at Saratoga in 1777. Margaretha's father is described on one ancestral website[277] as being related by marriage to "the former slave woman and colonial matriarch" Maaij Ansela van Bengali, "founding mother" of several Cape Dutch families. Perhaps this might explain Joan's humorous but rather cruel reference to Old Lady Hepburn as "the Hottentot".

Joan's correspondence with Lord John Campbell is scattered through several files in the Campbell Papers. The letters are sometimes in chronological order and sometimes not, and in fact many of the letters are undated. It will be obvious, therefore, that obtaining a clear picture of Joan's life from her writing is something of an exercise in "creating order

277 Website: "South Africa's Stamouers".

out of chaos". However, with patience, it is possible to gain some idea of her life at Letham, with her interests, social contacts, and her developing relationship with Lord John.

The first in the sequence of Joan's archived letters to John after her return from Europe[278] is undated but can be placed in August 1819. It is a scrawl in large letters, headed "Letham Friday", and gives the impression of having been written in haste, or under stress, or both. Seemingly Joan had heard from Lady Robert Kerr that John had set off from London for Scotland, but had been taken ill and had to turn back. She begs him to let Annie Mure know how he is, and Annie will pass the news on. "As two more days being not a word from Annie, I am certain you are very ill," she wrote. "I have no way of hearing, and Annie will if she does write only hear what the servants say at the door." The trouble was presumably a recurrence of the illness John had picked up during his army service in the Netherlands, which his son said plagued him all his life. The tone of this short letter is quite distraught, and Joan was clearly deeply concerned.

Her next letter, again undated, is marked in pencil "Received 27th", most probably 27th August 1819. It is another scrawl in large letters:[279]

> *"My Dear Lord John,*
>
> *I little intended troubling you with any letter when I have nothing to say, but I have heard by accident from Miss Adair that Miss Mure said you had been ill and gone back from Newark. I cannot wait and not say; do tell me how you are."*

He had apparently been intending to come to Edinburgh. Joan begged him again to write. "Is it the spasms?" she speculated worriedly. She had said goodnight to him only three weeks previously in London, presumably on her way home from her Continental Tour. "Now don't be angry at my plaguing you when you did not write me," she pleaded, "but I have no other way I can hear."

A few days later, however, Joan seems to have been reassured, and wrote from Letham on 30th August, "I am glad to hear you are continuing better, but I fear you are not so well, or have been worse than you say from your thinking you will be 'long' detained in Town… When you do set out, for any

278 Campbell Papers: Acc8508/47, Letter 2.
279 Accc8508/47, Letter 3.

sake take very short journeys." Mr Smith had apparently told her that Lord John was much better, but Joan was not quite sure that it was true. Her tone all the same is noticeably calmer, and she was able to write lightheartedly about her dog "Inver" who had run off but was later recovered, and was in "fits of joy" when reunited with his mistress.

The following day Joan sent off another letter, in which she apologised for the previous day's communication being "very dull stuff", as she had been "in the blue devils". She had obviously heard from John again, as she worries over his description of himself as "pale, thin, and yellow". However, this is a lively letter covering a range of topics, and Joan concludes with, "God be thanked, you are surely on the way to be well. Take care of yourself my dear Lord John, and believe me, affectionately yours, M. J. Glassell."[280] The "pale, thin, and yellow" reference may in fact be in response to verses John sent which he said he had found in a magazine. "It so curiously applies to my present appearance and to my chief subject of mental derangement, I could not help copying it out for your amusement."

"When your visage appears in its pale and its yellow
Like a guinea new coin'd from the mint,
At a distance I stare at so ugly a fellow
Surprised that your carcase has any life in't.

But when with confusion your wild thoughts transpire,
When your new mode of flight you attempt to explain,
When your pale cheek is flushed and your eyes dart forth fire,
Then I know you alas! For a maniac again.

There's a power of thought there, the Maniac replied
Which reptiles like you never knew.
I may still be thought wise by all others beside,
Though still deemed a maniac by you."

Although supposedly copied from a magazine, the rather shaky scansion and the reference to the "new mode of flight" arouse suspicion that the verses

280 Acc8508/47, Letters 4 and 5. "M. J. Glassell" seems to stand for "Miss Joan Glassell". There is no indication anywhere that Joan had an additional Christian name beginning with "M".

are John's own – the "new mode of flight" referring to John's enthusiasm for ballooning.[281]

Pale and yellow John may have been, but he was on the road to recovery. In an undated letter[282] probably from around the middle of September, he told Joan, "Tomorrow I go out for the first time". All the same, he clearly did not expect to make a quick recovery, as in another undated letter[283] from around the same time, he remarked stoically, "How cruel to be in England and in London till winter begins, but there's no help for it…". By 16th September he was able to conclude that day's letter to Joan, "There is Walpole come to help me to walk in the park, so I'll wish you guid bye for the present."[284] On 6th October he informed Joan that he had been walking every day, "and can now walk two miles and more without fatigue". Not only that, but his doctors had told him that he would "probably" be able to set off for Scotland the following week. "On Thursday," he wrote, "if all goes well I shall depart for Scotland, and on the Monday or Tuesday following hope to reach Edinburgh."[285] On 11th October, however, he wrote that his intention was now to leave on the Friday, and so he wrote, "I must, most unwillingly, desire you to stop that stream of intelligence and amusement with which you have so constantly cheered my tedious confinement… I am sure that I never can be sufficiently grateful to you for it."[286] Unfortunately business with a Mr Hope detained him further in London, and on the day he had intended leaving, Friday 15th October, John wrote again saying he could not after all leave until the following Tuesday. "I suppose there will be no possibility of getting a bed in Edinburgh during the Festival," he commented ruefully. (This was the second of three musical festivals held in Edinburgh during the early 19th century.)

There can be no doubt of the debt of gratitude Lord John felt he owed to Joan. "You say you have no claim on my gratitude," he chided. "Then I do not know what claims are on gratitude, for who is there that ever thought of me with the partial [i.e. sympathetic] view of all I do or say or write; or

281 Acc8508/23, Letter 8. This is undated, but a typed transcript says "Tuesday Sept 7th 1819" without offering any justification for attributing that date.

282 Acc8508/23, Letter 8.

283 Acc8508/24, Letter 9.

284 Acc8508/23, Letter 9.

285 Acc8508/24, Letter 2.

286 Acc8508/24, Letter 3.

who would or who could so constantly delight or amuse the tedious hours of sickness as you have done? Is there no gratitude for this?"[287]

The question of how Joan and John perceived their relationship at this time is intriguing. In the letter where he informed Joan that he expected to go out for the first time on the following day, he rebuked her gently for suggesting that answering her letters might be a "tax" on him. "You must know that to answer and to notice every part of them would afford to any person to whom they were addressed the greatest amusement and pleasure, and you may be certain that to me, who now begin to know the writer thoroughly, it is quite the most delightful way I could pass my time."[288] In her reply, Joan picked up on John's use of the word "now". "I am amused with your saying that you now begin to know me 'thoroughly'. Lord love ye!" Claiming modestly to have only a few "notes in her scale" compared to the many in John's, she states confidently, "Yet I am sure I knew what they might be nearly two years ago as well as I do now. It's not conceit of penetration, but I thought exactly of every atom of your character in December '17 as I do now, and will if I live till the millennium." Referring again to when she first knew him, Joan revealed that she had been astonished at the youthful appearance of one she knew to be a middle aged man. "My first exclamation to Miles was about yourself, 'My stars, what a perfect laddie he looks!'"[289]

Incidentally, Joan often uses Scots words and idioms in her letters, and occasionally breaks into sustained passages in literary Scots. She would of course hear Scots spoken constantly in the Longniddry of her childhood. Even her relatives among the East Lothian gentry would be perfectly familiar with it, and not above employing it themselves on occasion, although by the early 19th century English was thoroughly established as the superior mode of communication. All the same, Joan's Scots is sometimes more redolent of Scott and Hogg than the dialect of East Lothian.

Despite John's youthful looks, he was of course considerably older than Joan, having been born in December 1777, and in her letters to him during his illness, she begins to refer to him as "Papa". Bizarrely, he also occasionally

---

287 Acc8508/24, Letter 5.

288 Acc8508/24, Letter 8.

289 i.e. "A perfect laddie" in the sense of looking like "an absolute boy". Acc8508/47, Letter 10.

addresses her as "Papa", possibly in protest, or possibly because some private joke was involved.

Joan was obviously attracted to John's calm and rather introspective nature, and his quiet sense of humour. "I think there is something in your nature, an atmosphere of feeling like a home day, a soft grey that is not cloud, a predominance of serious feeling... God knows you have, and give out, more light than anybody... However, one might see you long enough in a party in London without knowing you as you really are."[290] She remembered a day in a "beautiful broomy glen" in Argyllshire: "I mind catching you quizzing me, Papa, for oh I ken your face weel, weel; and mony a time it laughs at a body when you're saying nothing."[291] There is obvious affection here, and it also comes to the fore in a dream she described to him. Joan was in the habit of enclosing rose leaves, sprigs of heather, and suchlike in her letters to John, and she dreamed that he had complained that she had sent him withered heather when he had plenty fresh heather to hand. "And oh Papa, I knew it was na true, but I had sent you the best I had. But I was like to greet, but my heart was ower sair to defend myself."

In her letters Joan was indeed sending John the best of herself, and he was very much aware of it. "I never can have it in my power to be half sufficiently grateful," he wrote, "but you will believe that I am very much so, and that with me is not a little."[292] But it was not only gratitude that John was feeling. His increasing admiration is plain. "You have too much imagination and too much feeling even to write upon the most trivial subjects without making them interesting," he observed.[293] As well as gratitude and admiration on Lord John's part, we begin to discern a little tenderness. When Joan half-seriously suggested that a comment of hers might have annoyed him, he replied, "Is it possible that any dream or any assertion could make you believe that I should be angry with you, or that anything could make me so distracted as to say anything to you willingly that could bring a cloud to your face? But I'm sure you do not. You cannot believe me suddenly become such a brute."[294] Their correspondence during John's illness certainly seems to have tightened the bond between the pair.

290 Acc8508/46, Letter 4.
291 Acc8508/46, Letter 16.
292 Acc8508/23, Letter 12.
293 Acc8508/24, Letter 3.
294 Acc8508/24, Letter 2.

In her last letter before he finally left London for Scotland, surmising that before he crossed the Tweed she would be "lodged at 112 George Street" in Edinburgh, she felt able to sign off with "Goodbye my dearest Lord John".

Deepening feelings there may have been, but as befitted correspondence between a lady and a gentleman in early 19th century Scotland, there is not a syllable about anything so untoward as sex. Those of a Freudian inclination however might find significance in Joan[295] remembering daydreaming while in Rome, imagining that she was back at Inveraray and carrying John's gun, when he had turned to her saying, "Give me that now, there's some pheasants, and they'll be saying 'Eh Lord man, will ye see till the Leddy wi the gun!'" Again, perhaps more explicitly, she dreamed one night of dining in a tent at Inveraray. A monster appeared with a horn a yard long on each foot, and the ability to poke a contraption out of its snout like the spokes of an umbrella. Joan was following John, carrying his gun, which grew into a cannon, and the exertion and terror woke her. Regency Britain has a reputation for sexual laxity, but for a respectable young woman like Joan Glassell, any such embarrassing urges would have to be held in check for a little longer.

A sure sign of their deepening mutual trust is the fact that Joan let John have the journal of her European tour to read. In an undated letter during his illness he admits that his progress with it "gets on but slowly". This he tactfully attributes to the fact that he has had so many letters to write, and also because of "the difficulty of reading it, for my eyes are weak and I cannot read it for long together." In fact the difficulty may have been not so much John's weak eyesight as Joan's atrocious handwriting. He hurriedly goes on to comment, "I envy you so much all the delightful scenery you describe (and wish so much I had been there)."[296] Also, "The journal is very interesting. There are many things in it I should like to talk to you about if I ever see you at Arden this winter… I shall be there, if I get strong, all winter." John is puzzled, though, about why she hated Florence so much – the "must see" destination of their times. On 19th September Joan promised to send him the "last sensible part" of her journal, which took her as far as Rome.[297] Although, as we have seen, there are many

295 Acc8508/48, Letter 8.
296 Acc8508/23, Letter 9.
297 Acc8508/46, Letter 15.

deletions in Joan's Continental Journal, she left enough of her comments about John to make her feelings plain. Allowing him to read the Journal surely demonstrates a growing confidence on her part that these feelings might be reciprocated.

In an even more explicit demonstration of her attachment, Joan also sent John poetry of her own, possibly as a consequence of the "thin and yellow" verses he had sent to her. The first poem is marked "Letham for Lord John MJG" and is undated. A pencil note says "Sept 1819". This is the poem already mentioned in Chapter 7, here given in full:

"Come gentle sleep and close these heavy eyes
That never tearless see the sun arise.
Come gentle sleep and calm that troubled breast
That only thy blind influence soothes to rest!
Oh come and calm this wildly throbbing heart,
Leave but of memory the softer part.
Oh linger late in that returning morn
When from that anguished heart its all was torn;
When the low accent of his last farewell
Rang on my soul of Hope and peace the knell!
My lips ne'er said farewell! The only tone
My soul could utter was a deep low groan.
Parting were sweet to this, had I dared say
With thee the sun sets on life's dreary day.
With Thee Beloved! The life [?] of life is fled.
May all that's left soon mingle with the dead.
Oh had I dared to leave the cold disguise,
Dared once to thee to raise my swimming eyes,
Dared to fold thy knees in one last wild embrace
And read forgiveness in that long loved face.
Forgiveness! And for what? My heart can tell!
For having loved not wisely but too well!
For having dared despite of every art
To wear thy image on my bursting heart.
Tho' many a time when haunted, wretched, lone,
I've tried to shake it from its burning throne.
Oh had I yielded to that heart's wild call,

That last wild moment would have told you all.
Oh kneeling had I dared that hand to kiss,
Drunk from these eyes a parting beam of bliss,
Dared to pour out the worship of my soul,
And from thy lips a sigh of pity stole.
But half-taught pride and crushed affection's power
Joined in wild tumult in that parting hour.
I dared not look on that beloved face
Without betraying all the dire disgrace
Of having given to thee, unwoo'd, unsought,
A heart that, trust me, never could be bought!"
Letham Septr 1819[298]

A cryptic note at the foot of the page says, "He may get it and say, 'So have the dead loved'. Tomorrow year past it was. Tomorrow year to come all may be deep peace and he eternal. MJG."

It would be easy to dismiss Joan's efforts as the conventional versifying of the day, and indeed troubled breasts, throbbing bursting hearts, and overemployment of the adjective "wild" were par for the course in the early 19th Century. Joan herself was not entirely confident of her literary ability. "Now mind," she urged, writing to Lord John on 4th September, "for pity's sake, in real earnest don't set me down for a poetising miss… I never attempted rhyme before, for I mind once wishing I could make some 'pottery' on a poor wee doggie who was so fond of me, and they hung it on a false accusation of madness, and I grat myself sick with grief and passion."[299] (Incidentally, is it not striking that another of the few childhood memories that Joan records is yet again an unhappy one?)

However, Joan's poem is better than merely conventional. It has some original touches and conveys vividly the emotions and thoughts of the protagonist parted from her lover. Of course both Joan and John could if necessary pretend that the poem merely described the imaginary parting of two imaginary lovers, but it would be perfectly obvious to John that Joan was in fact describing their parting at Rosneath the previous year.

It was probably in reference to this poem that John wrote, "The verses

298 Acc8508/47, Letter 8.
299 Acc8508/46, Letter 4.

are beautiful. I dare say some lines might be new measured, but the idea and feeling is Poetry." However, he made no admission of knowing that he was the object of "worship" in Joan's piece, but continued jocularly, "Upon my conscience ye's see nae mair o my ain Parodys except to be something outrageously ridiculous, for I see ye're a maister o pawetry."[300]

If Joan was disappointed by John's dodging the issue of what the poem was really about, there is no sign of it in her letters, and two or three weeks later she sent Lord John another poem, saying she had been up scribbling until the early hours of the morning:

Though many a time when weary, distant, lone,
I've tried to shake it from its burning throne,
But still the throbbings of that heart would tell
It still would love not wisely but too well.
The day returns and still my aching sight
From Home, home only, hopes the beam of light;
And why they say when time and youth are flying
Is that devotion never dying,
Which from cold clouded Home, thy eager eye
Drinks the warm sunbeams of a fairer sky.
And would the fervours of the burning zone
Blight the soft verdure of my love for Home?
Oh, only with my breath that love shall fly,
And then, even then, it surely cannot die!
Ill omened day! If still thy clouded brow
Another year of absence threatens now;
Soon may kind Heaven remove me to that shore
Where absence, sorrow, fear are felt no more![301]

Here in her imagination Joan is back in Italy longing for "Home". Or is it really Lord John who is the object of her "unsought devotion never dying"?

With a letter written on 1st October[302] Joan enclosed two wild roses, and another poem, which concludes:

300 Acc8508/24, Letter 4. Undated, but he mentions going out "for the first time".
301 Acc8508/46, Letter 19. Undated, but noted "Received Oct 11th".
302 Acc8508/48, Letter 47.

"To no foreign land
Are your pale blossoms going,
For no foreign eye
Will your last smile be glowing.
Feel now the smile
When ye first meet his eye
And drink in the beam
Of your soft native sky.
Go steal to his pillow
When languid and lone,
And your death sigh will be
Of the wild woods of home."

Below these lines Joan wrote "Prose run mad, or poetry on crutches." However, John's reaction was enthusiastic: "…and thon beautiful lines, did you make them or copy them from Moore?[303] They do indeed speak to me of Home, as much as the fading roses do of the wild woods there. They speak to me of all the elegance and feeling of your mind, but I must say no more lest you should think I am flattering you to get more incense offered to my own vanity."[304] And again, "You may be as vain as you please if my thinking thon lines beautiful will make you so. They are far superior to anything of Moore's I ever read. They are what I take to be the essence of all Poetry, natural feeling expressed as musical measure."[305]

Joan's apologetic dismissal of her verse as "poetry on crutches" is symptomatic of her feeling that despite her education, imagination and intelligence, she was Lord John's intellectual inferior. This was almost certainly an erroneous belief, but Joan was young, not yet independent, and John was a middle aged aristocratic Member of Parliament and man of the world. The same occasional lack of confidence can be traced elsewhere in her letters. Alluding to her mind, she wrote, "I never could make it do anything by an effort of will in my life… When it gets an impetus… it rolls straight on… Like

303 Thomas Moore 1779-1852. Popular Irish poet and songwriter. Composer of such perennial favourites as "Believe me if all these endearing young charms" and "The last rose of summer".

304 Acc8508/24, Letter 7. Undated.

305 Accc8508/24, Letter 9. Undated.

a Canadian sleigh it flies on down and up hill after the first propelling touch."[306] Impulsive, then, she seems to say, and incapable of organising her thoughts rationally. She recalled arguing with John in a drawing room, presumably at Ardencaple or Inveraray, where she was "in such a fury at your always getting some loophole, for I can't argue and you can. But God bless your heart, if you only saw how clear I see it all in my own head, though I can't bring it out in logical array."[307] Again, she remembered gazing at the Falls of Fernie and thinking how she might have found a piece of music to match them if she had not been "an idle idiot" all her "young days". She went on to comment regretfully (at the early age of 24) on lost opportunities to hone abilities and develop skills. "It's a very rare thing, in sober earnest, how many faculties we lose; how many strings that might have discoursed sweet music are left to rust, and we afterwards try in vain to wake them."[308] Joan even felt the lack of some of the very basics of education. "I wish," she wrote, "I could get the length of acquiring a competent knowledge of simple addition, and having by heart two or three lines of the multiplication tables, but counting and grammar are two things I have an unsurmountable stupidity in learning."[309] Joan is almost certainly exaggerating her mathematical blind spot, and if by "grammar" she means English grammar, she was misrepresenting her language skills, for though her handwriting was poor and her punctuation sometimes non-existent, her spelling and grammar are almost faultless. However, she is probably using "grammar" as a synonym for "Latin", which like mathematics would not have been considered an indispensable part of a young lady's education.

Joan credited John with opening her eyes and her intellect to possibilities beyond the merely mundane. "God knows, I could never flatter when there was room for it," she declared, "but it is deep self knowledge makes me say that every semblance of talent, every spark of imagination I have is as much the work of your mind, as ever dross formed gold could be of the chemist's hands." She subscribed to the conventional view that, "Feeling, deep unostentatious and sincere" was "the one rich vein in woman's mind which she can call her own." "Till you put it in my head," she assured John, "I had no more spark of fun, no more play of imagination, than there are

306 Acc8508/46, Letter 16. 6/7th October.

307 Acc8508/46, Letter 3. Undated.

308 Acc8508/47, Letter 9. Undated.

309 Acc8508/41, Letter 10. Postmarked 24th September.

green leaves on the wood I write on just now."[310] It is a little hard to believe that the girl who stole her cousin's clothes while he was swimming at Longniddry was devoid of a "spark of fun and play of imagination". Surely John was not so much the author of Joan's talents as a catalyst that helped to call them forth.

Joan, however, had been conditioned by her upbringing and education, and there was no escaping the opinions of the day, which were accepted by one and all as scientific fact. On "the rights of women", and a woman's "capacity" being equal to a man's, she wrote, "It's nonsense. Our strengths lie different ways, yours in the head, ours in the heart. You are born to rule and act and think, we are to all intents subjects; but nature has provided for our duties being in our feelings... There are women who take it in their heads they have got men's brains and live all their lives showing off, but depend upon it, they are not happy, whatever they seem." Alas for Madame de Staël, the foremost female intellectual of the day, of whom Joan remarked, "So much of man's talent, so much of the vanity of the weakest woman."[311] Joan's comments would cause outrage in many quarters today, but we can hardly expect 21st century insights from an early 19th century woman.

"I mind," Joan wrote,[312] "you and Mr Smith having a talk about cautious and sanguine tempers on the Boulevards one day, and you saying I had a sanguine temper." *Sanguine* is defined in Chambers' Dictionary as "ardent; confident and inclined to hopefulness". Leaving aside Joan's estimation of her abilities as inferior to John's, the dictionary definition agrees well with Mrs Grant's summing up of Joan's character nearly a decade previously. In Paris, her old acquaintance Dr Spurzheim had remarked, "Nature meant you for very gay." Spurzheim of course was an enthusiastic proponent of phrenology, which held that various character traits resided in particular parts of the brain, and that the bumps of these "organs" could be felt on the skull. Nature intended Joan to be gay, observed Spurzheim, but shaking his head and touching Joan's skull, he continued, "Thees and thees can make very unhappy."[313]

---

310 Acc8508/47, Letter 11.

311 Acc8508/46, Letter 3. Undated.

312 Ibid. Joan often uses the Scots idiom "I mind" in preference to the English "I remember".

313 Ibid.

What the ill-omened bumps on Joan's head signified she does not say, but one aspect of life that made her less than happy seems to have been the conventional social duties imposed upon a woman of her age and status. From Edinburgh, where she had presumably gone for the duration of the "Festival", she wrote to John that she was having to go out to make "calls".[314] "Oh what a thing is this world," she lamented. "What mere actors are we all... What a blank has it been to me this week, yet I have been in the whirl of blazing races etcetera." A day or two previously she had been talked into going to an "assembly". "Oh Papa, how mad at myself the minute after." She compared her situation in Edinburgh with "dear old Letham", and remembered with sympathy a "Mrs R." who had exclaimed at an Inveraray ball, "And this is pleasure!"

Before her visit to Edinburgh she complained to John that the following day she was obliged to go to Gosford and other places, and the day after that to visit Lady Elcho.[315] "There is always at least comparative pleasure in sitting at home looking at the falling leaves or the embers of a wood fire, but to be obliged to keep up eternally with all manner of people is what people call gaiety and I call misery... Oh Papa, are we not all slaves? ...It is a fine thing not to be obliged to dance about when one hates it, and I am sure had I had my senses I would have kept home all this while." Joan had told her aunt Lady Hepburn that she should sell the newly inherited estate of Smeaton and "go away to the back o beyont". Incidentally, Joan's uncle and host Sir John Buchan Hepburn not only owned Smeaton and Letham, but must have had a town house in Edinburgh, as Joan instructed Lord John that if he wrote to her after 18th October he was to address his letters to "JBH's 122 George Street".[316]

There is no doubt that Joan appreciated stimulating and thought provoking conversation, and enjoyed meeting interesting people, but she seems to have been exasperated by the bland humdrum conventional socialising expected of her. On September 6th she wrote[317] that the previous week Old Lady Hepburn had called at Letham. Joan had kept to her room,

314 Acc8508/47, Letter 7.

315 Acc8508/46, Letter 19. Marked "Received Oct 11th". Gosford, near Joan's property of Longniddry, was the seat of the Earl of Wemyss. Lord Elcho was the courtesy title of the eldest son of the Earl of Wemyss.

316 Acc8508/46, Letter 2. 18th October.

317 Acc8508/46, Letter 5.

and her aunt had pretended to the old woman that Miss Glassell was sleeping. Throughout her visit however, the old lady had persisted in asking, "Vel, is she vakin yet?" and eventually exclaimed, "My Got, vat a sleeper!" Ever since, whenever she saw Sir John or one of the boys, she had been asking, "Vel, vat is Miss Glassell about now? I never knew such a sleeper!" While Joan was writing, her aunt had left to "pay some veesits" and dine with Old Lady Hepburn. "She came up the noo," Joan informed Lord John, "to ask me what lee she's to tell for me not coming to pay my devotes to my venerable Hottentot but nevertheless much to be revered and never to be neglected Aunt." Her final comment was, "Go to make calls and dine with the old Lady and look piously sorry for her aches and ills (which are all inventions)! No, no."

In a similar vein, Joan wrote to John, probably in early October, that she was not looking forward to the Festival in Edinburgh. She mused that "living fast" was not just a matter of hard drinking, but rather a business of "consuming youth so as to permanently exhaust it". Pondering the acquisition of wisdom, she remarked wryly, "I wish I could be wise enough not to hate being dragged out to dance again tomorrow," and quoted Byron, "Oh that the desert were my dwelling place." Finally she lamented, "I think a populous country one of the greatest of miseries, where nothing but breaking a leg once a month can secure people peace to sit at home and follow their own devices."[318]

"Oh, I hate mobs," she sighed elsewhere,[319] and observed that as far as crowds were concerned, "The sort of glitter and motion catch our eye like the motes in the sunbeam. We look close and find them dust."

Certainly, Joan enjoyed solitude. Early on in the correspondence she told John how she loved the "wild walks" around Letham, adding, "I don't like things or people with all the corners smoothed down, each like their neighbours."[320] The miles of East Lothian countryside between Haddington and Tranent had been bleak inhospitable scrub and moorland, and had only recently been enclosed, cultivated, and planted with shelter belts and woods. In the early 19th century it would as yet not have "its corners smoothed down", and indeed patches of heather can be found in the woods there to this day. In her letter to John of 3rd September 1819 Joan talks of putting

318 Acc8508/46, Letter 1. Undated.
319 Acc8508/47, Letter 11. Undated.
320 Acc8508/48, Letter 5. 30th August.

on her "muckle cloak and highland bonnet to go out walking up the burn and into the wood" to look for heather on a windy night,[321] and in another around the same time she wishes she had a "fairy car" to whirl John up and set him down "in the Lamb Lair, the name of a wood here" so that she might take him for a walk among the heather.[322] Again, "I have been wandering for two hours in the wood eating brambles. I can't send you any, but here's some heather, such as it is, and some walnut leaves. What valuable gifts I bestow on you!!!!"[323]

The fact that Joan enjoyed solitude, however, should not make us assume that she was a solitary or antisocial person. More probably she enjoyed the company of like-minded people, but had little patience with the trivialities of run-of-the-mill social interaction, and did not suffer fools gladly. She had a lively mind and a wide range of interests. In her letter of 3rd September[324] she informed John that she had been reading a biography of John Philpot Curran, (the Irish orator, politician, duellist, Gaelic speaker, and champion of Catholic emancipation), and she devoted several pages to the thoughts and opinions stimulated by her reading. The previous day she had written to John enclosing an account of an experiment with the sun's rays which it was thought might have some bearing on the mysteries of magnetism.[325] She wrote indignantly of the treatment of the Jews in Rome where the Jews' Quarter had "not been enlarged for centuries and is now the most dreadful scene of crowd and filth". According to Joan, the Jews of Rome were forced to listen to sermons on Sundays "rating them as the refuse of creation", condemned to hell. Only in the time of the current Pope had they been released from the obligation to run a race along the Corso during Carnival "while the truly Christian spectators pelted and insulted them". Joan marvelled that they stuck to their creed and refused to convert, in spite of the fact that "no other faith entails such misery and contempt".[326]

When the actor Edmund Kean made a farewell visit to Edinburgh Joan wrote, "I am advising Lady Hepburn to go and see him, as she never has. I have often, and canna be fashed."[327] Familiar with the theatre, she was also

321 Acc8508/46, Letter 6.
322 Acc8508/23, Letter 8. Undated.
323 Acc8508/46, Letter 18. Undated. The four exclamation marks are Joan's.
324 Acc8508/46, Letter 6.
325 Acc8508/48. Letter 8. 2nd September.
326 Acc8508/47, Letter 10. 24th September.
327 Acc8508/46, Letter 4. Received 30th September.

familiar with poetry. Writing of Burns' early poem "Castle o Montgomery", Joan commented, "I think it so beautiful. It's a curious thing that the very first thing a boy of 17 or 18 wrote should be fully as much so as anything he wrote after his mind was more cultivated and his ear trained to the music measure…".[328] As for Byron, the poetic idol of the day, she condemned his "base" new poem which she saw as pouring out "a torrent of malice and invective against Lady B."[329]

We have already seen Joan busy picking up geological specimens in Italy. In her letter of 4th September[330] she ponders over the scientific evidence for the Carse of Stirling having been under water for a lengthy period in prehistory. "What a mere atom are our ages in time," she remarked. "When we have such a little drop of time given us for our portion (long enough, God knows, for all its pleasures!) we ought surely to make the most of it, and make the drop sparkle with as many colours as we can; and every new faculty we cultivate removes us from vegetating animals, and opens a new source of enjoyment…".

It was natural that Joan should include in her letters bits of news which she thought might interest John, and which were unlikely to appear in the London newspapers. As landowners, both would understand the implications of her remark to John on 29th August[331] that harvest was coming on, but there was a scarcity of "shearers", the seasonal labour required to cut and gather the grain harvest. In East Lothian the extra hands were usually supplied by itinerant Highlanders. A shortage of temporary labour meant that farmers had to offer higher wages to tempt the limited pool of local labour available, and the local labourers found they were able to coerce reluctant farmers to fall into line. On 4th September Joan related how an organised attempt against stingy farmers and blackleg labour came to a head.[332] "There was a serious battle in the village of Linton, by Smeaton, when some of them attacked the farmers. They, however, brought their own men on them, who seized a number and were like to fell them all to avenge their masters. I was amused to hear they began the attack by quizzing [i.e. mocking] one of the

328 Acc8508/46, Letter 25. Received 7th October.
329 Acc8508/47, Letter 9. Undated.
330 Acc8508/46, Letter 14.
331 Acc8508/47, Letter 4.
332 Acc8508/46. Letter 14.

farmers' sons as a 'Dandy'…". In Joan's opinion, "They are all discontented weavers who make this work and mischief, and not highlanders." However, it would seem that the farmers were more in danger of humiliation than of serious violence. "A farmer arrived home from market one day and found they had cut the skirts of his coat nearly off in the market for offering low wages."

The mention of "discontented weavers" is significant. The trade of handloom weaving had all but collapsed after the boom years of the Napoleonic Wars, and discontent was fuelled not only by poverty, but by the principles of the Rights of Man originating in Revolutionary France. On 6th October Joan wrote, "I hear today we are to have a revolution. They are forming yeomanry everywhere."[333] Later that month Joan reported to Lord John that there had been riots and serious unrest in the west of Scotland.[334] The 13th Regiment had been sent to Stirling to deal with potential sedition. This regiment had apparently last shown face in Scotland during the 1745 Jacobite Rebellion, and had been uneasy about the reception they would meet, particularly from Highlanders. As Joan remarked, however, the Highlands were now "becoming too civilized" to present any danger.

There was other news of purely local significance. "I have just heard of the death of the surgeon in Haddington," Joan wrote on 19th September,[335] "an invaluable man, and of 4 days' fever, quite a young man. I saw him the other day. God help us, how strange seems the choice of those who are taken in the midst of happy successful lives, and [those] who live on and on… It was Typhus, which is raging." The deceased was Dr John Welsh, a popular and able medical practitioner whose daughter Jane – a spirited and intelligent young woman of 18 at the time of her father's death – later became the rather mismatched wife of the literary lion Thomas Carlyle. Incidentally, Lord John replied to this piece of news that Welsh's death was "indeed awful", but "If the Typhus fever is about you, you will I hope go into Edinburgh."[336] Would Joan really have been safer in the city during an epidemic, than in the spacious and airy East Lothian countryside?

The death of "the poor Dr at Haddington" seems to have been a harrowing

333 Acc8508/46, Letter 26.

334 Acc8508/46, Letter 1. Undated.

335 Acc8508/46, Letter15.

336 Acc8508/23, Letter 10.

process, which Joan described a week later.[337] "Never was anything like the general consternation which it has produced. He came in on Wed from his visits, complained a little and went to bed, and never rose again. He became delirious next day and continued violent to the most dreadful degree. Yet they thought he would recover, and when he actually expired his poor wife became literally frantic. God help her, poor soul. It's not easy parting with what had been more than twenty years all her happiness… [In his] furious irrational state… his only recognition of her agonised attempts to soothe him, ordering her to get out of his sight as he could not endure her! It is dreadful to see force used to any creature. I just thought when poor Young had to be held by force in bed… what it would be to see that wild expression of hatred in an eye from which our own had once drunk all its joy." Joan concluded with, "We think this shock will go far to kill old Lady Hepburn, as she seemed to think Mr Welsh had the keys to life and death."

Both Joan and John had a lively interest in the sciences and allied topics. "Have you chanced to see in the newspaper anything of the keen contest in Edr for the Mathematical Chair?" she wrote.[338] Academic appointments to Edinburgh University in those days were not made by any committee of the university itself, but by the town council, as supervisors of the institution which had begun as "The Toun's College". The Council of course was vulnerable to political pressure, and one of the candidates for the Mathematical Chair, "Haldane of St Andrews", was being backed by the powerful Dundas family. The other candidate, William Wallace, "was backed by testimonials from the greatest names in Britain, and sent in to the Town Council the day they were deliberating, a barrow load of volumes of Encyclopedais (I can't spell it!) filled with articles on the different branches of mathematics all written by himself." It seemed to Joan that more interest was being shown in the appointment than would be shown in a General Election, and apparently "crowds" were waiting to hear the result. Eventually Wallace was chosen by a majority of 18 to 10, and burst into tears when he was informed of his appointment. "How fertile in talent the Scotch peasantry have been of late," Joan commented. "Leslie is the son of a smith in Fife and Wallace's father is a shoemaker in Hanover Street at this moment." William Wallace has been described elsewhere as "bald, with a strong Scots accent, and a grim and

337 Acc8508/47, Letter 10. 24th September.
338 Acc8508/47. Letter 10 24th September.

intelligent countenance".[339] John Leslie, Professor of Natural Philosophy at Edinburgh, was a prolific writer on scientific subjects, and the same source observes, "The blunt-mannered Leslie had moments of tenderness, usually in his amorous pursuits of unresponsive young ladies."[340]

It is perhaps worth observing that although the achievements of Scottish education have often been greatly exaggerated in the past, it was indeed possible, given determination and basic financial support, for talented boys of humble background, educated in parish schools, to graduate from university, enter the professions, carve out successful careers, and be accepted in the upper echelons of polite society.

It was only natural that Joan's correspondence should contain much in the way of gossip and comments about the sayings and doings of friends, relations and mutual acquaintances, with observations on passing fancies and mundane occurrences.

"All the talk just now is about Prince Leopold," Joan reported.[341] This was Leopold of Saxe Coburg, a German Prince who had married the daughter of the Prince Regent in 1816. He was adopted as King of the Belgians in 1831. On a visit to Scotland he had been to the Highlands and expressed himself "delighted". An attempt by Lord Huntly to impress the royal visitor almost went awry, when at a given signal 400 concealed Highlanders sprang up around the prince, who according to Joan, for a moment turned "quite pale".

Joan worried about her friend Annie Mure who was being pursued by Frederick Meade. Joan felt that Annie was trying to persuade herself that she was in love with him. "I really love Annie and would be heartily grieved to see her making a labyrinth to lose herself in," she wrote.[342] However, a month later, writing to John from Edinburgh[343] Joan observed that "poor Meade" had come to Town, but Anne was definitely not coming. "To be sure he laughs and jokes as before, but it is all hollow." Presumably Annie had failed to convince herself after all that "poor Meade" was husband material.

339 "Edinburgh, the Golden Age" – Mary Cosh. Birlinn. Edinburgh 2014. Page 504.
340 Ibid. Page 504
341 Acc8508/47, Letter 9. Undated.
342 Acc8508/48, Letter 8. 2nd September.
343 Acc8508/47, Letter7. Undated.

In an early letter in this sequence of correspondence with Lord John[344] Joan mentioned that a lady had asked her if Joan might let her have one of the peacocks from her property at Longniddry. Joan replied that there hadn't been peacocks there for years, but the lady was insistent that there were indeed two peacocks and two peahens at Longniddry. However, when the "Old Groom" came up to Letham from Longniddry he informed his mistress, "Oo yes mem, whan ye was in the wast kintrie last year the Marquis sent ye twa pair, an it's ill keepin them oot o the gaerdin." Joan then remembered being at Yester House and amusing herself with the peacocks there in June 1817, and the Marquis of Tweedale had said, "Since you're so fond of peacocks, I'll send you some when I get some from the farm at Lammerlaw." It might seem odd that Joan had never noticed peacocks on her own estate. The running of it was still in the hands of her Trustees, but it does seem as if Joan wanted as little to do with the place as possible. "I was to have gone down to Longlettery today," she remarked jocularly to John on 4th September,[345] "but so strongly was the spirit moved against it that I even bided at hame." "Hame", it seems, was her temporary abode with her relatives at Letham, while Longniddry, where she was born and spent her childhood, was a place to be avoided.

It is surely a sign of Joan and John's deepening relationship that they felt able to discuss awkward Argyll family matters frankly and without embarrassment. The profligate spending habits of John's brother the Duke of Argyll were well known, and had necessitated the selling off of parts of the ancestral landholdings. John explained to Joan that two or three years previously he had persuaded the Duke to sign a bond undertaking to sell no more land than would pay his "Trust Debts". "That bond exists," John affirmed, "and by the time the present sales are completed, the sum specified will be completed, and I mean to keep him to it. Some people say it's not binding in law; however it is in Honor, and I shall certainly try its strength if he proposes more sales."[346] Hinting that his brother the Duke might possibly be lacking in "Honor" is something that John most certainly would have expressed only to the most intimate of friends. We can sense his frustration when he mentions to Joan that his friend Dr Robertson had written to him

344 Acc8508/48, Letter 5. 30th August.

345 Acc8508/46, Letter 14.

346 Acc8508/24, Letter 9. Undated.

saying that he had visited the Duke and Duchess at Rosneath[347] and had found them "planning parterres and jets d'eau to be made in front of the new house when finished." All this, John fumed, together with all the other expenses incurred, was to be done on an income of £23 000 a year. "When the present sales are over," he continued firmly, I mean to protest against any more sales, so see what means then he'll get of paying his debts."

Perhaps the most significant example of Joan's sharing in intimate Argyll family matters is her discussion of John's sister Charlotte, who as already mentioned, had made an "unsuitable" marriage with a man much younger than herself. Joan had been constantly in Charlotte's company in Rome during her European tour, and obviously was very fond of her. At the same time, however, she was very conscious of what she perceived to be Charlottes weaknesses and character flaws, and of the imprudence of her actions. Nor was Joan afraid to express her opinions forcefully to Charlotte's brother Lord John, as she wrote at length in her letter of 1st October[348] when it was feared Charlotte had fallen ill.

> *"It is indeed a wretched termination to such a life as Lady Charlotte's, not I mean if she sinks fast now; I cannot think that, nor bear to think about it. Though when I look forward to all the painful and mortifying feelings she may [be] like to suffer from, I feel that to her, poor soul, length of days may be only length of sorrow. What an extraordinary fate! If she has erred more than almost anybody, she met with more to intoxicate and unsettle her reason than ever any woman ever did, and all acting too on a romantic imaginative character. She never calculated and built interested or ambitious views on the homage she could command anywhere. Had she been more coldly vain, she would have made to the eyes of the world a more respectable figure, without God knows, being a bit happier. But it's a cruel thing such a creature having been carried off her feet by the thirst of admiration, as she has shown she was capable of the most exclusive affection, and I believe sacrificed even the most natural amusements to humour Col C.*[349] *in his jealous fits. For oh, how easy it is to sacrifice when everything is valueless, and how easy to forgive even the unreasonable demands that still make us feel we were of consequence to those we love.*

347 Acc8508/24, Letter 7. Undated.

348 Acc8508/48, Letter 7.

349 Her first husband Colonel Campbell.

Surely it is a hard hard fate, such a creature falling from the very high ground she stood on. And it seems so strange her afterwards becoming so fond of admiration, after being attached too young and for so many years that she could not indulge the passion. I think her vanity was piqued into marrying Mr Bury by Mamie saying it was impossible so young a man could be in love with her. That I don't think, but God help us – if she had looked forward to the ordinary length of life, what is the proportion of the age of a woman above 50 when her husband is 40!![350] *And to a woman jealous of admiration, how eternally galling must it be watching for its decrease. For we all watch what we dread, and the most minute shades presaging evil, unseen by all other eyes, are as dreadfully plain to the microscopic eye of fear or affection. I don't think Mr B. will say anything to prevent her coming home if her health seems suffering. She has not an idea, I think, of his having any dread of creditors at least. She spoke about so many things to me, I am sure she would have told me had she known it. But she thinks it is for purposes of art he wishes to remain abroad (artful purposes, you'll say!). I don't know if I ever told you that she thinks the sort of cloud sometimes over him is about some lady he was in love with? And I see she has a strange sort of jealousy about it. I knew nothing of this, and one day she was saying she thought a man never cared for two people in his life, 'didn't I think?'. So I said I thought that nonsense, but about women I thought it very doubtful at least. I quite forgot that was not ground to touch on to a married widow! However, she went on with her own train of thought and asked me if I had ever heard Mr B. was attached to somebody. I never had, and certainly if I had I could not have told her. Now what I am afraid of is when they come back they may be jealous of each other. I know he can't bear her having 150 bosom friends, men. That I don't wonder at. It may be very savage, and certainly is very vulgar, unrefined, and unforeign, but I would have no idea of my wife reading poetry for hours to humble admirers, or doing as Mrs Ferguson Raith does, devoting every morning to their correspondence. Ae me, it's lucky Mr F.'s no like Annie. But what I fear is when Lady C. comes back Mr B. may be easily irritated or clouded rather, and she will feel it's sad change from the indifference she lived in for years before they*

350 Joan probably means, "How much of life is left to a woman over 50 with a 40 year old husband?"

went abroad. Oh me, it is melancholy to see a blight over people whom youth promised so fair. And it must indeed be a sad reflection to you, the days of her triumphant beauty and happiness, and think of her now in a sort of banishment. She has been haunting me these two days and I see that beautiful countenance looking so changed and emaciated, but still beautiful. How dearly I used to like to look at it. Many a time I have sat beside her, looking at it asleep, instead of on my book, and thought how much more lovely that pale face than any Guido, Raphael or Titian I ever saw."

We might think that Joan is being just a little judgmental and over-pessimistic in her views of Lady Charlotte's conduct and prospects. It is also rather ironic that the age difference between Charlotte and her husband Bury should bother Joan so much when there was a similar age gap between herself and Lord John Campbell. What is significant, though, is that Joan knew her criticisms would be acceptable to John.

10

"Not a do nothing body"

Lord John Campbell would arrive back in Scotland from London sometime in the second half of October 1819, and his correspondence with Joan Glassell seems to have ceased, presumably because they would then be able to see each other in Edinburgh, in John's home at Ardencaple, or in the homes of mutual friends and acquaintances. No written records seem to have survived to throw light on their relationship over the subsequent three months, but by the January 1820 John was back in London and the couple's correspondence resumed. Only Joan's letters from January to April have been preserved however, distributed among three folders of the Campbell Papers. As before, since many of the letters are undated it is not easy to place them in chronological order.

In January and February 1820 Joan was a guest at Carbeth near Strathblane to the north of Glasgow. In early spring, possibly from late February, she was with Mrs McCall at Ibrox Hill on the outskirts of the same city. In March and April she was either "in Town" (Edinburgh) or at her East Lothian estate of Longniddry, of which she was now in full control. There is barely a mention in her letters of the Hepburns, with whom she had spent the autumn of 1819.

In his autobiography, Joan's son wrote laconically, "In 1820 my father was married to Miss Glassell, and they settled down in their country house at Ardencaple."[351] This singularly uninformative statement gives no clue as to how the happy event came about, but obviously sometime between October 1819 and January 1820 John had proposed marriage to Joan and had been accepted. We might guess at the proposal being made around Christmas and New Year, but when and where it happened is never mentioned in Joan's letters.

What is clear from her correspondence is that their relationship was now on a different footing. Her letters are full of endearments and references to her feelings for John, and we can note the appearance of the sort of mildly embarrassing pet names that doting lovers will dream up for each other. Whereas in autumn 1819 Joan was still signing her letters to John "M. J. Glassell",[352] by spring 1820 she had become "your Mary" (John apparently thought Mary a particularly beautiful name), or "Pigeon", or "Pigie". This last seems to be a reference to the letter-bearing carrier pigeon rather than to the gentle and submissive dove. We also find the first appearance of Joan as "Tammie Norrie", which seems to have become her Argyll family nickname. "Tammie Norrie" is an old East Lothian name for the puffin, a small sea bird with a large rainbow-hued parrot-like beak. We might wonder that she did not find "Joan" rather more preferable.

One of the first letters in this sequence, perhaps the first, is dated "Carbeth, January 31st"[353]. Carbeth was the estate of William Smith, brother of James Smith who had overseen Joan's continental tour. At the time of writing John appears to have been at home in Ardencaple, and Joan was expecting him to visit her at Carbeth. "I wish you could have seen Mrs Smith's face today when I came. She literally could not speak for a while, or said anything, but look at me and kiss me again, and at last she said, 'I just could not believe I was to see you with a happy face on, and now you are the most perfect being that ever lived!'." This Mrs Smith is probably the companion of Joan's European trip, rather than the wife of William Smith of Carbeth. She would have had ample opportunity to observe Joan's unhappy face during

351 George Douglas 8th Duke of Argyll: Autobiography and memoirs, New York, E.P. Dutton and Company, 1906. Vol. 1, Page 55.

352 Presumably "Miss Joan Glassell". Her baptismal record shows no other Christian names.

353 Campbell Papers Acc8508/37, Letter 3.

the Italian jaunt. The reason for Mrs Smith's emotional welcome, and for Joan's happy face, was no doubt her engagement to Lord John.

Joan had been looking through a book of old maps printed in 1654, she told John, in which her estate of "Longstuffery" appeared to be in the sea. This prompted a long whimsical passage in which she imagined lobsters dwelling there, and she went on to relate her memories previously quoted of walking along the shore on a misty morning, and hearing the oyster fishermen's dreg-song drifting over the water. She also remembered John saying at Ardencaple, that Mary "was the most beautiful of all names; that it expressed every virtue under heaven".

Alluding to Mr Smith's "contraptions" for measuring and surveying, she affirmed that none of them could measure "the deep well of affection that will ever, in summer's heat and winter's cold, live in Pigeon's heart for you, and a happy Pigeon it will be when it sees you coming".

In another letter, undated, but which must have been written around the same time, she remarked, "I hear them now firing minute guns for the poor king. I hope the mourning will be over before April. It's a bore having to put on black things again. You like blue pigies better than black ones, don't you, love."[354] Joan was hoping the mourning period would be over by April because that month had been fixed for her wedding, although the exact date had not yet been decided upon.

No doubt anticipating her imminent (if rather belated) official coming of age, Joan had been studying the Haddington market grain prices, and wrote bitterly of "Steuart" (the lawyer Charles Stewart, one of her trustees) "making a Kirk and a Mill of the rents and bringing most of them for grist to his own mill". She continued indignantly, "I must say I would give a good deal to have an opportunity of bringing that fellow over the coals – mean rascal, taking advantage of the ignorance of a girl."

Joan gave a playful description of herself in another letter from Carbeth to John at Ardencaple, postmarked 5th February,[355] pretending she had seen an article in a recent issue of the transactions of the Royal Society:

> *"A new species of bird considered as a great natural curiosity discovered on the shores of the Firth of Forth by J.D.E. Campbell F.F.F.S.*[356] *in the*

354 Acc8508/46, Letter 21. George III died on 29th January 1820.

355 Acc8508/2, letter 6.

356 Fellow of the Flying Fools' Society – a reference to John's interest in ballooning.

course of investigations anent the flight of birds, and he has ascertained that this here wonderful hanimal unites many of the properties of the carrier pigeon, goose, and 'Tamie Norry' (The latter likewise a native of the Firth of Forth) and this bird will fly any given distance, even three thousand miles, retaining all the while a distinct recollection of the way home whither it will always return without any apparent inducement, and (apparently) remaining voluntarily for a considerable time among the pine woods and myrtle groves of Italy, seems discontented and unsociable, never becoming domesticated or assimilating its habits to others of the tribe, and though 'Foreign fowls have fair feathers', its plumage resisting the influence of 'fair and fervid Italy', finally returning as much resembling the grey goose as ever, with the same unenlightened attachment to former haunts and habits which in the end proves fatal etcetera. Now this bird having a remarkable enjoyment in the west wind sits for whole days on the moors of Stirlingshire watching the carry of the clouds which indicate the currents of air, and its large eyes seemingly marking with avidity those symptoms which are prognostics of a westerly breeze."

In Carbeth Joan was close to the Strathblane hills and happy to be once more among "something like mountains". "Oh dearest," she wrote, "the shifting lights falling on the dark woods, broom, fern, and all the varied brilliance of mountain vegetation are not more beautiful compared to red field and dull stubble rigs than I have always thought your mind and feelings more bewilderingly bright and soft compared with other mortals." Alluding to their forthcoming marriage, she observed, "You know what you have to expect, which let me tell you is more than most people can say. And when they say 'for better or worse' few can guess what that 'worse' is. But you have the comfort of thinking, 'The creature can't be much dafter than I think her, at least not much'."

On 16th February Joan was still at Carbeth, and John at Ardencaple. The Glasgow artist Millichip was painting her portrait. "Milliechap" or "Mealychops" as she rather cruelly called him, seemed to Joan to be a "strange creature". He seems to have thought much the same of her, telling her that he thought she "was afraid of what she admired for talent and would be afraid of what she much loved". After a long pause he said gravely, "Very few people are able to understand your character, I'm sure". Millichip and Mr Smith had been positioning her in different lights, insisting that she must be painted looking at the artist, which made Joan uneasy. "I don't like to have that man reading my eyes all the while," she commented. She was also afraid that Millichip would paint her not as she was "but much better". "I hate that," she complained, "as it will make you think the original an ugly beast, and I don't like that, though I never before cared what like I was."[357]

Turning her mind to her inheritance, she told John, "We must have some days at Longniddry and you must tell me what I am to do about some parks there… I may, I think, put some of the 100 old servants I know of into the house merely to keep it ready for us… but I wish to do nothing meanwhile till I have somebody to order me." They might, she thought, have Ardencaple painted in the summer, and go to Longniddry while the work was being done.

It is difficult to place exactly two undated letters from Ibrox which Joan sent to John, but it is possible that she took time off from her extended stay at Carbeth to spend a few days with Isabella Smith, the sister of James Smith her Italian chaperone. Isabella had married John McCall, a Glasgow merchant who had extended an old house at Ibrox Hill using plans designed by his brother in law James Smith.[358] (Incidentally, the site of this house is now occupied by the "House for an Art Lover" built 1989-96 to a design by the celebrated architect Charles Rennie Mackintosh.) At Ibrox Hill Joan had been pondering over Lady Augusta, John's elder sister. From other letters it would seem that Lady Augusta was becoming rather forgetful. Joan felt her a weight on her conscience. "If she would ever settle there we might give her Longniddry but I don't think it would suit her, and the sort of people would not do for her, tho' in so close a neighbourhood she would always be in a fidget going to visit somewhere."

Joan also suggested that if John were to come to Carbeth, Millichip might paint his portrait, if he was still in Glasgow. She addresses him as "Dearest Love" and "Beloved", and declares, "I cannot regret so much time flying when it is to bring the time, not when I am as before to leave you forever, but when your Pigeon is to be bound your slave for life…".

The other letter from Ibrox relates how Joan's dog "Inver" had strayed. Joan had put an advertisement in the Edinburgh papers. "Mrs McCall was

---

357 Acc8508/46, Letter 13.
358 Rootsweb – Duncan family of Strathblane, John McCall of Ibrox Hill.

so amused to see it the other day, well knowing my hieroglyphics to be the cause of the blunders. It calls him 'Turner' and says he strayed from 'Ibrow Hill'." [Anyone who has toiled to decipher Joan's handwriting will sympathise with the newspaper editor.] However, since the advertisement got Mrs McCall's name right, and the description of the dog, Joan had high hopes that Inver would be found. "Dearest," she concluded, "it is a dream of delight often to think you love me… there is only one thing I am very sure can never be exaggerated, my affection for you… Love ever, Your own Pigeon."

By 6th March 1820 John was back in London, no doubt attending to his parliamentary duties, and Joan was in Edinburgh. Her letter of that date[359] marks an important milestone in her life. (It is actually dated "Monday Feby 6th", but since it is postmarked "8th March" and marked "Received 10th March", Joan has obviously written "Feby 6th" in error for March 6th.):

> *"There was a curious gathering in my room this forenoon. Mr and Mrs Robertson, Mr Story, and in came Mr Kerr to congratulate me on being a free woman as the trustees had their last meeting. I expected whenever Mr S went away and the Rs, the old gentleman would say something. However, he wanted courage evidently, and merely significantly wished me all happiness. Lord Alloway[360] sent me a message to ask me to appoint an hour for his calling, which I am going to do. I am anxious to know whether he is leaving Town as I would give anything to have him deliver me over to execution 'talking devoutly to a Praest' or rather a Praest talking to me, for I don't think I'll have much to say to him. Kermack brought me all the papers and the accounts regularly made up to this date and audited by Scott Moncrieff. I shall take them out and look them over at Longniddry. I wish the Fletchers would change their mind about going, as I will have no time if they are there, and besides Mr F will be spying ferlies so much. Kermack is to bring me tomorrow the receipt from Sir Wm Forbes for the two thousand. Now, like a dear good soul, take it off my hands, for Pigies have no use for money in banks; so tell me you will. I hate having receipts or any things in my keeping. I wish to heaven you had Longniddry and everything in your own hands to make a Kirk*

359 Acc8508/46, Letter 20.

360 "Lord Alloway" – the judicial title of David Cathcart, Joan's senior trustee. He had been appointed a Court of Session judge in 1813.

or a Mill of (these are both there, only the Kirk is an auld one and like its mistress useless).[361] *One comfort if I were to die tomorrow, the ancient will I made before you came down, when I thought farewell was all I would ever say to you, will be as good now. But indeed, Love, there is nothing I less wish than to die now. Life is inexpressibly sweet when I can think it has value to you. Whenever your answer about the American agent's name comes, Kermack is to write to Grenan. He, I believe, is an honest man from what Kermack says was Cathcart's opinion of him, but General Shaw who was left in charge of some property in another state, is a scamp by all accounts and perhaps would be the better of a little rough handling. Since 1813 Steuart has received £1050 from America, I suppose all from Grennan, but I am not sure. £150 I think was within these 6 months. Now, judging by the effect on Steuart himself, I think it may have a very good effect on the American agents too, knowing that they have no longer to deal with trustees or a woman, the one too careless, and some would say the other too senseless to know anything of the state of things. I daresay Kermack thinks I have reversed the usual order of things and become more rational than I was in my life, as I never before could take anything to heart about business. The truth is, when I thought I had lost you, the only treasure earth held for me, I could not care for this world's gear and only wished to God I'd got a free passage out of it."*

John Glassell had directed that his daughter would not be "of age" till she was 25 years of age. Since she would not be 25 until 9th June 1821, Joan's trustees were in fact handing over responsibility ahead of schedule. The most likely reason for this was her impending marriage. The fact that Joan's intended husband was a Member of Parliament and the brother and heir of the Duke of Argyll may well have encouraged the Trustees to hand over their responsibilities with alacrity. It is interesting that as late as 1820 Joan's trustees were still receiving money from business interests in America. "Grennan/Grenan" is Daniel Grinnan the wealthy Virginian who, as we have seen, played a crucial role in sorting out "British Mercantile Claims", and married the daughter of Andrew Glassell, Joan's American uncle.

361 Joan seems to be referring to the fragmentary remains of a chapel in the grounds of Longniddry House known as "John Knox's Kirk". The Reformer is supposed to have publicly catechised his pupils there while acting as tutor to the sons of the laird of Longniddry.

In her letter to Lord John, Joan acts the part of the bird-brained "Pigie" who has "no use for money in banks" and wishes only to offload responsibility for real-estate and finances onto the manly shoulders of "Papa". In fact, she was far from devoid of business sense, and after marriage showed an ongoing interest in agricultural and estate matters. We get a glimpse of this towards the end of the letter where she reassures John, "Don't bother yourself about money. Though we had half the Duke's debts, even, I'll be hanged if we could not get rid of them, and it puts me mad you harrying and bothering yourself ill. You will say 'No fear', but I implore you to recollect your frequent illnesses in London…". Who comes over as the stronger partner here?

After responsibility for her estate at Longniddry was transferred into her hands from her trustees on 6th March 1820, Joan seems to have taken up residence there, although she also stayed frequently "in Town". Over half a century ago, a lady now long dead[362] related to me a brief anecdote about "Miss Glassell the heiress of Longniddry" which had been handed down in her family. Visiting her tenants not long before her marriage, Miss Glassell called at the home of Bett Merrilees, who lived at the Cooper's Close, the old farm on the site of the present Lorne Cottages in Longniddry. When the conversation turned to the impending marriage, old Bett observed, "If ye get a cat o yer ain kind, ye'll ken when ye're scartit!" Whatever was implied by this enigmatic statement, Miss Glassell apparently took offence and never spoke to Bett again.

Very shortly after her "free woman" letter, Joan wrote to John[363] saying that Lord Alloway had declared, "I would come from any part of Britain to your summons, so whenever the day is fixed, write to me, and I assure you few things can give me greater pleasure than to give you over to good guardianship." Lord Alloway, then, was secured to give the bride away in place of her deceased father John Glassell. Joan's faithful maid Aitken reflected what seems to have been the general opinion of the match. "She told Lady Robert," Joan reported to Lord John, "she never was so happy at anything, 'For I am sure my Lady they will be so happy. They are so alike, and his own people[364] are so fond of Lord John. He's the best master ever was'."

362 Mrs Pringle of Lorne Cottages, Longniddry.

363 Acc8508/46, Letter 10. Undated. Postmarked 8th March.

364 i.e. servants and tenants.

Joan was not without other admirers however. In the same letter she relates how she had seen two acquaintances while shopping in Edinburgh, "Colonel Napier and Crombie". In the course of conversation Joan asked Crombie if spring might tempt him back to Oban. Crombie, who had presumably not heard of Joan's engagement, replied with exaggerated gallantry, "No, but whenever you go there, depend upon it, I will go to secure you wherever I am." "I felt myself quite rouged," she admitted.[365]

Although the marriage was only a month away, Joan and John seem to have been reluctant to broadcast it to all and sundry. Perhaps they had set their minds on a relatively quiet occasion, and had no desire to stir up expectations among acquaintances that there would be a grand celebration to which the whole world would be invited. Joan wrote that Mr and Mrs Fletcher had called.[366] "Do tell me what shall I do if she asks me point blank, seriously? I don't think she will, but if she does I don't know how to deny it. Here I can avoid her and never call without a guard, but if they go out to Longniddry I shall be at her mercy."

As the wedding day approached, Joan's mind was not completely taken over by the prospect of marital bliss. "Shall I send in the caliche to have new wheels put on it, or rims to the old ones? …shall I send it into Edinburgh to have it done? Secondly, do you wish the parks which can be spared let by the season, or during the term of the rest of the lease, which is three crops? And can you give the gardener a house at Arden? Don't say 'Devil take her for bothering me with questions'."[367] Joan was giving John his place as her future husband, but was clearly not inclined to leave practical matters aside until he thought of them himself.

When Joan wrote again on 19th March from Longniddry[368] John was on the point of leaving London for Scotland. A general election was impending, and John would have to put in an appearance in Argyll. His re-election was a foregone conclusion however. "By this day fortnight you will be an MP again," Joan stated confidently, although previous letters suggest that John had hoped his kinsman Campbell of Lochnell might take on the job. "Tell

365 Ibid.

366 Acc8508/46, letter 17. Postmarked 10th March. Mrs Fletcher senior was a prominent Edinburgh hostess. Her son was married to Charlotte Clavering, Lord John's niece. It's not clear which Fletchers are meant here.

367 Acc8508/46, Letter 10.

368 Acc8508/46, Letter 23.

me the day and hour you will come," Joan pleaded. "Oh my me, the delight of having things ready for you, and seeing the carriage come down the long road." John's sister Lady Augusta was intending to come to Edinburgh, and Joan's letter makes it plain that although her presence at the wedding was desired, John had not yet invited her. "She will be there [Edinburgh] by this day week, and if your letter or yourself should inform her by that time, I am sure the prospect of the ploy of being at our execution will induce her to remain with perfect contentment till that time in Edinburgh… I might ask her out here for a few days between your going west and your return, but at the warning you gave me I will not do it till I see you of course." It is perhaps a measure of the couple's desire that their marriage should not be a great public event, that only two or three weeks before the wedding Joan could write,[369] "Lady Augusta was saying tonight very suddenly 'John need be in no hurry to come in. I suppose the marriage won't be for some time'." Joan was not keen to say too much to her about the wedding, because apparently Lady Augusta claimed to have predictive dreams, and Joan was terrified that if too much attention was drawn to the forthcoming marriage, she might be inspired to relate one of her ill-omened prognostications. "Poor good soul, she would not hurt a fly with her will, but she makes my hair stand on end by the long dreams she details circumstantially, that I know to be that instant made."

John's arrival was now imminent. "Oh, do not be later than Monday or Tuesday I entreat of you. I am weary to death to see you, and feel in such a frightened and anxious state till I do," she wrote. "Oh, never again, thank God a thousand times, will I try to shut my eyes to the only light they have. No, ever dearest; my existence, every power of my mind created by you is yours alone, yours eternally…". Joan rounded off her declarations of devotion with a short poem, presumably her own:

"To watch forever as thy wishes rise
And only read them in those well known eyes;
To serve thee! humble – as a trembling slave
But with such love as slavery never gave!
To woman's heart the tenderness is given,
The deepest curse, or brightest bliss of Heaven.

369 Acc8508/37, Letter 1, undated.

I would not now my hours of sorrow give
For all the bright ones that the happiest live
If my soul's worship tried by grief and time
Can ever give one throb of joy to thine.
Goodnight ever dearest Lord John… ever, ever, your Mary."

Finally, in her last letter to John before their marriage[370] Joan exclaims, "In two days I am to see you!" and informs him of where she will be, according to the time of day he arrives from Glasgow.

The details of the wedding day can be found in a letter Joan wrote on 1st April to her friend Mrs McCall. This letter, Acc8508/37, Letter 4, in the Campbell papers, is annotated "Just before her marriage, telling where it was to take place." It is dated "Longniddrie, April Day", beneath which Joan has commented, "Very appropriate!!!". Joan apologised for not having written earlier, saying John's arrival from England had put everything else out of her head. "I was at Lady R's on Friday night. I really did not expect him that night, when at 10 o' clock he walked in looking better than I ever saw him." She recounted how Lady Augusta had come to Town, and how John had left again (presumably on election business). Lady Augusta had been prevailed upon to stay with Joan at Longniddry until the wedding, which Joan said, "Will be on the 14th, I think." The "I think" is rather surprising. To have such a longed for and eagerly anticipated event only a fortnight away, and still not precisely fixed would seem just a little disorganised to the modern mind. There had also been a mix-up with the publication of the "banns" – the public announcement in church of the couple's intention to marry. The banns had been announced two weeks too soon. John and Joan had happened to be walking along George Street in blissful ignorance as the congregation exited the church, and no doubt would have to accept congratulations and lighthearted banter from friends and acquaintances while totally unprepared.[371]

"But I will tell you what has delighted me beyond measure," Joan continued. "The Hepburns are obliged to go out of town, the lease of the

370 Acc8508/37, Letter 2.

371 There is no mention of the banns being called in Gladsmuir, the parish church for Longniddry. The church mentioned is probably St Andrew's in George Street.

house being out, so I have got off in all honour and can have it at Lady Robert's, which rejoices my heart, and was what she had set her heart on. While in Edinburgh he [John] told everyone. He had written before to the Fletchers, Lady Augusta etc, and nothing can be more gratifying to me than the warm congratulations he meets from people whose interest is all to his happiness and every creature says he is a new creature from what he was in his youngest days even. We have had a long and dark winter , God knows, but may we not trust the more to the brightness and balm of a spring most warm in their approbation, and old Mrs Damer, who loves Lord John as her own son, never saw me but it seems has got some 'prejudice' in my favour second hand and sent her love to me… This is Lord John's election day. Rawdon and he went to Inveraray on Thursday, and we expect him here this day week, and on the Thursday or Friday following we will take our flight to the Land of the Sun. I believe your gloves and cake must go by coach, as we intend to breakfast in our respective holes before and immediately after the knot is tied. We will return to put on our boots and spurs while the party go to breakfast, and if we can we will escape without any more bother. I don't think we will manage that quite however. I will have charge with Miss Grant, of sending the cake etc. I thought he [Lord John] would be the most nervous and frightened of the two, but I suppose it is the usual desperate courage of men in awful situations, as he is quite the reverse of nervous, and I am beginning to quake about marching into a room full of people. I think [there] will be nearly 20 people

Lord Alloway	*Lady Augusta*
Lord Robert	*Mrs Fletcher*
Sir John Hepburn	*Lady Robert*
Rawdon	*Lady Hepburn*
Mr Fletcher	*Miss Grant*
Walter Campbell	*Miss de la Chaux*
The two men of law	*Lady E. Campbell*
	Elizabeth Kerr (My 2d).

Walter and Lady E we are not sure of, only if they are in Town he will ask them as he was at their occasion… I don't believe there ever were two victims led to the altar with lighter hearts than ours, as we have nothing, lose nothing, and know each other better than most people when they give their vows.

Aiken may thank her lucky stars she has Lady R and Miss Grant to apply to anent the weighty matters of 'Peertins', as she cannot get her mistress to give them due consideration. They had me arranged in my marriage dress 'tother night, and à la Heroine, 'never did I look so lovely' – that's not saying much."

It seems the marriage did not in fact take place on 14th April as Joan had "thought", but on the 17th, as indicated by a brief note of that date from Joan to Mrs McCall[372] marked "On her marriage day. Miss Glassell."

"April 17th.

My dear Soul, I cannot [illegible] signing my new name, but at this moment the people are coming to lead me to execution.

Yours ever,

1stly Miss J Glassell
2dly now J G G Campbell."

The two letters quoted above seem to be the only records of Joan's marriage preserved in the Campbell Papers. There appears to be no note of it in the National Records of Scotland, but under "Marriages May 1820" Blackwood's Edinburgh Magazine announced, "At the house of Lord Robert Kerr, the Right Hon. John Campbell to Miss Glassel of Longniddrie." "Lord Robert" is Major General Lord Robert Kerr, the youngest son of William Kerr 5th Marquess of Lothian. "Lady Robert" was born Mary Gilbert. Elizabeth Kerr, Joan's bridesmaid, was their daughter. Joan would be "given away" by David Cathcart, Lord Alloway, her former trustee. There is no mention of a minister conducting the marriage ceremony, but the mistimed banns in George Street might suggest that the minister of St Andrew's would officiate. The "two men of law" may have been official witnesses to the marriage contract, but on the other hand it was perfectly legal for a marriage to be solemnised without a minister, and it is just possible the "men of law" might have had a more important part to play. The honeymoon destination, the "Land of the Sun", was no doubt Italy, where we can assume Joan would be happier than on her previous visit. On their return the couple took up residence in John's house of Ardencaple on the outskirts of Helensburgh, where Joan was now "Lady John".

---

372 Acc8508/37. Folder 2, Letter 1.

The original castle of Ardencaple was built on a raised beach some 200 metres from the eastern shore of the Gare Loch, overlooking the opening of the loch into the Firth of Clyde. In the 16th century the Macaulay lairds of Ardencaple strengthened and enlarged the castle, but their fortunes deteriorated, their home became semi-ruinous, and the last Macaulay laird died penniless in Rhu. In 1787 the castle was bought by the Duke of Argyll, who had it restored. The architect Robert Adam was involved in comprehensive renovations and extensions. The Duke's brother Lord John took over Ardencaple in 1815 after the death of his uncle Lord Frederick Campbell, the previous occupant.

Lord John's son, the 8th Duke, describes his boyhood home as "built on the crest of the old coast line at a point where it was very steep and formed a projecting curve so that walls could have the benefit of a natural defence on two sides".[373] On each side "the same line of bank was covered with old trees, the home of an immense rookery". Behind the house was a "nearly level plateau of arable fields stretching to the foot of the mountain slope. On that slope was aa fine old wood, principally of oak…". "Mountain slope" is something of an exaggeration, as the hill behind Ardencaple, Tom na h-Airidh, is a mere 354 metres above sea level, but here we are on the southern edge of the Highlands, and as the 8th Duke pointed out, the hill commands extensive views over the Clyde and towards the higher hills to the north.

As for the house itself, "The lower part of the walls was of immense thickness, dating it is said from the 13th century. On top of these walls a modern house had been built… It had never been large or imposing and the more modern parts were simple and unadorned. But the southern front, facing the sea, was picturesque and included some variety of wall, of towers, and of turrets. The accommodation was limited, but a pleasant library looked inland over the lawn and to the wooded hill; there was a long narrow drawing room, a comfortable dining room, and a long narrow passage, almost another room. The castle was surrounded by trees on all sides but one."[374]

The interested modern investigator will search in vain for this "picturesque" house set in attractive rural surroundings. It was sold by the

373 George Douglas 8th Duke of Argyll, Autobiography and memoirs, New York, Dutton and Company, 1906. Vol. 1, page 50.

374 Ibid. P. 50.

Argyll estates in 1852, and eventually acquired by developers in 1935, who built a housing estate on the lawn. At the outbreak of the Second World War the house was requisitioned by the Royal Navy, and in 1957 demolished to build housing for Faslane Naval Base. A single tower was left as a mount for navigation beacons. This tower, in the middle of a swathe of modern housing, is all that remains of Joan and John's much-loved home. Their son the 8th Duke described it thus, "It was indeed perfect as a haven of rest from the troubles of life – situated in a beautiful country, with only a very few country neighbours, and otherwise a seclusion as complete as [they] might wish to make it."[375]

John's parliamentary duties compelled him to continue to spend time in London, but in 1822 he resigned his seat. It seems unlikely that he had ever felt much enthusiasm for the job, which he had inherited from his Uncle Frederick and probably only tolerated out of family duty. At heart he was not a politician, but an artistic craftsman who was happiest alone with his tools and materials. As his son explained, "Above the narrow drawing room my father had made a charming workshop, fitted up with all sorts of lathes for turning, and nests of drawers for the appropriate tools, with a store not far off of elephant tusks and of rare and beautiful ornamental woods such as could be combined with work in ivory and in metals. Large dormer windows let in abundant light and dominated the Firth of Clyde."[376] Apart from one small farm leased to a tenant, the whole estate was in John's own hands, and the management of its maintenance and cultivation "gave him plenty of occupation" as his son observed.

Under an arrangement with the Duke of Argyll's trustees Lord John also had responsibility for the management of the woods on the Inveraray estate,[377] and an annuity of £28000. The Argyll finances however were decidedly shaky. Luckily, Joan's fortune was substantial enough to allow the couple to live comfortably in accord with their position in society. How this may have been perceived by some is illustrated by a rather sour article, already mentioned, which was published in the "Newfoundlander" on 18th May 1883 after a visit to Richmond, Virginia, undertaken by Joan and John's grandson, the marquis of Lorne, then Governor General of Canada. After relating how John Glassell made his "enormous fortune", the

375 Memoirs, Vol 1, Page 50.
376 Memoirs, Vol 1, Page 50.
377 Memoirs, Vol 1, Page 90.

Newfoundlander turned to his daughter "Joanna Glassel [sic] who grew up a great beauty, and a most charming and attractive Scotch lassie." The article continued:

> *"Now it happened about the beginning of the twenties that the splendid estate of the Argyll family had been greatly burdened and exhausted by the reckless extravagance of [the 6th Duke] who was a famous fast man of London and a special friend of George IV then Prince Regent. The Duke's brother, Lord Campbell, in default of descendants of his own, would succeed to the titles and estates. But alas! How could they ever be cleared of the exhaustive burdens placed upon them by his dissipated elder brother? Only by marriage to some rich heiress. In seeking one, his attention was drawn to the beautiful and accomplished daughter of the rich old Virginia planter and merchant John Glassel. Joanna Glassel thus became the Duchess of Argyll[378] and proved the worthy wife of the most illustrious name in the history of the Scotch aristocracy."*

After extolling the virtues of the current Duke of Argyll and his son the Marquis of Lorne, the Newfoundlander article ended by claiming that Lorne's visit to Virginia was "in recognition of the obligations of his family to the soil and institutions through which his grandfather was enabled to rescue the family estates from ruin and extinction."

The Newfoundlander's insinuation that the marriage was a mere exercise in fortune hunting is a gross distortion of the truth. There can be no doubt that the union of "Pigie" and "Papa" was a genuine love match, although obviously Joan's money would not go amiss.

A son, presumably conceived immediately during the newlyweds' honeymoon in the "Land of the Sun", was born on 11th January 1821 and named John Henry. He was followed on 30th April 1823 by George Douglas, and on 12th March 1825 by Emma Augusta.

There is much that we can assume about Joan's life as "Lady John Campbell". After all, there is no shortage of accounts of life in landowning families in early 19th century Scotland, and Joan, for all her individuality of character,

378 Wrong. Joan died before her husband inherited the title.

would not stray too far from the norm. To learn about what was particular to her own life, however, we must turn again to her correspondence. Joan must have written many hundreds, perhaps thousands, of letters during the relatively short period of her marriage to Lord John Campbell, as letter-writing was an almost daily occupation in her circles. Some of these letters may still lurk in family archives, but such possibilities apart, we must rely on what is scattered through the various files of the National Library's "Campbell Papers". As observed earlier, these present occasional difficulties. Chronological order is not always observed, and folders sometimes contain more, or less, than what is indicated by their descriptions. Obviously, what we have there is only a fraction of Joan's total correspondence, but there is enough of interest to be worth pursuing.

The archive contains a mere three letters to her husband Lord John,[379] 17 to her cousin Hugh Francis Cadell of Cockenzie in East Lothian,[380] several from Mary Grant, the daughter of Joan's former mentor Mrs Grant of Laggan,[381] and several from her friend Bessie Mure.[382] Letters from Lord John's sister Charlotte are scattered through various different folders, and Acc8508/36 contains correspondence from Charlotte's daughters Emma and Adelaide. In addition, letters can be found here and there throughout the archive from a wide range of individuals, from the Duchess of Argyll to an aspiring wet-nurse.

Francis Cadell, Joan's cousin, was the son of her mother's sister. Mary Grant was one of Mrs Grant's two surviving daughters, on whose shoulders the care of her consumptive sister and elderly mother fell. Mary died in 1827 after a period of mental illness. Bessie Mure seems to have been an early acquaintance of Lord John's, and was probably Elizabeth, the daughter of William Mure of Caldwell, a soldier who had fought and been wounded in the American War of Independence. He later became Vice Lieutenant of the County of Renfrew and was rector of Glasgow University 1793-95. The west of Scotland connection suggests the Mures might have been part of the Smiths' circle, which would explain Bessie's original acquaintance with Lord John. Lady Charlotte, wife of the detested Mr Bury, we have already encountered.

379 Acc8508/49.

380 Acc8508/29.

381 Acc8508/30 and elsewhere.

382 Acc8508/15.

In Joan's correspondence with her cousin Francis Cadell[383] we begin to see a rather different woman from the impulsive scatterbrain of Mrs Grant's assessment, or the helpless "Pigie" of her letters to Lord John. Many a landowner's wife concerned herself solely with domestic matters and the social round. It is plain however that Joan developed an active interest in the business side of landowning. Whether or not Francis Cadell was Joan's official "factor" or business manager for her Longniddry estate, he certainly seems to have given his services in a supervisory capacity there. Living as he did only a couple of miles away from Joan's Longniddry property, it would not be difficult for him to keep an eye on things.

Writing to Francis only a month after her marriage,[384] Joan began her letter, "My dear Francis, many thanks for your report about the lime rock, and on submitting it to Lord John, he wishes a radical investigation of the quality as well as the depth of rock, and that a pump should be made to facilitate the object. I am quite of your opinion that one gang[385] should be sufficient, and as far as I can judge, Scot is the person to retain. I think therefore the sooner Pow is paid off the better, but if you will be so good, use your own opinion on the subject and draw whatever money is required from Kermack." Limestone had long been quarried to the south-east of Joan's property of Longniddry, and lime burning continued throughout the 19th century. Presumably this was a new venture being considered on her own ground. Her following two letters show that Lord John requested and received samples of the limestone which he subjected to "all manner of chemical tests", finding the samples to be "nearly pure limestone", and requesting that "another pit" should be sunk where Francis judged it best.[386] Lord John is portrayed here as the main mover, but Joan's words, "I am quite of your opinion", "as far as I can judge", and "I think" make it plain that in reality she is more than a mere go-between for her husband and cousin. In fact limestone was never mentioned again, and there is no evidence that it was ever quarried or mined on Joan's ground, so perhaps although initial investigations were optimistic, it was decided not to proceed with actual quarrying.

Previous to her coming of age and marrying, the management of Joan's

383 Acc8508/29.

384 Acc8508/29, Letter 1.

385 Gang: drainage channel.

386 Acc8508/29, Letters 2 and 3.

property had been, as we have seen, solely in the hands of her trustees, and she seems to have shown no interest in estate management or agriculture. After her marriage however a growing interest in such matters becomes apparent. In her first letter to Francis Cadell she tells him that she and Lord John have been busy "making new walks through the woods" at Ardencaple "marking them out ourselves". She remarks, "As most of them are through young woods of Lord John's own planting, it gives much more interest."[387] A month later she wrote to Lord John who was in Campbelltown that she had gone out "to look at the people" and found James Campbell and a boy "cutting stabs". It seems he should have been working on a "sunk fence" or ha-ha, but instead had decided to mend a barrier between the fat cattle and the cows. "I told him he had better go back to the fence today," said Joan. She had also had "Davie" filling up holes in the road and rolling it. "There will not be nearly enough of broken metal," she informed her husband. "I think the rain has made that part of the road so very deep and miry, the stones must be laid on pretty thick."[388] The new lady of Ardencaple seems to have already been showing confidence in issuing orders to estate employees, and although the repairing of an estate driveway was a relatively minor matter, "I think" once again indicates a woman not devoid of determination.

Less than two years later [389] Joan was able to write to her cousin Francis, "Tho' I never cared for farming when in E. L.[390] I have taken a passion for it now, and live in a field which we are draining and ploughing to bring it into order, taking down some old stone fences, levelling etc." "If your spring is anything like ours," she observed, "the Longniddry parks must have fine promise. I never saw anything so rapid and strong as the vegetation here. We have a field that was laid down with wheat last summer. It is to be cut this year. I really never saw so fine a sward as is on it now."

In her next letter, a month later,[391] Joan complained about the paltry financial returns she and John were getting for their farm produce, and about the annoyance caused by varying weights and measures. "You have no idea the bore it is here, the different weights and measures. Greenock, Glasgow, Helensburgh, Argyllshire (all near us) all have different ones." She then went

387 Acc8508/29, Letter 1.

388 Acc8508/49, Letter 3.

389 Acc8508/29, Letter 5.

390 East Lothian.

391 Acc8508/29, Letter 6. 28th March 1822.

on to discuss Longniddry. "When you have let the parks we will be able to guess the gross rental of Longniddry for the season. What a pity Stewart had the fingering of the rents when they were at their best. Do you think that including house and all we may make up £1700 by cottars rents and all? I am very anxious to dispense with all aid from other funds, and live on our land here and there this year, and give up the whole of Lord John's annuity from the Argyll Estate (£2800) for paying of debts; and if Longniddry can produce clear of burdens £1600, I will get it done, as I am Chancellor of Exchequer. You see what a fine miser I have become when you thought I would be a prodigal all my life." Joan's joke about being "Chancellor of Exchequer" is very significant. Pigie is not only bothering her pretty little head about domestic expenses – she is in charge of estate finances!

On 27th April 1822[392] Joan wrote to Francis that the Duke and Duchess of Argyll had been staying with them, and that the Duke had left "an ample commission to Lord John to act in all things for him." She emphasised, "The Duke wishes Lord John if possible to have the whole management of the estate. It would have been in a very different state had it been so all along." It seems the Argyll estates at that time brought in an annual income of £34000, and had debts of £120000, but Joan believed that with such an income it was perfectly possible to pay off the debts without selling land. Showing steady confidence in her own judgment she remarked, "I never saw two people so made to be a prey to lawyers as the Duke and Lord John. They never suspect any man of not being as free of self-interest as themselves. Tho' Lord John is quite a regular man in business matters, he has a degree of unsuspiciousness, that tho' very amiable, has been very hurtful to his interests and even those of his brother."

John, then, seems to have shouldered the burden of running the estates of his brother the Duke in 1822, and in the same year resigned his seat in Parliament, no doubt so that he could devote himself more fully to estate affairs. It should be remembered that John's health was not good. Early in 1822 Joan had confided to her cousin,[393] "Lord John has been rather unwell from stomach complaints caused, between ourselves, by grief at some proposed sales in Argyllshire. Poor dear, every one goes to his heart. Any uneasiness of mind immediately affects his health, but he is better,

392 Acc8508/29, Letter 8.

393 Acc8508/29, Letter 5.

thank Heaven." At the end of the year, writing to Francis from Inveraray,[394] she lamented that Lord John was "fagging himself to death going through the woods here marking wood to be cut, and he is so anxious to get a certain sum for his brother, and at the same time so afraid of any trees being cut that might not. He was out the whole of so many damp cold days, wet the whole time, that he got a bad attack of lumbago. I wish to heaven his Grace had a week of the hard work Lord John does for him all the year round!" Essentially John was a rather private retiring sort of man, happiest with his lathes in his workshop. We might begin to suspect the Joan was not only a comfort and support, but at times a much needed spur.

In early 1823 Joan was anticipating the birth of her second child and was very sensibly pondering the possibility, very real in those days, that she might die in childbirth, and what then might be the implications for family finances. She turned to her cousin Francis Cadell for advice, saying, "I can get no light from Lord John, as he is like to cut my head off if I mention the subject."[395] Regarding her fields in Longniddry which were let annually for grazing she continued, "When is the proper time to advertise the Longniddry parks…? If anything should happen to me this spring, would the rents of the current year be payable to Lord John naturally, and if not, could I by my directions make them so, as I should prefer his getting them to their laying up for Johnny[396]?" The difficulty seems to be that Joan's property was still governed by the terms of her father's entail, and by her marriage contract. At her marriage £500 a year was settled on Lord John, a quarter of the Longniddry rents at the time. The rents were now higher. Was Lord John therefore entitled to a quarter of the new rental? Was there any way, Joan wondered, of putting more of the rents into John's hands to pay for their son's education, and that of any future children?

It would appear from her letter to Francis of 5th April[397] that as an extra precaution Joan insured her life for a year for £5000. "They don't like short insurances," she remarked, "but as we are regularly and rapidly paying off debts, and will continue if the times and bairns will allow us, I do not wish to bind myself to continue; the only object being to get a sum to pay off debt should the Longniddry income suddenly be withdrawn."

394 Acc8508/29, Letter 9. 31st December 1822.
395 Acc8508/29, Letter 10. 3rd February 1823.
396 "Johnny" – her son.
397 Acc8508/29, Letter 12.

The birth of Joan's second son George was safely accomplished on 30th April 1823. However, in the summer of that year she was still chewing over the future of her Longniddry estate. She informed her cousin that there was "a most desirable property" for sale in Argyll, near Campbelltown, and selling Longniddry would be the easiest way of financing its acquisition. Objections from the heirs of entail, however, might scupper the project. Although Joan had apparent heirs in her two sons, if they were to die Longniddry would pass under the terms of the entail, not to Lord John, but to distant Glassell relatives, and those "heirs of entail" obviously would have an interest in any attempt of Joan's to dispose of her property. "From what we already know of them," she remarked to her cousin,[398] "I should think they would be rather disposed to give trouble from mere mischief… After what we have seen or rather heard of them before, I would do anything rather than have any personal intercourse with them – you will understand this." She copied to Francis the text of a letter she intended sending to her lawyers, adding the comment, "Tell me if this will do." The letter ran as follows:

"Dear Sir,

I have reason to believe that if I can obtain an Act of Parliament to sell Longniddry and rest the purchase money in lands in Argyllshire to be entailed on the same succession of heirs, a much greater rental can be obtained than that of Longniddry, and I conceive it to be much more advantageous to my children to possess lands in Argyllshire than elsewhere; and failing them, the interest of the other heirs of entail cannot in any way suffer, the rental of the lands proposed to be purchased being greater than Longniddry, and as the lands in Argyllshire must always be desirable to whoever is Duke of Argyll at the time, the Heir of Entail might always by a retransfer of the entail to lands in the low country make a highly advantageous sale to the Argyll family through whose interest another Act might at any time be obtained. I cannot anticipate any objection from the Heir of Entail, who I believe is in America, but I beg you will take the necessary steps for ascertaining that there will be no opposition to the proposed transfer, which if effected cannot in the slightest degree injure their interest. Of course every farthing recovered

398 Acc8508/29, Letter 11. 14th July 1823.

for Longniddry must be rested in lands strictly entailed on my children and the succession of heirs named in the entail, and the papers when completed will be shown to any agent of heirs if required, but indeed Parliament guard the interest of heirs of entail in such cases with the greatest jealousy, and were it not so, nothing would tempt me to injure the entail.

Dear Sir, Yours

J. Glassell Campbell."

We might be just a little surprised by Joan's eagerness to trade away Longniddry, but her apparent lack of attachment to her childhood home has been remarked upon before. Presumably the Campbelltown purchase fell through, however, as Longniddry was not disposed of until many years later.

Quite apart from important questions of financial management, Joan involved herself in more mundane matters of what nowadays would be termed "human resources". In her letters to Francis Cadell there are several references to "Robert" who seems to have been a sort of general factotum based in Longniddry. Robert brings a mare to Ardencaple in May 1820 and a cow in the spring of 1822. Joan frets that when he returns to Longniddry he may not have enough to do. "I hope poor Robert will not get into drinking when idle. Do contrive some work for him…" she instructed her cousin.[399] Since there was not much for him to do at Longniddry, Robert was drafted to Ardencaple when needed. "The Ardencaple grieve has much work on hand, and a man absent having scarlet fever in his house… He begs hard to keep Robert for 2 or 3 weeks. Robert wishes his wife to send his working clothes and a shirt or two."[400] On 31st December 1822 Joan wrote that she was keen to have Robert permanently at Ardencaple. She was aware that he would want to consult his wife, and she was also aware that his wife would be reluctant to move. "However, I must represent to Robert the necessity of servants not living so stationary as trees or hedges." Joan was not so keen to have one of Robert's sons, who was showing every sign of turning out to be "as good for nothing as his eldest brother". "I hope he is disposed to some

399 Acc8508/29, Letter 3.

400 Acc8508/29, Letter 8. April 27th 1822.

trade," she wrote, "and won't be transplanted to the west."[401] As Joan had anticipated, Robert's wife refused to move, and on 5th April 1823 she wrote testily, "It is quite nonsense his coolly saying his wife won't come and he is therefore to remain idle at Longniddry, or that I must pay his travelling and board here." She seems to have been resigned to Robert returning home, but was still determined to call upon him when she saw fit. "I may as well get Robert back in the summer," she decided, "as he will be totally idle and we have much to do."[402]

Another employee giving Joan food for thought was "Fairlie", who for some reason seems to have provoked the ire of Robert Howden, the tenant of a large farm on Joan's Longniddry estate. "At all events, I will have a house given to Fairlie as you suggest," she wrote to her cousin, "so be so good as to give Mitchell warning. It will be as well for Fairlie to be under our wing as Howden will make the place too hot for him if he were to remain in one of his houses."[403] By spring 1825 Joan seems to have been entertaining intentions of bringing Fairlie to Ardencaple, perhaps because she had given Robert up as a lost cause. "I have this morning received yours about Fairlie," she wrote indignantly to Francis Cadell.

> *"It is quite out of the question giving him board and washing, as we have more house people already than we know what to do with, but I would give him £24 or £25 per an, 6 bolls of meal and 3 or 4 of potatoes. Our gardener who is a first rate one and bred at Kew, yet so useful he works at all farm work, gets only £40 and 3 bolls meal. Now Fairlie getting £24 and board would be much more. Would we give his mother a free house and garden at Longniddry to induce him? But giving more wages could ruin all the others. He would get 3 carts of coals also. In short, I think:*

Money	*£25*
Meal. 6 bolls at say £1	*6*
4b potatoes at 10/–	*2*
2 carts coals at 9/–	*1 – 7*
House	*4*
	38 – 7

401 Acc8508, Letter 9.
402 Acc8508/29. Letter 12.
403 Acc8508/29. Letter 9. 31st December 1822.

> *should be enough for him at least till he is found on trial to be more valuable than ordinary. I certainly am very anxious to have him."*

After mentioning other matters Joan's letter finally returns to Fairlie. "Do you think it would make Fairlie happier having his mother here? If so, he might bring her. It might prevent his marrying if he had Mama to cook etc."[404] We might contrast Joan's quibbling over a yearly wage of £38 with the £120000 debt of the Argyll estates that her husband was heir to. No doubt her attitude was, "Every little helps."

However, Joan's management style was not all penny-pinching. When "Hercules's wife" was sent to Ardencaple with her furniture, she brought her father "old David" with her. "I mean to have him next season … installed in a new porter's lodge," she announced.[405] It will be a nice easy occupation for David attending to the gate and doing something in keeping the weeds round in subjection… The old man is heartily tired of farming and I am glad to have a berth for him." Then again, "I wonder," she asked Francis on 3rd February 1823, "if I asked you to give £1 – 1 to old Willy? If not, will you do so now. Poor body, this is a hard winter for him."[406] Joan's sympathetic generosity is also shown in the same letter when she requests her cousin to send a present of 5 bolls of meal and 5 bolls of potatoes to John Campbell of Craignure, sheriff clerk of Argyllshire, who had removed to Edinburgh "under rather circumscribed circumstances". She wished the gift to appear as if it were coming from Longniddry a little at a time, presumably to give the impression that it was surplus produce.

Joan's tact also appears in her relationship with her husband. Lord John seems to have been a worrier, not a man comfortable in a leadership role. His health was not robust, and he certainly was not one to be overbearing or aggressive. When he was away from home in the early months of their marriage Joan wrote to him describing how she and her guest Mrs McCall had been alarmed by some "blackguard Irishmen" skulking in the dark around Ardencaple.[407] "Poor Tammie Norrie was shaking at every noise for ever so long. What would I have given to feel your arm around me, Love,

404 Acc8508/29. Letter 15.
405 Acc8508/29. Letter 2. 9th August 1820.
406 Acc8508/29. Letter 17. 4th November 1825.
407 Acc8508/49. Letter 2.

to keep my heart from beating like an alarm watch." It was kind of her to suggest to John that she saw him as the strong protector.

The newly married couple were well matched, their characters complementing each other, with strong mutual love and affection. Writing of an acquaintance who had an "indifferent husband", a situation she described as "the cruellest of all the Pandora's box of human calamities", Joan declared, "What a pitiable wretch I would be if you were to take it into your head not to love me!"[408]

As already mentioned Lord John's fragile health seems to have been adversely affected in times of stress, causing Joan to feel protective towards him, and impatient and angry with those causing the upset. However, there was no escaping the fact that he was a senior member of one of Scotland's most important families and the heir to a dukedom. A letter to Joan from Mme de la Chaux[409] mentions Lord John and his brother the Duke attending the King on his visit to Edinburgh "in their glorious dress, kilt and all". John may have resigned his seat in Parliament, but he did not resign all interest in politics, no doubt feeling bound to support the landowning interest, particularly as it might affect the House of Argyll. A meeting in Haddington, East Lothian, to consider the movement towards abolishing the Corn Laws resolved, "At this moment it is unwise to interfere with a system under the operation of which the agriculturalists are thriving and no class suffering." Lord John was very much in agreement, and keen to have his name added to the petition produced by the Haddington meeting. Joan therefore asked her cousin Francis Cadell to sign for him if permissible.[410] The true direction of Lord John's inclinations however is probably indicated by the fact that during his attendance on George IV during his notorious Scottish visit, he presented the King with a wooden box of his own making.[411]

Writing to Joan on 12th February 1822 her friend Mary Grant thanked Joan for a packet delivered by Joan's Longniddry retainer Robert. "I was quite entertained," she remarked, "by Robert's volunteering his testimony to your conjugal happiness outlasting the honeymoon. He first said you were 'just as happy and comfortable as the first week', and a little after he said 'I never saw such lovingness between twa folk – at least so long after marriage'

408 Acc8508/49. Letter 3.
409 Acc8508/5. Letter 10. 10th September 1822.
410 Acc8508/29. Letter 16. 24th April 1825.
411 Acc8508/5. Letter 10.

was the discreet addition."[412] We could hardly ask for a better summing-up of Joan and John's relationship.

As previously noted, Joan gave birth to her first son John on 11th January 1821. A second son George was born on 30th April 1823, and a daughter Emma on 12th March 1825. Careful preparation would be made for the birth of the first child, all the more so since, if male, he was likely to be a future Duke of Argyll. Among the landowning aristocracy it was not customary for a lady to breast feed her own child, nor indeed to take much to do with the mundane and less appealing aspects of childcare. It was essential then that a nurse should be engaged, and a fascinating letter is preserved among the Campbell Papers on this matter. It was written to Joan by Jean Tolmie in Dalkeith on 28th November 1820.

"May Leday,

I having sin the reciepe of your letter to Mrs Dobson in foreames mie that your Leday Sheip may kipe yourselfe quiet on that account. If it pleis god to sper me I shal be sertenly reday for your Leday Sheip bie fore the 19th Janrey. Mrs Dobson in foreames mie that your Leday Sheipe wished a nurs as nay to your tim as possable. And when I was deseared to go to Ledy Robt Ker I told her Leday Sheip the latest tim I could count upon was the end of Decr and hear Leday Sheip was quiet satisfayed. And the next tim that I was desaried to go to Ledy Robt hear Leday Sheip ingaged mie for your Nurs and I med wp may mind and ingeded anurs for may on child. And Ledy Robt desired me to go to Dr Gream with may children and hie was perfectly setesfayed and was goeing to writ to Ledy Robt bay retureng of post. Mrs Dobson would a have ansered your letter hear selfe but on to hear bing verey purley in hear health for the siex wickes pas but is now geating beter agin or shie wold a have binn hapie to a have dunn this hear selfe.

I hope your Leday Sheip will rest setesfayed with what is hear stedit as abouve es [illegible] I fill may selfe that I will be in good tim for your Leday Sheip.

I remain your Leday Sheips
Most obedient and humble servent,
Jean Tolmie."

412 Acc8508/30. Letter 3.

Persevering readers who have struggled to the end of this communication will realise that in spite of her bizarre spelling, Mrs Tolmie was actually a fairly articulate woman. Her handwriting, it should be said, is almost all very legible, and vastly better than Joan's!

Joan was a healthy young woman and the birth of her first child seems to have been free of complications. Shortly afterwards she wrote to her cousin Francis Cadell saying she was "quite well", and had been told she had made a "supernatural recovery". "My boy is going on well," she announced. "Even his father allows he is not quite so ugly as infants in general."[413] The birth of "the boy", John, was an event of importance far beyond the domestic sphere, as he was the heir to a dukedom, and was seen as the future head of the house of Argyll, a position still viewed in terms of chieftainship by many Campbell lairds and tenants across Argyllshire and beyond. As such, it was imperative that his future should be secure. Writing of her husband, Joan commented, "I never saw any human being so little inclined to fight for his own. However, the boy has changed this a great deal."[414] Lord John's father, the 5th Duke, had been regarded with great respect (unlike John's brother the spendthrift 6th Duke), and during a visit to Campbell of Lochnell at Bonawe, Joan observed that her son, by then nearly three years old, was receiving a great deal of attention simply because he was the grandson of a man remembered with "gratitude and affection" by "all high and low". "Johnny never was so much made of," she remarked.[415]

From January to July 1825 Joan kept a diary[416] consisting of very brief entries, from which we see that Johnny was ill around the middle of April:

> *"14th April: Johnny little unwell.*
> *15th April: Johnny little unwell.*
> *16th April: Johnny unwell.*
> *17th April: Johnny became very ill with bilious attack.*
> *18th April: Johnny ill. Dr Hill came.*
> *20th April: Johnny rather better.*
> *21st April: Johnny better.*

413 Acc8508/29. Letter 4.
414 Acc8508/29. Letter 5.
415 Acc8508/29. Letter 13. 8th November 1823.
416 Acc8508/50.

22nd April: beautiful day. Johnny carried out a little.
23rd April: Johnny much better."

Alas, no sooner was Johnny on the road to recovery than his father fell ill, possibly with the same infection. A few weeks later, on 26th May, Joan noted, "Johnny got first lesson from Row schoolmaster."[417] Presumably it was never too early to begin the education of a future duke. However, Johnny was no stranger to the art of writing. Just before Christmas 1822, when he was approaching his second birthday, Mrs Elizabeth Low at Ardencaple wrote to Joan at Inveraray telling her that "Master Campbell" was "quite well". The letter contains half a page of scribbles, and Mrs Low (Johnny's nursemaid?) has added the explanation, "The above writing is Master Campbell to his Mamma."[418]

A second son George was born on 30th April 1823, and a daughter Emma on March 1825. Rather oddly, Joan's diary for that year makes no mention of Emma's birth, but under 6th June there is the bald statement, "Emma Augusta christened. McCalls came."[419] A pocket in the back cover of the diary contains a lock of very fine hair, possibly Emma's. A similar pocket in the front cover contains a small rectangular label on which is printed the word "LAUDANUM". A memento of Emma's birth perhaps?

There is very little mention of these children in Joan's surviving correspondence. Two months before George's birth Joan's friend Mary Grant wrote to her, "I hope and trust you do not mean to give Johnny two sisters from what you say of your size… Women are charming creatures, but little girls are very tiresome, at least until they are sixteen!"[420] In her next letter Mary advised Joan that she was sending her two books. "I think they will be fine intellectual provender for you when you are recovering, but I beseech you not to have them read to you the second day as was the case before with 'Kenilworth'."[421] It is fair comment on early 19th century attitudes to childbirth that Mary should be taken aback by the fact that two days after giving birth, a lady should feel strong enough to be read to! Early in May, Mary wrote, "We were delighted to read Mrs Smith's

417 "Row" is now known as "Rhu".
418 Acc8508/4. Letter 7.
419 Acc8508/50.
420 Acc8508/30. Letter 8.
421 Acc8508/30. Letter 9.

description of your brown haired boy. Long may he be spared!"[422] Implicit in Mary's lighthearted comment was the knowledge that in those days all too many children were not destined to be "spared". A fortnight after Emma's birth Joan wrote to her cousin Francis Cadell, "I go on quite well. It is only prejudice keeps me still in my room and on my sofa."[423]

In the first two years of his marriage to Joan, Lord John was still a Member of Parliament. He was also colonel of the Argyllshire Militia. After he resigned his parliamentary seat he took on much of the burden of running the Argyll estates. These duties involved visits to Inveraray, Campbelltown and other corners of the far-flung Argyll domains. Shortly after her marriage Joan wrote to her cousin from Inveraray,[424] "We came here on Saturday for a meeting and intended returning home on Wednesday, but another meeting takes place on the 11th... The militia are to be out for a month in summer, when we must return hither again, after which we propose making a tour to Mull, Lochend, Ballachulish, up the canal to Altyre, and round by the coast to East Lothian, as Lord John wishes to be a fortnight or three weeks at Longniddry in autumn." Incidentally, Joan's honeymoon in "the Land of the Sun" must have been of surprisingly short duration if she was married on 17th April, and was already in Inveraray before 5th May!

Although John's brother the Duke seldom graced his estates with his presence, he made occasional visits. "The Argylls are with us," Joan informed her cousin on 5th April 1822, "and we go to Inveraray on Monday with them."[425] Also, the Campbell Papers preserve an undated formal invitation to Joan in her capacity as "Lady John", signed by "Caroline Argyll" (the Duchess), inviting her to come and stay at Inveraray.

In the autumn of 1822 Joan and John were again at Inveraray, and were joined by "Islay", that is Lady Charlotte's son Walter Campbell, and his wife and sisters. Walter had married in 1820 Eleanor, daughter of Joan's East Lothian neighbour the Earl of Wemyss. Of the sisters, Joan wrote, "Two of them I had not seen since I went to Rome in 1819, and never did I see so lovely a trio." From Inveraray Joan travelled on to visit Campbell of Lochnell at Bonawe. At Connell Ferry Lochnell was awaiting them

422 Acc8508/30. Letter 10.
423 Acc8508/29. Letter 15.
424 Acc8508/29. Letter 1. 5th May 1820.
425 Acc8508/29. Letter 7.

"with his barge and six tartaned rowers, to Johnny's great delight." Lochnell obviously liked to keep alive the ancient tradition of Highland hospitality. "General and Mrs Campbell are the most agreeable and hospitable of all people," Joan enthused, "and there have been every day 5, 6, or 7 of the neighbours dropping in, besides a large party staying in the house."

In a letter to a Miss Ferrier in Edinburgh, written from Inveraray in July 1826, Joan describes taking Lady Charlotte's daughters Emma and Adelaide to the hill above Dalmally to show them the view of Cruachan and Loch Awe.[426] She also describes a drive they had taken before church the previous Sunday round "the high moors and Roebuck Park" near Inveraray Castle. "As we were walking down the wood above the Roebuck Park we heard a curious hum proceeding from a small heather hut. I went to see, and after opening a very crudely constructed door found nearly 30 boys and girls all reading in Gaelic. The children were all clean, and fine bold healthy looking creatures, very different from those in the town Sunday school where I had been some weeks ago. The master here was a young farmer and had never been visited or encouraged by either the clergyman or anyone. It was a beautiful sight." In the early 19th century of course the countryside around Inveraray was still solidly Gaelic speaking. It would not be surprising if nowadays the entire Gaelic speaking population of Inveraray and its surroundings would almost fit into Joan's "small heather hut". Incidentally, since Lord John was brought up at Inveraray and educated at home, he is bound to have been familiar with the Gaelic language, and may even have acquired a basic fluency. There is no indication is any of Joan's correspondence, however, that this was the case, or that he showed any interest in the language.

In the summer of 1825 Joan recorded an extended Argyllshire jaunt in her diary,[427] leaving on 6th June and arriving in Campbelltown on 13th June ("very hot weather"). Her diary then reads as follows:

19th June. Mr McLeod preached beautiful farewell sermon.
20th June. Called at Kildallaig.
21st June. Made calls in Town.
24th June. Dined at Kildallaig.
29th June. Ball on board Nimrod.

426 Acc8508/29. Letter 18.
427 Acc8508/50.

30th June. We dined at Line Craigs.
1st July. Cantyre Ball.
7th July. Our Ball.
8th July. At tea at Mr Campbell's Senr Kildallaig.
9th July. At Kildallaig. Saw Cove Keeran.
11th July. Provost's Ball.
12th July. Made calls. Regiment dismissed.
14th July. Came to Ballyshear.
16th July. Came to Keels Souther. Very unwell.
17th July. At Southend Church. Johnny with us for the first time.
19th July. Went to Saddel. Very hot. Lord John not well.
20th July. Dined at Carradale.
24th July. Came to Rhu Cottage. A paradise and Mrs C very agreeable.
25th July. Came to Oakfield.
2nd August. Came home.

While Joan was at Campbelltown her friend Mary Grant wrote to her, "I suppose you are not yet come home yet, but you gave me no hint how to direct to you, so this must await your arrival there. You have really been living a fine gay bustling Highland hospitable sort of life at Campbelltown, and must have been quite in your element."[428] Whether Joan was indeed in her element is debateable, for after all Joan had bemoaned the constant round of making calls and attending balls in Edinburgh, to the extent of quoting Byron's line "Oh that the desert were my dwelling place". As the wife of Argyll's heir, however, it was incumbent on her to fulfil her social duties. Perhaps she learned to enjoy the role.

References to social duties of another sort can be found in a letter to Joan from Janet Colquhoun of Rossdhu House[429] concerning the appointment of a minister to the parish of Rhu. In Lady Colquhoun's opinion the Reverend Mr Neilson was "a very unfit person for the charge". Instead she recommended a young man named Watt. "Should your ladyship and Lord John Campbell exert your influence with the Duke of Argyll in favour of Mr Watt Sir James and myself would be much indebted to you." Another letter[430] from John Campbell, Achalech, thanks Joan for the efforts she has

428 Acc8508/35. Letter 6.
429 Acc8508/4. Letter 12.
430 Acc8508/5. Letter 1.

been making to help his son to obtain a commission in the army. There must have been many such requests for Joan to use her perceived "influence". No doubt she became well able to sift the worthy causes from the chancers.

The social circles Joan moved in would require her to be on friendly, or at least politely sociable terms with a vast array of acquaintances, many of whom she would surely have found unsympathetic. From her surviving correspondence, apart from her cousin Francis Cadell, three stand out as genuine friends. Mary Grant seems to have been charged with shopping for Joan's requirements, and paying her Edinburgh bills. She mentions in a letter of 22nd February 1822[431] that Joan has sent her an order for £40 worth of goods, and informs her, "I have two parcels of books here from Carfrae and a large paper parcel addressed for Lord John which seems as if it contains prints. How shall I send them?" At the end of October 1822, she tells Joan that she has paid her bill of £30. Two pairs of "hose" have been sent to Lord John and Mary will pay for the other articles when she hears they have arrived.[432] On 10th May 1823 she wrote,

> *"Now, for your commissions. I must have more specific directions about them as I am really quite at a loss to act upon those I have in your letter. You wish to have some sewing silks. Query – what colour? Also – some narrow white ribbon and blue for the bairn. Whether is this ribbon satin or sarsent? What degree of narrowness and what quantity? A sash for Johnny. Query – what colour? What kind of ribbon and what quantity? Then, three ribbons for bonnets and sashes. What colours are they to be, what width, and what quantity of each? ...Aitken must be summoned to council and in her character of Prime Minister give orders in all these different points."*

Joan seems to have been keen for Mary to visit her at Ardencaple, but this was never possible, as Mary's surviving sister Isabella, "a fragile creature" as Mary described her, was a chronic invalid who was in fact dying, and Mary also had to care for her mother who was semi-crippled after a bad fall. Mary kept Joan informed about mutual acquaintances: "poor James Wilson" (a noted amateur naturalist) appeared to be dying. Henry Smyth, brother

431 Acc8508/30. Letter 3.
432 Acc8508/30. Letter 7.

of a former fellow pupil of Joan's at Mrs Grant's, had visited from Ireland. Mary had heard a "memorable" sermon from Dr Chalmers on the afterlife, a state of being which was apparently on no account to be confused with the Muslim conception of Paradise, for "it was not to be a sensual place of bliss". On a visit to Dollar Mary had taken tea with the parish minister Dr Milne, who had been a tutor of Joan's, and now ruled Dollar "with despotic sway". When Joan and Lord John sent her a box of woodcocks Mary was suitably grateful. "Many thanks for the woodcocks," she wrote, "which proved excellent, and which we were very glad to have for Isabella, who is only allowed to eat the lighter kinds of meat."[433]

Another friend was Bessie Mure, who seems to have taken charge of Joan's bills and purchases from Miss Grant. The death of Mary Grant's invalid sister Isabella in 1823 may have had something to do with this. Bessie seems to have been very particular about these minor commercial transactions. She wrote, for example, on 17th June 1825,

> *"I have paid all your bills except Anderson, Bookseller. I have £3–10s of yours on my hand and I shall pay it the next time I am that way. In the meantime I enclose the receipts. You will see that Spittal says his bill was £14-19-6, but you saying it was only £14–10s he got no more from me and was obliged to content himself the best way he could. Also Carfrae's bill was £42, but when I said you only mentioned £37, he said that was the bill he sent at the end of the year. So I said I would only pay that, and to prevent confusion I would have the articles stated. So he sent it, and it was £37-18s, but as you had put it down £37-8s I would give him no more. Don't I do things in a very business like way?"*[434]

Apart from such factual matters, Bessie Mure's letters[435] tend to be full of gossip about mutual acquaintances – a Mr Forbes is a "weak and wicked fool"; Bessie has heard from a "person" that Joan has fallen out with Mrs Fletcher; Lady Charlotte has flown into a "violent passion" with her daughter Lady Cumming when she criticised Mr Bury's rudeness; Mrs Forbes's two youngest daughters are beautiful, "especially the youngest in spite of red hair".

433 Acc8508/30. Letter 8.
434 Acc8508/35. Letter 11.
435 Acc8508/35. Letters 1-14.

In an undated letter of 1823, Bessie sent a harrowing account of the death of Isabella Grant:

> *"Mrs Morehead saw Isabella on Saturday, and never did she witness so wonderful a scene. That poor girl with death written in every line of her countenance, conversing with as much interest and cheerfulness, tho' more feebleness, than when in perfect health. Miss Grant [i.e. Mary] quite as usual from powerful effort and abstracting her mind from all but the great end of soothing, composing and comforting the sufferer. Mrs Grant just as usual, and even jests passing in that chamber of death. Mrs Mercer said she was sure she never thought she was dying herself. Miss Grant was quite aware for some time, and only anxious she should not suffer. Which she did not… As soon as it was over, Mrs Mercer took [Miss Grant] upstairs and put her to bed She was quite patient and quiet till poor old Mrs Grant, agitated and restless, went up to her room. Then she was dreadfully overcome and hysterical."* [436]

In the same letter but in lighter mood, Bessie describes a gathering at Mrs Fletcher's where the celebrated Anglo-Irish novelist Maria Edgeworth was present:

> *"Everybody was introduced to her, and she talked to them all till the poor authoress was like to drop from fatigue. She is the wee-est woman ever was seen, and has a long beard which has been reckoned a sign of wisdom. As such perhaps she preserves it, but having given more equivocal ones, were I her I would take it off. She has one sister, and another very fat and coarse but with a pleasant countenance. She herself they say is very natural and entertaining."*

Early portraits show Maria Edgeworth to have been a rather attractive young woman. A later portrait does indeed show the elderly Ms Edgeworth sporting a beard.[437]

Lady Charlotte Campbell, the mature society beauty encumbered with a low-born second husband, figures prominently in Bessie Mure's

436 Acc8508/35. Letter 9.
437 See Wikipedia, "Maria Edgeworth".

gossip. "When Lady Cumming[438] came to town, she at the first interview with her mother held out her hand to Mr Bury and asked how he did. He exactly behaved to her as he had behaved to Lady Uxbridge last autumn – turned his back upon her without speaking…"[439] (This is the incident that led to Charlotte shaking her daughter in a "violent passion".) "It is said Bury and Charlotte are going abroad never to return," Bessie concluded. Not so, however. In July 1825 Charlotte and Bury were in London "living in Grosvenor Street in a house of Lady Lambert's", and apparently being asked to "all the first parties in London".[440] In the autumn of that year Charlotte was still in London and Bessie had seen her. She was "in great good looks and spirits" and "very magnificent in dress now." Her daughter Eleanor was apparently having marriage problems, and Charlotte advised her to "bear and forbear". She asked Eleanor if her husband ever beat her, to which the daughter replied that if he had done any such thing, "she would have left his house that moment". Surprisingly perhaps, Lady Charlotte then apparently revealed that "she had suffered that often and had never complained". Obviously growing impatient, Charlotte finally advised Eleanor that the only thing for it was to "run away with the first man she could get, be divorced, and marry her lover". "Was there ever such advice from a mother to her daughter?" exclaimed the scandalised Bessie Mure.[441]

Lady Charlotte and Joan had of course become great friends during Joan's Italian tour. They remained on friendly terms, in spite of Charlotte's difficulties with her relatives, and several letters from Charlotte to Joan survive in the Campbell Papers. On 11th February 1822 Charlotte wrote recalling "the remembrance of the dear Palatine and of Porta Pia", and declaring how happy she would be to see her brother John "for the first time in his stormy life really happy, and happy in a wife and child". As to the child, however, "Why did you call him Johnny?" she inquired teasingly, and reminded Joan of an ancient prophecy regarding Iain the son of three Iains ["Iain" being the Gaelic equivalent of John], in whose lifetime one white horse would bear away the only two Campbells to survive a bloody carnage. Charlotte's little daughter Beatrice had died not long before, and

438 Charlotte's daughter Eliza.

439 Acc8508/35. Letter 1. 18th July 1822. "Lady Uxbridge" is Charlotte's daughter Eleanor.

440 Acc8508/35. Letter 6.

441 Acc8508/35. Letter 8. 26th October 1825.

in her letter[442] Charlotte enclosed some verses she had written at the time.

As we have seen, Charlotte's relations with her family were stormy. "I never hope to live again with my relations," she wrote in April 1822. "They behave in such a way to my husband that I never can." Her brother the Duke of Argyll had behaved kindly towards her, she said, but the Duchess had given cause for grave offence. "But she, Oh! Dear Lady John, I am not apt to be chilled, but such repulsive coldness I never met with. She literally never spoke to me and hardly even answered me when I addressed a speech to her."[443] In July of that year Charlotte reported that she now never saw the Duke. "We are dead to each other. It is astonishing how well one does without people whom we thought most dear and necessary to us." She hoped to see Joan the following year, as her son Walter had invited her to Scotland then. "What are your readings," she asked, "and what your chief pursuits? You are not a do nothing body."[444]

In spite of Walter's invitation, at the end of the year Charlotte sent Joan a lengthy and impassioned rant against him. He was legally required to make his mother an allowance of £750 a year, and resolutely refused to give her any more. She was, she said, on the point of being "turned out homeless and shelterless" from "Westwood", her "little home" in Kent, and asked Joan to beseech her husband to persuade Walter to settle the house on her for life with an allowance of £1200. She complained that she had experienced a hard life with Walter's father, but was "a good and faithful wife to him under very trying circumstances", then at his death had been left homeless "to fight through the world with my eight children".[445]

Joan seems to have been particularly fond of Lady Charlotte's daughters Emma and Adelaide. The Campbell Papers preserve a series of letters from 1825 written by Emma to "Dearest Tammie Norie".[446] The earliest, written from Montague Square, London, on 26th April, is begun by Emma, continued by Adelaide, and finished by Emma. The Caledonian Ball had caused much excitement, and Emma's Mary Queen of Scots costume had made a good impression. Emma, Adelaide confided, was still pale and thin, but "not quite as much tormented about Mr Russell". In June Emma was

442 Acc8508/35. Letter 15.
443 Acc8508/3. Letter 11.
444 Acc8508/3. Letter 10.
445 Acc8508/5. Letter 4.
446 Acc8508/36. Letters 1-10.

staying with Miss Mayou in Sydenham. Joan had asked for news of Lady Charlotte. "But indeed," replied Emma, "we know so little ourselves that I can scarcely tell you anything." Bury had been in London house-hunting, but, said Emma, "We never had the misfortune of falling in with him."[447] Emma's letter seems to have been enclosed in one from Miss Mayou, who worried that Emma was thin, pale, coughing, and "so unlike what I could desire". Miss Mayou continued, "If she does not love that young man, I am indeed deceived. When I can I will write more fully of this and of him, urging on you that what I say will rest with yourself alone, for Mr Campbell is so very violent that I am afraid of any wind escaping." The violent "Mr Campbell" was Emma's brother and legal guardian Walter, and "that young man" was presumably the Mr Russell previously mentioned. In spite of Walter's apparent disapproval, Emma eventually married him.[448]

Walter Campbell had stepped into the shoes of his uncle Lord John as MP for Argyllshire. He had also inherited the island of Islay, to which he travelled with his younger sisters in August 1825, where they remained until at least December. Emma seems to have hoped Joan would pay a visit, but was disappointed. Regarding her sister Eleanor's marital woes, Adelaide wrote from Islay, "I suppose you must have heard long ere this of the melancholy news… namely Eleanor's separation from Uxbridge… Pray do not mention the subject to anybody till we hear further accounts… I dare not think of the consequences. I know not how she will endure parting with her children."[449] The final letter in this series is dated 18th January 1826, from Inveraray, where there had been three days of theatricals, singing, and dancing. Emma had been "danced off her legs" and at the time of writing was "so completely knocked up" that she could "hardly speak". Much of this letter deals with Joan's falling out with her friend Mrs Fletcher, already briefly mentioned. Joan seems to have asked Emma if she could remember Joan ever saying anything derogatory about Mrs Fetcher, "Chatty" as they called her. "Chatty" is probably Charlottte Catherine Clavering, daughter of Lord John's sister Lady Augusta. She had married in 1814 Miles Fletcher, son of the prominent Edinburgh hostess Eliza Dawson, an Englishwoman who had married a much older Scottish lawyer. Emma could not remember

447 Acc8508/36. Letter 6. 14th June 1825.

448 William Russell, youngest son of Lord William Russell, a long-serving Whig politician who was murdered by his valet in 1840.

449 Acc8508/36. Letter 8. 12th September 1825.

Joan ever disparaging Mrs Fletcher, but suggested that Joan's "not quite liking" Mr Fletcher was the cause of the rift. Whatever the cause of the quarrel, Joan and Mrs Fetcher seem to have made up. "I am so glad," Emma wrote, "that you and Chatty are no longer on the horrible terms you have been. Pray give her my kindest love."[450]

As Lady Charlotte remarked in one of her letters, Joan was not a "do nothing body". We have already seen evidence of her interest in agriculture and estate management. Much time was also taken up with visits, sometimes social, sometimes accompanying her husband on Argyll family business. Indeed, much of what would appear to be mere socialising might be classed nowadays as "networking", the keeping up of contacts and the cultivation of those with influence. "What in the world are you staying always at Inveraray for?" asked Bessie Mure.[451] The answer might well have been, "Family and estate business, and polishing the Argyll image". As the wife of "the heir to a dukedom" Joan had an important role to fulfil. A dowdy frump incapable of intelligent conversation would have done her husband no favours.

Scientific and mechanical matters fascinated Lord John, and their surviving letters to each other show that Joan shared his interests to a certain extent. Her Continental journal shows a keen interest in landscape, in nature, and in people. She certainly had an inquiring rather than a merely accepting mind. There is an interesting letter to her in the Campbell Papers from James Wilson.[452] Wilson was the brother of John Wilson the renowned editor of "Blackwood's magazine". Although a lawyer by profession, James was a respected amateur naturalist with an international reputation. Joan had presumably found an injured or exhausted bird at Ardencaple and had written to Wilson to find out what it could be. "Dear Lady John," he began, "I was honoured with your ornithological communication yesterday morning." In a long, friendly, and amusingly droll letter, he explained that the bird was probably not a sandpiper as Joan had thought, but more likely to be a redshank. "It is called 'Le chevalier aux pieds rouges' by the French, 'Rothfussingen Wasserlaufer' by the Germans, and 'Gambetta' by the Italians. Colonel Campbell of Knock would probably call it 'Culach

450 Acc8508/36. Letter 8.
451 Acc8508/35. Letter 2.
452 Acc8508/6. Letter 6. 6th January 1824.

Traich',[453] which being interpreted signifies 'shorecock'." Wilson then gave a short account of its habits, and asked Joan to put the bird in a box and send it to him. He thought it would survive the journey. (It might not have survived Wilson's attentions, however. He had a famous collection of stuffed birds and preserved butterflies and insects.) He went on to mention various invitations: "I have been asked to pass the coming summer with a Dutch naturalist in Amsterdam and by another in Paris, and I had also some thoughts of circumnavigating Scotland with a very civil engineer who annually visits the Aurora Borealis and Northern lighthouses." The Arctic explorer Parry had also sent him all the specimens from his recent expedition for examination and classification. In spite of all this he was "cut off from the world" by ill health. (Indeed two years previously Mary Grant had written to Joan that "poor James Wilson" appeared to be dying.) However, "Lady Charlotte's fair daughters have irradiated my prison walls with their bright happy eyes and startled the very spiders in their inmost cell with their glad voices." Wilson concluded by assuring Joan, "I shall always look back at my stay at Ardencaple with pleasure." Here we see Joan on friendly terms with a naturalist with a European reputation. His letter is good humoured, but certainly not condescending, and he seems to be aware that he is addressing a knowledgeable and intelligent woman.

Was Joan particularly interested in birds? Perhaps not, although an undated letter from W. J. Hooker to Lord John tells that he has sent Wilson's "Ornithology" containing the account of the passenger pigeon for Joan to read. He also sent his own "Reminiscences of Iceland" in the hope that she would "do him the honour" of accepting it. Joan had a lively mind, and was probably interested in "anything that was interesting". She seems to have been an avid reader, and her correspondence contains many references to poets and authors. "What a deal you spend on books!" remarked Bessie Mure[454], who had the task of settling Joan's Edinburgh bills.

According to the 8th Duke's "Memoirs", Joan gave birth to a fourth child in 1827, a daughter Elizabeth. "My mother never recovered well from this last confinement," he wrote.[455] The child did not survive long, and Joan's

453 Properly "coilleach traghad".

454 Acc8508/35. Letter 2.

455 George Douglas 8th Duke of Argyll, Autobiography and memoirs. New York, E.P. Dutton & co. 1906. Vol. 1, Page 55.

health did not improve. The 8th Duke related, "For better access to the best medical advice, my father removed her from Ardencaple to a villa on the Clyde close to Glasgow." Johnny the elder son went with his mother, but George the second son and future Duke was sent to stay at Portkill on the Rosneath peninsula with Lorne Campbell the Rosneath estate manager for the Duke of Argyll. "After a time," George later remembered, "the weary fight which my mother had long maintained was evidently drawing to a close. Wishing to see all her children before she left them, she sent for me, and the messenger was my pet cousin Adelaide Campbell, the youngest of the many beautiful daughters of my aunt, Lady Charlotte Campbell, and one of the two to whom my mother was most attached. She had been for some time helping to nurse my mother in her illness."[456] George and Johnny were taken in to see their mother for the last time. George dimly remembered her instructing her sons to read the Scriptures each night and morning. Two copies of the Bible were given to the boys. Although he had no recollection of his dying mother's face or voice, George vividly recalled that his Bible was a single volume, whereas Johnny's was in two volumes. He remembered later being taken to see his dead mother in her coffin, and having to kiss her brow.

In fact, Joan gave birth to her daughter Elizabeth on 8th January 1828 and died on 22nd January 1828. Her child survived her by some three weeks, dying on 19th February. The date of Joan's death is stated unambiguously in the records of the Court of Session and the dates of her daughter's birth and death can be found in Debrett's Peerage.[457]

Joan was laid to rest in the Argyll family mausoleum beside the church of Kilmun, overlooking the Holy Loch. The funeral party proceeded to Kilmun by steamer, and Joan's coffin was laid beside that of Lord John's father the 6th Duke. The bearers then retired, closing the mausoleum door behind them, leaving the mourners inside. "I still recall the panic which then seized me," George remembered, "and the tall deeply craped figure of my cousin Adelaide Campbell trying to pacify my terrors by assuring me we were not to be there long. I recollect too my father kneeling on the slab

456 Ibid. Page 59.

457 Decisions of the Court of Session. 21st May 1831. J.H. Glassell Campbell against Lord John Campbell (regarding Lord John's annuity from the entailed estate of Longniddry). The same date is given in Debrett's "Peerage". The dates of her daughter's birth and death are given in Debrett's and Cacroft's "Peerages".

beside my mother's coffin, and seeing that it was carefully adjusted with reference to the position of the other mouldering remains... A few days later we all left the fateful villa near Glasgow, and drove to our old home at Ardencaple."[458]

Joan died in 1828, at the age of 32, never having attained her expected position of Duchess of Argyll. What mark this active and talented woman might have left on the Dukedom and the county of Argyll (or indeed on Scotland) we can only surmise.

Ardencaple Castle in the late 19th century.
(Source: "Annals of Garelochside" – William Charles Maughan.)

In his "Memoirs" the 8th Duke recalled Lord John's "favourite niece" keeping house for him at Ardencaple after Joan's death. Presumably this was Adelaide Campbell. In 1831, however, Lord John married as his third wife Anne Colquhoun, the widow of Dr George Cunningham Monteith who had attended Joan during her final illness. The two sons, Johnny and George, were educated at home. Neither of the boys enjoyed good health, and Johnny died in April 1837. The 6th Duke died in 1839, and Lord John at last became Duke of Argyll, inheriting what has been described as "an

458 "Autobiography and Memoirs", Vol 1, Pages 60, 61.

The site of Ardencaple Castle today.
(Author's photograph).

Kilmun Church and the Campbell Mausoleum.
(Author's photograph).

appalling financial mess", a situation which in spite of his best efforts, he was never quite able to remedy.

At the death of the 7th Duke the Argyll estates were still in debt to the tune of some £232000. The pressure was eased a little by the sale of the Glassell property of Longniddry to the Earl of Wemyss who already owned much of the surrounding countryside. George's marriage to Elizabeth, daughter of the Duchess of Sutherland, brought in additional funds from her fabulously wealthy family.

When his father took his seat in the House of Lords on his accession as 7th Duke, George had accompanied him to London where he had become fascinated by politics, attending debates as an observer in both the House of Lords and the House of Commons. Early ambitions to represent Argyll in the House of Commons were thwarted, and his inheritance of the Dukedom on his father's relatively early death denied him the political career he coveted. He duly took his place in the House of Lords, however, and from initially taking an independent political position moved to the Liberal Party. He was known as a powerful debater, was three times Lord Privy Seal, and in between these stints was Postmaster General and Secretary of State for India. He was a prolific writer on scientific subjects, and an outspoken supporter of the Abolitionist cause and of the North in the American Civil War. He finally broke with the Liberal Party in 1886 over Gladstone's support for Irish home rule.

George 8th Duke of Argyll was married three times, first to Elizabeth Leveson-Gower who bore him five sons and seven daughters before she died in 1878. Secondly, he married Amelia, widow of a Colonel Anson, and thirdly Ina McNeill, the daughter of McNeill of Colonsay. His third wife edited (and some have suspected, manipulated) his memoirs. There were no children of the second and third marriages, and when George died in 1900 he was succeeded by his eldest son John who for long had been known by his courtesy title of Marquis of Lorne.[459]

Lorne had made little impression as M.P. for Argyll, and was rather cruelly described at the time as a "nonentity". He married Louise, the artistic and

459 An excellent and detailed account of he life of the 8th Duke of Argyll can be found in "The Intellectual Duke: George Douglas Campbell 8th Duke of Argyll 1823 – 1900", Ph.D. thesis by Kirsteen Mairi Mulhearn, University of Edinburgh, 2006. http://www.era.lib.ed.ac.uk/handle/1842/6918 .

mildly bohemian daughter of Queen Victoria. He was appointed Governor General of Canada in 1878, a post he occupied with undoubted success until 1883. Later, he was M.P. for Manchester South, until he succeeded as 9th Duke of Argyll. There were no children of John and Louise's marriage, and he was widely supposed to be homosexual. At his death in 1914 he was succeeded as Duke of Argyll by Niall, son of Captain Archibald Campbell, son of George the 8th Duke. Niall was therefore the great grandson of Joan Glassell and her beloved Lord John, and great great grandson of John Glassell the wealthy American merchant who began life as the son of a humble Dumfriesshire tenant farmer.

11

"Noble, generous, gentlemanly." Andrew Glassell and his descendants

WHEN JOHN GLASSELL RETURNED TO SCOTLAND IN 1775, HIS brother Andrew remained in Virginia, and eventually became sole owner of the Glassell plantation in Madison County, paying John the full value of the property after the peace settlement. In 1776 Andrew married Elizabeth, daughter of Erasmus Taylor of Orange County, Virginia. His marriage bond is preserved in the archives of the Virginia Historical Society.[460]

> *"Know all men by these Presents that we Andrew Glassell and Erasmus Taylor are held and firmly bound unto the Common Wealth of Virginia in the sum of Fifty pounds curt. Money, to which payment well and truly to be made we bind ourselves our heirs executors and admnrs. Jointly and severally by these presents sealed with our seals dated this 21st day of Octr. Anno dom 1776.*

460 Mss1G8855d3.

Whereas there is a marriage suddenly intended to be solemnized between the above bound Andrew Glassell and Elizabeth Taylor spinster, the condition of the Present Obligation is such that if there be no lawful cause to obstruct the same then this obligation to be void or else to remain in full force.
Sealed and delivered in the presence of *Andrew Glassell*
Eras: Taylor "

Andrew, baptised in Torthorwald parish in Dumfriesshire, Scotland on 8th October 1737, would be 38 years of age at the time of his marriage. Elizabeth was born on 22nd September 1755,[461] making her 21 when she married Andrew, seventeen years her husband's junior. Andrew and Elizabeth raised a large family of nine children. They were:

Millie Glassell, born 21st June 1778,
John Glassell, born 29th October 1780,
Mary Kelton Glassell, born 4th May 1783,
Helen Buchan Glassell, born 28th July 1785,
Jane Moore Glassell, born 17th November 1787,
James McMillan Glassell, born 1st January 1790,
Andrew Glassell, born 15th May 1793,
Robert Alexander Glassell born 18th June 1795,
William Erasmus Glassell, born 17th May 1797.[462]

It is stated in Hayden's "Virginia Genealogies" that Andrew built "a large brick residence on his fine estate on the Upper Robinson River". This estate he named "Torthorwald" after the parish of his birth in south-west Scotland. Andrew's house burned down in 1892, long after it had passed from the Glassell family's possession, but there is a description of it on file at the Library of Virginia:[463]

"Torthorwald was built of bricks which were burned on the plantation.

461 Letter from Martha Breeden (Madison County Historical Society), a direct descendant of Andrew Glassell.

462 "Virginia Genealogies" – Horace Edwin Hayden, Wilkes-Barre, Pa., 1891. Page 7, quoting Andrew Glassell's family Bible.

463 Works Project Administration of Virginia Inventory, May 3, 1937. Information supplied by Martha Breeden, Madison County Historical Society.

The house was rectangular with wings on the north and south; three and a half stories with a gabled slate roof. The house had four chimneys of brick, thirteen rooms, with a double door entrance with fan lights. There was an open stairway in the front hall, with basement entrance under. Closed stairways were in the north and south wings. There were four large rooms in the cellar, three fire places with Dutch ovens. The main house consisted of walls with 30 inch wainscoting and plaster. Door knobs were brass, and all do the hinges [sic] were made in Andrew Glassell's blacksmith's shop. The floors were six inch-width of pine. There were eight mantels, very handsome, made of walnut. There were four columns supporting the front porch which were 36 inches in diameter."

According to Hayden's "Virginia Genealogies"[464], Andrew Glassell "imported mechanics from Scotland" to build his house at Torthorwald. It might seem at first sight rather odd that he should do so, as there must have been numerous tradesmen and labourers in Virginia capable of doing the work. However, the Torthorwald plantation lay in what was still at the time a relatively remote area, possibly not attractive to builders from the more developed areas of Virginia. Perhaps it was easier and cheaper to secure a deal to recruit a squad of eager immigrants through family or commercial connections in Scotland, than it would have been to find a Virginia builder capable of the work, who was also willing to operate at the back of beyond at an affordable price.

The house was "a beautiful mansion completed in 1795… located on a hill on the east side of the Robinson River in Hebron Valley".[465] Hebron Valley lies just below the Blue Ridge Mountains, and many of the original settlers were German, often (confusingly to a British ear) referred to as "Dutch" by English-speaking Virginians.

Torthorwald Farm was put on the market in 2018 at a price of $1 130 000 for 78 acres or $1 510 000 for 116 acres.[466] The estate agent's description of the property includes the following:

"Welcome to Virginia's Hebron Valley, a location renowned for its beauty, fertility and proximity to some of the nation's best outdoor recreation. In

464 Virginia Genealogies, Page 6.
465 Letter from Martha Breeden, Madison Historical Society.
466 Gayle Harvey Real Estate Inc., Charlottesville Va. http://www.gayleharveyrealestate.com/hebronvalley/virginia.php .

the heart of this lovely valley is Torthorwald Farm, 78 acres set between a driveway lined with Bradford pear trees in front, and the Robinson River, a trout fisherman's dream, in back."

After describing the modern main residence and the "cute quiet cottage", the advertisement continues:

"The property is within one of the most desireable farming areas in Virginia. The valley floor is exceptionally flat, the soil extremely fertile, and the climate mild. The land is currently being cropped by a local farmer for winter wheat, soybeans, corn and hay. It could easily be fenced for horses, cattle, sheep, goats, or more exotic livestock.

Outdoor sports opportunities begin at the edge of the property which fronts the Robinson River. The state of Virginia stocks the river with rainbow and brook trout, so your next fish dinner could be the freshest of your life. Some stretches of this river are Class II whitewater. A short drive away are the scenic Blue Ridge Mountains, where you'd find biking and hiking trails, camping, boating, horseback riding, cavern exploring and just about any other outdoor enjoyments you can think of. In particular, Old Rag Mountain in Shenandoah National Park, which can be seen from the property, is a popular hikers' destination."

Martha Breeden from Madison Historical Society confirms, "The Hebron Valley is the most beautiful place in Madison C. Va. The view is amazing with beautiful pasture fields and the Blue Ridge Mountains all around." In this rural idyl, "Tobacco was the main crop on the [Torthorwald] plantation, and later they planted corn and wheat crops."

Tobacco production in early 19th century Virginia was dependent on slave labour. The Federal Population Census for Culpeper and Madison Counties of 1810 lists the white residents on Andrew Glassell's property as 2 males aged 10-16, 1 male 45+, 1 female 10-16, 2 females 16-26, and 1 female 45+. In addition, there are 30 slaves. The properties of Andrew's adult sons John and James contained 9 and 2 slaves respectively.

"Andrew Glassell," says his descendant Martha Breeden, "was a very aristocratic man and also very religious. He would travel from Madison to

Fredericksburg to worship with his family at a Presbyterian church where he was an elder." According to Hayden's "Genealogies", Glassell was, "A man of great force of character, firm convictions, large benefactions and earnest piety. At the age of fifteen he united with the Presbyterian church in Scotland, and remaind a zealous consistent Christian throughout the remainder of his life." Quoting Foote's "Sketches of Virginia", Hayden repeats the recollections of one who worshipped in the Fredericksburg Presbyterian Church from 1816 to 1818. He recalled:

> *"that genuine Scotch elder from Madison, tender of heart, but unconquerable in spirit, Andrew Glassell, with his short grey hair and Scottish accent, his long boots, and his small-clothes buckled at the knee, bending with age, but quick in his step; a full believer in his own creed, yet kind to those who differed, and charitable if their minds were correct."*[467]

We have already seen in an earlier chapter, Andrew Glassell's disapproval of his kinsman William Glassell's enthusiasm for debt collecting, and his acts of kindness towards several of his brother John's debtors. Hayden relates another example of "Mr Glassell's generosity, justice and integrity". Apparently in the summer of 1816 Virginia was ravaged by drought, and the corn (maize) crop failed. The price of corn rose to the "exorbitant" height of two dollars a bushel. Andrew Glassell and another Madison County planter, Mr Fry, were among the very few whose crop had not failed, but instead of taking advantage of the soaring prices, they sold their corn exclusively to the poor at a mere 50 cents a bushel.

Hayden also quotes *part* of what he terms a "lengthy paper" composed by Andrew Glassell for the benefit of his children and left to them after his death. It is hardly what might be termed light reading.

> *"I do here in the name of the Lord, lay upon your own shoulders those solemn engagements that we, your parents, have come under on your behalf in baptism; and you are to seriously consider now that the vows of the Lord are upon you, and to prepare for a solemn render of yourselves to Him by fulfilling your covenant with God in commemorating His dear Son's sufferings and death, in obedience to his commands. This you are not*

467 Virginia Genealogies, Page 9.

to do rashly or ignorantly, for it is a sealing ordinance between Christ and his followers to which you are to be admitted. Therein you are to engage yourselves in the most solemn manner to be for Christ and Him only; to fight against the world, the flesh and the devil; to avoid every appearance of evil, and to prove yourselves faithful followers of our own blessed Lord. O what a glorious and honourable thing it is to be members of Christ's family, heirs of God and joint heirs with our Lord Jesus Christ. And now, my dear children, lay these few instructions to heart, keep them in mind and practice them in life, that so your aged parents may have the joy of meeting you in the mansions of everlasting bliss beyond the grave, where we shall be eternally happy with the Lord.

I come now to give you a few directions how you are to conduct yourselves through this world and not be stained and polluted by it. First, do justice to all men. Make it a point to pay all your just debts. Make it a fixed rule never to go into debt for anything except when you have a visible prospect of paying at the time appointed. Be sure to conform your living below your income, as by this means you will keep yourselves in easy circumstances. Be always content with your lot in whatever state the Lord may place you. Be much in the habits of industry and economy, that you may have it in your power with ease to relieve the distressed, and the Lord will bless you if you do it purely out of charity. Shun evil company and associate with the precious ones of this earth, that is, those whom you judge to be followers of the Lord, and you will find great comfort from it, if you be one of the Lord's dear children. In closing, I commend for your perusal the 35th chapter of Jeremiah. This will point out to you the ready obedience the Rechabites gave to their father's command, and for that the Lord sealed unto them a perpetual blessing. The Lord grant that my children may do likewise."[468]

What we find here are the principles of the "Presbyterian work ethic" which stood so many Scots emigrants in good stead. It manifestly worked well for Andrew Glassell who commanded respect and standing in his community, and enjoyed property, posessions and comfort beyond the reach of many a country laird in the land of his birth. The modern reader might well of course wonder how a man of such "earnest piety", a man insistant on

468 Virginia Genealogies, Page 7.

"justice for all men", squared his beliefs with the ownership of thirty slaves. Andrew is unlikely to have seen any contradiction, however. In Scripture, slavery is taken for granted in the Old Testament, and in the New Testament Paul specifically urges slaves to be obedient to their masters.

It is not unlikely that in his own eyes Andrew saw his position in life as something akin to an Old Testament patriarch, presiding over an extended household of wife, sons, daughters, "manservant and maidservant, ox and ass". It is unlikely that a man of Andrew Glassell's principles would be deliberately cruel and oppressive towards his slaves, and he was probably not the sort of master to force himself on his female slaves and father children by them. He may even have been kind and considerate in his dealings with his "negroes", and it is not beyond the bounds of possibility that they may have come to revere and even love him. Such planters did indeed exist. All the same, a man so keen on "ready obedience" from his children would have tolerated nothing less from his workforce, and any slave inclined to offer anything less than that "ready obedience" would find life difficult indeed. And then, of course, it does not necessarily go without saying that the overseer in direct daily contact with the slaves would share the same high principles as his employer.

Andrew Glassell died on 4th July 1827 at the age of 89,[469] and was probably laid to rest in the burial ground on his property at Torthorwald. Martha Breeden informs us, "There is a family cemetery located on the property. However it is overgrown and on private property now. The cemetery is about 40 feet square surrounded by a rock wall built of river rock. It is believed to have only graves of the Glassell family. The only stone with an inscription states, 'The fifth child of Andrew Glassell'."[470]

Andrew Glassell's will, and the inventory of his possessions at the time of his death, are preserved in the archives of the Virginia Historical Society[471] and it is worth giving these fascinating (and admittedly lengthy) documents in full.

> *"In the name of God, Amen. I Andrew Glassell of the County of Madison and State of Virginia, in perfect health and memory (God be praised) do make and ordain this my last will and testament in manner and form following, that is to say –*

469 A history of St Mark's Parish, Culpeper Co., Virginia: Rev. Philip Slaughter, 1877.
470 Letter dated 4th November 2014 from Martha Breeden, Madison Historical Society.
471 Will – Mss 1G8855 d4. Inventory – Mss 1G8855 d5.

First – I recommend my soul to my Creator hoping and assured by believing through the only merits of Jesus Christ my saviour to be made partaker of life everlasting, and my body to the earth from whence it was taken.

As to my worldly goods with which it has pleased God to bless me, I do dispose of the same in manner following:

First of all I do desire that all my just debts be paid.

Item: I lend to my beloved wife Elizabeth Glassell and to my son Andrew Glassell during the widowhood of said Elizabeth in lieu of her dower, that part of the tract of land on which I reside, adjoining to the lands of Gamble, the tract purchased of John Hoffman and other persons, together with the tract of land aforesaid bought of John Hoffman.

Item: I give to my son John Glassell and to his heirs and assigns forever the tract of land on Fleshman's Run on which he formerly resided, supposed to be 250 acres together with a slip of land in an angular form supposed to contain twenty or thirty acres adjoining the said tract and the land of Abraham Tanner.

Item: I give to my son James McMillan Glassell and to his heirs and assigns forever the tract of land I bought of Maj. Towels, about 450 acres in the County of Madison.

Item: I give to my son Andrew Glassell, after the death of my wife Elizabeth Glassell, his heirs and assigns forever, all the lands loaned to him and my said wife, together with the land I bought of Moses Samuel, except the tract of land bought of John Hoffman.

Item: I give to Jas M. Glassell the two slaves Moses and Whitfield, and two stills; to Andrew Glassell two slaves named James and Charity his wife; to William E. Glassell two slaves Anthony and John forever.

Item: I give to my daughters Miley Smith, Helen Grinnan, my son Jas M. Glassell, the children of my late daughter Mary Wallace, and Jane M. Cave daughter of my late daughter Jane Cave all my remaining personal estate, negroes included, to be divided in the following manner:

One eighth part thereof to Jane M. Cave, and one fourth of the remainder to Milly Smith, Helen Grinnan, Jas M. Glassell, and to the children of Mary Wallace, that is, one fourth part to the said four parties.

I also give to Milley Smith, Helen Grinnan, James M. Glassell, and the children of Mary Wallace one fourth part each, their heirs and assigns forever, all my land in the state of Kentucky, and should a majority of the four parties prefer a sale of this land to retaining it, it may be sold by my executors, hereinafter to be named, and the proceeds thereof paid to the said four parties.

I also give to Milley Smith, Helen Grinnan, Jas M. Glassell and the children of Mary Wallace, each party one fourth part of all the tract of land I bought of John Hoffman, which land my executrix and executors John and William E. Glassell are hereby authorised to sell to my son Andrew Glassell at valuation by disinterested and competent judges of the value.

It is my desire that should any of my children or my granddaughter Jane M. Cave depart this life without leaving issue at his or her death, that their portion of my estate herein devised, or the proceeds of it, should be equally divided between my now surviving children and the children of Mary Wallace, her children taking the portion she would have had.

It is also my desire that the portion given to Jane M. Cave or allotted to her shall remain in the possession of my wife Elizabeth and Andrew Glassell until she shall marry or arrive at age.

It is also my desire and will that in settling and dividing my personal estate between my two daughters and the children of Mary Wallace, each party one third, reference should be had to their respective accounts in my ledger to equalise the three accounts.

Lastly, I appoint my wife Elizabeth Glassell my executrix, and John, Andrew, and William E. Glassell my executors.

In testimony whereof I have hereto set my hand and affixed my seal this fourth day of September Anno Domini one thousand eight hundred and twenty six.

Andrew Glassell.

Signed, sealed and acknowledged before us: Sampson Hoffman, James F. Blankenbaker, Belfield Cave, Elliot Blankenbaker.

Madison County 4th Sept 1826. Codicil to my foregoing will:

Whereas a suit is depending now on the Court of Appeal between myself and Robert Thomas, and myself or my heirs or executrix or executors be thereby compelled to pay the said Thomas his heirs or assigns any money on that score or account, I hereby burthen my four sons, Viz: John, James M., Andrew, and William Glassell, and my two daughters Milley and Helen and the children of mary Wallace being one party, in all seven portions, to pay each one seventh part of whatever sum of money said Thomas shall recover as foresaid, and I do hereby subject the property herein devised or above given to each of the seven parties to the payment of said claim or demand that may be against me or my heirs, executrix or executors when finally decided.

Andrew Glassell.

Signed, sealed and acknowledged before us: Sampson Hoffman, Jonas F. Blankenbaker, Belfield Cave, Elliot Blankenbaker.

4th September 1826: Codicil to my foregoing will: I hereby subject the property devised to my son Andrew Glassell to the expense of building a good brick wall four feet high around our family burying ground, and request him to have it done.

Andrew Glassell.

Signed, sealed and acknowledged before us: Sampsonn Hoffman, Jonas F. Blankenbaker, Belfield Cave, Elliot Blankenbaker.

At a court held for Madison County the 26th day of July 1827:

This last will and testament of Andrew Glassell deceased was produced into court and proved together with the Codicils thereto by the oaths of Sampson Hoffman and Elliot Blankenbaker witnesses thereto, and ordered to be recorded.

Teste: Belfield Cave CMC.

A copy –o Teste A. H. [Cave?] Clerk of the Circuit Court for Madison Co. Va."

"An inventory and appraisement of the estate of Andrew Glassell deceased taken on Saturday the 15th September 1827, by Leonard Barres, Thomas Clore and John Fray, agreeable to an order of the County Court of Madison, bearing date the 23rd of August 1827.

Negroes Viz				
Frank	*Suppo.*	*48*	*years old.*	*$200.00*
Randle	"	*10*	"	*220.00*
Coatney	"	*7*	"	*130.00*
Hartley	"	*15*	"	*250.00*
Hannah	"	*70*	"	*000.00*
Chas (butler)	"	*50*	"	*125.00*
Edmond		*21*	"	*350.00*
Ezekiel		*42*	"	*150.00*
Bob		*12*	"	*300.00*
Ben		*75*	"	*000.00*
Charles		*10*	"	*200.00*
Julia		*20*	"	*275.00*
Eddy & Child (Delpha)		*25*	"	*300.00*
Frances "				*100.00 [sic]*
Linah & child (Sylvia)		*40*	"	*175.00*
Vina c				*80.00 [sic]*
Nancy		*90*	"	*00.00*

1 sorrel mare and colt	*60.00*
1 sorrel horse (1 eye out)	*20.00*
1 mare (blind)	*5.00*
1 mule	*50.00*
1 bay horse	*12.00*
7 work steers	*105.00*
1 work bull	*10.00*
1 bull	*10.00*
8 cows	*64.00*
5 beef steers	*50.00*
12 young cattle	*36.00*
1 white bull	*7.00*
1 young calf	*1.50*
2 yearlings	*6.50*
1 horse cart and gear	*5.50*
1 wagon	*15.00*
28 head of sheep	*28.00*
1 cast iron bark mill	*39.00*

1 smith's bellows, anvil. Vice & hammers	*12.00*
5 hilling hoes	*1.67*
8 hay and manure forks	*2.67*
3 shovel ploughs	*1.50*
3 axes	*1.50*
1 grubbing hoe	*0.50*
1 shovel	*0.25*
1 frow	*0.34*
1 stone hammer	*0.34*
1 tan yard skimmer	*0.25*
1 whip saw and hand saw	*2.00*
1 wheel barrow, axle iron &c	*0.50*
2 pr. hames, 4 clivis and 2 pins	*1.00*
Parcel of old trace chains	*0.50*
1 log chain	*1.00*
3 augurs & foot adze	*0.75*
1 old wheat fan	*5.75*
Parcel of old irons on bench	*0.25*
1 old gig bridle	*0.25*
4 cotton wheels and pr old cards	*4.00*
4 flax wheels and Do.	*2.00*
1 loom warping bars and boxes	*5.00*
1 hackle	*0.50*
1 soap jar	*3.00*
1 meat chest	*0.50*
1 safe	*4.00*
8 large stone pots	*4.00*
1 keg	*0.25*
1 case of white bottles	*4.00*
1 tight hogshead	*1.00*
7 jugs and 2 pewter measures	*4.00*
1 cooper's adze and 2 funnels	*0.25*
2 stone pots	*0.50*
2 pairs and-irons	*1.25* [472]
4 brass cocks and weights	*1.25*

472 Andirons: firedogs, iron bar to support the end of a log in a fire.

1 paint stone and pots	*1.00*
1 decanter	*0.25*
2 pair steelyards	*4.25*
1 glass lantern	*1.00*
1 butter churn	*1.00*
2 iron pots and 3 ovens	*4.00*
1 roasting hook	*0.25*
2 skillets	*1.25*
2 bread bakers and tongs	*1.00*
1 ladle, skimmer, and 2 bread toasters 1	*1.00*
1 coffee mill and brass skillet	*2.00*
1 waffle iron	*1.20*
3 pair pot hooks and pepper box	*0.50*
3 bread trays	*0.50*
13 old Windsor chairs	*4.00*
1 walnut press	*6.00* [473]
1 old walnut folding table	*2.50*
	$3476.02

1 pr sugar nappers and brush	*0.50*
1 pr and-irons	*1.00*
1 bureau	*5.00*
1 old trunk	*1.00*
1 looking glass	*1.00*
1 desk and book case	*9.00*
Parcel black bottles &c &c	*1.00*
2 pr sheep shears, skillet & cleaver	*2.00*
2 pr hand bellows	*0.25*
1 pr old scales and weights	*0.75*
1 pr gold scales and seal	*1.00*
1 tin safe	*3.00*
I small folding table	*2.00*
1 bed and bedstead	*15.00*
1 truckle Do.	*2.00*
7 pair sheets	*7.00*

473 Press: cupboard.

10 pillow cases	*1.00*
6 cotton counterpanes	*12.00*
	$3540.52
1 sheet	*0.50*
2 bolster cases	*0.50*
1 pair coarse sheets	*1.00*
2 floor carpets	*5.00*
2 table cloths	*0.75*
1 fender, shovel & tongs	*1.00*
1 large folding table and 2 half rounds	*12.00*
Knives and forks with a box	*1.00*
1 claw hammer	*0.25*
A parcel Liverpool china ware	*9.50*
1 side board	*20.00*
1 eight day metal clock	*40.00*
2 silver tumblers	*2.00*
1 waiter with custard pans &c	*4.00*
1 waiter with glass salver &c	*5.00*
1 box with 1 doz knives and forks	*4.00*
4 pewter basins & 3 plates	*4.00*
4 brass candlesticks & snuffers	*3.00*
	$3654.02
3 tin waiters & 3 bread do.	*0.50*
1 pair ridged decanters	*0.70*
1 arm chair (writing)	*0.75*
11 Windsor chairs	*7.00*
1 pine table	*0.50*
1 hand vice, pincers and saw	*0.75*
Parcel old earthen ware	*3.00*
4 small stone pots &c &c	*0.75*
Parcel milk pans, water jug &c	*3.00*
1 brass mortar and pessel [sic]	*1.00*
3 trippets	*0.33* [474]

474 Trippet: trivet, tripod for a pot or kettle.

1 clock reel	*0.75*
1 small table	*1.50*
1 large looking glass	*10.00*
1 shot gun	*1.50*
1 large US map	*10.00*
1 tester bedstead	*3.00*[475]
1 common do.	*1.00*
	$3700.00

1 candlestick & cradle	*1.00*
2 armchairs	*1.50*
1 bed, bedstead &c	*8.00*
1 dress table, cover and glass	*1.00*
6 chairs with covers	*3.00*
2 plated candle sticks	*0.50*
4 large window curtains	*1.00*
1 small bed and mattress	*4.00*
1 wash stand	*0.25*
1 looking glass	*0.50*
1 bed, bedstead and furniture	*17.00*
1 do. do.	*8.00*
1 Scotch carpet	*15.00*
1 common do	*1.00*
1 dress table and cover	*1.00*
2 old looking glasses	*0.50*
9 Mobby hogsheads	*6.75*
2 stills, boiler &c	*50.00*
1 iron kettle	*4.00*
	$3824.10

Life of Washington 5 Vol.	*10.00*
Henry's commenteries – 2 Vos	*2.00*
Britania Encyclopedia – 3 Vos	*6.00*
Tillston's Sermons – 12 Vos	*6.00*
History of England – 12 Vos	*3.00*

475 Tester: canopy over a bed.

Family Bible	*3.00*
43 volumes old books	*6.50*
Religious pamphlets &c	*1.00*
1 set tongue and groove plains [sic]	*0.50*
3 pair H. hinges	*3.00*
Mill peck, chisel & ps lead	*0.25*
1 inkstand	*0.25*
1 desk	*0.25*
4 old maps	*2.00*
1 set surveying instruments	*25.00*
1 small pine table	*0.75*
1 pine shovel and tongs	*0.75*
1 pair tongs	*0.25*
	$3902.35

A parcel of bottle corks	*0.50*
1 hone and strap	*0.75*
1 pair razors	*0.25*
1 warming pan	*2.00*
1 do. bed pot	*1.00*
Lumber in store room	*4.00*
1 money purse	*0.12½*
1 spy glass	*0.75*
218 bushels corn at [sic]	*327.00*
	$4238.72½

[Signed] *Jno. Fray* *Thomas Cave* *Leo Barnes*

Twenty two shares of stock of the bank of Virginia.
Six shares of stock in the Swift Run Turn Pike Company.
Cash in testator's desk ninety two dollars and ninety three cents.
Credit of testator's on the books of Virginia Bank at Fred'g. Fifty two dollars.
Daniel Grinnan's bond for two hundred and sixty dollars dated 13th Sept 1826 and payable on demand.
Yager Smith's bond for fifteen dollars.
Jeremiah Morton, Adminr, with the will annexed of Andrew Glassell,

July 24th 1828.

At a court held for Madison County, the 25th day of September 1828: This Inventory and appraisement of the estate of Andrew Glassell, deceased, ordered to be recorded.

Teste: Belfield Cave C.M.C.

A copy – Teste: A. H. Cave C.M.C. "

We can imagine the assessors beginning with the slave quarters, moving on to stables and outbuildings, then progressing from room to room of the house of Torthorwald, carefully noting the contents down to the most insignificant trifles. Andrew Glassell was a man in very comfortable circumstances, as is obvious from his "tracts of land", commodious house, large workforce, cash in hand, bonds and investments. His house appears to have been well furnished, but not lavishly so. We will search through the inventory in vain for much in the way of luxury or self indulgence. His library might be taken as an indication of a man who read for instruction rather than entertainment, and it would be surprising if his 43 "old books" contained a wide selection of poetry and light fiction.

The inventory also gives us glimpses of agricultural and domestic activities in a largely self-sufficient economy; the raising of cattle and sheep, the storage (and presumably the cultivation) of "corn", that is, maize. The "bark mill" might indicate the tanning of leather; the cotton and flax wheels show that thread was being spun, and the loom demonstrates the weaving of cloth. The listing of "bellows, anvil, vice and hammers" suggests that Torthorwald had a resident blacksmith, and the two stills point to the production of alcohol.

What is most likely to give the modern reader pause for thought, however, is the fact that Andrew Glassell's single most valuable possession, apart from house and land, was another human being, a young man named Edmond, valued at $350. When this valuation is compared to that of Glassell's other livestock, it is immediately obvious that slaves were an important and costly investment. It might be argued therefore that a prudent slave owner would take pains to treat his investment with care, and have its wellbeing never far from his attention. Unfortunately, as we are well aware, not all slave owners were thus motivated. Septuagenarian readers might feel some indignation at the valuation of Hannah, Ben and

Nancy at zero! Their continued presence on the plantation could be seen as kindness, or at least as Christian charity on Andrew Glassell's part.

It will be noted that none of Andrew's "negroes" have surnames. After all, a dog or a prize bull may be given a name, but it would be thought ridiculous to give it a surname. Slaves were as much possessions of their master as a dog or a bull. Indeed, we might wonder whether Randle, Hannah, Ezekial & co. had their names bestowed on them by their parents, or imposed on them by their master. On liberation, slaves often assumed the surname of their plantation owner, particularly if the family's blood had mingled with theirs. It would be interesting to know if there are any black Glassells today in the USA. Andrew's will bequeaths the slaves Moses and Whitfield to his son James, the slaves James and his wife Charity to his son Andrew, and Anthony and John to his son William. We need not bother asking whether these slaves were consulted as to where and to whom they should be allocated after Glassell's death. Note that the allocations were made "forever". At least "James and Charity his wife" were to be kept together. Many plantation owners did not recognise that a slave could have such a thing as a "wife".

His descendant Martha Breeden is quoted above describing Andrew Glassell as "a very aristocratic man". In fact he was the son of a humble Dumfriesshire tenant farmer, but having made a fortune and fathered a large family, he founded a dynasty of upper-class Virginians. Although there was of course no titled elite in the United States, such families did to all intents and purposes exist as Virginian "gentry" or "aristocracy".

Andrew Glassell's daughter Mildred

Andrew Glassell's eldest child Millie was born on 21st June 1778. Little is known of her beyond the meagre details given in "Virginia Genealogies" and "A history of St. Mark's Parish". She was married on 3rd September 1796 to Reuben Smith. She had three children, Jane, George and William. Jane married Jeremiah Morton, member of Congress, in 1822, and had one daughter Mildred who married J. J. Halsey. George married Julia, the daughter of James Somerville of Culpeper County, and lived latterly in Bell County in Texas. He had four daughters and "several" sons. William (Dr William R. Smith), was twice married, first to a Mrs Middleton and secondly to Mary Mayrand. He fathered two children and lived latterly in Galveston, Texas.

In her father Andrew Glassell's will, "Milley" was left a share of a quarter of all his personal estate, "negroes included", remaining after the payment of his debts and the deduction of legacies to his widow and his sons John and James, and the deduction of one eighth of what remained, which was reserved to his granddaughter Jane Cave. Millie also inherited a quarter of Andrew's land in Kentucky, and a quarter of the land he bought from John Hoffman, which was to be resold to Hoffman.

Andrew Glassell's son John, and descendents

The second child of Andrew Glassell and Elizabeth Taylor was born on 27th October 1780, and named John. When John was nine years old his father took him to Scotland, and placed him in the care of the Rev. James McMillan to be educated at Dumfries Academy, where, according to Hayden's "Virginia Genealogies", he remained for nine years. This seems an unusually lengthy school education, as "academy" pupils in 18th century Scotland would usually have begun their university studies, or have been apprenticed in some professional capacity, before the age of eighteen. Perhaps after leaving Dumfries Academy John had private tuition from McMillan, or, as his cousin Joan did, from "masters" specialising in one field or another. A letter written in 1898 by one of Andrew Glassell's descendants states, "Mr James McMillan was a Presbyterian minister, a particular friend of my grandfather. He had a large school in Dumfries which your grandfather attended the nine years he was in Scotland".[476] McMillan was the minister of Torthorwald, Andrew Glassell's native parish near the town of Dumfries. If he also ran a school, it was not Dumfries Academy, as during the nine years that young John Glassell was in Scotland the rectors of that establishment were James Wait (1774 – 1794) and James Gray (1794 – 1801). It is more than likely, as already suggested, that John attended the Academy and perhaps had extra tuition from McMillan. According to "Virginia Genealogies", "The principal of the academy would often on Saturdays invite some eminent person to lecture to the boys. Mr Glassell thus frequently heard the poet Burns who was among the lecturers."[477]

John, then, presumably arrived in Dumfries in 1789 and returned to

476 Letter quoted in online "Biography of Frances Toy Glassell Ware" – Judith Ware, 2009, Updated 2013.

477 Virginia Genealogies, Page 9.

Virginia in 1798. On his return, according to Judith Ware, his father gave him a farm near the town of Haymarket[478], which he eventually sold, and bought another near the family plantation of Torthorwald. On 11th September 1806 he married Louisa Brown, aged 21, daughter of Alexander Humphrey Brown of Prince William County in Virginia. A letter from Louisa to her fiancé, written a month before the wedding, was printed long afterwards in the "Alexandria Gazette" as a historical curiosity.[479] She begins her letter addressing him formally as "Respected Glassell". "Our neighbourhood," she says, "has been thronged with visitors, and in the course of two weeks we partook of two barbecues in Haymarket, where we had an assemblage... of all the belles and beaux from the adjacent counties of Loudon, Fairfax and Fauquier."

John and Louisa had children as follows:

- Andrew McMillan Glassell, born 29th October 1807. Married Francis Anne Downing.
- Francis Toy Glassell, born 25th July 1809
- Marian Glassell, born 16th April 1811. Married William Henry Conway.
- Elizabeth Taylor Glassell, born 31st January 1813. Died aged 16, 7th May 1829.
- Cecelia Brown Glassell, born 24th December 1814. Died 18th December. Died 18th December 1817.
- Louisa Brown Glassell, born 4th October 1816. Married Joshua Ware Eno.

John's wife Louisa died at the early age of 33 on 20th August 1818. Three years later John married his second wife Margaret Lee (neé Scott), the widow of an uncle of the famous Confederate soldier Robert E. Lee. This marriage resulted in a further two children:

- Mildred Smith Glassell, born 12th January 1823. Married Edward Matthew Covell.
- John Glassell, born 16th August 1828.

---

478 Biography of Frances Ware – Judith Ware.

479 Ibid,

Margaret died aged 60 in 1843, and two years later John married Sarah Scott Ashton as his third wife.[480]

The 1810 Federal Population census for Madison County, Virginia, lists John Glassell's household consisting of one male aged 26 – 45, one female aged 26 – 45, one male under 10, one female under 10, and nine slaves. The children mentioned will presumably be Andrew and Frances. It is not quite clear where John and Louisa were living at that time, but at his father Andrew's death in 1827 John was bequeathed "the tract of land on Flashman's Run on which he formerly resided, supposed to be 250 acres, together with a slip of land in an angular form supposed to contain twenty or thirty acres adjoining to the said tract Abraham Tanner." A derelict house near Haywood in Madison County, known at one time as "the Rouse House", and thought to date from the 1820s or earlier, stands near Fleshman's Run. It is believed to have belonged originally to the Glassells, and may have been John's home. A spot in the neighbourhood was apparently once known as "Glassell's Quarters", and would presumably indicate the location of former slave quarters.[481]

When John married his second wife Margaret Lee, he moved his family into her home at Waverly Farm, northwest of Haymarket in Prince William County (to the west of Washington D.C.), and here Margaret raised her stepchildren along with her own two children by John. After Margaret's death John bought "The Glebe", north of Madison, where he lived with his third wife Sarah Ashton till his death on 30th September 1850.[482]

John Glassell's eldest child Andrew McMillan Glassell was born on 29th October 1807 at Torthorwald, Madison County, Virginia – the "McMillan" of course bestowed in honour of the mentor of his father's youth in Scotland. As a boy Andrew was sent to the town of Winchester to be educated under the supervision of his great-uncle the Rev. Alexander Balmain.[483] It is not quite clear whether this involved attending school while living with the Balmains, attending boarding school with the Balmains keeping a watchful eye on him, or possibly being tutored exclusively by his uncle. Perhaps a

480 Details of John's wives and children from online "Biography of Susan Ware" – Judith Ware.

481 Information from Beppy White of Madison County Historical Society, and "Madison Place Names" – Dove, Page 82.

482 Online "Biography of Frances Ware" – Judith Ware.

483 Hayden's "Virginia Genealogies".

different regime was applied at different times. At any rate, Andrew began medical studies under a Dr James Somerville in Madison County, before attending the University of Pennsylvania, where he graduated M.D. in 1831 after submitting a thesis on "Acute Dysentery". He spent two years as physician to the Baltimore Almshouse, then set up as a general practitioner in Bowling Green, Caroline County, Virginia. After another course of study at the University of Pennsylvania he returned to Bowling Green where he remained in medical practice for the rest of his life.

In 1840 Andrew married Frances Downing, and fathered a large family of nine: John Downing Glassell, Frances Ware Glassell, Mary Eugenia Glassell, Ada Glassell, Andrew McMillan Glassell, William Glassell, Robert Taylor Glassell, Louisa Brown Glassell, and Marion Conway Glassell.[484] In 1845 he built an imposing brick house in Bowling Green which he named "Glasselton House", and which stands to this day. He was baptized into the Baptist Church in 1871, and in 1879 was elected mayor of Bowling Green, occupying the position for two years. Andrew died in June 1888 and was succeeded in his medical practice by his son Dr Robert T. Glassell[485].

Frances Toy Glassell, the second child of John Glassell, was born on 25th July, probably at Torthorwald. She has been the subject of extensive research by her descendant Judith C. Ware, from whose online "Biography of Frances Toy Glassell Ware"[486] the following details are culled. Frances was known to family and friends as "Fanny" and after her mother's death and her father's remarriage to Margaret Lee, lived at Waverly Farm in Prince William County, Virginia. Like her brother Andrew, Fanny was sent to her great-uncle Rev. Alexander Balmain to be educated in Winchester. In a letter to her father of 12th December 1822, when she would be 13 years old, she informs him that she has "quit school" due to a relocation of the school into unsuitable premises. However, she reassured her father, "I intend to pursue my studies in the same manner I would at school." It should be said that Fanny writes a very literate letter. In it, amusingly, she says that her aunt wishes her father to stop sending pocket money to her brother Andrew, as he was generally spending it on confectionary, which "takes him from his studies".

In Winchester Fanny became acquainted with Josiah Ware, a young

484 Ibid. Pages 22, 23.

485 History of Caroline County Virginia – Marshal Wingfield.

486 Biography of Frances Toy Glassell Ware – Judith C. Ware 2009, updated 2013.

man from a wealthy family living at Riverside near Berryville in Clarke County, just east of Winchester. Ware was seven years older than Fanny, with a taste for amateur dramatics. He had a position as Deputy Court Clerk in Winchester, and was commissioned as a captain in the Virginia Militia. In 1827 Fanny and Josiah Ware were married, and in the same year Josiah began the construction of their house "Springfield" on land inherited from his mother. Springfield was an imposing white stucco mansion with a cupola, "one of the most beautiful houses in the valley".

The couple's first child James was born on 16th February 1831, and his cradle, skilfully crafted by a slave named Henry, is still preserved by Fanny and Josiah's descendents. James died at the age of only eight months, but a further four children followed: James Alexander Ware, John Glassell Ware, Lucy Balmain Ware, and Charles Alexander Ware. Fanny died on 10th May 1842, at the age of only 33, a year after the birth of her son Charles. Three years later Josiah married Edmonia Jacqueline Smith, and several more children were born.

Josiah Ware had become a noted agricultural improver, importing superior strains of livestock, particularly sheep and horses. He was a breeder of champion stallions, the founder of the Maryland and Virginia Agricultural Association, and was instrumental in founding Clarke County. He was a magistrate of the county, and a militia colonel, one of the social elite of the Shenandoah Valley. Describing [487]these men, a local historian commented, "They became models for a group of prosperous self-made men with origins not in the Tidewater, but in the Valley".

Fanny's house at Springfield still stands, and her grave and headstone can be found in Grace Episcopal Church Cemetery in Berryville, Virginia.

The youngest child of Andrew Glassell's son John was also called John, and was born on 16th August 1828. He was educated at Fredericksburg Preparatory School and the prestigious University of Princeton, from which he graduated in 1847. After graduation he engaged in farming in Virginia,[488] before moving to Louisiana. An interesting letter has been preserved[489] from

487 "A separate place – the formation of Clarke County Virginia": Warren T. Hofstra, White Port, Va., 1986.

488 Princeton Alumni Weekly, Vol 10, No 18, Page 2. Obituary.

489 Huntington Library, San Marino, California; Banning Co. Addenda 1, Box 4, Letter 43.

John's uncle Andrew Glassell to his mother-in-law. Writing from Mobile, Alabama, where he had settled, on 29th April 1859, Andrew wrote,

> *"I have just had a visit from John Glassell. He arrived here from Louisiana on Saturday morning and remained with me on Sunday to avoid travelling on that day. He is really a blue stocking and more particular, I think, than my father ever was as to the observance of that day in a Judaical manner. He has made a large purchase of land near Dr Gibbs who resides in Mansfield the county seat of Desoto Parish. He returns home to affect a sale of his land in Culpeper in order to move next winter. He is about to settle in a new country among new men and I fear sharpers. He says he is forewarned by dear bought experience. He is so unsophisticatedly honest that he can never suspect others of duplicity."*

John's house near Mansfield, De Soto Parish, in north-west Louisiana, still stands – a Greek revival building named "Wood Park".

John had married Mary Thom in 1850, and although already the father of five children, served as a private in the Confederate army during the Civil War. John and Mary eventually had nine children, namely:

- Ellen Footes Glassell, born 2nd June 1851, Culpeper County, Va. Died 26th November 1929.
- Susan/Margaret [Sic.] Scott Glassell, born 21st May 1853, Culpeper County, Va. Died 18th September 1932.
- William Erasmus Glassell, born 29th July 1855, Culpeper Co. Died 20th October 1933, Shreveport, Caddo parish, Louisiana.
- Virginia Thom Glassell, born 18th March 1857, Culpeper Co. Died 24th November 1897, Benton, Bossier Parish, Louisiana.
- Eudora Swartwout Glassell, born 23rd August 1858. Died 23rd August 1907, Mansfield, De Soto Parish, Louisiana.
- Ann Frances Glassell, born 8th August 1860, Mansfield, De Soto Parish, Louisiana. Died 6th April 1863. Mansfield.
- John Glassell, born 28th December 1861, Mansfield. Died 14th January 1939, Shreveport.
- Mary Stuart Glassell, born 26th April 1864, Mansfield. Died 3rd June 1947, Shreveport.

- Reuben Thom Glassell, born 23rd April 1867, Mansfield. Died 14th January 1950.

In 1886 John Glassell was ordained as a minister in the Presbyterian Church by the Presbytery of Red River. He suffered from paralysis for some years before his death, and had to rely on an assistant to perform his pastoral duties. The Rev. John Glassell died at the home of one of his sons in Shreveport on 17th April 1907.

Rev. John Glassell's son William Erasmus began work in 1879 as overseer on a large plantation in Bossier parish, Louisiana, owned by J. M. Foster. He was also manager of the plantation store. Around 1889 he set up a wholesale grocery business with a partner in Shreveport. He had the financial backing of his former boss J. M. Foster, and the firm subsequently became "The Foster and Glassell Company Limited", a prosperous business trading across northwestern Louisiana and neighbouring states. Glassell was a long-standing elder of Shreveport's First Presbyterian Church (which has a "Glassell Memorial Window"), served as president of Shreveport Chamber of Commerce and served also as chairman of the finance committee of Caddo Parish School Board. William married Janie Adger from Charleston, and had five children, including William Erasmus Glassell Jr and John Richmond Glassell.

Rev. John Glassell's son John married Annie G. Currie. Their three children were John Glassell, born in 1896, Alfred Currie Glassell, born in 1889, and Reuben Ashton Glassell, born in 1895. Alfred Currie Glassell was the owner of Cuba Plantation in northern Louisiana. His son Alfred Currie Glassell Jr was a man of distinction, who will feature in the final chapter.

Andrew Glassell's daughter Mary.

Andrew Glassell's third child was Mary Kelton Glassell, born on 4th May 1783. Little is known of Mary, apart from the fact that she married Michael Wallace, and was the mother of seven children: Ellen (later Mrs Somerville), Gustavus, H. Nelson, Elizabeth (later Mrs Goodwin), James, and Marianna (later Mrs Conway).[490] By the time her father Andrew Glassell drew up his

490 History of St Mark's Parish.

will in 1826 Mary was already dead, as is plain from his legacy of a portion of his personal estate and land in Kentucky to "the children of my late daughter Mary Wallace".

Andrew Glassell's daughter Helen and family.

Helen Buchan Glassell was born on 28th July 1785 and raised on the family property at Torthorwald. On 20th November 1815 she married Daniel Grinnan of Fredericksburg, an eminent Virginian whom we have already met in his capacity as investigator of "British Mercantile Claims" in the aftermath of the struggle for American independence. Grinnan was the second son of Daniel Grinnan Sr who had served in the Virginia Brigade in the "Revolutionary War". As a young man Daniel Jr moved from Culpeper to Fredericksburg to work as a clerk for the Scots merchant James Somerville, and after Somerville's death Grinnan succeeded to the business. In 1799 he was tasked with settling the many claims of British merchants who were still owed money from before the war. Grinnan concluded this difficult assignment successfully, to the satisfaction of both sides.

Around 1810 Grinnan formed a partnership with John Mundell of Fredericksburg and George Murray of Norfolk Va. which carried on an extensive shipping trade both in the United States and abroad. Although he lived mainly in Fredericksburg, Grinnan was also the proprietor of several estates elsewhere in Virginia, including Presque Isle at the confluence of the Rappahanock and Hazel rivers in Culpeper County, a house described as a "rare gem" and a "historical marvel".[491]

Helen Glassell was Daniel Grinnan's second wife. He had previously been married to Elizabeth Green, daughter of the proprietor of the Fredericksburg newspaper, the "Virginia Herald". She had died in 1813. The only child of Grinnan's first marriage, a son named Walter, died in 1817 aged 7. Helen Glassell and Daniel Grinnan had seven children: Robert, Eliza, Cornelia, Helen, Daniel, Andrew, and Daniella.

Hayden's "Virginia Genealogies"[492] informs us:

> *"Foote in his 'Sketches of Virginia' speaks thus of Mr Grinnan... 'Here came always at the hour of worship the manly form and benevolent face*

491 Blog "Today at Brandy Station: blogslot.co.uk". Mike Black, 26th July 2010.
492 Page 11.

of Daniel Grinnan, leading his lovely and devout wife, a daughter of the mountains; the man that felt himself obliged by having an opportunity of showing kindness. He sat half way from the right hand door of entrance to the pulpit with that peculiar contemplation seated on his face that lacked but a single touch of enthusiasm to have made him a chosen leader of God's host in perilous circumstances. How many in his quietness he was the means of leading to Christ can be known only at the Great Day...'."

Daniel Grinnan died at the age of 58 on 25th March 1830, after an illness "protracted and exhausting", bourne with "patient resignation". His youngest son recalled, "When my father found death nearly approaching he requested his wife to call in the children, and as they knelt one by one at his bedside, he put his hands on their heads, and prayed for and blessed them. As I was very young, my mother, fearing I would disturb him, did not bring me in, but, noting my absence, he asked for 'the boy', and had me brought in for his blessing."[493]

"Few men," his obituary stated, "passed through life with a more unblemished reputation, and none will be remembered with more sincere and tender affection. His undaunted integrity, his intelligent and well-cultivated mind, his polished manners, his friendly disposition, his open-hearted and generous benevolence and his unfeigned piety will be all remembered by all who knew him, and prove that the memory of the just shall be blessed."[494]

Helen Glassell survived her husband by over three decades, dying in 1863. Her headstone in Fredericksburg's Masonic Cemetery is inscribed in memory of:

"Our mother Helen B. Glassell, relict of Daniel Grinnan of Federicksburg.
Died October 16th 1863 in the 69th year of her age.
Living the life of the righteous,
Dying in the triumphs of the Gospel.
Her last word
All is well – All is well with me now and forever and forevermore."

Helen's daughter Cornelia Grinnan was known in her lifetime as a lively

493 Virginia Genealogies, page 12.
494 Virginia Genealogies, Page 11.

and intelligent woman with an enquiring mind and wide interests. In the mid 1850s she visited Britain, and met her kinsman the Duke of Argyll. She seems to have made the acquaintance of many of the Great and Good and been "received" by Queen Victoria. According to Hayden, she "was received and visited by a number of the nobility, and was especially intimate with the Duchess Dowager of Argyll, whom she visited at Ardencaple Castle and with whom she corresponded."[495]

Hayden quotes in full a letter from the "Duchess Dowager", who would be Ann, the third wife of Joan Glassell's husband "Lord John".

"Tetwood, Somersetshire,
13th Feb. 1855.

Dear Miss Grinnan,

I am indeed much gratified at your kind remembrance of my very hasty visit to you last July in London. It was alike my duty and my pleasure to endeavour to see a cousin of my dear departed friend [i.e. Joan Glassell], whose place as wife to one of the best of men I after her death had endeavoured to supply. Everything I could have done to have made your visit to Scotland happy by seeing you at Ardencaple, where she and I lived so long in the society and affection of him we loved would indeed have afforded me the most heartfelt satisfaction. But another time, if God wills, it shall be so, for I have no doubt you will try and come over to see us all. Your young cousins, the Duke and his children, and Emma, are ties which you feel, I see, and I really believe they were truly happy to see you, as they often spoke of you to me. And you see how well in the estimation of Englishmen George [the 8th Duke] stands. He is again in the new modelled government in the same office of Lord Privy Seal. Of course they are very dear to me, both for the love I bare to their mother and father, and I rejoice in seeing the Duke so gifted. Many thanks for the apples you have sent to me. I shall value them as YOUR KINDNESS. I have sent to my steward at Ardencaple to forward them immediately to me here. I am here generally from the end of January till the end of June. All are less or more suffering from the extreme cold this season – a Canadian winter. The frost was intense last night for England, for this, you know, is very far southwest. Emma is in Edinburgh. She is so fond of 'Auld Reikie'

495 Ibid. Page 11.

as Sir Walter Scott used to call Edinburgh. When you can spare a few minutes I shall always be glad to hear from you, my dear Miss Grinnan.
And ever believe me one of your affectionate Scotch friends,
C. Argyll."[496]

A close reading of this letter might lead us to wonder if Hayden was exaggerating a little when he stated that Cornelia was "especially intimate" with the Dowager Duchess. The letter is courteous and kind, but "another time it shall be so, if God wills" is hardly an enthusiastic heartfelt invitation from one intimate friend to another, and the Duchess's declaration that she will always be glad to hear from Cornelia if she "can spare a few minutes" might suggest that she suspects (or even hopes) that the ebullient and opinionated American will not have that amount of time to spare from her busy life.

Apparently Cornelia was shocked during her visit to Britain by the "wholesale execration of slavery, as if it could be swept away easily and speedily as a parlour table is dusted over."[497] She set herself to redress the balance, and according to Hayden, "By her correspondence with the London Times before the War, Miss Grinnan changed the tone of that paper towards the South."[498] Also, says Hayden, Cornelia "formed an intimate friendship with Lady Amelia Matilda Murray, Maid of Honour to the Queen, and changed her anti-slavery views into pro-slavery, and influenced her to take a trip through the United States… ". This lady, a granddaughter of the Duke of Atholl, published an account of her American tour as "Letters from the United States, Canada and Cuba".[499] In these letters she makes her opinions on slavery and Afro-Americans very plain. If, as is highly likely, they reflect the opinions of Cornelia Grinnan and the American Glassells in general, they might make uncomfortable reading for their present day descendants. Readers in Scotland will be forewarned of the nature of Amelia's view of the "facts" by the following:

496 Since the Dowager Duchess's name was Ann, it is puzzling that she should have signed it "C. Argyll". Perhaps Hayden, or his correspondent, misread the original signature.

497 Virginia's Civil War – Ed. Peter Wallenstein and Bertram Wyatt-Brown, University of Virginia Press, Charlottesville and London, 2005. Page 66.

498 Virginia genealogies, Page 11.

499 New York, G. P. Putnam & Company 1856.

"Really we in England know as little about the domestic arrangements of the Southerners as they do about our great landholders in England. I have been several times assured that the present Duchess of Sutherland depopulated the Highlands for the sake of raising sheep there. They confuse dates and facts and confound the present Duchess with the old Countess Duchess, whose energetic plans aided the starving Celts she caused to emigrate, and that outlay of money may perhaps now tend towards the improvement of the estates of the present Duke."[500]

As for Amelia's opinions on the "Negroes" of the Southern States, it will be sufficient to offer a few more excerpts without comment:

"As to the Negroes, they are the merriest most contented set of people I ever saw; of course there are exceptions, but I am inclined to suspect that we have as much vice and more suffering than is caused here by the unfortunate institution of Slavery; and I very much doubt if freedom will make the black population in the mass, anything more than a set of grown-up children. Even as to the matter of purchase and sale, it is disliked by masters; and I find compassion very much wasted upon the objects of it. An old lady died here lately, and her negroes were to be parted with. Mrs S., an acquaintance of mine, knew these blacks, and shed tears about their change of fate, but when they came to market, and she found all so gay and indifferent about it, she could not help feeling her sorrow was greatly thrown away."[501]

"I find that the term 'slave' is rarely made use of in the South. The blacks are called 'our servants' or 'our people'. We must remember that when slaves are to be disposed of, people in this country do not consider that they are literally buying men, but services, and what we hear of are the abuses, not the laws, of the system. Should a master ill-treat a slave, the law protects the latter, and I am inclined to believe cases of such treatment are rare. If a slave violates the law, a judge sends to his master and says, 'This is your servant; if you do not punish him, I must.' Of course the culprit much prefers to be corrected by his own master by whom all extenuating circumstances are understood and allowed for, and he is usually left in his hands.

500 "Letters" Page 207.
501 Ibid. Page 195.

As I have said before, the blacks are children of larger growth. They are tricky, idle and dirty. An excellent English housekeeper who has the management of this house, tells me that it is impossible for them to get on with the motives that would influence whites. She is very averse to reporting any of the darkies as requiring correction (alias a whipping), but without the power of doing so, they would be utterly unmanageable. As it is, one white servant would do the work of three blacks. 'Tom', perhaps, has no other vocation than to light fires. I have been amused to observe the slow roundabout way in which he performs the operation, never having all he wants at hand. This morning he brought no light; so before preparing to light the fire he takes my wax candle, lights it, and lets it stand burning uselessly. Then after lighting the fire, he keeps the candle burning for half an hour in broad daylight, while he goes through various evolutions about the cinders and the dust till he has settled it all to his satisfaction. I must repeat, over and over again, our ideas of negro character, and its capabilities, are little grounded upon truth.

We have cast aside the evidence of people who, with clear unbiased judgment, have watched the African from his cradle to his grave, and taken the opinion and the advice of well-intentioned but hot-headed zealots, until we have damaged the cause of civilisation, checked the progress of individuals of the black race, and at the same time done mischief to ourselves, and to fine islands and colonies which are now again tending towards barbarism… Barbadoes has already much deteriorated, and unless the power of landed acquisition by negroes receive some legal check… the blacks will slowly but certainly gain possession of the island. The same process will follow in others… ".[502]

"There is no doubt the blacks are susceptible of education and improvement, to a certain extent, under white influence. The darkies of Baltimore and Virginia are a shade higher in the scale of improvement than those of Georgia, from being more in approximation with whites in a mass; but you never can change the Ethiopian character or wash white his skin. 'The pig will never grow into the lion.' Under good direction, it is a light-hearted, merry, unreflective race, excitable and impulsive; but it has a sense of justice, and can be attached and be made an honest,

502 "Letters". Pages 209, 210.

useful, and highly respectable servant by judicious management and early training. They are apt at any mechanical employment. Some of them are very orderly, but put them out of a track to which they have been accustomed, and they rapidly lose themselves. A lady here has taken great pains with a negro boy in her family. I was amused to observe him standing behind her chair with a tray under his arm like a little black statue. He never forgets to come at a particular time for her orders, but the teaching him to read is no small order. He goes on the box of the carriage and well performs any accustomed duty; but if you ask him to take a knife and dig up a plot, he looks utterly bewildered."[503]

"Instead of being surprised that these slave proprietors feel themselves insulted and aggrieved by the manner in which English philanthropists have vilified and abused them, I am only astonished at the patience and gentleness with which they have endured our calumnies. They are just and kind to us in spite of our faults, and for the sake of good intention they forgive... I have observerved a noble generous gentlemanly spirit in this part of the Union. I feel assured that if the Southern proprietor, as a class, found reason to believe that the institution of slavery was predjudicial either to the Christian or temporal interests of the blacks, they have chivalry enough in their composition to have cast aside mere motives of private interest; but they knew, and we did not know – that was the difference."[504]

Cornelia Grinnan died on 20th November 1864, aged 43, in Goochland County Va., when, according to a eulogy penned by the Rev. John Leyburn of Baltimore, "a brief illness brought her to the grave". Mr Leyburn continues, "Her well stored sparkling mind, her brilliant conversational powers and ready wit rendered her the life of every circle. During a visit to England some years since she was received without formal introduction into the society of the nobility, where she made a most favourable impression. But few who have been abroad have been able to afford more entertainment by subsequent narration of what events they had met with. Though her physical structure was feeble, she was so exhuberant with life that she bid fair for many days. But God has ordered it otherwise, and his will be done."[505]

503 "Letters", Pae 211.
504 "Letters", Pages 211, 212.
505 Virginia Genealogies, Page 11.

Andrew Glassell's daughter Jane.

Jane Moore Glassell was the fifth child of Andrew Glassell and Elizabeth Taylor. She was born on 17th November 1787, and grew up to marry Benjamin Cave, a planter, the descendant of a Benjamin Cave who came to Virginia from England in 1725, and eventually, with a business partner, became proprietor of a thousand acres on the Rapidan River. His son Benjamin had a son Belfield Cave, who was the father of Jane Glassell's husband. Jane and Benjamin Cave had two children, one of whom died in infancy. The other was a daughter, Jane Moore Cave.

Jane Glassell died on 23rd April1812 aged only 24. It is probably her grave in the burial ground at Torthorwald which is marked by the only stone with a surviving inscription. It commemorates "...the fifth child of Andrew Glassell".[506] Jane's husband Benjamin Cave died on 24th June 1822.

In Andrew Glassell's will of 1826, Jane is described as "my late daughter Jane Cave". Andrew bequeathed to her daughter Jane M. Cave one eighth of his personal estate after deduction of the bequests to his sons. He ordered, "It is also my desire that the portion given to Jane M. Cave, or allotted to her, shall remain in the possession of my wife Elizabeth, and Andrew Glassell, until she shall marry or arrive at age." One of the witnesses to Andrew's will was "Belfield Cave". It is not clear who had the care of young Jane after her parents' deaths, but she married a John B. Gray, and had eight children: Robert Atcheson Gray, Lucy Robb Gray, Agnes Gray, Margaret Gray, Jane Glassell Gray, Gertrude Gray, Isabel Bowie Gray, and John Bowie Gray. Jane herself survived until 1890.[507]

Andrew Glassell's son James.

James McMillan Glassell was born on 1st January 1790 at the family home of Torthorwald in Madison County. His name reflects his father's friendship with James McMillan, minister of Torthorwald in Dumfriesshire, Scotland. According to Hayden, in 1810 he married Eudora Swartwout[508], a native of New York, in St Augustine, Florida.[509] There was only one child of the marriage, a girl Eudora Swartwout Glassell who died aged seven in Baton

506 Letter from Martha Breeden, Madison Historical Society.

507 Details from "Virginia Genealogies". Jane's death date from "Ancestry.com".

508 Virginia Genealogies.

509 Genealogy.com.

Rouge, Louisiana.[510] In the 1810 census of Madison County James is shown as the owner of two slaves, and the 1826 will of his father Andrew gifts him "two slaves Moses and Whitfield, and two stills." His father also left him "the tract of land I bought of Maj. Jos. Towels, about 450 acres in the County of Madison." James also inherited a fourth part of his father's land in Kentucky, and a similar share of a tract of land his father had bought from John Hoffman. Under the terms of the will this land was to be sold on to James's younger brother Andrew.

James embarked on a career in the U.S. army. According to Hayden, "He entered the U.S. Army during the war [with Britain] of 1812." A posting to Florida might have explained why he married there, so far from his home in Virginia, and his wife's home in New York. However, if indeed he married in 1810, and joined the army in 1812, that cannot be the case. Perhaps one of these dates is wrong, or both. By 1812 James would be 22 years old, which seems just a little late in life to begin an army career. To complicate matters, Eudora's date of birth is given on several genealogical websites as 1798. If she and James were indeed married in 1810, that would make Eudora twelve years old on her wedding day, which to say the least, is rather unlikely!

According to Hayden's "Virginia Genealogies", James began his military career as a recruiting officer. During the 1812 war with Britain he was posted to Lake Ontario. Having been warned that sleeping beside a campfire would expose him to enemy snipers "he frequently slept in the snow, and often awoke to find a foot of snow covering him". After the war he applied for promotion to the rank of captain, but President Madison turned him down on the grounds that promoting him might appear as favouritism, as the President was a relative. James was compelled to content himself with the humbler rank of seond lieutenant.

He was ordered to Georgia, and participated in a campaign against the Cherokees and Choctaws. He was then posted to Florida, where he impressed General Jackson to such an extent with one of his reports that he was drafted onto the staff at the General's headquarters. James was judge advocate at the controversial court martial of two Englishmen who were hanged for supplying arms to the Seminole tribe. He was also given the task of superintending the building of forts at Fort King and Key West. If

510 Virginia Genealogies, Page 7.

in fact he married Eudora Swartwout in St Augustine, Florida, it would make sense to place the marriage during his period of military service in that state; in other words , nearer 1820 than 1810.[511]

Again according to Hayden, Glassell was promoted to Captain in 1818, and was Assistant Adjutant General from 1818 until 1821. He was made Brevet Major in 1828, and major in 1837. "After spending some time in Europe," says Hayden's informant, "he was stationed in Philadelphia, when he was made Brevet Major and ordered to Baton Rouge under Col. Zachary Taylor".

As regards the European trip, on 10th June 1825 James Madison wrote a letter supporting an application by Captain Glassell for leave of absence to make a trip to Scotland to "aid an object in which he has an eventual interest".[512] Permission presumably having been granted, Captain Glassell arrived in Liverpoool on 9th September 1825, and embarked for home from the same port on 2nd August 1826. During that time he kept a diary, which is preserved in the "Special Collections" of the University of Virginia Library.[513]

For at least some of the time, James seems to have been travelling with a small party of Americans, but it is not usually clear who the "we" in his journal actually includes. The impression given is that various acquaintances went their own way at some times and met up again at others. We might guess that the composition of the party varied as its members paid visits or attended to business of their own, as necessity or their fancy took them. A Mr A. M. Crutchfield seems to have been a fairly frequent companion.

On the evening of Friday 9th September 1825, James landed in Liverpool, and put up at the "Waterloo". The following day he dined at "the most fashionable resort in Liverpool", the "Pig and Whistle", which for all its fame was a "dirty looking house" in a filthy lane. The small, cramped, low-ceilinged room he dined in had apparently been converted from a stable. On the Sunday he attended church at the Blind Asylum, and was most impressed by the blind organist and his blind choir. Two days later he again

511 Much of the foregoing information comes from a note supplied to Hayden by "W. E. Glassell", who is more likely to have been a nephew of Major Glassell's than his brother of the same name.

512 Website "Founders Online". Letter from James Madison to Jacob Brown, 10th June 1825.

513 University of Virginia, University Library, Albert and Shirley Small Special Collectios Library, Papers of Grinnan and related families, MSS 49, Box 49.

visited the Blind Asylum, and was astonished at the skill of the inmates in making shoes and baskets, and weaving carpets.

On 17th September, Glassell and Crutchfield left Liverpool, and breaking their journey in Manchester, travelled on by Stockport and Sheffield to arrive in Doncaster late in the evening of the 18th. The town was inundated with visitors, there for the horse racing, and Glassell and Crutchfield found themselves having to pay 30 shillings ("upwards of 6 dollars!") for a shared bed in a "coarse looking house" in a "miserable alley". However, James seems to have enjoyed the races, including the famous St Leger, and was greatly impressed by the magnificent coaches of the nobility with their squads of outriders, attendants and postillions. Although the road to the racecourse was festooned with religious placards, and grave-looking men were handing out leaflets inveighing against horse racing, "the bells of St George's Church chimed at eleven o'clock as a signal for the commencement of the races" (a turn of events which evoked three exclamation marks from Captain Glassell). He also noted that women hawking race programmes had other leaflets concealed beneath, "containing the most obscene notices of the girls of the town". James does not seem to have been tempted. He did note, however, that English women had excellent complexions, but rarely had well-shaped legs. These were on frequent view as ladies boarded their coaches. "Not infrequently," James admitted, "have I loitered for that purpose where a carriage was standing steps down before the door of some handsome house."

After Doncaster, Captain Glassell proceeded to Sheffield. There he visited a cutlery showroom, and the ruins of Manor Castle where he saw the room where Mary Queen of Scots was imprisoned. On 23rd September he arrived in Birmingham, and took lodgings at the "Hen and Chickens", which he thought "a most excellent house, and among the best in England". The streets of Birmingham were wide and handsome, but the sidewalks were paved with small round stones, and "disagreeable to walk on".

Warwick was the next stop, where St Mary's Church impressed with the marble monuments of the Earls of Leicester. Warwick Castle was open to the public, and James was able to view Queen Anne's bed, which had not been slept in since last used by that monarch. He also saw various relics of the semi-mythical Guy of Warwick, whose fleshpot was being used by the current Earl's family as a punchbowl. From Warwick James was able to proceed in a "carr" to Kenilworth Castle, where he was "highly gratified with the stupendous ruins". Later in the day he took another "carr" to Stratford on Avon. He was suitably awed by Shakespeare's tomb, and sat for a time in the very church pew in which the Bard himself had worshipped. He also visited the playwright's birthplace, a small low chamber entered up a narrow stair from a butcher's stall. He found every wall, and the very ceiling, covered with the names of visitors, and eventually, after falling on his knees, found a small space to inscribe his own.

From Warwick, James travelled on to Oxford where he visited the various colleges, halls, libraries and galleries, noting that the "Baudelin" Library had 200000 volumes and 160000 manuscripts. He also paid a visit to Blenheim Palace, where he was shown round by "a female housekeeper who expects 3 or 4 shillings from each party". Notwithstanding this expense, James was awestruck by the magnificent house and extensive parkland. "The house covered 7 acres," he marvelled, "and the park contains 2700, the stone wall around which is 12 miles in length and about 8 or 10 feet high. It contains about 200 deer with a broad expanse of water on which float numerous swans. The walls of many rooms are handsomely ornamented with fresco paintings and stucco, most of the former by the best artists, the forms exhibiting allegorical and historical subjects. The various victories of the great Duke are represented on tapestries, and every room is profusely garnished with paintings and statues by the best masters." In one wing of the palace there was also a private theatre, and the Titian Gallery containing "a large collection of lascivious paintings on leather by that celebrated artist". Regarding the current Duke of Marlborough, James noted, "He is 60 years old, but nevertheless keeps 5 or 6 mistresses at and about Blenheim. He is so much involved by gambling and debauchery, both in purse and character, that they will not credit him in Woodstock for a loaf of bread, and his house has frequent visits from the Bailiffs to search for what they can seize, as they cannot touch anything belonging to the Palace and parks, which is all entailed."

From 27th September to 16th October James was in London. He saw all the requisite sights – the Tower of London, East India House, the British Museum, Westminster Abbey, St Paul's and the Houses of Lords and Commons. He took a boat trip down the Thames to see the ongoing works of the projected tunnel under the river, and continued to Deptford to view the naval dry docks. However, he found there that "foreigners could not be admitted".

He visited an extensive menagerie, and ventured to handle a "prodigious boa constrictor", but was unable, he admitted, when so doing, "to conquer either my aversion or apprehension". Several of James's evenings were spent at the theatre – Drury Lane, Covent Garden, and Haymarket where he saw the actor Liston in "Paul Pry" twice. He also attended the "English Opera" where his companion Mr Boardman of Boston was relieved of £30 by a pickpocket.

On 11th October Captain Glassell procured a passport from the American "minister" (ambassador), and the following day had it signed by the French equivalent. On the 17th he crossed from Dover to Calais, and the following day left for Paris in the "diligence" or stage coach, passing through "Boulogne, Montreuil, Abbeville, Beauvais, Beaumont and St Denis, as well as many other smaller towns and villages, most of which have a shabby and filthy appearance".

On his arrival in Paris James put up at the Petit Hotel de Montmorency, and the following day, 20th October, undertook a taxing schedule, visiting the Palais de Bourbon, Les Invalides, Notre Dame, the Church of St Geneveive, the Pantheon, and the Chambre des Députés. He dined "sumptuously" for 2 francs ("about 38 cents") and proceeded to the Italian Opera to hear Madame Pasta sing in "Romeo and Juliet".

There follows a blank in Captain Glassell's diary until 2nd November when he was rejoined by his compatriots Crutchfield and Robinson who had been touring the Netherlands. On 3rd November he departed the Hotel de Montmorency for a "fashionable boarding house", which he left a week later after finding it "troublesome". He and Crutchfield, and another by the name of Siegbert, took rooms with a Madame de Ligny "who also contracted to furnish us with breakfasts". Glassell again neglected his diary until 19th December, when he and Crutchfield set off to visit by invitation the French hero of the American War of Independence, General Lafayette.

Gilbert du Motier, Marquis de Lafayette, had become convinced as a young army officer of the justice of the American cause, and sailed to America to participate. He served with distinction, went back to France to lobby for more concrete French support, and after returning to America was rewarded with senior military commands. On his eventual return to his homeland he was elected a member of the Estates General of 1789 and helped to write the "Declaration of the Rights of Man". He had attempted to steer a middle course in the French Revolution, until more extreme factions ordered his arrest, and he was forced to flee. He was arrested by Austrian troops and imprisoned until his release was secured by Napoleon in 1797. He became a member of the Chamber of Deputies after the Bourbon restoration in 1814. His wife had inherited the Chateau de la Grange-Bléneau in the commune of Courpalay in the department of Seine et Marne, and here Lafayette lived from 1802 until his death in 1834. In 1824, the year previous to Glassell and Crutchfield's visit, he had toured the United States, and was rapturously received in all 24 states of the then union.

Glassell and Crutchfield arrived by stage coach at "Rosay" (Rozay en Brie) and hired a "cabriolet" to take them to Lafayette's mansion at La Grange. They found the family at dinner, and Lafayette, who had one side of the table to himself, placed them one on his left and one on his right. Next morning after breakfast the Americans strolled in the grounds with the General's daughter Madame Mauberg, his son George Washington, and the "young ladies" of the family. In the afternoon James was given a conducted tour by the great man himself of Lafayette's farm, a complex which housed an impressive array of livestock. The general's sheep, James noted, were all merinos, 800 of them, descended from an original gift from the King of Spain to the French King. In the evening, there was a "sumptuous dinner in the French style", then after adjourning to the parlour, singing to the piano by the young ladies, and "conversation and the exhibition of prints". At ten o' clock the company reconvened in another parlour and the young ladies handed round tea.

Glassell and Crutchfield had intended to leave on the following day, but were pressed to stay another night. Early on the morning of 22nd December they were driven to Rozay in the General's coach, arriving just in time to catch the diligence to Paris. James took the trouble to list in his diary all those present at La Grange, amounting to 20 persons, all members of the General's family, apart from the two Americans. "The young ladies," he noted, "are almost all of them handsome, and Miss Segur, with the two youngest of George W's daughters, and one of Madame Lasery's, very much so." The young ladies had apparently exerted themselves to make their guests' time pass agreeably. "Mine," said James, "passed delightfully."

Another gap follows in James's journal, before his departure from Paris on 20th January 1826. He presumably then returned to Britain. It will be remembered that he had originally been granted leave from his military duties to attend to business in Scotland and we may suppose that this was indeed undertaken. What business this was, unfortunately, must remain a mystery, as this part of his diary is missing. What remains takes up again in the middle of a sentence where he records visiting a ruined abbey and returning to Dumfries, which is of course the town adjacent to the parish of Torthorwald where the Glassell family's roots were.

The following day, 17th July 1826, James visited the widow of the poet Robert Burns, then departed for Carlisle. He arrived in Liverpool on the 19th and paid a short visit to Dublin, where he thought "the Irish character was not very prominent". He left Dublin on the 24th, sailing back overnight to Liverpool. On 2nd August he "got on board this morning, and with a fine breeze left Liverpool" for the United States.

According to Hayden's "Virginia Genealogies" James was promoted to Brevet Major in 1828, and to Major in the 6th Infantry on 6th September 1837. He was posted to Baton Rouge in Louisiana, where his health broke down, and he died from a "dropsical affection" at Fortress Monroe on 3rd November 1838. He was interred at Hampton, Virginia. His only child, a daughter Eudora, also died in Baton Rouge, aged only seven. His wife, Eudora Swartwout, survived him by many years, dying in 1865 in Winchester, Virginia.[514]

Andrew Glassell's son Andrew.

Andrew was his father's seventh child, born on 15th May 1793.[515] He was educated in Winchester, and on 1st February 1825 married Susan Thornton. Susan was the daughter of William Thornton, and Eleanor Thompson whose father was a prominent Virginia Lawyer and politician. Andrew and Susan had six children:

- Ellen Elizabeth Glassell, born 1825,
- Andrew, born 1827,
- Philip Rootes, born 1829,
- William Thornton, born 1831,
- John Henry Hobart, born 1833,
- Susan Thornton, born 1835.[516]

514 Genealogy.com. "The updated Swartwout chronicles."
515 "Virginia Genealogies".
516 Banning Company Addenda. Glassell family tree.

Philip presumably died in infancy or early childhood, as there seems to be no further mention of him after his birth.

Under the terms of his father's will Andrew and his mother inherited the land around the family home at Torthorwald, and "the tract purchased of John Hoffmann and other persons". After his mother's death Andrew was to become sole proprietor of all except the Hoffman tract, which was to be shared equally among Andrew's siblings Millie, Helen and James, and the children of their deceased sister Jane. This land they were then required to sell back to their brother Andrew. Andrew was also to have the land his father had bought from Moses Samuel.

His father also bequeathed to Andrew "two slaves named James and Charity his wife", and bound him to enclose the family burial ground with "a good brick wall five feet high".

Hayden's "Virginia Genealogies" confirms that Andrew inherited part of the family estate of Torthorwald, but then sold it, and moved to the plantation of Richland in Culpeper County. "This he sold to his brother William, and bought 'Fleetwood' where he lived until 1836 when he bought an estate near Livingston, Alabama."[517]

Why Andrew decided to move to Alabama is not clear, but the move was by no means as simple as might be assumed, and was to have tragic consequences. Different sources give different dates for the move to Alabama, but a letter to her mother in March 1833 shows Andrew's wife Susan still living at Fleetwood, Virginia. Much of the letter is taken up with religious matters, including the unhappy possibility of one of their acquaintances becoming an Episcopalian. The letter was to be delivered by her husband Andrew, who was setting out "directly" in search of a new overseer, and he would leave the letter for Susan's mother at "the Ct. House".[518]

On 18th December 1834 Andrew wrote to Susan from Huntsville, Alabama. "I arrived here this morning to breakfast," he informed her, "after spending two nights on the stage without sleeping, except what I got by nodding." Andrew was obviously in Alabama hunting for a suitable property. He had been speaking to a "Judge T-n", who had advised him not to buy but to rent. The search for another property seems to have been long and arduous. "Oh! That we were once more settled somewhere," he

517 Virginia Genealogies, Page 16.
518 Banning Co. Addenda 1, Box 4, Letter 59.

lamented. "Nothing will ever induce me to ever move again, certainly never to separate us so long again. I now look forward to the Spring with a great deal of anxiety. But I have a great deal to do before I can turn my face toward home." To compound the misery, Andrew had been ill. "I am now nearly as strong as ever, not entirely clear of the mercury out of my system."[519] Mercury is well known as the remedy of choice for syphilis in pre-antibiotic days. However, it was also used in cases of typhoid, cholera, parasites, skin conditions and other ailments, to the extent that in the USA in the first half of the 19th century, mercury was used "as a universal medicine for almost any disease".[520] It is also, of course, a powerful poison. "I take care of myself," Andrew continued, "have a double set of flannels on me, and although the other stage passengers complain of cold, I never feel the least inconvenience on that account."

In January 1836, in spite of his earlier intentions, Andrew had still not managed to find a new home for his wife and family. On 19th January he wrote to Susan from Greensborough, Alabama, bemoaning the "uneasiness and misery" he felt at not having seen her for so long. The price of good land in Alabama was continually rising, he informed her, and those who held good land were not pressed for money, and thus not inclined to sell cheaply. "I have been riding about the country, and just got into this neighbourhood last evening," he reported. "The immediate vicinity of this town is by far the most desirable country to live in that I have seen yet. But a good home here could not be purcheased for less than 25 or 30 dollars per acre. Its lands are like the Rappahanock bottoms and very productive, but too dear for me."[521] It had become obvious to Andrew that many Alabama landowners preferred to buy their slaves from Virginia. "Negro fellows will readily command here $800, and in Mississippi $900 & 1000, but say nothing about this. That property [i.e. "negro fellows"] will rise still higher next fall, as the great demand for money on account of the late public sales of land has hitherto kept that property down, if down I can say." He intended, therefore, to advise Susan's brother to buy his cook's husband as soon as possible – presumably to prevent him being snaffled by some predatory purchaser from Alabama or Mississippi.

519 Banning Co. Addenda 1, Box 4, Letter 37.

520 https://art-bin.com/art Article: "A hundred years of misuse of mercury and dental amalgam." – Mats Hanson.

521 Banning Co. Addenda 1, Box 4, Letter 38.

That same year, 1836, as indicated by Hayden's "Virginia Genealogies", Andrew acquired a property at Livingston, Alabama, and made arrangements for his family to join him – his wife Susan, and children Ellen, Andrew, William, John (known by his middle mame of "Hobart") and Susan. The move did not go to plan however. Writing of Susan the youngest child, "The Washingtons – a family history" states, "Susan Thornton Glassell (born in Virginia March 2 1835). That same year she was carried as an infant from Virginia on a long trek to a new home in Alabama. Along the way Susan's mother and sister died of yellow fever, and she was nursed on mare's milk…"[522] As shown above, the move was almost certainly 1836, not 1835. As already mentioned, a son Philip had probably already died in Virginia, and another, Hobart, was to die in 1853 at the early age of 30.

By 1854 Andrew seems to have been resident in Mobile. It is not clear whether he was still the proprietor of the plantation at Livingston, but in 1853, visiting Livingston from Mobile, Andrew's daughter Susan wrote to her cousin, "Livingston has undergone so many changes that it is almost impossible to feel at home."[523] Andrew by this time appears to have been a contractor hiring out gangs of slaves. "I am happy keeping house in this city," Andrew wrote to his son William. "I have old Nelly to cook and wash for me. I always have one or two invalids to attend to. I have other negroes besides my own to hire out." In the same letter he mentions that their relative Cornelia Grinnan "has been in London since before winter and has visited the Argyle family".[524]

Andrew's son William had become a naval officer, while his son Andrew had become a successful businessman in California – we shall become more familiar with them in the final chapter. Andrew Jr. was keen for his father to join him, but Andrew Sr. had raised various objections, including his reluctance to sell "the family negroes". On 4th June 1857 his son reassured him,[525] "As to your objections on the ground that you would dislike to sell the family negroes, that may be soon avoided. I observed that Sue and Grandma were anxious to have Nelly and Betsy about them. Let

522 "The Washingtons – a family history" – Justin Genn. Vol 2 "Notable members of the presidential branch", Page 3207. Saves Publishing, El Dorado Hills, California. 2014.

523 Banning Co. Addenda, Box 7, Letter 21.

524 Banning Co. Addenda, Box 4, Letter 39.

525 Ibid, Letter 40.

them have them, and such others as you would not sell, and dispose of the balance. If you could realise 12 or 1500$ and bring it to this place I know you make it safer and more profitable than are the negroes in whom it is now invested. The present high value of negroes is tenfold more precarious than the present value of property in California, to say nothing of the risk to their lives." Andrew Glassell Jr. was a shrewd and prescient businessman who perhaps realised that the writing was on the wall for the way of life of the gentry of the Old South. They were on the eve of the Civil War, and an investment in slaves was even more drastically "precarious" than young Andrew predicted.

However, a year and a half later Andrew Sr. was still in business in the same old way. On 19th January 1859 he wrote to his mother-in-law Eleanor Thornton from a steamboat approaching Selma on the Alabama River, that he had been able to get no news of his negroes until some of the deck hands on the boat told him that they had seen them often and had no "evil intelligence" of them. There is much in this letter about financial wheeling and dealing which Andrew obviously expected his mother-in-law to understand. "For a man unaccustomed to business as I am," he observed modestly, referring to the sale of a negro, "I think this was brisk work. What do you think of it?"[526]

Later that year in another letter to Eleanor Thornton[527] we get another glimpse of his old cook and cleaner Nelly:

> *"I do not know what to say in answer to your proposition to carry Nelly and Meadi to Virginia. She seems to be very much opposed to leaving 9 children behind to be with only two. Here she also hears from Gus. She is not able to do the work she formerly did, owing to the continual running from her breast. With Mr Henshaw she has but little to do. There is some time yet to think about it before I leave, which will not be until July."*

Andrew had just received an unexpected tax bill, backdated three years. "The city taxes on negroes are enormous; half percent on their value," he fumed. He was contemplating a journey, but, as he said, "My presence here is very necessary to the profit of my negroes." His daughter Susan by this time was married and living in Kanawha, West Virginia, near her

526 Banning Co. Addenda, Box 4, Letter 42.
527 Ibid. Letter 43.

grandmother Eleanor. "Give my love to Sue and George and kiss the baby for me," Andrew requested.

Andrew's health continued to decline. A letter of 27th October 1857 had observed that his intention had been to be "over the bay" by that time, but had not felt well enough with his bowels "in their present inflammatory state". "I am still obliged to take small doses of morphine to keep down the pain," he admitted. "This does not seem to abate. I much fear it will become cronic. It is so hard for an old man to recuperate.[528] My digestion is good and every other symptom appears good except for the pain and the transparent mucus attending evacuation."[529]

By 1866 Andrew was blind. A letter of 24th June in that year from Andrew jr. to his brother William mentions "our dear father's blindness", but observes that "our father's health and spirits were improved".[530] The reason for Andrew's low spirits, health problems apart, may have been poverty and disillusion. The Civil War had ended, and as one writer commented, "Old Mr Glassell had already given his worldly goods to the Confederate Cause."[531]

Andrew Glassell Jr. had become a wealthy entrepreneur in California, and in 1866 he sent for his father, his brother William, and his now widowed sister Susan and her children. In California, the land of burgeoning opportunity, the family would attempt to rise from the ashes of the calamitous Civil War. "Old Mr Glassell" survived until 1873. His children we shall meet again in the final chapter "American heroes".

Andrew Glassell's son Robert.

Robert Alexander Glassell, was born on 18th June 1795, the 8th child of Andrew Glassell of Torthorwald and his wife Elizabeth Taylor. Of the two main sources of information on the Virginia Glassells, the "History of St Marks Parish" is seemingly unaware of Robert's existence, and omits him entirely. Hayden's "Virginia Genealogies" has the bald statement, "Robert Alexander, born June 18th 1795. Served in the US army during the war of 1812. Contracted fever while in the discharge of his duty as a soldier. Died

528 He was 64.
529 Banning Co. Addenda. Box 4, Letter 40.
530 Ibid. Letter 50.
531 "Patton – A genius for war": Carlo D'Este. Washington post books. Chapter 1.

October 6th 1814 at Mr Wilcox's, Charles City County, Virginia, where he was buried." There seems to be no further information about him.

Andrew Glassell's son William.

William Erasmus Glassell, the ninth and last child of Andrew and his wife Elizabeth, was born on 17th May 1797. His unusual middle name was in honour of his maternal grandfather Erasmus Taylor. On 4th February 1819 he married Margaret Anne Somerville, the daughter of a wealthy family with Scots mercantile roots. William and Margaret had children as follows:

- Mary Jane Glassell, born 29th February 1820. She died in 1845, only six weeks after her marriage to Captain Joseph Halsey.
- Robert Alexander Glassell, born 11th April 1822, died 9th November 1840.
- James Somerville Glassell, born 5th July 1824. A soldier in the Confederate Army during the Civil War, he was killed "while gallantly storming Cemetery Heights at Gettysburg, Pennsylvania".
- Albert Somerville Glassell, born 10th June 1826. Graduated M.D. at Jefferson College Pennsylvania 1847, and died in 1853.
- Walter Glassell, died in infancy.
- Julia Somerville Alexander Glassell was born on 11th June 1829, and died 8th January 1834.
- Margaret Ann Glassell, born 14th October 1831. She married Charles Conrad Weeks, who was a U.S. senator 1842-43, a brigadier general in the Confederate Army, and latterly a sugar planter in Louisiana.[532]

In 1832 William's wife Margaret Ann died, and the following year he married Harriet Scot. This second marriage was childless, but it fell to Harriet to bring up William's large family.

The eulogy submitted to "Virginia Genealogies" by the Rev. J. Calvin Stewart relates how shortly after his marriage William became a member of the Presbyterian Church at Fredericksburg of which his father had been a founding member. William succeeded his father as an elder of that church,

532 Details of all the above from "Virginia Genealogies", Page 16.

and later helped to set up a Presbyterian church at Litchfield where he was presumably living. About 1862 he moved to a new home, "Meadow Grove", at Marshall, Fauquier County. He served as an elder in the Presbyterian Church at Marshall for the rest of his life, and taught the church's Bible Class. "Mr Glassell's everyday life," wrote Mr Stewart, was a beautiful and powerful exemplification of true religion – love towards God and towards our fellow men shining through consecrated thought and action. His piety was very pure, and pervaded his whole nature. There was a peculiar magnetism about him for all. To the young he was friend, counsellor, father; to the old, brother, counsellor and servant for Christ's sake."

William's second wife Harriet died in 1880, and William Erasmus himself, the last surviving child of Andrew Glassell, the planter of Torthorwald, died in his sleep after a year of failing health on 26th August 1885, at the age of 88. "Thus," said the Rev. Mr Stewart, "closes the life of one of the most faithful and vigorous elders in the Presbyterian Church in Virginia." He was laid to rest in the family burial ground at Meadow Grove.

12

American heroes

The Civil War

Since several of the Glassells were affected personally, and in some cases traumatically, by the American Civil War, it may be helpful to provide a summary of that rather convoluted conflict. However, since understanding of its complexities is not absolutely essential, some readers may prefer to skip the next few pages, and resume with "Andrew Glassell – a Californian tycoon".[533]

Slavery in the northern states of the U.S.A. was abolished shortly after independence was won from British rule. New states north of the Ohio River joined the Union without slavery, and never adopted it. In the South, however, slavery remained an essential part of the region's economy and culture, and as settlement expanded from there into vast swathes of territory appropriated from Native Americans or captured from Mexico, slavery spread westwards from the Old South. The drive for abolition had

533 The summary of the Civil war was put together from my reading of "Battle Cry of Freedom: the American Civil War" – James M. McPherson, Penguin Books 1990. First published By Oxford University Press, 1988.

early 19th century religious roots in New England. By mid-century the campaign had become politicised, and had begun to to polarise the Union, where there were already significant cultural differences between North and South. To mention only the most obvious divergencies, 80% of the population of the Southern States worked in agriculture compared with only 40% in the North. A quarter of the Northern population lived in urban areas, as opposed to a tenth in the South. A mere 6% of the inhabitants of Northern states were unable to read, while in the South nearly half the population was illiterate.[534] The South was also commercially dependent on the North, where almost all of the USA's manufactures were produced.

Chaos in the new territory of Kansas caused by violence between pro and anti slavery factions did much to bring matters to a head, as did the hanging of John Brown in Virginia for attempting to incite a slave rebellion. In 1860 Abraham Lincoln came to the fore as the presidential candidate of the recently formed Republican Party, which was execrated in the South as a vehicle for the horrors of racial equality. The prospect of Lincoln as president sparked hysteria in the South, and his victory in the election made it inevitable that North and South would go their separate ways. Within three months of his election South Carolina withdrew from the Union, quickly folloed by Mississippi, Florida, Alabama, Georgia, Louisiana and Texas. There were scenes of rejoicing across the South, with crowds literally dancing in the streets. On 4th February 1861 delegates from the seven seceding states met in Montgomery, the state capital of Alabama, to set up the Confederate States of America. Jefferson Davis was unanimously elected president.

When a Northern garrison in Fort Sumter off the coast of South Carolina was bombarded and forced to surrender, a spontaneous outburst of Confederate support in Virginia sparked an official declaration of secession, and Virginian militia seized Union military and naval bases. Arkansas, Tennessee and North Carolina followed Virginia into the Confederacy, and Richmond in Virginia was declared the Confederate capital. Neighbouring Maryland hesitated over seccession until elections resulted in a decisive Unionist victory later in the year. Missouri and Kentucky also opted for the Union, although, bizarrely, alternative legislatures in each state were admitted to the Confederacy. In West Virginia a convention rejected the

534 "Battle cry" page 40.

Confederacy, an invading Union army drove out a smaller Confederate force, and Confederate attempts to redress the situation failed. West Virginia not only remained firmly under Union control, but was admitted to the Union as a new state in June 1863. Notwithstanding, the Kanawha Valley of West Virginia remained mostly sympathetic to the Confederate cause.

At the beginning of the war the Union army was a relatively small force, mostly scattered through remote frontier posts west of the Mississippi, and many of its officers resigned to support the Confederacy. Volunteer companies sprang up on both sides, with widely varying capability and effectiveness. Senior officers were often elected by their men, and rank often reflected social position rather than military expertise. Nevertheless, such companies, along with established state militias, coalesced into the Army of the South, and formed an important part of the Union military machine. Most of the action in the Civil War took place in the South, making it necessary for the North to maintain long supply lines. However, northern industrial capacity was incomparably greater than that of the South, and Northern transport systems were more developed and efficient. Thus, although Southern forces were theoretically closer to their sources of supply, it gave them little advantage, and the tattered scarecrow "Johnny Reb" familiar to us from films was often near enough to reality.

Public opinion in the North demanded an immediate invasion. In July 1861 an attack was directed towards Manasas, an important railway junction in northern Virginia. Initially the outnumbered Confederate forces were pushed back, until Thomas Jackson brought up a brigade of Shenandoah Virginians to reinforce the retreating line."There is Jackson standing like a stone wall!" came the cry. The line stabilised and held, and Jackson was known as "Stonewall" Jackson for ever after. The Northern attack falttered, and a Confederate counterattack, accompanied for the first time by the spine-chilling "rebel yell", resulted in a Yankee rout, the Battle of Bull Run.

This setback, although initially discouraging, resulted in renewed determination on the Union side. General McClellan was put in charge of a successful military buildup. McClellan created a formidable force, but he was cautious rather than aggressive. Initial reverses in the Western sector were discouraging, but from a base in Cairo, Illinois, Union gunboats soon began to dominate the Tennessee, Cumberland and Mississippi rivers. A force under Ulysses S. Grant forced the Confederates to surrender first Fort Henry, then Fort Donelson. Remaining Confederate troops were widely separated by Grant's victorious army, and in February 1862 Nashville and Columbus were abandoned to the Yankees. Kentucky and most of Tennessee were now under Union control.

In an attempt to defend Corinth, a surprise early morning Confederate assault was launched at Shiloh on 6th April. The brunt of the attack was bourne by William Tecumseh Sherman, who rallied his men with exemplary courage. Next morning reinforcements under Generals Buell and Grant pushed the Confederates back, and their General Beauregard ordered a retreat to Corinth.

Meanwhile, in the east, McClellan's troops forced a Confederate evacuation of the York Peninsula between the York and James rivers, and brought his army to within six miles of the Confederate capital of Richmond. Its fall seemed only a matter of time. Confederate general Robert E. Lee conceived the idea of a diversion further west, and so Stonewall Jackson took Confederate troops into the Shenandoah Valley where he pursued a Union force as far as Winchester, where they turned to fight. They were routed. Jackson managed to outwit the much larger Union forces sent to eliminate him, and successfully diverted thousands of Union soldiers from other duties. Nevertheless, Union troops were closing in on Richmond. Robert E. Lee attacked on 26th June, resulting in the "Seven Days Battles". Paradoxically, initial Southern setbacks were followed by Union withdrawal, and the immediate threat to Richmond receded.

In the summer of 1862 the Confederacy launched an invasion of Kentucky. The expected flood of recruits never materialised, and the ensuing Battle of Brandston was undecisive. The Confederates withdrew, and the Union commander was replaced by William C. Rosencrans. Also in the summer of 1862, Confederate troops moved north from Richmond. McLellan's Army of the Potomac failed to come to the aid of General Pope's Army of Virginia, which dug in near the former Manasas battlefield. A subsequent attack by Pope met fierce Confederate resistance, and he withdrew to Washington, which itself was now under severe threat.

The Confederates then embarked on an invasion of Maryland under Robert E. Lee, but the hoped-for support from its inhabitants was not forthcoming. The Confederates were attacked at Antietam Creek by McClellan, who was now in sole charge of the Union forces. The ensuing battle resulted in a devastating slaughter of the Confederate centre, but McClellan failed to follow up his advantage, and Lee was able to withdraw into Virginia. The Confederacy was seriously weakened, however, and Antietam was not only seen as a Union victory, but came to be regarded as an important turning point in the war.

Initially the abolition of slavery had not been an officially stated Union war aim, but pressure in the North to make it so gradually became irresistible, and on 1st January 1863 Lincoln issued a Proclamation of Emancipation under the powers allowed to the President in time of war to seize enemy resources. The proclamation therefore applied only to those states in rebellion. It also allowed for the recruitment of black soldiers into the Union army.

Lincoln finally lost patience with McLellan's continuing hesitation and delay in advancing on Richmond, and replaced him with General Burnside. Burnside moved to Falmouth, on the opposite bank of the Rappahannock facing Fredericksburg, hoping to cross there and push on to Richmond. His efforts to cross the river on 11th December 1862 were initially frustrated by Confederate snipers, but after an artillery bombardment and fierce hand-to-hand fighting the Confederates were driven from Fredericksburg, and Union soldiers looted the town in a frenzy of deliberate destruction. Unfortunately for the Union cause, the successful capture of Fredericksburg was followed by stunning defeat as they moved out of town to attack General Jackson on Prospect Hill. The Union right was mown down by Confederate soldiers firing from behind a wall at the foot of Merye's Hill. They suffered nearly 13000 casualties, and Burnside decided to withdraw back across the river.

Further west on the Mississippi, marauding Confederate cavalry had considerable success in disrupting Union communications. A Union attempt to capture Vicksburg was beaten back with heavy casualties among the attackers. Another Union attack on General Bragg at Stones River, 31st December 1862 – 2nd January 1863, resulted in stalemate with heavy Confederate casualties. Foul weather frustrated further Union attempts to take Vicksburg, and by the spring of 1863 public opinion in the North was displaying increasing dissatisfaction with the litany of failure in Virginia and the Mississippi valley.

However, the Union blockade of shipping, increasing breakdown of

Confederate transportation, conquest of productive Southern farmland, and a serious summer drought all conspired to produce severe food shortages in the South, and rising inflation increased the prices of such food as was available. There were bread riots in the spring of 1863, and in Richmond a mob a thousand strong looted shops and warehouses. The difficulties were compounded by thousands of refugees expelled forcibly from their homes, or fleeing Union advances.

In the spring of 1863 General Grant decided on a further attempt to take the still defiant Confederate stronghold of Vicksburg, the "Gibraltar of the West", on the east bank of the river. He marched an army down the west bank of the Mississippi to a point south of Vicksburg. A flotilla of gunboats was sent downriver to liaise with the troops and ferry them over to the east side. After two failed attacks the Union army dug in to besiege Vicksburg, which was finally compelled to surrender on 3rd July 1863, awarding the North a crucial strategic victory.

Meanwhile, in April 1863 the Confederates had 60 000 men strung along the Fredericksburg side of the Rappahannock River in a network of trenches. Union troops feigned an attack on Fredericksburg while an army was sent to cross upriver. By 30th April the Union General Hooker had 70 000 infantry nine miles west of Fredericksburg at Chancelorsville, in an area of second growth forest known as "The Wilderness". The following day the Confederates attacked through the woods, routing the Yankees. In confused fighting during the night the renowned Confederate hero Stonewall Jackson was shot by his own side. His arm had to be amputated and he died a week later. Fighting continued for several days, but in the end Hooker pulled his men back over the Rappahannock. Although this was a humiliating defeat for the North, the Confederates had suffered severe casualties, and had lost Jackson, one of their most competent generals.

With unfortunate overconfidence, in the wake of the Confederate success in the Wilderness Robert E. Lee proposed an invasion of Pennsylvania. In early June 1863 he advanced up the Shenandoah Valley, steamrollered Union garrisons at Winchester and Martinsburg, and erupted unimpeded into Pennsylvania. Hearing of a supply of shoes held in a depot at Gettysburg, a Confederate division moved to secure them. Unknown to them, however, two brigades of Union cavalry had arrived at the depot the previous day, and they held off the Confederates until reinforcements arrived. Soon around 24 000 Confederates were facing 19 000 Union troops in a semicircle north and west of Gettysburg. Lee ordered an attack on the strong Union position on Cemetery Ridge, but it petered out after furious Union resistance and counterattack.[535] A two-hour Confederate artillery bombardment on the following day, 3rd July 1863, proved ineffective and the ensuing Confederate assault was decimated by artillery and rifle fire. Within half an hour the South had suffered total defeat. However, General Meade, the victor of Gettysburg, was over cautious in following up his triumph, and Lee was able to escape over the Potomac River to Virginia, much to the displeasure of President Lincoln.

Little Rock, the state capital of Arkansas, fell to Union forces on 10th September 1863. General Rosencrans had secured Tennessee in June, and Knoxville and Chattanooga were abandoned by the Confederates later in the summer. A bloody battle at Chickamauga Creek on 19th and 20th September ended in a Union retreat to Chattanooga on the Tennessee River, where they were besieged by the Confederates. Lincoln was able to send massive reinforcements south through an unbroken swathe of Union-held territory west of the Appalachian Mountains. On 29th November 1863 the Confederates were driven from their position on Lookout Mountain, and two days later from their remaining defences on Missionary Ridge, thus allowing the relief of Chattanooga and causing another serious setback for the South.

In the spring of 1864 Lincoln gave Grant overall command of the Union Army. Grant put Sherman in command of the western sector, while he supervised Meade in the east himself. Philip Sheridan was sent east to command the Union cavalry. Meade and Sherman were ordered to move aggressively against the Confederates. Meanwhile, subsidiary operations were faltering. Nathaniel Banks' Army of the Gulf failed to take Mobile. Benjamin Butler's Army of the James was attacked south of Richmond and bottled up between the James and Appomattox rivers. Franz Sigel in West Virginia and the Shenandoah Valley was forced into retreat in an action at New Market which featured a heroic charge by 247 teenage cadets of the Virginia Military Institute.

535 James Somerville Glassell, son of William Erasmus Glassell, and grandson of Andrew Glassell the Torthorwald planter, was killed during the attempted storming of Cemetery Ridge.

At the same time the Union Army of the Potomac was facing the Confederate Army of Northern Virginia across the Rapidan River. Grant intended to cross the river and engage the Confederates in a showdown battle to the south of the Wilderness. Lee allowed him to cross with the intention of engaging him in the woods where Grant's superior numbers would be less of an advantage. The Union advance was indeed halted and pushed back. Grant then decided to advance round Lee's flank to seize the village of Spotsylvania while Sheridan's cavalry severed Lee's communications to the rear. On 12th May 1864 a day of savage and bloody hand-to-hand fighting in atrocious weather resulted in the Confederates falling back to a new line of defence during the night. Further Union attacks during the next few days failed to drive the Confederates from Spotsylvania. Grant then unsuccessfully attempted manoeuvers to lure them out from their defences. The situation then was that two entrenched armies were facing each other in a state of exhaustion. A dawn assault by Union troops on 3rd June 1864 was firmly repulsed and Grant was forced to turn his mind to devising a new course of action.

The new plan was for General Hunter in the Shenandoah Valley to move south, cross the Blue Ridge Mountains, eliminate the Confederate supply depot at Lynchburg, and head for Richmond, cutting railway communications as he went. Sheridan's cavalry were to raid westwards, also wrecking railroads. Sheridan was then to rejoin the Army of the Potomac south of Richmond, and meanwhile Grant himself would seize the railroad hub of Petersburg. Hunter indeed took Lexington and left it in flames, then moved on to Lynchburg. Sheridan clashed with Confederate cavalry at Trevilian Station, then tore up the railroad. Meanwhile the Army of the Potomac crossed the James River. The Confederate troops defending Petersburg were pushed back almost to the outskirts of the town, but the exhausted Union soldiers failed to press home the advantage, and their half-hearted assaults on the Confederate trenches were called off. However, the Confederates had suffered severe casualties, their communications had been disrupted, and they were now pinned down in Petersburg and Richmond.

In the meantime, Sherman's cavalry was advancing through Georgia, threatening Atlanta. The Confederates held off an attack on their entrenchments on Kennesaw Mountain, but were forced back to Peachtree

Creek, only four miles from the centre of Atlanta. Their commander Johnston was replaced by the more aggressive General Hood, but he too was forced to pull back, and the Union forces settled down for a siege of the city. Hood evacuated Atlanta on 1st September 1864, and Sherman entered the city with bands playing, to raise the stars and stripes above City Hall.

Back at Petersburg, Union tunnellers blew up a Confederate fortification, causing the destruction of an artillery battery and an entire Confederate regiment. The explosion left a vast crater which unfortunately lay in the way of the ensuing Union attack. A helpless confused mob of Yankee soldiers found themselves trapped in the crater, bombarded with shot and shell until they were finished off by a brutal Confederate counterattack.

On 4th August 1864 the Union navy defeated a Confederate flotilla in Mobile Bay, and a combined army and navy operation took the forts guarding the entrance to the bay. The city of Mobile itself remained in Confederate hands, but it was finished as a port and crucial gateway for Confederate supplies. The taking of Atlanta and the loss of Mobile Bay were lethal blows to the Confederacy.

In Virginia, Sheridan overwhelmed General Early's Confederates at Winchester, and a few days later again at Fishers Hill, forcing him to retreat sixty miles south into the Blue Ridge Mountains. Sheridan then laid waste the Shenandoah Valley. However, on the night of 18th/19th August 1864 a surprise Confederate attack at Cedar Creek near Winchester sent the whole Army of the Shenandoah scurrying down the valley in retreat. Returning from a trip to Washington, Sheridan ran into fleeing stragglers, and with a dazzling display of leadership organised and inspired his men into a counterattack which resulted in a decisive Union victory. Meanwhile, Grant was pressing the Confederate defences hard at Petersburg and Richmond, and an attempted Confederate invasion of Missouri aided by local guerrillas ended in disaster.

After the capture of Atlanta, Sherman headed for Savannah, cutting a swathe of devastation across the South. As he neared Savannah in mid-December 1864 its Confederate defenders fled, and Sherman entered in triumph. Also in the winter of 1864 the Confederate Army of Tennessee under General Hood was thrown back at Franklin, south of Nashville, then finally smashed at Nashville on 16th December. The fleeing survivors were pursued into Alabama and on into Mississippi.

By January 1865 Robert E. Lee's Army of Northern Virginia was the only remaining viable Confederate force. After the Union capture of Fort Fisher at the mouth of the Cape Fear River, Lee was no longer able to bring supplies upriver. On 1st February 1865 Sherman headed north from Savannah, burning Colombia, the North Carolina state capital on 13th February, and brushing off all Confederate attempts to stop his inexorable progress northwards towards Virginia.

Grant was determined to finish off Lee's Army of Northern Virginia himself, before Sherman arrived to share his glory. He forced the Confederates to abandon Petersburg and Richmond, and entered Petersburg on 3rd April 1865 accompanied by President Lincoln. Grant then headed west to finish off Lee, while Lincoln strolled through the streets of Richmond with a small naval escort, surrounded by a rapturous crowd of black residents shouting, "Glory, glory!"

The remains of Lee's army found themselves surrounded near Appomattox Courthouse on 9th April. Faced with overwhelming odds and no escape route, Lee surrendered. Wisely, there were no prosecutions for treason, and Confederate officers and men were allowed to lay down their arms and go home.

During the course of the war an estimated 360 000 Union soldiers and 260 000 Confederates were killed. Wide areas of the South had been devastated, with unknown but probably significant numbers of civilian casualties. Slavery was formally abolished everywhere in the U.S.A. by Lincoln's "13th Amendment" of 31st January 1865. Reality had overtaken the rosy Southern illusion of a self-confident white yeomanry gently governed in a rural idyl by a wise and benevolent white gentry, and served by happy and grateful blacks. The notion survived a while, however, in romantic and nostalgic Southern imagination.

Andrew Glassell – a Californian tycoon.

Andrew was the son of Andrew Glassell, who in turn was the son of the Torthorwald planter of the same name. He was born on 20th September 1827, his parents' second child. His siblings were Ellen Elizabeth (born

1825), Philip Rootes (born 1829), William Thornton, (born 1831), John Henry Hobart (born 1833), and Susan Thornton (born 1835). Andrew's father inherited part of Torthorwald, which he sold, and moved to "Richland" in Culpeper County, Virginia. Later, he sold Richland to his brother William, and bought the plantation of Fleetwood.

As already detailed in the previous chapter, Andrew's father moved the family to an estate near Livingston, Alabama, in the mid-1830s. Andrew's mother Susan Thornton and his sister Ellen died on the way.

Andrew entered the University of Alabama at the age of seventeen, and graduated in 1848.[536] He was attracted to Law as a career, and studied under the supervision of Hon. Samuel W. Inge before entering the legal practice of Hon. John A. Campbell, a former judge of the U.S. Supreme Court. "His experience with this learned judge was one of the greatest assets he had in his work of learning the law," states "Los Angeles County Biographies", and continues, "In 1852 he came to California, bringing with him a letter from his good friend Judge Campbell, which missive immediately gave him recognition, and also admission to the bar before the state supreme court." California at that time was America's "Land of Opportunity", and Andrew, at the age of around 25, was about to prove the worth of the advice to "Go west, young man."

California had been a remote northwestern area of the Spanish colony of Mexico. In 1821 Mexico achieved independence from Spain. Until then, under Spanish rule, land grants to individuals in California had been few and far between. After independence these became more frequent, and the Mexican government also allowed foreigners to hold land in California. Previously, much of California had been administered by Franciscan missions, which in theory held their lands in trust for the natives living there. The Mexican government was keen to "secularise" the mission lands, most of which they granted to white Hispanic Californians, or wealthy incomers from elsewhere in Mexico. After 1834 over 600 land grants were made in California. As compensation the native peasantry were allowed small plots, most of which were quite inadequate for the support of their occupants. There was a steady influx of immigrants from the United States,

536 California of the South, Vol 5 – John Steven McGroarty. Los Angeles County Biographies: Andrew Glassell Sr. Clarke Publ., Chicago, Los Angeles, Indianapolis, 1933.

but they were as yet a small fraction of the whole – perhaps some 2 500 out of a total Californian population of 114 000.[537]

War between Mexico and the United States ended in 1847 with vast tracts of northern Mexico being ceded to the U.S.A. – including California. At that time most of the foreign immigrants were concentrated around Los Angeles and Monterey in southern California, with small settlements at San Francisco and Sacramento. Mountainous northern California was still sparsely populated, occupied in the main by surviving Indian tribes.

The discovery of gold in 1848 transformed everything. In a single year 100 000 immigrants flooded into California, not only from the United States, but from all over the world. The tiny port of San Francisco boomed. A year after California was officially transferred to American rule, delegates met in Monteray to draw up a state constitution. It was modelled on those of New York and Iowa, and slavery was expressly forbidden. On 9th September 1850 President Phillimore signed the bill granting statehood to California.

California was far from the theatres of war between Union and Confederacy. Most enlisted Californian volunteers never left the state and spent the war years guarding U.S. military depots and instalations – although a Californian battalion did see service in Virginia, and other troops served in New Mexico. California's agricultural produce helped to support the Union, but it was only after the war was over that the east and west coasts of the U.S.A. were firmly and finally linked. Work had begun in January 1863 on the Central Pacific railway line running east from Sacramento, but it was not until 1869 that it met the Union Pacific line extending westwards from the Atlantic coast.

The "Wild West" ambiance of the Californian gold rush took a little time to evolve into law-abiding respectability. Vigilante committees were a feature of the early years of statehood, and notoriously, in 1858, the prominent San Francisco politician James Casey was tried and hanged by a vigilante committee for shooting down a newspaper editor who had offended him.

The rule of law, however, ultimately prevailed, and one of the law's foremost and most formidable tasks was to make sense of land ownership in the new state. Much of California's best agricultural land was tied up in

537 California History Collection: http://memory.loc.gov/ammem/abhtml/cbrush.html.

early Spanish and Mexican land grants, often vague and even contradictory in content. Not only that, but Mexico's last governor of California, Pío Pico, signed a flood of land grants at the time of the American takeover, bearing fraudulent dates from the days of Mexican rule. Land ownership cases were to provide decades of lucrative work for busy Californian lawyers.

Andrew Glassell arrived in California in 1852[538] as a young recently qualified lawyer, with a letter of recommendation from his former boss Judge John Campbell. He was immediately admitted to the California bar and soon afterwards appointed as a deputy to the U.S. District Attorney in San Francisco.

Generally speaking, the duties of a United States District Attorney are to manage the prosecutor's office, to investigate alleged crimes in co-operation with law enforcement, to file criminal charges, and to bring evidence before a Grand Jury. In carrying out their duties as prosecutors District Attorneys have the authority to investigate individuals, file formal criminal charges, plea bargain with defendants, and grant immunity to witnesses and accused criminals.

Andrew spent three years in the District Attorney's office in San Francisco. In 1851 Congress had set up the United States Land Commission with the specific purpose of settling titles to land in California. Andrew was assigned the task of working on large numbers of cases pending before the Commission.[539] (His obituary in the Los Angeles Herald[540] claims that he undertook this work as D.A. in Sacramento. Perhaps his duties involved work in both cities, but certainly his letters from the pre-Civil War period are addressed from San Francisco.) "His name," said the Los Angeles Herald half a century later, "is indissolubly linked with the settlement of the almost interminable litigation and out of court adjudications that had their origins in the old Spanish land grants."[541] In conducting this work Andrew acquired a deep knowledge of land law and a particular expertise in that field, and according to the Los Angeles Herald, developed "legal talent of a high order". After his three years in the District Attorney's office, Andrew left to embark upon private legal practice on his own account.

538 According to "Los Angeles County Biographies". Other sources say 1851 and 1853.
539 Los Angeles County Biographies.
540 29th January 1901.
541 Ibid.

In 1855[542] he married Lucy Toland, the daughter of Dr Hugh Toland of San Francisco. She was apparently a Roman Catholic[543], something which would certainly not have pleased Andrew Glassell's devout Presbyterian grandfather the planter of Torthorwald. This marriage, all the same, is an indication of how Andrew Glassell's star was rising in California. Dr Toland was the fourth of ten children of an Irish immigrant who had become the owner of a plantation in North Carolina. He graduated in medicine in Lexington, Kentucky, in 1832 and subsequently studied surgery in Paris for two years. He settled in California in 1852, and by 1861 he was enjoying an annual income of $40 000. In 1866 he founded the Toland Medical College in San Francisco, and when the college was subsumed into the University of California as its medical department, Dr Toland was appointed Professor of Surgery. At his death he was in possession of "considerable" real estate in the interior of California and an extensive ranch at Rio Vista, the whole with an estimated value of between one and two million dollars.[544]

Andrew and Lucy had a large family of nine children:

- Susan Elinor. (Born 4th October 1856. Married Henry Milnor Mitchell. Died 31st December 1907.)
- Mary F., known as "Minnie". (Born 14th February 1858. Married Harington Brown. Died 24th February 1933.)
- Hugh. (Born 11th July 1859. Married Lala Roberts. Died 21st July 1938.)
- Andrew. (Born 20th October 1860. Married Rietta Ring Richter. Died 12th July 1924.)
- William Thornton. (Born 14th January 1863. Married Lillie Solomon. Died 25th January 1918.)
- Louise. (Born 17th November 1864. Married James de Barth Shorb. Died 1st June 1945.)
- Philip Hobart. (Born 1867. Died 15th April 1907.)
- Alfred Leigh. (Born 21st August 1876. Married Ivy Gardner. Died 1st November 1905.)

542 The Los Angeles Herald's obituary says 1857, which is unlikely given the date of birth of their first child.

543 Los Angeles County Biographies.

544 San Francisco Genealogy: Obituaries and death notices – Toland. www.sfgenealogy.org/sf/vitals/sfobit.htm

- Lucien. (Born 1897. Died 1st March 1899.)

Letters preserved in the Banning Company records make it possible to get glimpses of Andrew's life during the early years of his marriage to Lucy.[545] On 20th May 1856 he wrote to his father that San Francisco was in a "state of revolution" and that the "Vigilance Committee" were now the "rulers and uncontrolled tyrants" of the city. He blamed the situation on the poverty and distress prevailing in much of the state, which its victims in turn blamed on "corruption in high places". Andrew had offered his services to the proper authorities to resist the growing agitation, but commented pessimistically to his father, "It is now no use to say or do anything, and I endeavour to have as little to do and say on the subject as possible." He expected that Casey the disgraced politician would soon be hanged, as indeed he was.

Interestingly, in the same letter he refers to a former friend Miss Inge who had attacked him in a newspaper article, and appeared to be "little short of derangement". "Poor fool," he commented loftily, "I pity her and forgive her." Was this a political or legal disagreement, or could Miss Inge have been a former romantic attachment put out by Andrew's recent marriage?[546]

On 19th December 1856 Andrew wrote to his grandmother Eleanor Thornton.[547] She was then living near Andrew's sister Susan in Kanawha, in what was to become the state of West Virginia. He informed Mrs Thornton that he had been busy with "the most arduous litigation concerning most of the land titles in the state". "In regard to my professional business," he observed, "I think I have reason to congratulate myself." At the time of writing he was sharing accommodation with "Uncle Robert's family". Both families , he explained, "have rooms in the same building and mess together, having a common dining room, kitchen, cook, diningroom servant &c... making each family perfectly independent." Andrew had heard from his father that there was a possibility that Mrs Thornton might pay him a visit in Alabama that winter. He also mentioned his sister Sue, "Mr Patton" her husband, and "the young stranger", their first child. He was keen to introduce his wife to them, and to meet the husband of his "dear little sister" for the first time, but he was so busy that a visit was "barely possible". He

545 Banning Co Addenda 1, Box 4, Nos 45-54.
546 Banning Co Addenda, Box 4, No 45.
547 Ibid, No 54.

had received a letter from his brother William, a naval officer, who was about to embark on an expedition to survey the coast of Texas.

In a letter to William on 19th February 1857[548] Andrew complained that although he wrote to him every month or six weeks, he hardly ever heard from William. He also expressed sorrow over the changes affecting the family. "About four years have passed since I saw you… Our family as it used to be is no more. Its individual members are either far from this world or personify different characters. Father is an old man living alone, thousands of miles separated from his children. Grandma is a boarder in the family of Mr and Mrs Patton. Sue is a wife and mother and mistress of an independent family household. You are a citizen of the world, now on a strange coast, now on the briny deep. Last of all, I am a husband and father, having a family of my own on the distant shore of California." As to his working life, his law practice Glassell and Leigh was "still gaining ground". "I have been modestly successful in laying up some of the treasures of this earth, and hope soon to be quite independent. How happy I would be to afford a home to you or Father or Grandma or Sue." We can probably understand from this that Andrew was no longer employed by the District Attorney's office and had been building up a law practice with a partner, but had not yet acquired sufficient wealth to be able to lead a life of leisure.

Evidence of Andrew's further progress can be found in a letter to his father of 4th June 1857.[549] He had, with his father's help, disposed of his wife's property in South Carolina and invested the proceeds. "The current interest on this, with what I had besides, makes me very comfortable and independent, and I can now practise law like a gentleman and an amateur." Property prices in California were low: "I believe that a speculator could very safely invest money in the purchase of property, with the assurance that in a few years he would realize a handsome advance." Here we have a pointer towards Andrew's future business dealings, and the substantial fortune he would eventually amass.

He urges his father to sell his "negroes", come to California, and invest his money safely and profitably there, where the climate is "the most salubrious and delightful on earth, the agricultural portions of the state must continue for our time at least to be the most luxuriantly productive in the world, and

548 Ibid, No 45.
549 Banning Co Addenda, Box 4, No 46.

the gold mines cannot be exhausted for the next twenty years if at all."

Two years later, in a letter of 19th March 1859, Andrew regretfully tells his father that he is unlikely to be able to visit him. His "professional engagements" are "more imperative instead of less", he has an "increasing and helpless family", and, tellingly, "I am now the owner of so much land, and this land requiring in some instances suits to be brought to eject the squatters, in some instances partition of individual interests, some for sale and some for lease." In passing, one cannot help wondering who were these hapless "squatters" who were to be ejected. The reference suggests an unfortunate parallel between Andrew's land dealings in California, and the notorious contemporary "clearances" in the Glassells' ancestral Scotland.

Finally, on 4th November 1859, Andrew informed his father,[550] "I feel quite a confidence however that I am constantly gaining ground, and unless some unforeseen event turns up, I think I will eventually find myself well off and very comfortable." He hoped his father might yet be able to join him, and be introduced to Andrew's "dear little family". His family were all well, but Andrew had found difficulty in finding a suitable wet-nurse for his son. He had not succeeded in procuring one who was prepared to reside with the family, and so the infant had been boarded out. "Such a thing," observed Andrew, "may shock the nerves of some mothers, but in California even the ladies have to become philosophers." In closing, Andrew asked his father to send the letter on to "our family in Kanawha".

Apart from the direct purchase of land, Andrew's position as a landowner was probably due to the practice of taking his legal fees partly or wholly in land, something which, as we shall see, he certainly did later in his career. At the end of the 1850s Andrew was in his own words (and in more than one sense) "constantly gaining ground". However, an "unforeseen event" was indeed about to bring his progress to a temporary halt. That unfortunate circumstance was the outbreak of Civil War.

California, of course, was firmly in the Union camp, but far from the theatre of war. Andrew's Southern background and ancestry made it impossible for him to feel comfortable with an oath of allegiance to the United States. His refusal to take the oath debarred him from practising his profession

550 Banning Co Addenda, Box 4, No 48.

as a lawyer. Accordingly, he went into the lumber business, and operated a steam powered sawmill near Santa Cruz, employing "a large force of men", and producing barrel staves and other sawn timber.[551]

When the war ended in 1865 with the defeat of the Confederacy there was little point in holding out against swearing the loyalty oath to the United States. Andrew therefore resumed the practice of law, and moved with his family to Los Angeles. He formed a partnership with Alfred Chapman, who was apparently an old boyhood friend. In 1870 Colonel George H. Smith joined the practice, which then became known as "Glassell, Chapman and Smith", Andrew being the senior partner. When Chapman retired in 1879 Andrew Glassell's nephew George Patton was admitted as a partner in his place.[552] The firm's speciality was "dealing mostly with real estate transactions involving land partition suits",[553] in other words smoothing the process of breaking up the vast estates conferred in Spanish and Mexican land grants and redistributing their constituent parts for commercial development. "With every final decree on partition," it seems, "the firm would take their compensation in land."[554]

The Civil War had been a mere blip in Andrew Glassell's upward trajectory in the world. By contrast, the effects of the war on his nearest relatives had been catastrophic. His sister Susan's husband had been killed in action, fighting for the Confederacy; his brother William, a Confederate naval officer and war hero, emerged from the conflict broken in health; their elderly father, blind and also beset with health problems, had not heeded Andrew's advice to dispose of his "negroes" and invest in property, and was now penniless. With exemplary generosity Andrew sent for them all and established them in a new life in California.

While William was still hesitating over the move, Andrew assured him in a letter of 24th June 1866, "If you all were here we would have no difficulty in making a living for ourselves and furnish the children [i.e. their sister Susan's children] with the facilities for good education." Gently

551 Annual Publication of the Historical Society of Southern California and Pioneer Register, Vol 5, No 1 (1900), Page 98. University of California Press, Los Angeles.

552 "Los Angeles County Bigraphies: Andrew Glassell Sr." in California of the South, Vol 5 – John S. McGroarty, Clarke Publ, Chicago, Los Angeles, Indianapolis, 1993.

553 Wikipedia – Andrew Glassell.

554 Ibid.

piling on the pressure, Andrew continued, "Now, supposing it settled you are coming…".[555]

A year later, with William clearly already established in California, Andrew wrote to him to inform him that they were now the sole owners of "the Ranch &c". He would not be able to see Wiliam for a month or two, he said, but when he had the opportunity, he would explain his ideas for this investment, which he expected to be worth between thirty and fifty thousand dollars after ten years. It seems there was some small doubt about some element of the title deeds to the ranch, which Andrew warned William to keep quiet about. "All I ask is that you assume that the title is perfect, and in the course of this year when I have the opportunity, some little flaws will be fixed up." William seems to have expressed an interest in raising cashmere goats. "Beware of experiments!" Andrew warned. They could not afford experiments, and there were many other ranches in California more suitable for goats. "Ours is otherwise far more valuable," he insisted. The whole tenor of the letter reflects Andrew's confidence in his own skill both in legal and business matters. He encouraged the less worldly William, "You have now, my dear Brother, a good field in which to exercise your energies and ingenuity in the way of developing & bringing into notice &c the extensive numerous and valuable resources of the property you own."[556]

Letters from Andrew to William later that year[557] make it clear the William was at that time based in Santa Cruz, and since there is a mention of an order for barrel staves it seems likely that William had been put in charge of Andrew's sawmill. He had also become involved in lime burning. Lime of course is a necessary ingredient in cement and concrete, an absolute essential in a state in the throes of a building bonanza. Andrew warned however, "The business requires the exercise of the greatest energy and economy and experience." In his next letter Andrew advised his brother not to sell his lime to San Luis Obispo: "Believe me, San Francisco is the only market that should be considered." He rebukes William for not listening to the advice of more experienced men, as he is an "inexperienced sailor", and he should not imagine that he can improve on the practice of "sharp Yankee business men". Taking more risk will not guarantee more profit. "Slow and

555 Banning Co. Addenda, Box 4, No 50.
556 Ibid. No 51.
557 Ibid Nos 52, 53.

sure is the better policy." Andrew obviously had a finger in many pies – there is also mention in the letters of cattle and "the title to our tin mines".

These few letters in the immediate aftermath of the Civil War give some idea of the spread of Andrew Glassell's business interests. His philosophy in business is best expressed in his dismissive comment on his brother's interest in cashmere goats, "It may be very good, but it is not a certainty, and I now only go in for certainties."[558]

As a result of their efforts in a lawsuit over the partition of the Rancho San Rafael near Los Angeles, in 1871 Glassell and Chapman became owners of a section of the property in a hilly district northeast of the city. In 1879 Andrew bought the neighbouring Rancho Tujunga, and eventually settled in the area. His heirs subdivided and sold off the property in the early 20th century, and it evolved into the community of Glassell Park, which was soon subsumed into the city of Los Angeles. Present day Glassell Park is a predominantly working class suburb of the city, with a "latino" majority.

Another Glassell acquisition was part of the Rancho Santiago de Santa Anna. This enormous property had originally been granted to Juan Pablo Grijaba, a retired Spanish soldier. By the mid 19th century it was occupied by his descendants the Yorba and Peralta families. A member of the extended family defaulted on a loan for which he had put up his share of the ranch as collateral. This sparked off a complex lawsuit involving Glassell and Chapman. Eventually the ranch was divided into a thousand units and parcelled out among family members and creditors, and Glassell and Chapman took part of their legal fees in land.[559]

William Glassell was put in charge of developing the new acquisition. He drafted the plans, took charge of sales and advertising, and laid out the larger farm plots around the projected town, which was to be named "Richland" after the Vrginia plantation where the Glassell brothers spent part of their childhood. Glassell Street met Chapman Street in a central plaza, and the development was bounded by Maple, Grand, Almond and Lemon Streets. When application was made for a post office, a problem arose, as there was already a "Richland" in Califonia, and so another name had to be found.

558 Banning Co Addenda, Box 4, No 51 (26th June1867).

559 http://socialhistoryland.mystic.com/Orange
So. Cal. Historyland – "Orange, California – my hometown" : Phil Brigandi.

There is a legend that the name "Orange" was substituted for Richland as a result of a poker game. The story is that Andrew Glassell, his partner Chapman, and two other interested parties argued over a new name but were unable to come to a decision. Glassell favoured "Orange", Chapman "Lemon", and the others "Walnut" and "Olive". A game of poker was proposed, with the winner awarded the privilege of naming the town. Andrew won, and Richland duly became "Orange". Local historians now consider this story to be almost certainly apocryphal, and it seems more likely that the town was simply named Orange after Orange County in Glassell's native Virginia.[560]

Orange in its early days was something of a rural backwater. Local ranchers would herd their livestock through the streets, and it has been noted that "An early problem was roaming flocks of chickens that created a hazard to horse and buggy traffic."[561] The arrival of the railway created a boom in the area, however, leading to expansion and improvement. By the time the community was incorporated as the City of Orange in 1888 it was already a town 3.1 square miles in area with a population of 600, and the dusty unadorned Plaza was in the process of becoming a park with fountain, trees, shrubs and flowers. Sadly, William Glassell did not see the work he had begun come to fruition. His health had never been robust, and in 1875 he was forced to retire to Los Angeles where he died in 1889. Today, many of the original buildings still remain in what was the town centre, but Orange has been engulfed in the vast Los Angeles conurbation, which now fills the plain between the Pacific Ocean and the San Gabriel Mountains and spreads far to the south.

Andrew Glassell's business interests continued to be many and varied. He was one of the incorporators of the Farmers' and Merchants' Bank, and acted as its attorney. He was the first president (1878-80) of the Los Angeles County Bar Association. He helped to develop the Los Angeles and San Pedro Railroad, and was active in its management until it became part of the Southern Pacific Railroad, which Andrew then represented as its official counsel in Southern California.[562] "Los Angeles County Biographies" states

560 Skegit River Journal of History and Folklore: Andrew and James DeBarth Shorb. Go West Young Man, Part 2.

561 http://www.cityoforange.org/localhistory/plaza/history.htm

562 Wikipedia.

that "It is an unquestionable fact that Mr Glassell had one of the largest and most lucrative practices among the lawyers of his day. He was known over the whole state, and, as the records show, he was an attorney on one side or the other of almost every important civil suit during his career." He was also an expert in naturalisation law, and was active in encouraging immigration into California with a view to its development.

In June 1879 Andrew's wife Lucy gave birth to their ninth child Lucien, and died two months later at the age of only 39. Andrew retired from his law practice in 1883, and in 1885 married Virginia Micon Ring, a cousin, and lifelong friend of his sister Susan. Virginia died in 1895, and Andrew himself died at his home at 352 Buena Vista Street, Los Angeles, on 28th January 1901. "Mr Glassell had been ill for ten weeks prior to the end," reported the Los Angeles Herald,[563] "and his death was expected at any time. He had reached such an advanced age that death cannot be attributed to any specific disease, but rather to a general breaking down." In fact Andrew was only 73, which most septuagenarians nowadays would hardly consider an "advanced age". The report of his death concluded, "For ten years Mr Glassell has lived an exceedingly quiet life. Possessed of an ample fortune well invested, he has mixed but little in the life of the city."

On 7th February 1901 the Los Angeles Herald reported that the value of Andrew's estate was $700 000, including real estate in Los Angeles, Orange, San Diego, Solano, San Francisco and Tulare counties, as well as "notes, mortgages, bonds, stocks and other personal property". He left fifteen hundredths of his estate each to his children Susan, Minnie and Andrew, and thirteen hundredths each to Louise, Hugh, William, Philip and Alfred (his youngest child Lucien had died two years previously). Several codicils to his will left special bequests to family members.

Andrew was interred in Rosedale Cemetery, Los Angeles, where an impressive obelisk marks the Glassell burial place. His nine children are also buried there. After his death his fellow lawyers issued the following obituary:[564]

"As a lawyer and as a man he was scrupulously honest, direct in his

563 Vol. XXVIII, No 120, 29th Jan 1901.

564 Los Angeles County Biographies – Andrew Glassell.

> *methods, open and frank in all of his dealing, and towards the members of the bar always extremely courteous and affable, but at the same time, at the trial of a case, bold and vigorous. He was generous to those who were associated with him in his cases, and was always quick to recognise their services rendered to the common cause. He was liberal to the young men who entered the profession through his office, and more than one member of your committee remembers with gratitude his kindness, helpfulness and generosity, and it is most pleasing now to remember that in all their intercourse with him they cannot recall one single course of expression or single instance in which even for a moment he laid aside the bearing of a gentleman. He was a sound lawyer, deeply versed in the principles of his profession, and thoroughly posted as to precedents affecting questions on hand. He was a safe adviser, and practical rather than brilliant. He was not an orator, but always terse, clear, and forceful in argument. In his business dealings with his debtors he was merciful and forbearing, often reducing or remitting the debt when its enforcement might have seemed to be harsh. By devotion to his profession and by rare business sagacity he accumulated a large fortune, but by far the richest legacy he leaves behind him is the reputation which he earned by a lifelong course of honest dealing in his professional and business career."*

It is a pity for one who never "laid aside the bearing of a gentleman" and steered a "lifelong course of honest dealing" that the only one of his children to achieve any degree of fame did so as a result of distinctly ungentlemanly behaviour. It is perhaps indicative of his character that when Philip Hobart Glassell was named as a co-executor of his father's will, he declined the duty and requested the court to appoint his sister Louise in his place. Responsibility does not seem to have been Philip's forte.

The Los Angeles Herald of 3rd March 1901 reported a "Sad suicide on Bonnie Brae Street", where "A handsome young woman shoots herself through the head in front of Dr Shorb's residence because Phil H. Glassell had gone back on his promise to marry her." The woman in question was Rhoda M. Eddo. Two days later the same newspaper carried a very full report of the inquest into her death, headed, "Due to love for Glassell: coroner's inquest on Miss Eddo's death." Coming as it did just over a month after their father's death, this scandal must have caused excruciating pain and embarrassment to Philip Glassell's brothers and sisters, all but one of whom resided in Los Angeles.

Rhoda M. Eddo was a native of Connecticut, and at the time of her death, according to the Herald, "about 19 years of age". She was one of the six children of James Eddo, a painter, then living in Los Angeles. Rhoda's mother presumably was dead, as she is never mentioned and Rhoda's aunt was acting as her father's housekeeper. At the time of her first encounter with Philip Glassell only Rhoda and her brother Frank still lived at home with their father.

Rhoda first met Phil Glassell when she was working in a lodging house on North Broadway. She was rather lame in one leg, but as the Herald said, "a handsome young woman". Although she was "scarcely 17 years old", and Glassell was around 34, he persuaded her to come and live with him. Since his father was still alive Phil could not do this openly, for fear of parental disapproval, but set her up in rooms in Bumillar Park. Her father, who was understandably vehemently opposed to the affair, forcibly removed her to his home in Chicago Street and threatened Glassell with violence. However, Rhoda was apparently besotted with Glassell, returned to him at the first opportunity, and for the next year or so occupied rooms in a succession of lodging houses and hotels where Glassell would visit her.

After the death of Phil's father, Rhoda began telling her friends that she and her lover would soon be married. She was well aware however that his family and friends were putting pressure on him to break off the relationship. Not only that, but Glassell was a heavy drinker and apparently was in the habit of verbally abusing her when drunk. One evening towards the end of February 1901 he left her in her room in the Kenwood Hotel and never returned.

Rhoda grew increasingly distraught, and after Glassell had been absent for four days she hired a horse and buggy and scoured the city, visiting all his known haunts in vain. She became convinced that he was hiding from her at the house of his sister Louise in Bonnie Brae Street. Louise was married to Dr James de Barth Shorb. Shorb's father was a wealthy tycoon who had made money first in mining and then in grapes and wine. The Shorbs claimed kinship with the Hohenzollern kings of Prussia who became emperors of Germany, and on his mother's side "Barty" Shorb was connected to the Yorba ranching dynasty.

On 2nd March neighbours had noticed a young woman in a buggy passing and repassing the Shorb residence, staring at it intently. At one point apparently Dr Shorb came out and told Rhoda that if she continued her behaviour he would have her arrested for vagrancy. An acquaintance Rhoda spoke to on North Main Street later reported that she said Glassell had promised to marry her, but had now "gone back on his word like a coward" and had "left her without a cent". That same day Rhoda visited her father's house on Chicago Street. Her father and brother were at work, but she told her aunt that she intended to come home on the following Sunday and requested that her brother retrieve her clothes from the Kenwood Hotel.

Rhoda then drove back to Bonnie Brae Street, tied up her horse, and walked into the Shorbs' front garden where Lucy Mitchell was sitting reading. Lucy was the daughter of Susan, the elder sister of Mrs Shorb and Phil Glassell. Rhoda asked Lucy if Philip was in. Lucy knew very well that he was indeed in the house, but told Rhoda that he wasn't there. Rhoda then drew a long-barelled Smith and Wesson revolver from the folds of her dress, placed it to her right temple, fired, and fell dead to the ground. Lucy rushed into the house hysterical.

As she fell, Rhoda had dropped a letter. One of Dr Shorb's servants attempted to pick it up, but was prevented by neighbours who had witnessed the tragedy and sent for the police. The letter read:

> *"Dear Sweetheart Philip,*
>
> *I will do as you have heard. You asked me to pray for you, that you would get back that night, and this is the way you came back. Well dear, I hope we will meet at home or hell – which it is I don't know, but it sure cannot be worse dear. I love you and I cannot live without you. Please see that my body gets in the ground.*
>
> *As ever, your wife as you must always call me,*
>
> *Mrs P. H. Glassell*
>
> *Rhoda M. Eddo.*
>
> *Goodbye dear."*

Another letter was found tucked into her dress:

> *"Dear Father,*
>
> *I hope you will forgive me for what I have done, but all the hope in*

life is gone from me. I have lived with Philip H. Glassell for a year or more as his wife. Now he has left me. Mr de Barth Shorb this morning said a thing to me I cannot bear. My things are at the Kenwood on Broadway, between First and Second, Room 45. I am sorry. All those we love – all – have got to go sometime; why not now?

I am as ever your ["daughter" scored out]

Rhoda M. Eddo

Formerly Mrs P. H. Glassell

Goodbye."

At the inquest into Rhoda's death the Coroner stated that he had been unable to serve a subpoena on Glassell requiring him to attend, and thus "was unable to determine whether he had heartlessly made up his mind to desert the girl after he came into money left him by his deceased father, or had simply gone on one of his habitual carouses, during which he forgot all about her and the rest of the world". The inevitable verdict of the court was, "Death from the effect of a gunshot wound inflicted by herself with suicidal intent while labouring under excitement caused by the desertion of one Philip H. Glassell." The Los Angeles Herald gave the last word to Rhoda's father:

"She had been a good girl, he said, until she listened to the wiles of Glassell, whose baneful influence on the girl had been so great that she had twice returned to him after witness had forcibly taken her to his home on Chicago Street again."[565]

Philip Glassell's erratic lifestyle no doubt hastened his premature end. The disgrace of public exposure would do little to help. He died six years after Rhoda Eddo's suicide, on 17th April 1907, aged only 40, and was buried in the family plot at Rosedale. Coincidentally, his protector Dr Shorb died in November of the same year, and his elder sister Susan, Mrs Mitchell, on 31st December.

565 The account of Rhoda Eddo's suicide is based on reports in the Los Angeles Herald, Vol XXVIII, 3rd March 1901 and 5th March 1901.

Captain William Thornton Glassell, Confederate States Navy.

William was born on Fleetwood plantation, Culpeper County, Virginia, on 15th January 1831, the fourth child of Andrew Glassell and Susan Thornton. In 1836 the family moved to Livingston, Alabama. William's mother and his elder sister Ellen died on the way. Nothing seems to be known of his childhood or education, but in 1848 at the age of seventeen he entered the United States Naval Academy at Annapolis, Maryland.[566]

U.S.N.A. Annapolis was founded in 1845. The students were classed as "midshipmen", and the first class of "passed midshipmen" graduated in 1851. The format of the course was somewhat unsettled in the early years. Initially a course of five years was intended, with the first year at school, followed by three years at sea, and the final year back on shore in Annapolis. In 1850 the course was changed to two years at Annapolis, three years at sea, and two final years at school. Only a year later the course was altered again to four consecutive years of study. The three years at sea were abandoned and replaced by practice cruises during the course of study.[567] Since William graduated as a passed midshipman on 15th June 1854[568] his course must have lasted six years. Obviously, due to the unsettled format of the course during these six years, it is difficult to fathom when he would be at sea and when he was on shore.

However, a letter survives from William to his grandmother Eleanor Thornton. Dated 17th April 1848, in the first year of his course, from Germantown, Norfolk, Virginia, it shows that William's naval education must have begun with a sea voyage:

> *"I got on board ship last Friday and have been almost constantly on duty. But I like the life very much. Every midshipman has four hours to keep watch every night (rain or shine). One takes it at eight o' clock and watches till twelve, and then another and so on. I have been most all today on boat duty... I am now writing in the midst of the greatest bustle and confusion you ever heard, as they are at this time taking powder on board... It is not known when or where the ship will sail. Everything in*

566 "The Washingtons. A family history" – Justin Glenn. Vol. 2, Page 3205.
567 Wikipedia.
568 Hayden's "Virginia Genealogies", Page 30.

> *Norfolk is very dull… Does Father stay at Livingston much and how is his health? I felt bad at leaving him unwell, but I hope he will get over his fever."*[569]

William would be aged 17 at the time of writing. His spelling (corrected above) is sometimes less than perfect.

Three years later, in 1851, William was serving aboard the "St Laurence", a U.S. Navy "war steamer" which was sent across the Atlantic to the "Great Exhibition" or "World's Fair" in London. While the ship was lying off Portsmouth it was visited by Lady Byron, the widow of the poet. Much to the surprise of the other officers, she invited young Glassell to dine with her the following day. He accepted, and enjoyed "a very pleasant interview with her".[570] Lest it be suspected there was any sort of impropriety, the reader should be aware that William was aged 20, while Lady Byron was 59, and has been described as a "stiff religious woman with strict morals". Perhaps William interested Lady Byron because he was the son and grandson of Southern slave owners, and she was an enthusiastic abolitionist. Another factor may have been his distant connection to the ducal house of Argyll.[571]

In 1852, still a midshipman, William visited Constantinople. His sister Susan wrote to her cousin Virginia Micon in New Orleans:

> *"I received a long letter from Brother Willie while he was at Constantinople. He enjoyed himself very much, was presented to the Sultan (by our minister in that place) and went through various forms before being ushered into his majesty's presence. He was first conducted into a large saloon where pipes were handed round. They were splendidly set with diamonds and other precious stones. The mouth piece was of amber, also set with diamonds (I should have been tempted to have bitten it off and accidentally swallowed it) then coffee was served in small porcelain cups enveloped in a network of gold, also set with diamonds. After many more follies being performed he was taken before the Sultan*

569 Banning Company Addenda 1. Box 4, No 62.
570 Hayden's "Virginia Genealogies", P. 30 – 32.
571 Lady Byron, "Arabella" to her friends, married the poet Byron in 1815 and was legally separated from him the following year. They never lived together again, but they never divorced and she continued to style herself "Lady Byron".

> *whom he said was 'quite a natural looking animal' with his pants so long they were soiled at the bottom."*[572]

Although according to Hayden's "Genealogies" William graduated in June 1854, in December of that year he was still in Annapolis. On Christmas Day he wrote to his grandmother Eleanor Thornton, who was visiting friends in Richmond along with William's sister Susan:

> *"I was invited to dine with a very pleasant family today where I might have enjoyed the society of a number of pretty young ladies. But not being partial to dinner parties I concluded to dine with my companions in the Fort, where everything in the way of nice eatables was provided that the heart could wish."*

William was quietly enjoying a good cigar as he wrote. His grandmother had sent him an obviously impressive Christmas cake which he had shared with his friends. He continued:

> *"For the past three or four days Annapolis has presented quite a different picture from its usual dull monotony. After we found we could not get back to visit our friends, the midshipmen put their heads together and got up quite an extensive ball which was attended not only by all the elite of Annapolis, but a good many persons from Washington and Baltimore."*

William had also been to church twice the previous day and once on Christmas Day, when he had "enjoyed intelligent preaching and music".

It is plain from William's letter that his younger sister Susan had just become engaged to her future husband George Smith Patton. "I am happy to hear that you are becoming more and more pleased with Patton," he observed to his grandmother. "I was sure he would prove a first rate fellow." (Susan married Patton the following year and settled in Charleston in what is now West Virginia, where he practised law.) William's letter mentions that Susan had been taking French lessons along with her "pretty cousin Sallie Taylor". He hoped Susan would take care of "the pretty little creature" until the following June, and "keep away

572 Banning Co. Addenda 1. Box 7, No 23, 4th October 1853.

all such fellows as that Powitan Clark". Perhaps he had Sallie in mind when he wrote:

> *"The fact is, since all my Dear Sister's affairs for future happiness &c have been arranged to her perfect satisfaction, about as good a way she can employ herself now will be in mustering up a wife for her brother… I am the more persuaded to allow her to choose for me a wife such she has shown such good taste in helping you [i.e. Mrs Thornton] to a grandson-in-law."*[573]

William was joking of course, but was he also dropping a hint?

Nearly three years later and now aged 25, William was still on the lookout, still single, and was writing to his grandmother from the fashionable resort of White Sulphur Springs, Greenbrier County, in what is now West Virginia. White Sulphur Springs had begun as a summer refuge for wealthy Virginians from the heat and humidity of the coastal plain, but it quickly gained status as "Queen of the Watering Places" and attracted visitors from the upper echelons of society right across the South. William was clearly enjoying his vacation, but

> *"I have been disappointed however in my expectations of meeting that fair auburn haired creature of whom you heard me speak in such glowing terms – that being who is beautiful notwithstanding freckled skin, crossed eyes, and turned up nose. But then I have had a very pleasant time with new acquaintances, once or twice have almost imagined myself in love with a young lady from S.C. who is about the age and professes to have been a school mate and intimate friend of Lucy Toland.*[574] *She is very intelligent, appears aimiable, possesses many accomplishments, and though not beautiful is very good looking and able to pay her own Mess Bill. But then I think she is a little too fat, and I suppose it is more than probable she would think me a little too lean. The fact is there are too many pretty girls here for anybody to fall in love with one in particular."*[575]

On 6th June 1855 Susan had written to one of her cousins, "I received a

573 Banning Co Addenda 1, Box 4, No 62.

574 S.C. – South Carolina. Lucy Toland was the wife of William's brother Andrew.

575 Banning Co. Addenda 1, Box 4, No 64. 17th August 1856.

letter from Brother Willie a few days ago. He has been very ill, but was then convalescent. I would not be surprised if he were compelled to go to some Springs for his health…". Later in life, William's health was to cause him serious problems, and it would not be entirely surprising if we glimpse the beginning of the trouble here. Quite apart from meeting "pretty girls" the purpose of "taking the waters" was to improve health, and perhaps William's "leanness" was not entirely due to youth and an exacting profession. "I have gained no flesh since I left," he continued in his letter to Mrs Thornton, "but hope the water is preparing my system to imbibe more nourishment as soon as I leave here".

Finally, "Taz" Patton, the brother of Susan's husband, had just left White Sulphur Springs, and unless William received orders to report for duty, he expected to join his grandmother and sister in Charleston the following week. Since Mrs Thornton was "care of Mr G. S. Patton", it looks as if she was now living with Susan and her husband in Charleston, Kanawha County, in what was later to become the state of West Virginia.

By the time of his vacation in White Sulphur Springs, William was already making progress in his naval career, having been promoted to Master on 15th September 1855, and apparently to Lieutenant the following day, 16th September. It is of course difficult now to follow closely the course of William's life in the U.S. Navy, but his brother Andrew wrote to their grandmother on 19th December 1856 that he had received a letter from William, who was in Philadelphia "just on the eve of sailing on his cruising or rather surveying expedition on the coast of Texas". Andrew continued cryptically, "I am glad to see he is so much better contented than he used to be".[576] The following year, 1857, Andrew wrote to his brother on 19th February, complaining that William so seldom wrote to him. "Months often pass without my knowing where you are, and what you are doing or have done."[577] Andrew's mild rebuke does not seem to have had much effect, as he wrote to his father on 4th November 1859, "I have not heard from my brother William for some months. I suppose he is somewhere near the Horn by this time on his way to visit you all".[578]

At the outbreak of the Civil War, Lieutenant Glassell was serving

576 Banning Co. Addenda 1, Box 4, No 54.
577 Ibid, No 49.
578 Ibid, No 48.

as a deck officer on board the U.S.S. *Hartford* in the China Sea with Commodore Stribling's East Indies Squadron. The *Hartford* was a "screw sloop", a wooden ship built in Boston in 1858, able to employ both sail and steam. She carried 28 guns and a crew of over 300.[579] When the *Hartford* returned to Philadelphia in December 1861 Glassell was disconcerted to find that he and other Southern officers were required to swear a new oath of allegiance to the United States of America. In his own words:

> *"I had served, I believe faithfully, as a lieutenant in the United States Navy, and had returned from China on the United States Steamer "Hartford" to Philadelphia some time in 1862 [sic] after the battles of Manassas and Ball's Bluff had been fought. I was informed that I must now take a new oath of allegiance or be sent immediately to Fort Warren. I refused to take the oath on the ground that it was inconsistent with one I had already taken to support the constitution of the United States. I was kept in Fort Warren about eight months, and then exchanged as a prisoner of war on the banks of the James River. I should think that even Mr President Hayes would now acknowledge that it was my right, if not my duty, to act the part of a belligerent.*
>
> *A lieutenant's commission in the Confederate States Navy was conferred on me with orders to report for duty on the ironclad "Chicora" at Charleston. My duties were those of a deck officer, and I had charge of the first division."*[580]

Thus, William refused the new oath as a matter of principle. He wrote a letter of resignation from the U.S. Navy dated 4th December 1861 which apparently was never delivered.[581] Instead he was formally dismissed on 6th December, a process intended as a mark of disgrace, and imprisoned in Fort Warren, a pentagonal fortress on an island in Boston Harbour which,

579 Details from "Prisoner of the Civil war" – Douglas Westfall, Ed. Pedro Garcia, The Paragon Agency, Orange, California. 2013. (A fictionalised account of William Glassell's adventures.)

580 "Reminiscences of torpedo service in Charleston Harbor" – W. T. Glassell, Commander Confederate States Navy. Southern Historical Society Papers, Vol. 4, Page 225. Richmond, Virginia, 1877.

581 Civil War Navy Sequicentennial October 2013. "The official blog dedicated to the dissemination of information surrounding the history, events and activities during the Civil War Navies Sequicentennial Anniversary."

apparently, was haunted by the ghost of a young woman who had come to the fort armed with a pistol to rescue her husband, accidentally shot him dead in the attempt, and was subsequently hanged for her trouble.

It is likely that while William was held in Fort Warren, friends or relatives made arrangements for him to be offered a commission in the Confederate navy. This would presumably alter his status from U.S. Navy traitor to "prisoner of war", and allow him to be exchanged as such. He was then, as described above, ordered to the *Chicora* at Charleston, South Carolina. The *Chicora* was an "ironclad", a ship with a conventional wooden hull sheathed in iron plate. Writing a dozen years later Willian remembered his imprisonment as lasting "about eight months". An article in the Los Angeles Times of March 30th 2003 places his release in "July 1862".

In the summer of 1862, then, Lieutenant Glassell resumed his naval career, opposing his former comrades as a deck officer on the Confederate ironclad *Chicora*.

The prime objective of the U.S. Navy in the Civil War was to prevent supplies reaching the Confederacy and to prevent the export of cotton, the mainstay of the South's economy. A successful blockade was no easy task. As well as ten major ports, the Confederate States' 3500 miles of coast contained innumerable bays, inlets and river mouths. At the beginning of the conflict the North had only two naval bases, one at Hampton Roads opposite Norfolk at the mouth of the James River, and another at Key West off Florida. However, the North quickly seized Hatteras Inlet in North Carolina, Ship Island off the coast of Mississippi, and in November 1861, Port Royal, South Carolina. In February 1862 the Union navy took Roanoke Island "the key to Richmond's back door", and went on to capture all the North Carolina ports, including Beaufort, which became an important blockade fleet base. By April 1862 every significant harbour on the Atlantic coast except Charleston and Wilmington was in Union hands and barred to blockade runners.

The blockade was not an impenetrable barrier however. It has been calculated that at the beginning of the war, nine out of ten blockade running vessels were getting through. Even by 1865, one out of two attempts were successful. Indeed, in 1863 Charleston's foreign trade was greater than it had been in the year previous to the outbreak of war. Cotton was still being shipped out, and a wide range of supplies, including rifles, powder, and even cannons were coming in. However, most blockade runners were built for speed, not capacity. Shortages in the South were soon apparent, and the blockade was certainly a crucial factor in the ruinous inflation which drove the Confederate dollar down to one percent of its original value by the end of the war.

The undeniable superiority of the Union navy generated some innovative thinking in the South, resulting first of all in the *Virginia*, which was basically the salvaged wooden hull of a frigate equiped with a sloping iron plated superstructure, ten guns, and an iron ram. She was described by an observer as resembling "a barn floating with only its roof above water". This vessel caused some trepidation in the North, but she proved to be slow, difficult to manoeuvre and impossible to deploy in shallow water. The news of the construction of the *Virginia* inspired the bulding of the *Monitor* for the U.S. Navy – a wooden hull sheathed in iron, covered by an armour plated shell protecting all vital machinery, and equipped with a revolving armour plated turret housing two guns. The *Monitor* may have looked like "a raft", but she was easily manoeuverable and could fire in any direction.

On 8th March 1862 the *Virginia* attacked the Union base of Hampton Roads, and before nightfall had managed to sink two warships, killing at least 240 sailors. However, the following day the *Monitor* arrived. The ensuing duel between these two productions of naval ingenuity ended inconclusively, but the *Virginia* withdrew to Norfolk, and when Norfolk fell to the North two months later, she was blown up by her crew to prevent her falling into enemy hands. The *Monitor* fared little better, sinking in a gale on 31st December 1862 while being towed to begin blockade duty.

When William Glassell arrived in Charleston, then, it was one of only two ports remaining in Confederate hands, and was subject to ever tightening blockade by the United States Navy. As deck officer on the *Chicora* William saw action in an engagement with the blockading fleet in the early hours of 30th January 1863. "It was my part on that memorable morning," he later wrote, "to aim and fire one effective shell into the *Keystone State* while running down to attack us".[582] This single shell killed 21 men and severely wounded 15. The *Keystone State* hauled down her flag in token of surrender, and later limped off out of harm's way. The blockade continued,

582 "Reminiscences of torpedo service…" – W. T. Glassell.

but as Glassell remarked, at a "respectful distance", being disinclined to risk further casualties.

Privately, Glassell believed Confederate tactics were wrong, and thought charging into the enemy vessels with iron rams would be much more effective. Meanwhile, a Major Frank Lee was working on a rather less heroic but potentially more lethal means of attack – the torpedo. This was not quite a torpedo as we picture it today. Lee's torpedo could not be launched from a safe distance, but had to be taken to the target. An explosive charge encased in copper, and equipped with a percussion fuse, was fixed to the end of a long pole weighted and suspended beneath a rowing boat from cords at the bow and stern. The pole floated horizontally around six feet below the keel, with the "torpedo" at the end of it, some ten feet ahead of the boat. In theory, a boat could be rowed quietly up to its target under cover of darkness. The torpedo would explode on impact, holing the enemy vessel below the water line. An experiment was tried on an old hulk in Charleston Harbour, which resulted in the destruction of the target without damage to the torpedo boat.

Lieutenant Glassell was most impressed and immediately became an enthusiastic proponent of the torpedo. He urged the Confederate naval commander Commodore Ingraham to have forty boats constructed with protective iron shields, and capable of carrying torpedos. Ingraham's reaction was lukewarm, but he eventually gave Glassell permission to mount an attack with a single boat. Thus at one o' clock in the morning on a moonless night with a calm sea, Glassell directed his crew of six oarsmen towards the U.S. ship *Powhattan* with a torpedo containing 50 pounds of rifle powder.

While still two or three hundred yards from the *Powhattan* they were spotted and ordered to identify themselves. In spite of repeated orders to stop, and threats to open fire, Glassell forged ahead, giving evasive answers and expressing the intention of coming aboard. As they neared the *Powhattan*, however, one of the oarsmen, Murphy, suddenly "backed his oar" bringing the boat to a stop. In confusion the other oarsmen stopped rowing. Murphy then threw his pistol overboard and attempted to do the same with his neighbour's weapon. He later claimed to have been so terror-stricken that he didn't know what he was doing, but as he eventually deserted to the enemy Glassell suspected ulterior motives.

The torpedo boat now drifted helplessly past the *Powhattan*. Armed men appeared on her deck and an officer ordered a boat to be lowered.

Glassell then drew his revolver and ordered his men to cut the torpedo loose and pull away with all their might. To his astonishment they were not fired upon, and swallowed up in the darkness, they were able to reach safety unscathed. Shortly afterwards Glassell was ordered to Wilmington to supervise the fitting out of the Confederate ironclad *North Carolina*.

Undeterred by his rather farcical adventure with the *Powhattan*, while he was in Wilmington, Glassell began pondering the possibility of attaching a torpedo to a small steam tug. However, he suddenly received orders to return to Charleston by rail with the crew of the *North Carolina*, who were to be redistributed to gunboats. As for himself, he discovered, "There was nothing in particular for me to do."

Lieutenant Glassell was not the only one persuaded of the potential of the torpedo. Thirty miles up the Cooper River from Charleston, on a secluded plantation belonging to Dr St Julian Ravenel, a privately financed team including Theodore Stoney and David Ebaugh were working on a vastly improved conception of the torpedo boat. This was a small iron plated cigar-shaped craft, weighted with iron ballast to make her ride very low in the water. She was driven by a screw powered by a small steam engine. This prototype has sometimes been wrongly called a "submarine", but having an open cockpit and a smokestack, she obviously could not be submerged. The craft was at best a "semi-submersible". The torpedo was no longer to be suspended beneath the boat, but was placed at the end of a boom projecting from the bow of the "cigar" – imagine a swordfish with an explosive charge at the end of its "sword".

In his "Reminiscences" Glassell refers to Stoney as an "esteemed friend", so it is perhaps not surprising that as a naval officer with torpedo experience and "nothing in particular to do" he was thought the very man to try out the new invention. The craft was nicknamed the *David*, referencing the biblical tale of David and Goliath, and perhaps also the name of one of her designers David Ebaugh. Eventually the *David* was ready and was shipped by rail to Charleston to acquire the finishing touches. The new naval commander in Charleston, John Randolf Tucker, was more open minded than his predecessor Ingraham, and was firmly convinced of the effectiveness of the spar torpedo. He gave his approval for a torpedo attack on the Union fleet, and General Beauregard also gave the venture his blessing.

Under Lieutenant Glassell's command, the *David* was crewed by J. W.

Cannon as pilot, J. H. Toombs as engineer, and James Stuart as fireman – Stuart for some reason apparently also used the alias of Sulliven. Just after nightfall on 5th October 1863 the *David* left Charleston Wharf. The tide was ebbing and there was a slight breeze from the north, but the sea was calm. Silently, the torpedo boat passed Fort Sumter. "I had a good opportunity", Glassell later wrote, "to reconnoitre the whole fleet of the enemy at anchor between me and the campfires on Morris Island".[583] The thought struck him that with a dozen torpedo boats attacking simultaneously, the entire Union fleet could have been destroyed, leaving the 20 000 Yankee soldiers on Morris Island abandoned. Glassell waited quietly until the "lights out" gun was fired, then made his way cautiously towards the Union flagship *New Ironsides*. Glassell took the helm, ordered the engineer and fireman to keep below out of sight, and gave a double-barelled shotgun to the pilot. Also armed with a shotgun, and now steering with his feet, Glassell edged closer tho the starboard side of the *New Ironsides* exposed before them. Some three hundred yards from their target they were spotted and challenged. The *New Ironsides'* deck officer appeared and ordered them to identify themselves.

Forty yards from the *New Ironsides*, Glassell felled the deck officer with a blast from his shotgun,[584] and gave the order to stop the engine. The *David* ploughed forward under its own momentum, and moments later the torpedo struck and exploded. A great column of water shot into the air, broke, and cascaded down upon the *David*, flooding down her hatchway and smokestack. Glassell gave the order to reverse the engine and back off, but received the dismaying news from engineer Toombs that the fire was out and the machinery jammed!

By then the alarm had been sounded and the whole Yankee fleet alerted. Glassell gave the order to abandon ship and swim for it. Later he "thought" he recalled ordering Toombs to scuttle the *David*. Without a second's delay, Glassell grabbed a cork lifesaver, plunged overboard, and swam off amid a hail of bullets from the *New Ironsides* and her neighbours.

The pilot Cannon, who could not swim, scrambled into the water and clung to the sheltered side of the *David*, as she drifted off into the darkness.

---

583 "Reminiscences of torpedo service…".

584 This unfortunate young man, Ensign Charles Howard, was the only fatality of the encounter, dying of his wound on 10th October. He was granted posthumous promotion to Acting Master and was buried in Beaufort National Cemetery. (American Civil War Forum – The attack on USS New Ironsides.)

After quarter of an hour or so he hauled himself back on board, and shortly afterwards, to his delight he spotted Toombs in the water and picked him up. They managed to relight the *David's* boiler, got up steam, and proceeded warily towards Charleston. Although they were fired upon several times they eventually reached shore and berthed at Atlantic Wharf at midnight. The fireman Stuart, not fancying his chances in the open water, clung to the *New Ironsides'* rudder chains until he was discovered and brought aboard as a prisoner.

William Glassell, meanwhile, had hoped to swim to Fort Sumter, but found the wind was against him. After an hour in the water, numb with cold and exhausted, he had the good fortune to be noticed and picked up by the ship's boat from a Union transport schooner. He was brought on board, and as he later wrote, his rescuers "found to their surprise that they had captured a rebel".

The New Ironsides, although not sunk or crippled, had been sufficiently damaged to make it necessary to withdraw her from the blockade to be put into dry dock for repairs. As has been observed,"This was the first successful torpedo attack in history".[585] The *David* continued in service and several other "Davids" were built – how many is not clear, as different sources give widely varying numbers. Although these craft failed to make much impression on the course of the Civil War, they were of course the forerunners of the modern submarine.

After his rescue William was taken on board the schooner, where the Captain saw that he was provided with whisky and blankets, and made as comfortable as possible before being brought before Rear Admiral John Dahlgren, the commander of the union navy blockade of Charleston. Publicly, Dahlgren fumed that Glassell and his fireman should be tried and executed for using "an engine of war not recognised by civilised nations", but privately he seems to have been rather impressed by Gassell and his unconventional new weapon.[586]

Glassell was sent to be confined on the guard ship *Ottawa*, which lay apart from the fleet, with orders that he should be put in irons, and "double irons" should he prove obstreperous. However, he was immediately

585 www.csslhunley.com : The David Semi-submersibles. 27/02/15.
586 The Washingtons – a family history, Vol 2 : Justin Glen.

recognised by the captain of the *Ottawa*, William Whiting, a former brother officer in the U.S. navy. On being informed of Dahlgren's orders, Glassell smiled and told his old comrade that Whiting's duty was to obey orders and Glassell's to adapt himself to circumstances. Whiting immediately took himself off to see Dahlgren, and when he returned Glassell was released from his chains on giving his word not to attempt to escape.[587]

William spent over a year as a prisoner of war in Fort Lafayette and Fort Warren. During that time he was promoted to the rank of Commander, Confederate States Navy, for "gallant and meritorious service". Eventually he was exchanged for the second time in his Civil War service, late in 1864.

After a brief spell in Charleston, William was ordered to Richmond to command the Confederate ironclad *Fredericksburg* in the James River Squadron. By that time however the war was all but over. At the evacuation of Richmond, William was forced to blow up his ship to prevent her falling into enemy hands. He and his crew were hurriedly drafted into a Naval Artillery Brigade, which first attempted to join Robert E. Lee's retreating army, then hearing of Lee's surrender at Appomattox on 19th April, Glassell's brigade headed south into North Carolina. There they joined General Johnston, with whose troops they laid down their arms shortly afterwards.

Just before the outbreak of war William Glassell's sister Susan had moved with her husband George Patton and their children from Charleston, in what was to become West Virginia, to Patton's ancestral home at Spring Farm near Culpeper, Virginia. The war devastated much of Virginia and left Susan a widow with four children. She spent the winter of 1864/5 in a state of destitution at Goochland near Richmond, caring not only for her children but for her blind and infirm father. It was probably while she was at Goochland that she was joined by her brother William.

William was now suffering from tuberculosis and his health seems to have broken down completely. It has been stated that he had picked up the infection during his incarceration as a prisoner of war, but it will be remembered that back in 1855 he was taking the waters at White Sulphur Springs after having been in his sister's words "very ill". Perhaps the

587 "Remeniscences" – W. T. Glassell.

privations of his war service and imprisonment exacerbated a problem that was already latently present.

It seems the family was rescued from its desperate situation by a young Patton relative who arrived driving an old horse-drawn Confederate ambulance and ferried them to an old Colonial mansion near the town of Orange where they were joined by other members of the Patton family. A patch of land nearby was cultivated to provide enough food for their survival, and William seems to have recovered strength enough to perform the duties of a "field hand".[588] According to "Virginia Genealogies" William was offered a command in South America with the navy of either Chile or Peru: perhaps both – the details are vague. He turned the offer down, however, because he felt bound to stand by his old and infirm father and his widowed sister and her family. Perhaps he also suspected that his precarious state of health would not be up to the job.

William's brother Andrew, as we have seen, had prospered in California, and well before the outbreak of war had already been trying to persuade William to join him. On 17th February 1857 he wrote to his brother, "I wish, my dear Will that I could welcome you into the embrace of my family and talk with you of things present and the future prospects of us all… How happy I would be to afford a home to you, or Father, or Gma or Sue."[589] Painfully aware of his relatives' post-war circumstances, Andrew's entreaties became more urgent. In a letter to William of 24th June 1866 he expressed himself gratified that William had recovered from the "maladies" that had affected him over the previous six months, and pressed him to make a final decision on whether the family was to stay on in Virginia, or join Andrew in California – which he thought "best for all parties". "I feel confident," he said, "that if you all were here we would have no difficulty in making a comfortable living for ourselves and furnish the children with the facilities for good education &c". Applying a little none too subtle pressure, Andrew continued, "Now, supposing it settled that you are coming…" and gave advice on the best time of year to set out, and the necessity of the travellers supplying themselves with quinine for their passage through "the tropics". Incidentally, the legend of family destitution while scraping a living outside

588 The Washingtons – a family history.
Patton, a genius for war – Carlo D'Este. Harpercollins, 1995.
589 Banning Co Addenda 1, Box 4, No 49.

Orange, Virginia, has perhaps been exaggerated a little, as Andrew's letter also contains the information, "Your money in my hands is loaned out at one and a half percent per month in mortgage, due next May. Sue's $800 is out also at the same rate."

The dilemma was indeed soon settled, aided by a donation of $600 from Andrew to pay for the passage of William, their elderly and infirm father, and their sister Susan and her four children, from New York to San Fransisco. It is possible to trace the voyage from letters written by Susan. The party travelled by rail from Washington to New York, and boarded the steamer *Arizona* on 10th November 1866. William had a cabin to himself, old Mr Glassell and Susan's eldest son George shared another, while Susan and her three younger children shared a third. By 15th November they were "off Cuba", and all of the party except William had been seasick for two days. Presumably William's immunity was the result of his naval experience. The family had to disembark at Panama, cross the isthmus, and board another steamer on the Pacific coast to take them to San Francisco. From there they travelled on to Los Angeles, where by 19th December they seem to have been living as the guests of Andrew and his wife Lucy.[590]

On 15th January 1867 Susan wrote to her sister-in-law Sally Patton, "Brother Willie has gone to Brother's ranch in Santa Cruz, where he expects to remain for a while until he makes other arrangements."[591] An interesting letter to William from his brother dated 26th June 1867 shows Andrew expressing mild impatience. William must have been considering the prospect of other employment. "I really think you can do better to devote your energies on your own property than by taking employment from anyone," observed Andrew pointedly. Of a scheme to raise cashmere goats, Andrew was equally dismissive. "I would not trouble myself about cashmere goats unless some rich person will stand all the expenses," he wrote, and elaborated, "In reference to your goat speculation, it may be very good but it is not a certainty, and I now go in for certainties." He also informed William, "The purchase is completed and you and I are now the sole owners of the Ranch &c... You have now, my dear brother, a good field in which to excecise your energies and ingenuity in the way of developing and bringing into notice the extensive numerous and valuable resources of the property

590 Patton family papers, Box 1, MssPF317-330, N58-E.
591 Ibid.

that you own." Although Andrew and William would appear to be co-owners of the property in question, there can be no doubt that Andrew was the boss. "Until I have an opportunity to go over it with you," he wrote, "I cannot make you fully understand my ideas".[592] *My ideas* suggests that William's thoughts on the matter were not Andrew's first priority.

In another letter a month later Andrew warned William about getting personally involved in lime burning:

> *"I see plainly that you do not give due credit to the wisdom and experience of men whose lives have been devoted to business on land. You are an inexperienced sailor. Do not falsely imagine that you can improve on the rules and habits of sharp Yankee businessmen. Your improvement? on the plans that your brother urged on you when you took charge of the ranch, by which you expected it to make more profit by taking more risk, should warn you that slow and sure is the better policy."*[593]

It is not explained what William's "improvement" on his brother's plans can have been, but Anrew's bedecking of the word with underlining and a question mark suggests that the changes had not been much of a success.

Fortunately, the right outlet for William's "energies and ingenuity" was eventually found. Andrew and his partner Alfred Chapman had been professionally involved in a complex lawsuit over the vast Rancho Santiago de Santa Ana. Glassell and Chapman took part of their legal fees in land, and had apparently also been buying up sections of the ranch for several years. By 1870 they had acquired some 5 400 acres and had decided to develop the area as a new town. It was not far from Los Angeles, the soil was fertile, and a water supply could be provided from the nearby Santa Ana River. William was put in charge of surveying and marking out the parcels of land, and selling the plots. As explained in the previous section of this chapter, the new town, originally dubbed "Richland", was renamed "Orange" when it was discovered that there was already a Richland in California. The first building on the site was Wiliam's house and office. As a local historian has neatly put it, "Alfred Beck Chapman sometimes declared, 'I am the father of Orange.' But if Chapman was the father, William T. Glassell was the midwife."[594]

592 Banning Co Addenda 1, Box 4, No 51.
593 Ibid, No 53.
594 Phil Brigandi: So Cal Historyland, http://socialhistoryland.mysite.com/Orange.html

Larger farm plots were laid out around the projected town, and William supervised the construction of an irrigation canal to supply them. By the end of 1871 there were a dozen houses on the site of the town, a school was completed in the summer of 1872, and the following year the Fisher brothers opened the first store. Also in 1873 the Methodist Episcopal congregation met in the first place of worship. A post office was initially refused on the grounds that there was already a community named Richland in California, and so in early 1875 the settlement was renamed "Orange". By then Orange had become an established community inhabiting streets grouped round a central "plaza"[595].

William's health was now rapidly breaking down, however. In early 1874 there was a flaring up of the tuberculosis that had beset him before his move to California, and he spent the summer of that year resting in Los Angeles in an attempt to regain his health. Much missed, he was welcomed back in the summer with "heartfelt gladness".[596] Sadly, in those pre-antibiotic days, there was no effective cure for "consumption". In 1875 William's failing health forced him to leave Orange for the last time and he retired again to Los Angeles. In 1877 his "Reminiscences of torpedo service in Charleston Harbor" appeared in the Southern Historical Society Papers.[597] William brought his account to a close as follows:

> *"I may have been a fool. I supposed or believed that the people of the south would never be conquered. I hardly hoped to live through the war. Though I had no intention of throwing my life away, I was willing to sacrifice it, if necessary, for the interests of a cause I beleved to be just. I was more regardless of my own interests and those of my family than I should have been. A large portion of my paper salary was never drawn by me. Nearly every thing I had in the world was lost – even the commission I had received for gallant and meritorious conduct, and I possess not even a token of esteem from those for whom I fought, to leave when I die to those I love.*
>
> *But the time has arrived when I think it my duty to grant pardon to the government for all the injustice and injury I have received. I sincerely hope that harmony and prosperity may yet be restored to the United States of America."*

595 City of Orange Ca. www.cityoforange.org

596 Paul Brigandi, quoting a "local newspaper".

597 Southern Historical Society Papers, Vol 4, Page 225. Richmond, Virginia.

Surely, there spoke the ideal of the Southern Christian gentleman. William died in Los Angeles on 28th January 1879, days after his 48th birthday. In spite of his youthful interest in "pretty girls", he had never married. His grave can be found in the Glassell plot in Rosedale Cemetery, Los Angeles.

Hayden's "Virginia Genealogies" contains a tribute to William from an acquaintance who had fought on the opposing side during the Civil War:

> *"Captain Glassell was a man of singularly modest and retiring character – a man of pure and blameless life, and one whose manner was ever marked by a gentle courtesy that made friends of all he met. He had, I believe, no personal enemies. Withal, he was possessed of a quiet uncomplaining fortitude which, whether the endurance of the soldier, or the patience of the Christian, led to few murmurings during the sufferings of his long and hopeless illness."*

Susan Glassell and the Pattons

Susan Thornton Glassell was the sixth and youngest child of Andrew Glassell and his wife Susan Thornton, and was the granddaughter of Andrew Glassell the original planter of Torthorwald. She was born on 2nd March 1835,[598] probably at her father's plantation of Fleetwood, Virginia. Susan's father decided to move the family to Alabama, but on the way, in 1836, her mother and elder sister Ellen died of yellow fever, and according to a family story, the infant Susan had to be "nursed on mare's milk".[599]

Susan's father had acquired a property at Livingston, Alabama, probably a cotton plantation, but by the mid 1840s appears to have been resident in Mobile, investing in "negroes". He seems to have been hiring out gangs of slave labourers, but it is not beyond the bounds of possibility that he was also dealing in slaves. From the constant mentions of "Grandma" in later letters, it seems likely that Susan's maternal grandmother Eleanor Thornton was drafted in to supervise the household, which consisted of father Andrew, Susan, and her brothers Andrew, William and Hobart (John Henry Hobart). Another brother Philip Rootes had died in infancy or childhood. Andrew

598 The Washingtons – a family history: John Glenn, Vol 2. Sevas publishing, Eldorado Hills Ca. 2014.

599 Ibid.

became a successful lawyer and businessman in California, William became a naval officer, and Hobart died at the early age of twenty.

There appears to be no extant information about Susan's childhood and education. We do not know whether she was sent to school or educated at home, but as the daughter of Virginian "aristocracy" she would certainly be taught to acquire the accomplishments and attitudes befitting a lady familiar with the upper echelons of Southern society as manifested in Alabama.

Some idea of Susan's teenage years and her life as a young wife and mother can be gleaned from her letters to her cousin Virginia Micon in New Orleans.[600] In the first of these, written a month after her 16th birthday,[601] she had just arrived by boat in Livingston with "Brother" and her grandmother. There is no mention of where she had been, but, "I now hasten to fulfil my promise of writing to you" might suggest she had visited "Virgie" in New Orleans. She had in fact little of interest to say.

By the summer of 1853[602] it would seem that Susan was by then normally resident in Mobile, but was spending a week back in Livingston. She was now eighteen, and her social life was making heavy demands on her time. She had been hoping that the visit to Livingston would provide "a rest from the turmoil of society in which I have been so much last winter". According to "The Washingtons – a family history" she had been in Virginia "where she immediately attracted many admirers".[603] As for relaxing in Livingston, unfortunately, "my friends have been calling continually, and sending for me to go here and there and everywhere with them". Livingston had apparently changed so much that Susan no longer felt at home there. She was expecting to travel on to Tuscaloosa, and wished that Virgie could come with her. "What a jolly old time we should have flirting and carrying on with those college boys," she remarked. (Modes of expression may change, but the focus of a teenage girl's interest apparently does not.) Susan was not looking forward to going home to Mobile. In an interesting aside, she draws attention to the precarious health of so many young women in the mid 19th century Southern States. "Really Virgie, there seems to be no end to delicate young ladies. I know at least half a dozen in Mobile that are young,

600 Banning Co Addenda 1, Box 7.
601 Ibid, Letter 20, 6th April 1851.
602 Ibid, Letter 21.
603 The Washingtons, Vol 2, Page 3207.

beautiful, intelligent and interesting, and are so weak that they cannot sit up more than an hour at a time."

It seems Susan did not manage to visit Tuscaloosa's college boys after all. Later that summer[604] she wrote to Virgie saying that instead she had spent six weeks at Livingston with her grandmother, then her father had summoned her to accompany him to Bladen. Back at "Selton Cottage" outside Mobile she had been studying French with her brother Hobart. She had been in receipt of letters from her naval officer brother William in Constantinople, and from Andrew, whose star was rising without impediment in California. Mobile was in the grip of an epidemic of yellow fever. Susan felt that as they were living outside the city, they were safe from "the dreadful ravages of that awful plague" as long as they kept out of town. However, panic in the city was driving many people out of Mobile into surrounding neighbourhoods, and although Susan does not say so, there was an obvious risk that some would carry the infection with them.

In her next letter,[605] reflecting on her recent social life, Susan remarked, "I am afraid I was a little wild last winter, but I had a great deal of enjoyment and pleasure." Considering the many restraints on the behaviour of young Southern ladies, it would be surprising if her "wildness" would raise many eyebrows nowadays. Susan was still studying French, and her brother Andrew was writing every second week – "Every letter brings us news of fresh success". Her brother William, meantime, had been presented to the Sultan in Constantinople. The yellow fever epidemic appeared to be almost over: "Oh Virgie," she wrote, "how thankful we should be that through all the devastation of that terrible plague we have had our dear friends and relations spared to us… None of us here have been sick, though there have been some cases of the fever in the neighbourhood… We keep very constantly in the house, never expose ourselves to the sun, and I think that is one reason we have kept so well." Here of course Susan was displaying the contemporary confusion regarding the nature of infection. Staying at home would certainly have helped, but fearing infection from sunshine was a little wide of the mark.

Alas, Susan spoke too soon, as her letter of 17th November shows.[606] "Oh! My darling Virgie, can it be or am I dreaming, that my Hobart, my dear brother has gone, yes gone forever from my earthly vision." Susan

604 Banning Co. Addenda, Box 7, Letter 22. 31st August 1853.

605 Ibid, Letter 23. From Selton Cottage, 4th October 1853.

606 Banning Co. Addenda, Box 7, Letter 24.

and her grandmother had also been "very sick", and her father was only then recovering from "a very severe attack of that dreadful plague". He had decided to move the family back into town after their recovery, and they were in the process of moving to rooms in "Miss Preston's", a private boarding house in Mobile, "a very genteel and pleasant house" where they would spend the winter.

The loss of Hobart, the sibling closest in age to herself, affected Susan deeply. She tried to comfort herself that he had "been taken in his youthful innocence from the troubles of this miserable and trying world, and although it is our loss, it is his gain". This was plainly cold comfort however. "Oh Virgie, had you known him as I do, had you watched by his pillow while he was sick, and beheld the manly fortitude with which he bore his pains, and seen his forbearance – then Virgie you could well know the struggle it was, and oh my Virgie is, to give him up."[607] Susan surprised herself by putting her thoughts on her brother's death into a poem. "What was my astonishment to find that I had written three verses of poetry, when I never could write a rhyme before in my life." Daily life went on however, and on 5th December[608] Susan informed her friend, "Grandma and father are both pleased with boarding, and I like it very well." She had also begun guitar lessons, but Hobart was still on her mind. "Poor darling, he has been lamented by all and every one that knew him."

After December 1853 there is a long gap in Susan's communications to Virgie. The next letter in the series was not written until 14th September 1854,[609] and opens with, "How can I begin a letter to one whom I have seemingly so long forgotten. What can I say to extenuate myself!" She was writing from "Montpelier", Rappahanock County, Virginia, which she explained had been built almost seventy years previously by her great grandfather Thornton, a large house "situated on a hill surrounded by beautiful mountains". She had come to Montpelier some three months previously from Richmond, with her grandmother and brother William. Her cousin Mary lived nearby with three daughters, the eldest of whom was about Susan's age, and accompanied Susan "riding on horseback all over the mountains in every direction". On one of these expeditions Susan had been

607 Ibid, Letter 25. From Mobile, 29th November 1853.

608 Banning Co Addenda, Box 7, Letter 26.

609 Ibid, Letter 30.

thrown from her horse and injured her ankle, which necessitated "some days" confined to bed.

It was intended that she should proceed with William and her grandmother to Fredericksburg at the end of September, then after a month there, back to Richmond, but life at Montpelier must have suited her, for she remarked, "I frequently find myself with a violent fit of the Blues in anticipation of our departure." While at Montpelier she had been unwillingly dragooned into making up a party for a visit to Fauquier Springs. "As it happened," she revealed, "I never enjoyed myself more in my whole life. I made some of the most charming acquaintances whom I shall ever remember. One in particular I think of as superior to all whom I have ever seen."

In Richmond Susan's grandmother had fallen ill, and they decided to spend the winter in Virginia.[610] In her letter of 24th November there is mention of "Cousin Corney" (Cornelia Grinnan), and an intriguing reference to a letter from Susan's brother Andrew which would seem to indicate that he had designs on Virgie. "I trust you may make each other happy," Susan wrote. "There never was a more noble, high minded and generous man than my brother Andrew." The real news in the letter however was of a different love match:

> *"And now I come to tell you of the one and only individual, the one that I 'liked better than all the rest'. You will be astonished when I tell you that to this individual I have given my entire heart. He is one of God's own noblemen, a work of his own hands. He is the son of Mr M. Patton[611] of this place, his name is George. I met with him last spring and liked him from the first moment I saw him. I again met with him at Lee's Springs, and then he went to Montpelier to see me. I have been engaged to him now for rather more than six weeks and every day develops some new and noble trait… He is very fond of fun and we keep up a most incessant chatter. Grandma likes him very much… almost equal to Andrew."*

The family origins of this "one of God's own noblemen" were rather similar to the Glassells' own. The original American Patton was Robert, a

610 Banning Co. Addenda, Box 7, Letter 31. From Richmond 24th November 1854
611 Not so. His father's name was John.

Scotsman who crossed the Atlantic indentured to the mercantile syndicate of William Cunninghame. He apparently served in the Cunninghame depots of Falmouth and Culpeper before moving to Fredericksburg, where he prospered as a merchant on his own account.[612] He was in partnership with a local merchant by the name of Williamson until 1805, after which he ran the business himself. Around 1800 Robert Patton built a mansion house north of Fredericksburg overlooking the Rappahanock River, and named it "White Plains".[613] In 1792 he married Anne Mercer, the daughter of Dr Hugh Mercer, a brigadier general in the War of Independence, who fell at the Battle of Princeton in 1777 and had been a friend of George Washington's.[614] There was apparently a family legend that Robert Patton had fought in the 1745 Jacobite Rebellion, and that his real name was not Patton, which was a cover for his true identity. Another tall tale had him arriving in Virginia after fleeing from Bermuda where he had shot the governor after that dignitary had dared to insult him.[615] Whatever his origins, Patton became wealthy and respectable, a pillar of the Fredericksburg Presbyterian Church, who, like his countryman Andrew Glassell, founded a dynasty of Virginian "aristocrats".

The third child of Robert and Anne Patton was John Mercer Patton. Born in 1797, he studied medicine, graduating from the University of Pennsylvania in 1818. He never practised as a physician however, but instead embarked on a career in law, before serving as a Virginia congressman 1829–1838. He was a member of the Executive Council of Virginia for four consecutive terms, and at one point stood in briefly as acting Governor for thirteen days. His most significant work was in helping to revise the Virginia civil and criminal law codes.[616] John Patton married Peggy French Williams and had eight sons and a daughter:

> *Robert (b. 1824), John (b. 1826), Isaac (b. 1828), George (b. 1833), Tazewell (b. 1835), Eliza (b. 1839), Hugh (b. 1841), James (b. 1843), William (b. 1845).*[617]

---

612 Patton Family hon.comcast.net/~nea/patton.htm

613 "Patton, a genius for war" – Carlo D'Este, Harper Collins Inc., New York, 1995.

614 "Patton – legendary commander" – Martin Blumenson and Kevin Hynel, Potomac Books Inc., Washington D.C., 2008.

615 Carlo D'Este 1995.

616 Ibid.

617 http://www.pattonhq.com/pattontree.html

The fourth child of John and Peggy Patton, George Smith Patton, attended the Virginia Military Institute, graduating in 1852 second in his class overall, but first in Tactics, French, Mathematics, Latin, and Geology.[618] He began a career in law but retained an interest in military matters. This George Patton was the young man who had so impressed Susan Glassell. They were well matched, both coming from families whose humble Scots origins were quickly overtaken by their firm establishment in wealthy Virginian society. Susan seems to have been considered quite a catch. Her humble Dumfriesshire farmer forebears might have been surprised to learn that "Susan Thornton Glassell was descended from a distinguished family that could trace itself to George Washington's great grandfather, King Edward I of England, and France's King Philip III. Even further in the dim recesses of time were sixteen barons who signed the Magna Carta, all of whom the Pattons believed were their direct ancestors."[619] It is rather ironic that in a country whose founding principle was that "all men are created equal", families should feel such a need to dream up mythical antecedents festooned with titles.

After Susan Gassell's letter of 24th November 1854 there seems to have been another gap in her correspondence with Virgie. Her next letter was written on 3rd January 1856 from Charleston, Kanawha County, west of the Blue Ridge Mountains. Kanawha was at that time still part of Virginia, but was soon to be included in the new state of West Virginia. Susan was now married. The wedding had taken place in Richmond on 8th September 1855.[620]

Susan apologised in her letter for not writing before the wedding. There had been so much going on that she had decided to wait, but then after the wedding she had been busy with "so many various little odds and ends", and then she had been ill over the Christmas period, "in bed, with a doctor pouring medicine down my unwilling throat". "How I wish dear V," Susan enthused, "that you could know my dear husband. He is the very best fellow in the world. You would like him I am sure for he is so full of fun and spirits... We spend a very quiet life here, tho there is a considerable amount of visiting among the ladies. One day I received no less than ten calls, a great

618 Carlo D'Este 1995.

619 Carlo D'Este 1995.

620 "The Washingtons – a family history"

many in a place like this. In the evenings we are generally very domestic. George reads aloud to Grandma and self while we do a little fancy work. I am happier than I ever was…".[621]

Susan's first child was born on 30th September 1856 and named George William. "Does it not sound strangely to hear of me being a mother?" she wrote shortly afterwards.[622] Two years later she was writing of her "two little jewels [who] improve every day and hour". However, she observed regretfully, "I find that two children and the necessary time engrossed by house-keeping leaves me very little time for anything else, and I often look back and remember how much precious time I used to waste away in various foolish ways, that I should value so much now."[623] At the time of writing Susan was still only 23. She reflected that she was greatly changed in appearance, and that Virgie would probably not recognise her immediately. While sympathising with Susan's subjection to domestic duties, we should bear in mind that as the wife of a wealthy up-and-coming lawyer, she would not be without household staff – more than likely of the unpaid enslaved variety.

Susan's husband George had set up a law practice in Charleston, and it was now flourishing. He was apparently a "well liked citizen", and something of a "dashing romantic figure", nicknamed "Frenchy" because of his goatee beard. No doubt it was his education at the Virginia Military Institute which inspired him to set up a company of militia volunteers, the Kanawha Rifles, in which he assumed the rank of captain. He was joined, it seems, by "many young aristocrats of high standing in the community like himself".[624] We might be forgiven for dismissing the Kanawha Rifles as a gang of wealthy young pups playing at soldiers, but their testing in battle was to come all too soon.

By 1860, George and Susan Patton were the parents of four children – George, Eleanor, John, and Andrew. The clouds of war were already gathering, and a series of letters from Susan to her husband in early 1861 gives a clear indication of her political sympathies and her reaction to the outbreak of hostilities in the Civil War. Susan, her children, and her grandmother were in Richmond. Her husband George seems to have been

621 Banning Co. Addenda 1, Box 7, Letter 35.

622 Letter 36.

623 Banning Co Addenda, Box 7, Letter 40, 10th May 1858.

624 Details in this paragraph from Carlo D'Este, 1995.

occasionally at home in Charleston, but it is obvious from the letters that he was elsewhere for much of the time, possibly on military duties. By the outbreak of war in the spring of 1861 George's militia company of Kanawha Riflemen had become Company H of the 22nd Virginia Army.

Susan's letter of 11th February 1861 from Richmond[625] tells us that George had written to her from Washington. She was missing him "most painfully" and was thinking of him almost constantly. Baby Andrew had been vaccinated against measles, but if had "not taken". Her next letter[626] was addressed on 17th February to George at Charleston. "I think," she wrote, "if tomorrow's mail comes without a letter from you I shall return to Kanawha, for I certainly cannot stand it." Delegates from South Carolina were due to address the "Convention" in Richmond and the city was crowded. "What the result will be God only knows. I pray that he will order all things for our ultimate good." George's brother John and his wife Sally were insisting on Susan staying with them, and then accompanying them when they went "up the country", but she was not sure whether she would go or not. "Someone sent me a 'Kanawha Report' with the returns of the Election in it," she related indignantly to her husband. "I suppose it was someone who was crowing over me. I wish I knew who it was."The Kanawha Valley's sympathies lay largely with secession and the Confederate cause, but western Virginia as a whole supported the Union, and later joined it as the newly constituted state of West Virginia, hived off from "old" Virginia. Susan and her husband were enthusiastic secessionists, and their opinions would be well known in Charleston. The Confederacy had been formally proclaimed on 4th February 1861, but Virginia did not join until 17th April.

Susan wrote again from Richmond on 27th February,[627] relating an unfortunate encounter with "an abolitionist lady", an admirer of Lincoln who hoped to see slave owners driven from Virginia, and looked forward to the happy day when Northerners would come and make it the greatest state in the Union. "I was so agitated," Susan admitted, "that I scarce know what I said. Grandma says that my eyes flashed fire and that I was very rude to her, but I don't care if I was." She also related a conversation that must have done wonders for her self esteem: "I was in a store yesterday kept by a woman, making a few little purchases for Andrew. The woman looked at me

625 Banning Co. Addenda 1, Box 7, Letter 15.
626 Letter 16.
627 Letter 17.

very hard and said, 'You surely have not got a baby.' I told her I had had four. I never saw one so amazed as she was." Susan at the time of writing was just a few days short of her 26th birthday. She left this letter unfinished, and a postscript added by George's sister Eliza tells why:

> *"My Dear Brother, 1st March, Richmond.*
> *Since Sue wrote the first part of this letter the most melancholy and heart rending affliction has happened to her. Mrs Thornton [Susan's grandmother] was taken suddenly ill last night about eleven and notwithstanding prompt and active remedies she died before twelve. Her death was so sudden they could not send for Sue, and she did not know of it until about an hour ago, 8 o' clock this morning. Her distress is perfectly heartrending... Bro John told her, and her shrieks were most distressing."*

Susan's grandmother, of course, had supplied the place of the mother she had never known, and her death would indeed be a severe blow.

On 13th April Susan wrote to George, "I cannot tell you how very sad I feel. The news came today that war is indeed inaugurated...". She was suspicious of Virginia's politicians, saying, "I am firmly convinced that these creatures are afraid and are going to try and preserve a neutral position in this great struggle." While she was writing this letter Susan was startled by the sound of cannon fire. She and George's mother went out to investigate, and eventually learned "the joyful news that Fort Sumter had been taken". The people of Richmond filled the main square, a salute of a hundred guns was fired, and there were torchlight processions, fireworks and bonfires. Speeches were made from the porch of the Capitol, including one from George's brother John. "The people are wild with excitement," Susan affirmed on her return home, "and the old fogeys of the Convention thoroughly scared out of their wits."[628]

By the time Susan wrote again on 5th May, Virginia had seceded from the Union, and the consequent disruption was making it sifficult to plan ahead. "The times are so changing that ere my letters reach you, something else turns up causing all of our plans to be worthless." Apparently George had been "ordered east" and Susan had decided to

628 Banning Co Addenda 1, Box 7, Letter 19.

remain in Richmond. Now it seemed that he would be kept in Charleston after all. "I am ready to come home whenever you say it," she announced loyally, but if she did not hear from her husband within the following ten days, she thought he would go "up to Culpeper".[629] The destination there was presumably Spring Farm, the Pattons' "ancestral home" in Culpeper County.[630]

Susan never returned to Charleston. She wrote to her father on 1st June 1861 from Spring Farm, having arrived there with her children three days previously.[631] She had travelled part of the way in a packed train, sharing a carriage with Confederate troops. "They are all in fine spirits and seem almost crazy for a fight," she enthused. At Spring Farm everything was "calm and peaceful", but a clash was expected at Manassas Junction. "They say if we are defeated at Manassas, that Culpeper would not be tenable for ladies," she observed, while obviously having full confidence in Confederate arms. "Lee has set a trap for the vandals which will inevitably catch and crush them all," she declared.

Susan also mentioned to her father that all the Patton brothers had now gone off to war except Robert, the eldest, and William, who was a mere boy. Excluding Robert and William, the brothers were John, Isaac, Susan's husband George, Tazewell, Hugh and James. Their mother Margaret (Peggy) was a woman of strong character who on the outbreak of war "gave each of her sons a thoroughbred horse for himself and a nigrow body servant, with a second less well bred horse for the nigrow".[632] The eldest brother Robert, it seems, had a drink problem and lived in a back room of Spring Farm with a bulldog.[633]

Susan seems to have been as enthusiastic for the Confederate cause as her mother in law. It was told of her that at some point during the war, a Union sergeant jokingly put his cap on her son George's head, telling him he was now a Yankee. When she heard of this Susan indignantly cleansed him of the perceived insult by vigorously scrubbing the boy's head.[634]

629 Banning Co Addenda 1, Box 7, Letter 19.
630 "Patton – a genius for war" – Carlo D'Este.
631 Banning Co Addenda 1, Box 7, Letter 12.
632 Carlo D'Este, quoting an unnamed grandson of Mrs Patton's.
633 Carlo D'Este.
634 "Patton – legendary commander" – Martin Blumenson and Kevin Hynel, Potomac Books Inc., Washington DC, 2008,

George Patton's Kanawha Riflemen, as already mentioned, became H Company of the 22nd Virginia Infantry When the regiment was absorbed into the Confederate Army, George became a lieutenant colonel. He saw action for the first time at Scary Creek in July 1861, where he was wounded in the arm, taken prisoner, and then parolled. Although the wound never healed properly, he returned to duty serving under "Stonewall" Jackson, again as a lieutenant colonel in the 22nd Virginians. He was wounded again on 10th May 1862 during the Battle of Giles Court House.[635]

The circumstances of this second injury are curious. It seems that Susan had given her husband a money belt with a $10 gold piece sewn into it to be kept for emergencies. If he were taken prisoner again, for example, "the gold might buy him some kindness from a guard". During the action at Giles Court House Patton was shot in the belly. Knowing that such wounds tended to be fatal, George waved away the attentions of a military surgeon, propped himself against a tree, and began a letter of farewell to his wife. However, General Henry Hath asked to be shown the wound, probed it with his finger, and extracted Susan's $10 dollar coin. The musket ball had apparently struck the gold piece and glanced off, driving the coin into George's flesh. This was indeed a lucky escape, but not surprisingly George contracted blood poisoning and was returned to his family in Richmond to recuperate.[636]

In August of the following year, 1863, Susan and her children were at Greenbrier Resort near the famous White Sulphur Springs watering place. Union General William Averell launched a raid on White Sulphur Springs with the intention of cutting the railway linking Richmond and Chatanooga. Confederate cavalry and George Patton's brigade beat Averell off and forced him to retreat. White's hotel was requisitioned to receive the wounded from both sides, and Susan Patton volunteered her services as a nurse. Her son George later remembered following her around with a bucket and sponge, and recalled that the stench was so overpowering that his mother fainted and had to be carried out.[637]

In the summer of 1864 Patton was with Jubal Early's army threatening Washington, and General Philip H. Sheridan was sent to stop them. The

635 Carlo D'Este.

636 Carlo D'Este.

637 "The Washingtons – a family history". However, Carlo D'Este places this incident in November 1863 after a Confederate defeat at Drop Mountain.

two sides clashed on 19th September at Winchester. At some time prior to this, George Patton had been able to visit Susan at the house of his brother John, "The Meadows", near Abermarle. He was able to stay for a few hours, then left on a troop train. "I remember," his son George later wrote, "seeing a soldier on a car gave him a hand to get aboard, and as the train moved out he was leaning against a gun and waved us goodbye. I never saw him again."[638]

The engagement at Winchester degenerated into a Confederate rout. Vainly trying to rally his men as they streamed through the streets of Winchester, George Patton was badly wounded in the leg by a shell fragment, and was carried to the house of his relative John Williams. According to one version of the story, he refused amputation offered by a Union surgeon.[639] Another version claims that the surgeon did not believe the wound to be life threatening[640], and that six days later George seemed "cheerful, even buoyant". However, later that day, 25th December 1864, his condition deteriorated drastically and he died from "a combination of fever and gangrene". Susan apparently only learned of her husband's death four days later from a newspaper report, and by the time she reached Winchester he had already been buried.

Long after the war had ended George was reinterred in Stonewall Confederate Cemetery, Winchester, along with his brother Tazewell who had been mortally wounded at Cemetery Ridge during the Battle of Gettysburg. The reburial apparently involved a solemn silent moonlight ceremony with veterans dressed in now illegal Confederate uniform. The occasion was seemingly marred by an unfortunate accident during the interment when Tazewell's corpse fell from its coffin. George Patton's son remembered that his uncle "looked little different in death than he had in life".[641] Since poor Tazewell had died after having part of his jaw sheared away by a shell fragment, this seems, to say the least, rather unlikely.

Susan was now left a widow with a young family. Her son John seems to have died in early childhood, but the family now included an infant Susan Glassell Patton who had been born on 23rd February in the year of her

638 Carlo D'Este.
639 "The Washingtons..."
640 Carlo D'Este.
641 Carlo D'Este.

father's death.[642] As the war ended, much of Virginia lay devastated, the fields uncultivated and the economy in ruins. Susan spent the winter of 1864-65 at Goochland near Richmond, and was joined by her elderly father and her brother William. Both were in a precarious state of health. Her father was now blind and William was suffering from tuberculosis. Both were incapable of contributing financially. As we have seen, old Mr Glassell had supposedly "given his all" to the Confederate cause. It is perhaps more likely that his "all" had been invested in "negroes" – an investment which would evaporate with emancipation. William had been officially dismissed from the U.S. Navy, and there would be no pay-offs or pensions for the naval officers of the defeated and obliterated Confederacy. Susan and her family had speedily descended from the privileged life of Southern "aristocrats" to a state of near destitution.

At some point after the end of hostilities, Susan's brother-in-law William Patton arrived, driving an old horse-drawn Confederate ambulance, and took the family to an "old Colonial mansion near Orange" where they were joined by other members of the Patton clan, including the Patton brothers' mother Peggy. There the family managed to cultivate enough ground to supply their basic needs until Susan's brother Andrew sent $600 to enable Susan, her children, her father, and her brother William to join him in California.[643]

Susan had undoubtedly fallen on hard times, but it is difficult to imagine that the extended Patton family was entirely devoid of resources. Not all "destitute" victims of Confederate defeat would be able to find refuge in a "Colonial mansion near Orange", and as we have already seen, in California Andrew had invested "Sue's $800"[644] – a substantial sum in 1866. Nor was Susan without domestic assistance. Regarding Susan's departure for California, we read in "The Washingtons – a family history":

> *"It was especially difficult to leave behind Mary, a dear friend, who in antebellum times had been given to Sue as a playmate and her property. Susan gave her a portion of the $600 as a parting gift. Later, as Susan left for the train station, Mary ran up to her with a box of toys for the children, purchased with the money Susan had given her."*

642 "The Washingtons – a family history."

643 Carlo D'Este.

644 Banning Co Addenda 1, Box 4, Letter 49.

Apparently, for the rest of her life Susan had a recurring dream in which Mary was busy packing her mistress's bags as she prepared to join her wounded husband. In the dream, as in reality, she never managed to join him, and in the dream, as in reality, she never saw his face again.[645]

On 15th November 1866 Susan wrote to her sister-in-law Sally Patton from the steamer "Arizona", off Cuba, describing her journey so far.[646] She had been unable to get berths in a sleeping car for the overnight journey to New York, and had been continually disturbed by ticket inspectors and sellers of pies and sandwiches. She left New York on board the "Arizona" on 11th August with her four children, her father, and her brother William. They were all comfortably accommodated, but all except William suffered from seasickness. Southerners were very much in the minority on board, although the captain was a Virginian, and as Susan said, "We Southerners are all seated at his end of the table." She continued, "The rest of the company are rather radical I expect. Mr McDonald told one lady I was from the Confederacy at which information she raised her hands in horror." There were two U.S. Army generals among the passengers, "both Yanks". One, General Fry, "whose countenance denotes relentless cruelty", she believed to have "distinguished himself as a villain" during the war. The wife of the other general took a fancy to Susan's son George, saying she was sure he had never been kissed by a Yankee before, and she wished to show him what a nice kiss she could bestow. The boy retorted that he would never kiss a Yankee, which fortunately amused the lady greatly. Also among the passengers was a Catholic archbishop, a priest, and twenty Sisters of Charity, all bound eventually for Oregon. The nuns were greatly taken with Susan's toddler Susie, and made a great fuss of her, giving her a holy medal, and teaching her to kiss a crucifix.

The "Arizona" took the party to Panama, where they had to cross the isthmus and take ship again on the Pacific side for San Francisco. They spent ten days in San Francisco, then sailed down the Californian coast to San Pedro, the port for Los Angeles, some 25 miles from the city. Susan was met in San Pedro by her brother Andrew. She recognised him immediately from a distance. He was "unchanged in appearance and manners" she wrote

645 "The Washingtons – a family history".

646 Patton family papers, Box 1, Mss PF317-320.

to her old friend Virgie[647] "but he declared that he never would have known me".

Susan informed her sister-in-law that she had met with a "most cordial reception" in California.[648] "The splendour of everything amazed the poor half starved Confederate," she enthused. "Everything was so new and different to what I had ever seen; the customs and manners so different that I felt as if I had been transferred to another world." She was astounded at the variety of fruit and vegetables on sale in San Francisco. Strawberries were available eleven months in the year!

On reaching Los Angeles Susan and her children initially lived with her brother Andrew and his large family, in what seemed to Susan to be the best house in town. Andrew's wife Lucy had only one servant, but, (and here we glimpse another side of the Californian paradise) she also had "a little Indian girl" that Lucy's father Dr Toland "bought and gave her". "But," Susan commented, "they are universally scropulous[649] and nearly always die when taken from their savage state and civilized. This child is able to do but little and Lucy intends getting another Irish girl to wash and do chamber work."[650]

Susan suspected that Andrew had lost substantial sums of money during the war, and was therefore determined to put her "shoulder to the wheel" and do all she could to avoid being a burden to him. To that end she decided to "get work teaching". In a letter of 15th January 1867 to Sally Patton[651] she updated her sister-in-law on her plans. "I have every prospect of getting a very nice school composed of little girls from 8 to 13 years old. I may get from 18 to 20 in number at three dollars per month. If so I shall rent a small house in the course of this year, and go to housekeeping." Andrew and Lucy were very kind, she admitted, but she preferred to live independently if possible. She hoped to open her school about the middle of February 1867. It is not absolutely clear whether Susan was intending to take over an existing private school as a going concern, or whether the school was an entirely new venture.

On 19th December 1868 the "Los Angeles Star" carried a report on the

647 Patton family papers, Box 1, Ms PF 320.
648 Ibid. Ms PF318. 19th December 1866.
649 Scrofulous? Scrofula is tuberculosis of the lymph nodes in the neck.
650 Patton family Papers Box 1, Ms PF318.
651 Ibid. Ms PF319.

public examination of the pupils of the Boys' Grammar School. This was followed up by a reader's letter from "Looker on", who commented:

> *"Press of business seems to have caused you to overlook the examination which took place on Friday at the private female school of Mrs Patton on Main Street. Had time permitted you might there have witnessed the bright faces of some forty children whose deportment alone would have excited the liveliest admiration. The system pursued by Mrs Patton seems to be one of order and punctuality, enforced by gentle kindness and judicious appeals to self respect and pride of the children, instead of that severe austerity which renders the schoolroom so irksome (to use no harsher term) to the children."*[652]

Among the Patton Family Papers[653] are transcripts of an undated newspaper cutting and a "circular" advertising Susan's school, both probably from the summer of 1869. The newspaper advertisement announces:

> *"PRIVATE SCHOOL: Mrs Patton, who has ably conducted a private school for the past year, has yielded to the solicitations of her numerous patrons and made arrangements to supply the demands of the community for a Young Ladies' Seminary, and will reopen her school on the 20 of July with a talented corps of teachers, the school house enlarged and otherwise improved, and all the higher branches, including music and the languages, will be taught upon the most liberal terms. Parents and guardians wishing to educate their daughters and wards have an opportunity of doing so upon terms within the reach of all."*

The "circular" announces that the school will reopen on Monday July 20th, and it is to comprise three sections. Pupils will spend two years in the "Primary" department, four years in "Intermediate", and four years in "Collegiate". The subjects taught develop from "Reading and spelling" in the first year of primary, until the curriculum of the final year of "Intermediate" covers "Reading, Spelling, Written Arithmetic through vulgar fractions, Geography, Grammar commenced, History of the United States, Composition and writing". In the final year of the Collegiate department

652 Ibid. Box 17, Ms PF350.
653 Also Box 17, Ms PF350.

the students would tackle "Review of Arithmetic, Algebra, Parsing in 'Paradise Lost', Geometry (finished), Moral Philosophy, Kame's 'Elements of Criticism', Butler's 'Analogy', and Composition". French and music were also available at an extra charge.

Fees were $3 for the Primary Department, $3 for Intermediate, and $4 for Collegiate. "Music on piano" was $5, "Use of instrument in practising" was $1, French $1, and the "Vocal class" was free of charge. Presumably these are annual charges.

The "Literary Department" was to be taught by Susan herself and Miss Ann Chapman. Miss Chapman may well have been a relative of Susan's brother's partner in the legal firm of Glassell and Chapman. It might be remarked in passing that the spelling in Susan's letters is often less than perfect. For example in the letter describing her voyage to California she has the nuns travelling to "Origen" and teaching her daughter to kiss the "crusafix". Hopefully she was more careful in her teaching.

Susan was now able to support herself independently, and rented a house for herself and her children. It would take a while, however, to put the trauma of the Civil War behind her. "I think so much of you and all my dear people of the South," she wrote to her old friend Virgie early in 1867. "Would to God they had the power to resist the opressor's iron hand, but I fear there is no hope left. And yet at times I feel that God cannot permit his people to be so entirely crushed as at present seems the intention of the Yankee government. It makes my heart sick when I think of these things or read the News Papers… Tho we may never again meet, dear Virgie, I shall never cease to love you, and you must not forget me; and remember my poor crushed heart when you pray, and ask God to help me to be submissive to his will and to be brave and strong for the battles of life."[654]

In the autumn of the same year Virgie's brother informed Susan of the sad news of the death of Virgie's husband. "None can sympathise with you more deeply than I can," Susan wrote to her old friend, "for by bitter experience I know full well the pangs you suffer… Life has lost its charm for me, and when autumn comes I can but think of the October days when the light of my life went out, and the cold earth received the form of one who was my idol, and I long to lie down by his side and be at rest."[655]

654 Banning Co Addenda 1, Box 7, Letter 41, 24th February 1867.
655 Ibid. Letter 42. 5th October 1867.

Stress was also telling physically on Susan. In 1867 she described herself as "thin as a rail from constant work",[656] and later lamented, "I am so thin now... I don't think the climate and confinement agrees with me, for I had never since I was grown weighed so little."[657]

Help was at hand however. In April 1867 Susan had remarked to her sister-in-law Sally, "Cousin George looks well and gives entire satisfaction to the firm of Glassell and Chapman. I suppose he will be taken into the firm as a partner very soon."[658] "Cousin George" was in fact the cousin and close friend of Susan's deceased husband. They had attended the Virginia Military Institute together, and both had apparently been rivals for the attentions of the young Susan Glassell. George Smith, like George Patton, had served in the Confederate Army, and like his cousin had been seriously wounded. He was subsequently appointed colonel of the 62nd Virginia Mounted Infantry, and before the end of hostilities was captured and held as a prisoner of war. On his release he made his way to California, and as we have seen, was given employment in the law firm of Glassell and Chapman.[659]

California was of course the land of opportunity, and he was already acquainted with the Glassells, but one source also claims that George Smith went to California in search not only of employment, but of Susan Glassell.[660] Be that as it may, Smith was soon accepted into Glassell and Chapman as a partner, as Susan had predicted. Having achieved financial security, he then proposed marriage to his old flame. Susan and George Smith were married in Los Angeles on 1st June 1870, and the couple went on to have two children of their own, Anne and Ettinge Hugh. George Smith was greatly loved and respected by Susan's four children by George Patton, to the extent that her eldest son George discarded his middle name William, and took the name George Smith Patton. It is not clear what happened to Susan's school after her marriage, but one might suspect that it would be passed on to other hands with a sigh of relief. Susan herself died of breast cancer on 16th November 1883 at the relatively early age

656 Patton Family Papers, Box 1, Ms PF320.
657 Banning Co Addenda 1, Box 7, Letter 42.
658 Patton Family Papers, Box 1, Ms PF320.
659 "The Washingtons – a family history".
660 The fighting Pattons – Brian Sobel.

of 48.[661] Two years later Susan's brother Andrew married her old friend Virgie.

George, the eldest son of George Patton and Susan Glassell, was born in Virginia on 30th September 1856. As we have seen, his father was mortally wounded in a Confederate defeat at Winchester and died not long after his son's eighth birthday. Young George was brought to California by his mother in late 1866, along with his three siblings, his maternal grandfather and his mother's brother William.

On 24th February 1867 his mother wrote to her friend and cousin Virgie, "George is going to school to a Southern man."[662] Presumably this was Dr Rose, whose Boys' Grammar School was publicly examined in December 1868. The Los Angeles Star of 19th December 1868 carried a report on the examination, and mentioned George Patton as one of the boys who "excelled" in 1st Grade Grammar, and as one of four "particularly well posted" in Geography. He also participated in a demonstration of "Physiology" with a diagram of the human heart pinned to his chest. Overall, the "Roll of Honor" for his year ranked twelve names in order with George Patton placed third. The examination proceedings were closed by an address from "that promising young orator George Patton". This appeared in the newspaper report in the form of a lengthy poem in blank verse, capitalised at the beginning of each line, but in fact it reads rather better as a piece of prose: "… And do you wonder much that timid boys such as those you see should shrink from being marshalled out before this gazing crowd to sing, declaim, and answer all the questions plain and right?" He wonders how the Board of Education and the audience would feel if the same were to be required of them. "I think you'd say as did the mouse of old to Pussy-cat, 'This may be fun to you, but tis death to me'." "Say then, do you not pity us?" he concluded, "I know that these ladies do. I see it in their eyes. Our wise committee too look kindly on us while from our very hearts we thank you." No doubt Susan was suitably impressed with her son's performance.

As noted above, George's mother remarried in 1870, and young George became attached enough to his stepfather to take his surname as a middle name, becoming George Smith Patton. Since both father and stepfather

661 "The Washingtons – a family history".
662 Banning Co Addenda 1, Box 7, Letter 41.

had been Confederate officers and graduates of the Virginia Military Institute it is hardly surprising that George's education was continued there. During his time at V.M.I. he became 1st Captain of the Corps of Cadets, and commanded the corps as they paraded at the Philadelphia Centenial Celebration Exhibition in 1876.[663] This attracted some attention, as it was the first parade of Southern military personel in the North since the Civil War. George graduated in 1877 at the age of around 21, then returned to Los Angeles to learn Law from his stepfather and uncle. He became a partner in the firm in 1880. In 1903 Henry E. Huntington purchased the Shorb estate and appointed George Patton as its general manager. Patton also served two terms as Los Angeles District Attorney, and was "well respected" in the political circles of the Democratic Party.

In 1884, at the age of 28, Patton married Ruth, the daughter of Benjamin Davis Wilson. Wilson was what might be called a "colourful character". From humble beginnings in Tennessee he moved west and spent time as a fur trapper and Indian trader in Santa Fe. He apparently came to southern California with the intention of taking ship to China, but decided to remain. He became a storekeeper, a rancher, and married Ramona Yorba, daughter of a prominent and wealthy Hispanic landowner. He was made a Justice of the Peace for the "Inland Territory" and was given oversight of Indian Affairs. It is said that he acquired his nickname of "Don Benito" among the Native Americans because of his "benevolent manner" towards them. Be that as it may, one source reveals that in 1845 he was asked to pursue a band of marauding Ute Indians who had stolen horses from local ranchers. In the course of his mission he led 22 men into the San Bernardino Mountains where he massacred "hundreds" of Serrano Indians he had mistakenly believed to be Utes.[664] Don Benito became the first non-Hispanic owner of the vast Rancho San Pascual, now occupied by the towns of Pasadena, Altadena, South Pasadena, Alhambra, San Marino and San Gabriel. His business investments were many and varied, and he helped to develop the first orange groves and vineyards in the area. He served a term as mayor of Los Angeles and three terms as a California state senator. After the death of his first wife Ramona, Don Benito remarried and had two daughters by

663 "Patton, legendary commander" – Blumenson and Hynd Page 4.

664 Benjamin Davis Wilson. World Heritage Encyclopedia https://www.hawaiilibrary.net/article/WHEBN0001780104/Benjamin… I should say that I have been unable to find any other reference to this massacre.

his second wife Margaret Hereford, one of whom was Ruth, the future wife of George Patton.

General George Smith Patton

George and Ruth Patton lived in San Marino, where their two children were born – George in 1885, and Anne (known as "Nita") in 1887. George, the elder child, was the grandson of Susan Glassell, the great great grandson of Andrew Glassell, the planter of Torthorwald, and great great great grandson of Robert Glassell, tenant of the farm of Howgate, in Roucan, Dumfriesshire. This boy was to become almost the caricature of the larger-than-life American Hero. What follows is the briefest of summaries of his achievements and eccentricities, but his life has been extensively documented elsewhere, and interested readers will find it easy to investigate him further.

George's boyhood in southern California allowed him to live a healthy outdoor life and develop an abiding interest in horses and riding. After attending a private school in Pasadena, at the age of eighteen he entered the Virginia Military Institute, like his father and grandfather before him. After only a year there he won a place at West Point through a competitive examination. In spite of this examination success, George Patton was not gifted academically, and was required to repeat his first year at West Point. Indeed, according to his daughter Ruth Ellen, he was dyslexic. (It has been facetiously observed that his statue at West Point faces away from the Library.) On the other hand, Patton was an enthusiastic athlete, excelling at "track", swordsmanship, and polo.

Graduating from West Point in 1909, Patton married Beatrice Ayer the following year and began his army career at Fort Sheridan near Chicago. His wife was a member of an immensely wealthy and influential family of Massachusetts industrialists, and the connection was to stand the young army officer in good stead. Patton was selected for the American team competing in the 1912 Stockholm Olympics, where he came 5th in the "Modern Pentathlon". In 1915 he was transferred to the 8th Cavalry based in Texas near the Mexican border, and participated in the punitive expedition into Mexico to capture Pancho Villa after he had shown the temerity to launch a raid into the American state of New Mexico.

In 1917 the U.S.A. joined in the First World War, and General Pershing led the American Expeditionary Force across the Atlantic to

France. Patton was on Pershing's staff, and developed an interest in tanks. He became the Expeditionary Force's acknowledged expert on the new motorised weapon, and formed an American tank school. He was wounded in action near the end of hostilities, and received the Distinguished Service Cross.

Patton was determinedly ambitious and believed he was destined to become an acclaimed leader of men. He strove consciously to act the part of the hardened warrior, believing that a leader must always appear larger than life. His daughter Ruth Ellen later observed, "He was built like a hero, and acted like a hero, and was a hero worshipper." Apparently he believed in reincarnation, and according to his daughter, claimed to remember drinking his own urine out of his helmet in Hannibal's army. Seemingly he could also recall being wounded as a Viking warrior, and retreating with Napoleon from Moscow.[665]

In the inter-war years Patton progressed up the career ladder through several staff positions, aided at least to some extent by his wife's family's wide network of social contacts, which allowed him to hobnob with influential politicians and high ranking military men. He had retained his interest in armoured warfare, and at the time of American entry into World War II Patton commanded the U.S. 2nd Armored Division.

In June 1940 Italy entered the war on the German side, and France signed an armistice, leaving the vast swathe of French North Africa in the hands of the collaborating Vichy regime. An Italian invasion of Egypt in early 1941 was repulsed and crushed by the British, prompting Germany to send the formidable General Rommel with his Afrika Korps to the aid of the flagging Italians. British and Commonwealth forces were forced into retreat, but in late 1941 and early 1942 they began to push Axis troops back through Libya, before being driven back again to El Alamein in Egypt. Here the tide turned, and the British 8th Army under the charismatic Bernard Montgomery pressed steadily westwards through Libya with the Axis forces in constant retreat before them.

Although the U.S.A. had entered the war in December 1941, it did not join the North Africa campaign until November 1942. Russia had been pressing for the opening of a second front. The U.S.A. would

665 "The fighting Pattons" – Brian Sobel.

have preferred an invasion of France, but Churchill managed to carry his strategy of an invasion through North Africa into Europe's "soft underbelly" via Sicily and mainland Italy. The planned campaign was designated "Operation Torch", and put under the overall command of the American General Eisenhower. George Patton's 2nd Corps was an integral part of the strategy.

The untested American troops were only too well aware of the enormity of the task before them, and of their inexperience and dearth of achievement compared to the battle hardened British 8th Army. Patton was therefore determined to whip his men into shape, and enforced rigorous discipline. "Kicking butt," one commentator observes, "was the activity of choice for the autocratic, flamboyant, frequently coarse, pistol-packing Patton."[666]

Patton landed at Fedola in Morocco under Vichy French fire, secured the beaches and surrounded the port of Casablanca, which surrendered on 10th November 1942. A deal was subsequently struck with French forces in North Africa to support the Allies. Axis troops caught between American and British and Commonwealth armies were eventually herded into a pocket around Tunis before surrendering on 13th May 1943.

The way was now clear for the invasion of Sicily. Under the overall command of General Eisenhower and his second-in-command Sir Harold Alexander, two task forces were planned – an Eastern Task Force consisting of the British 8th Army under Montgomery, and a Western Task Force under Patton. Amphibious landings went ahead along the south and east coast of Sicily on 10th July 1943, and good progress was made. The following day Patton ordered his reserve parachute troops to drop. Unfortunately the arrival of the transport aircraft coincided with an Axis air raid, and the American planes were fired on by Allied naval vessels causing many casualties.

Both Montgomery and Patton pushed northwards, and Patton took Palermo on 22nd July after fierce fighting. He then pushed two divisions eastwards, forcing continued Axis withdrawal. Soon a full-scale evacuation of German and Italian troops from Sicily was underway though Messina, which the Allies were unable to prevent. When they entered Messina in mid

666 The path to victory: the Mediterranean Theater in World War II – Douglas Porch, F.S.G, May 2004.

August they found the enemy had gone. A brutal campaign on mainland Italy was to follow, but in that Patton would play no part.

Before the final capture of Messina General Patton visited a tented evacuation hospital in Nicosia on 31st August, speaking to several wounded patients, and giving words of encouragement and commendation. Approaching a soldier who appeared to have no physical injuries, Patton asked where he was hurt. In fact the man had been evacuated because of "battle fatigue", and made the mistake of telling Patton, "I guess I can't take it." Patton exploded with rage, slapped him with his gloves, dragged him to the tent door by the collar, and kicked him out, yelling, "Don't admit this son of a bitch!" He demanded that the soldier should be sent back to the front, saying, "You hear me you gutless bastard? You're going back to the front!" In fact Patton's victim was later found to be feverish, running a high temperature, and was diagnosed as being infected with malarial parasites.

A week later Patton again visited an evacuation hospital, and again spoke to several patients. Sitting among them was a soldier with four years of service who had been brought in suffering from fever, fatigue, confusion and listlessness. He had been hospitalised in spite of his own request to be returned to his unit. Patton asked him what the trouble was, and got the reply, "It's my nerves. I can't stand the shelling any more." Again, Patton exploded, slapping the man and yelling, "Your nerves! Hell, you are just a goddamned coward!" When the soldier began to weep, Patton slapped him again, bawling, "Shut up that goddamned crying! I won't have brave men who have been shot at seeing that yellow bastard here crying!" He told the man he was going back to the front to fight, and if he didn't fight he would be shot by firing squad. "In fact," he continued, "I ought to shoot you myself, you goddamned whimpering coward!" He then pulled out his pistol, and at that point the hospital commander intervened. As Patton left he continued grumbling about the "yellow bastard being babied".

Reports of Patton's outrageous behaviour reached Eisenhower and eventually leaked out to the press, causing something of a furore, and prompting calls for Patton to be dismissed. Eisenhower ordered an unofficial investigation and wrote to Patton rebuking him for brutality and uncontrolled temper, questioning his judgment, and "strongly suggesting" that Patton should personally apologise to the two soldiers and to medical staff. Patton complied with his commander's "suggestion", but he was removed from battlefield command and eventually ordered to the U.K. to participate in preparations for the invasion of Normandy. Although the confidence of his superiors had been temporarily shaken, and although his British allies tended to regard him as something of a joke, it must be said that his popularity remained undiminished among the men he had led through North Africa and Sicily.

Through a campaign of deliberate misinformation the Germans were led to believe that Patton was in England to lead an invasion of north east France from Dover. This was to divert attention from "Operation Overlord", the Allies' true plan to launch an invasion of Normandy. In fact Patton's allotted task was to prepare and command the U.S. 3rd Army, which was to act as a follow-up force after the initial landings on the Normandy beaches. Most of the 3rd Army were raw inexperienced troops newly arrived from the U.S.A., and Patton attacked his assignment with gusto, making a series of inspirational speeches to vast audiences of over a thousand men at a time, orations delivered extempore and without notes. He was a commanding figure, with cavalry boots, riding crop, highly polished helmet, and grim-faced scowl. Basically his inspiring harangues were all the same speech, dwelling on his main motivational points:

> *"An army is a team. It lives, sleeps and fights as a team."*
> *"The quicker things are whipped, the quicker we go home."*
> *"Keep moving."*
> *"We're advancing constantly."*
> *"My men don't surrender."*

He would end with the certainty that one day his hearers would be able to tell their grandchildren with pride that they "rode with the Third Army and a son of a goddamned bitch named George Patton."

The gist of these speeches was later collected from soldiers who had written them down from memory and sometimes reproduced them in published memoirs. The historian Terry Brighton later reconstructed a full text based on these recollections. Patton's words were certainly received with enthusiasm by his audiences, but would surely have brought a blush to the manly cheeks of his forebears, the Christian gentlemen officers of the

Confederate army. Part of the appeal of the speeches was the crudity and profanity of Patton's delivery:

> *"I don't give a fuck for a man who is not always on his toes."*
>
> *"This individual hero stuff is bullshit."*
>
> *"[Let's] clean the goddamn thing up and then get at those purple-pissing Japs."*
>
> *"We're not going to shoot the bastards, we're going to rip out their living goddamned guts and use them to grease the treads of our tanks. We're going to murder those lousy Hun cocksuckers by the bushel-fucking-basket."*
>
> *"We're going to hold him by his balls and we're going to kick him in the ass, twist his balls and kick the living shit out of him all the time."*[667]

The invasion of Normandy began on 6th June 1944. Patton's 3rd Army was shipped to France during the month of July, and began operations on 6th August, attacking west into Brittany and also to the south-east and north, trapping several hundred thousand German soldiers in the "Falaise Pocket". Patton's tactic was rapid aggressive advance, with air reconnaissance and timely delivery of supplies. The Third Army made speedy progress to Lorraine, where they halted at the Moselle River outside Metz, as their fuel supply ran out due to Eisenhower's unfortunate prioritising of a projected invasion through the Netherlands. Metz fell to the Third Army in mid November, but progress was slow thereafter.

In December 1944 Germany suddenly launched a devastating attack through Belgium, Luxembourg and northern France, catching the Allies off guard. Eisenhower summoned his commanders to an urgent council of war at Verdun. At the time, Patton's Third Army was engaged in heavy fighting at Saarbrucken. Patton foresaw that Eisenhower might require him to disengage part of his force to counter the German "bulge", and prepared accordingly. He was thus able to assure Eisenhower that he was ready for immediate action, and was given the task of relieving Allied troops besieged at Bastogne. In what has ever since been regarded as a remarkable achievement, Patton took six divisions out of his front line and sent them

667 Wikipedia. Patton's speech to the Third Army.

north in midwinter to Bastogne, where they were able to open up a corridor for relief and supply of the beleaguered Allied forces.

The momentum of the German advance petered out, and by February 1945 they were in full-scale retreat. Patton pushed into Germany, taking city after city. On 22nd March a pontoon bridge over the Rhine was completed and Patton took a division over, pausing, it is said, to urinate into the river as he crossed – the alpha male marking his territory (albeit in a rather transitory way)!

The Third Army was ordered to Bavaria and Czechoslovakia, but was not allowed to proceed beyond Pilsen. Much to Patton's disgust, eastern Europe, and eastern Germany itself were to be left to the tender mercies of the U.S.S.R. After V.E. Day, 8th May 1945, Patton requested a transfer to the Pacific, but was instead given home leave to the U.S.A. On his return he was appointed Military Governor of Bavaria.

As Military Governor, Patton irritated his colleagues and superiors by allowing former Nazis to take up political posts. It was said that his behaviour was becoming erratic, and there were rumours of a scandalous liaison with his niece. After a "heated exchange" with Eisenhower he was removed from his post on 28th September, and a week later removed from command of the Third Army. He was posted to Bad Neuheim to command the U.S. "15th Army", which in fact consisted only of a small headquarters staff tasked with compiling a history of the war.

Patton quickly lost interest in his new job. On 8th December 1945 he set off with others on a hunting trip organised by his chief of staff Major General Hobart Gay. Both men were sitting in the back seat of Patton's Cadillac staff car. The driver stopped at a railway crossing near Mannheim-Käffertal to allow a train to pass. As they moved off and were crossing the tracks, an approaching American army truck suddenly veered across the road in front of them. Patton's driver swerved and slammed on his brakes, but was unable to avoid hitting the truck, albeit at a low speed. Patton was thrown forward, and struck and gashed his head on the glass partition in front of his seat. The other passengers were only slightly injured, but on examination in hospital in Heidelberg, Patton was found to have a compressed fracture of the skull, two dislocated vertebrae in his neck, and a damaged spinal cord. He was also paralysed from the neck down. He was put in spinal traction and appeared to be making progress, but died in his sleep on 21st December 1945 from fluid on the lungs and heart failure. He was buried in the Luxembourg American Cemetery at Hamm, Luxembourg.

The circumstances of the accident, Patton's removal to a hospital twenty miles off in Heidelberg instead of nearby Mannheim, and his death after an initially optimistic prognosis, have given rise to conspiracy theories ever since. Patton deeply mistrusted the Soviet Union, and bitterly resented the handing over of eastern Europe to Stalin. His emphatically stated objections distinguished him from most other prominent Allied figures. Was he the victim of a Russian plot? Was he eliminated as a dangerous nuisance by his own superiors? Probably not, but to this day there are nagging doubts and unanswered questions in the minds of many people.

There is no doubt that General George Patton was an inspirational leader and tactician – his achievements were compared to those of Napoleon by the French leader de Gaule. Patton had obvious personal flaws, but in spite of them (or perhaps because of them) there is no doubt that he was one of the outstanding military leaders of the Second World War, a legend in his own lifetime and a true American Hero.

Alfred Curry Glassell Jr.

Anyone embarking on an internet search by googling "Glassell" will quickly come upon the Glassell School of Art in Houston, Texas. This institution is named after Alfred Curry Glassell Jr. who financed it with a generous donation. Glassell was a wealthy Texas oilman with a phenomenal range of intellectual, artistic, scientific and sporting interests. He was also a bountiful philanthropist in the heroic American tradition of Andrew Carnegie.

Alfred Curry Glassell Jr, the billionaire philanthropist, was yet another descendant of Andrew Glassell the planter of Torthorwald in Madison County, Virginia. Andrew Glassell's eldest son John, educated in Scotland, was a planter in Virginia like his father and had a son John by his second wife Margaret Lee. This John grew up to farm in Virginia, but moved to De Soto Parish in Louisiana and was ordained as a Presbyterian minister late in life. The seventh of the nine children of the Rev. John Glassell and his wife Mary Thom, also John, was born in 1861. John grew up to marry Annie G. Curry, and their son Alfred Curry

Glassell in adult life owned the Cuba Plantation in northern Louisiana, and married Frances Elvira Lane.

The son of Alfred C. Glassell and Frances E. Lane, Alfred Curry Glassell junior, was born on 31st March 1913 at Cuba Plantation. He had three sisters, Lillian, Joanna and Emily.[668] Alfred was educated at Bird High School, Shreveport, Louisiana,[669] and Louisiana State University, where he served as president of the Student Body and president of the Kappa Alpha Fraternity. After graduating B.A. in 1934 he embarked on a business career in the energy sector, exploring and developing oil and gas fields along the Texas and Louisiana coasts of the Gulf of Mexico. Quickly coming to prominence in the industry, he was one of the founders of the Transcontinental Gas Pipeline Corporation which brought gas directly from Texas to New York for the first time. He also served on the boards not only of Transco but of other powerful corporations such as El Paso Natural Gas and First City Bank.

In World War II Glassell saw active service in North Africa and in Europe and attained the rank of major. On discharge from the U.S. Army he took up residence in Houston, Texas, and returned to the petroleum industry with notable success, in the post-war drive to supply the United States with cheap and plentiful energy. Alfred Curry Glassell amassed a vast fortune from oil, but in the best traditions of American billionaire philanthropists, he gave away substantial sums of money to support the causes and institutions that reflected his wide range of interests.

Glassell was an enthusiastic and renowned big game fisherman, inducted into the International Game Fish Association Hall of Fame. On 4th August 1953, of the coast of Cabo Blano, Peru, he hooked a black marlin weighing 1560 pounds, a world record for hand-held rod and reel. He donated the corpse of this monster to the "Life at sea" hall of the National Museum of Natural History in New York. He subsequently appeared on the cover of "Sports Ilustrated", and footage of his battle with the "Mighty Marlin" was included in the film version of Hemmingway's "Old Man of the Sea".

His interest in the sea went far beyond mere killing and record breaking

668 See "From Roucan to Riches", Chapter 11, "Andrew Glassell's son John, and descendents".

669 Much of what follows is based on Glassell's lengthy obituary in the Houston Chronicle

however. He contributed to the science of marine biology and conservation, and organised and participated in scientific expeditions aboard his own vessel the "Argosy". In 1957 he led the Yale University Seychelles Expedition to the Indian Ocean and east coast of Africa, and in 1971 he received the International Oceanographic Foundation Marine Science award for his outstanding contributions. His involvement with biology and conservation was not limited to marine life, as he also had an abiding interest in the fauna of Texas and its preservation, and he was instrumental in establishing a Professorship in Quail Research at the Caesar Kleberg Wildlife Research Institute.

Glassell was also a life long collector of golden *objets d'art*, particularly from pre-colombian America, Asia, and Africa. Recognising the need to stimulate public interest in, and involvement with, the fine arts, he made a generous donation to the Museum of Fine Arts in Houston to finance the Glassell School of Art as the museum's teaching institution. Opening in 1979, it has now been superceded by a new building, but retains the name "Glassell School of Art".

In 1990 Glassell was elected chairman of the board of trustees of the Houston Museum of Fine Arts. He oversaw an ambitious programme of expansion and donated his own extensive and valuable collections to the museum. Also, as his obituary in the Houston Chronicle enumerates, "Over a lifetime he dedicated his time and resources to the Houston Museum of Natural Science, Houston Symphony Society, Society for Performing Arts, Houston Ballet Foundation, Houston Chamber of Commerce, Texas Children's Hospital, the American Museum of Natural History in New York City, Smithsonian Institute, and Archaeological Institute of America."

Alfred Glassell and his wife Clare Atwell had two children, a son Alfred Curry Glassell III, and a daughter Curry. Glassell died at the age of 95 on 29th October 2008, leaving the bulk of his vast fortune to charity. However, as often transpires with the disposal of family wealth, not everyone was happy. His son Alfred Curry Glassell III was left in charge of the Glassell Family Foundation and Glassell Producing Company Inc. and was quite content with his inheritance. Not so his sister Curry, "Houstonian millionaire, life coach and Democratic supporter", who contested the will, claiming that her father had come under undue influence to change his will shortly before his death. The courts rejected Curry's challenge, leaving her with a mere three million dollars of her father's fortune. She later sued her brother over the sale of some of Glassell Producing's oil and gas interests, insisting she had been tricked into agreeing to the deals. The court finally decided that the resolution of her claims should go to arbitration.[670]

670 https://warptown.com/life-coach-curry-glassell-is-fighting-with-he…

Postscript

THE URGE FOR SELF-IMPROVEMENT, THE DRIVE TO "GET ON" IN LIFE, IS not an exclusively Scottish trait. It is one however that has often loomed large in the Scottish psyche, and one that is well illustrated by the achievements of many of the Glassells – descendants of a humble Scots tenant farmer. Success does not always go hand in hand with happiness, however, as is made plain by the lives of several of those who feature in "From Roucan to Riches."

Perhaps Matthew's Gospel should have the last word on fame, fortune and "getting on":

"What will a man gain by winning the whole world at the cost of his true self?"[671]

671 Matthew Chapter 16, verse 26. New English Bible translation.

Bibliography.

THE FOLLOWING WILL BE FOUND USEFUL FOR SETTING THE SCENE FOR the Glassell origins in Dumfriesshire:

A history of Dumfries: an introduction to the history of Dumfries by Robert Edgar – Ed. R.C. Read, J. Maxwell and Sons, Dumfries 1919.

The book of Dumfriesshire – James Anderson Russell, Blacklock, Ferries and Sons Ltd, Dumfries, 1964.

History of the burgh of Dumfries – William McDowell, First published 1867, Adam and Charles Black, Edinburgh.

Dumfries's story – David Lockswood, T. C. Ferries & Co Ltd, Dumfries 1968.

A history of everyday life in Scotland 1600 t0 1800 – Ed Elizabeth Foyster and Christopher A. Whatley, Edinburgh University Press, Edinburgh, 2010.

Memorials of Torthorwald Parish – George Gilchrist, Published George Gilchrist c/o Town Hall, Annan, 1968.

Early records of an old Glasgow family – "W. H. H.", Glasgow University Press' Glasgow, 1903.

The history of Glasgow – John McUre, "A new edition", Macvean and White, Glasgow 1830. First published 1735.

National Records of Scotland.

Old Parish Records: Torthorwald baptisms and burials.
Dumfries Commissary Court CC/6.
Gifts and Deposits GD26/7/355, GD86/446.
Register of deeds:
RD 274; DAL LXXXX 1; MACK LXXIX; RD2/74 fol 733; RD2/92 fol 555,721; RD4/86 fol 519; DAL LXXXVIII 1030, 1200; RD2/81/1/232; RD2/81/2/773; RD82/215, 630, 657, 667; RD3; RD4; RD2/94 fol 733.

Early Glassell associations with Virginia

"Virginia Genealogies: a genealogy of the Glassell family of Scotland and Virginia. Also of the families of Brown, Ball, etc etc." – Rev. Horace Edwin Hayden, Wilkes Barre, Pennsylvania 1891. (Reprinted for Clearfield Company Inc, Baltimore Maryland, 2004). (Essential for an understanding of Andrew Glassell's establishment in Virginia. Much information also about his 19th century descendents.)

"A history of St Mark's Parish, Culpeper County, Virginia, with notes of old churches and old families, and illustrations of the manners and customs of the olden times" – Rev Philip Slaughter D.D., Rector of Emmanuel Church, Culpeper County, Virginia, 1887. (Much information also about 19th century Glassell descendents.)

Diary of John Harrower 1773-1776 – American Historical Review, Vol 6, Issue 1, Pages 65-102, October 1900.

John Glassell's Ledger 1769-70. Special collections and archives, James Branch Cabell Library, Richmond, Virginia.

A Scottish firm in Virginia: W. Cuninghame & Co – Scottish History Society 4th Series, Vol 20, Ed T. Devine Ph.D., Clark, Constable (1912) Ltd, 1984.

British Mercantile Claims – Articles published 1962-1992 in the Virginia Genealogist, J. F. Dornan, Falmouth, Virginia.

The Chimneys, HITI Success Story – Helen Makarechian. Fredericksburg.com, 3/11/2006.

An unlikely ghost – Barbara Crookshanks. Newspaper article in "Town and Country", The Free Lance Star (Fredericksburg), Saturday 26th October 2002.

Virginia Ghosts – Jenny Lee and Marguerite du Pont Lee. (online article).
Alum Spring Park, a walk through history – Librarypoint (website), Central Rappahannock Regional Library.
Fredericksburg Hustings Court, Will Book A 1782-1817.
To the ends of the earth – T. M. Devine, Alan Lane, London 2011.

John Glassell of Longniddry

"Reminiscences and notices of the parishes of the county of Haddington" – John Martine. East Lothian County Library Srvice, 1999. Originally in 2 volumes 1890 and 1894.
"Longniddry in transition" – Betty M. Third. Transactions of the East Lothian Antiquarian and Field Naturalists' Society, Vol VI, D. & J. Croal, Haddington 1955.
New Statistical Account, Vol 2, Parish of Gladsmuir, 1836.
National Records of Scotland:
Gladsmuir Kirk Session Cash Book CH2/169/10.
Gladsmuir Heritors' Records HR115/1.
Register of Deeds RD4/260, 270; RD3/311/1935.
Register of Deeds (John Glassell's legal papers): RD3/3111/1111, 1235, 1430, 1530.
Haddington Sheriff Court Records SC40/20/22; SC40/1/41.
Court of Session Records (John Glassell v. Earl of Wemyss) CS/235/G/127; CS/232/G/12/31.

Joan Glassell and the Campbell of Argyll connection

National Library of Scotland – "The Campbell Papers", ACC8508.

The Campbell Papers are absolutely crucial as a source of information on all aspects of the lives of Joan Glassell and her husband Lord John Campbell. However, it should be noted that Joan's correspondence with Lord John is scattered through several files in the Campbell Papers. Letters are filed sometimes in chronological order and sometimes not, and in fact many are undated. Creating a clear picture of Joan's life from her correspondence is very much an exercise in "creating order out of chaos". Similarly, Joan's fascinating journal of her European tour is presented in a rather disordered state – for example, most of ACC8508/41 should actually precede 40. The various bundles in 41 are not in sequence, and the entries for 19th-27th May rightly belong in 40.

Edinburgh, the Golden Age – Mary Cosh, Birlinn, Edinburgh, 2014. (An excellent guide to the social and cultural scene in late 18th and early 19th century Edinburgh.)

Memoir and correspondence of Mrs Grant of Laggan (3 Vols) – Ed. J. P. Grant; Longman, Brown, Green, Longman; London, 1844.

A group of Scottish women: Mrs Grant of Laggan 1755-1838. www.electronicscotland.com .

Biography of Anne Grant – Pam Parkins. Corvey women writers on the web CW3 Sheffield Hallam University.

Wikipedia: Anne Grant.

The Intellectual Duke, George Douglas Campbell 8th Duke of Argyll – Kirsteen Mulhearn. Ph.D. thesis University of Edinburgh, 2006. http://www.era.lib.ed.ac.up/handle1842/6918 .

"Draft": John D. E. H. Campbell 7th Duke of Argyll – Anne Gaillard. (Printout of her research kindly forwarded by Ms Gaillard.)

The lessons of Walcheren fever 1839 – John Lynch, Military Medicine.

Walcheren 1839, a medical catastrophe – Martin R. Howard, British Medical Journal, 18th December 1999.

The history of parliament: the House of Commons 1770-1820 – R. G. Thorne, Secker and Warburg, London, 1986. (Article on Lord John Campbell).

Stately Passions: the scandals of Britain's great houses – Jamie Douglas Home, Michael o' Mara Books Ltd, London, 2012.

James Smith of Jordanhill. www.clanmacfarlanegenealogy .

"Rootsweb" website. Duncan family of Strathblane: John McColl of Ibrox Hill.

Debret's and Cacroft's "Peerages".

National Records of Scotland. Decisions of the Court of Session 21st May 1831.

Andrew Glassell and his American descendants

Banning Co. Addenda 1. Boxes 4 and 7. Huntington Library, San Marino, California.

Archives of the Virginia Historical Society. Mss 1G8855 d3, d4, d5.

California History Collection (website) http://memory.loc.gov . Information on Mexican and early U.S. California.

San Francisco Genealogy: Obituaries and death notices. www.sfgenealogy.org .

Annual Publication of the Historical Society of Southern California and Pioneer Register, Vol 5, No 1 (1900). University of California Press, Los Angeles, California. (Re. Andrew Glassell's law firm.)

Orange, California: my hometown – Phil Brigandi (Online publication.) http://socialhistoryland.mystic.com .

Skagit River Journal of History and Folklore – Go west young man, Part 2. Andrew and James de Barth Shorb.

Benjamin Davis Wilson. Article in World Heritage Encyclopedia https://hawaiilibrary.net .

Los Angeles Herald Vol XXVIII No 120, 29th January 1901 (Andrew Glassell's death). 3rd and 5th March 1901 (Rhoda Eddo and Phil Glassell).

Prisoner of the Civil War – Douglas Westfall, Ed. Pedro Garcia, The Paragon Agency, Orange, California, 2013. (Fictionalised account of William Glassell's adventures.)

American Civil War Forum (website). The attack on USS Ironsides.

The David semi-submersibles. Online article www.csslhunley.com

Reminiscences of Torpedo service in Charleston Harbor – W. T. Glassell, Southern Historical Society Papers, Vol 4, Richmond, Virginia, 1877.

Patton Family Papers, Box 1, Mss PF 317 – 320, 350. Huntington Library, San Marino, California.

Patton, Legendary Commander – Martin Blumenson and Kevin Hynel, Potomac Books Inc., Washington D.C., 2008.

The Fighting Pattons – Brian Sobel, Praeger, Westport Connecticut and London, 1997.

The path to victory: the Mediterranean Theater in World War II – Douglas Porch FSG, Farrier Straus and Girvin, New York, 2004.

Wikipedia: General George Patton.

Houston Chronicle. Obituary of Alfred Curry Glassell October 31st 2008.

Meet Curry Glassell (website) https://wwwcurryglassell.com .

Online article on Curry Glassell's legal battles: https://warptown.com . ("Life coach Curry Glassell is fighting…").